HOW GOD CHANGES
YOUR BRAIN

HOW GOD CHANGES YOUR BRAIN

Breakthrough Findings from a Leading Neuroscientist

ANDREW NEWBERG, M.D.,

AND

MARK ROBERT WALDMAN

BALLANTINE BOOKS

NEW YORK

Copyright © 2009 by Andrew Newberg and Mark Robert Waldman

Published in the United States by Ballantine Books,
an imprint of The Random House Publishing Group,
a division of Random House, Inc., New York.

BALLANTINE and colophon are registered trademarks of Random House, Inc.

ISBN 978-0-345-50341-1

LIBRARY OF CONGRESS CATALOGING-IN-PUBLICATION DATA

Printed in the United States of America on acid-free paper

www.ballantinebooks.com

2 4 6 8 9 7 5 3 1

FIRST EDITION

Book design by Mary A. Wirth

TO OUR STUDENTS, PATIENTS, AND
RESEARCH PARTICIPANTS:

You have helped to redefine the religious landscape of contemporary American society by demonstrating the beauty, diversity, optimism, and health benefits associated with the spiritual practices of the world.

CONTENTS

THREE. TRANSFORMING YOUR INNER REALITY

AUTHOR'S NOTE

Throughout most of this book Mark and I will be speaking to you with a united voice, for we have closely collaborated on the research we present. Thus, we liberally substitute *I* and *we,* and only occasionally specify ourselves as individuals, since the anecdotes we relate tend to reflect our shared experiences and values. However, when *I* is used to talk about the brain-scan research conducted at the University of Pennsylvania, it is in reference to myself, as are most of the anecdotes that refer to childhood and college experiences. But research is never a solitary venture, so you'll often find references to *our* work, which includes not just Mark, but also the members of my research staff at the university, without whom I could not possibly conduct the work I do. For a list of those who have contributed to the research gathered in this volume, please see the acknowledgment page at the end of this book.

Of all the fields of science and medicine, neurophysiology is one of the most difficult topics to talk about in simple terms, especially when it comes to issues concerning consciousness, logic, emotional processing, and the reality-processing mechanisms of the brain—issues that are essential to address when dealing with the neurological correlates of spiritual experiences and religious beliefs. We have made the information as "user friendly" as possible, but generalizations often leave out important qualifications and concerns. Therefore, for those who desire additional information, we have provided extensive peer-reviewed references—over a thousand—in the endnotes to substantiate the conclusions we have drawn.

ONE

RELIGION
AND THE
HUMAN BRAIN

*Our time is distinguished by wonderful achievements
in the fields of scientific understanding and the technical application of those insights. Who would not be
cheered by this? But let us not forget that knowledge
and skills alone cannot lead humanity to a happy and
dignified life. Humanity has every reason to place the
proclaimers of high moral standards and values above
the discoverers of objective truth. What humanity owes
to personalities like Buddha, Moses, and Jesus ranks for
me higher than all the achievements of the inquiring
and constructive mind.*

—ALBERT EINSTEIN, *THE HUMAN SIDE*

1

WHO CARES ABOUT GOD?

Prelude to a Neurological and
Spiritual Revolution

God.

In America, I cannot think of any other word that stirs up the imagination more. Even young children raised in nonreligious communities understand the concept of God, and when asked, will willingly draw you a picture—usually the proverbial old man with the long hair and a beard. As children grow into adults, their pictures of God often evolve into abstract images of clouds, spirals, sunbursts, and even mirrors, as they attempt to integrate the properties of a reality they cannot see. In fact, the more a person thinks about God, the more complex and imaginative the concept becomes, taking on unique nuances of meaning that differ from one individual to the next.

If you contemplate God long enough, something surprising happens in the brain. Neural functioning begins to change. Different circuits become activated, while others become deactivated. New dendrites are formed, new synaptic connections are made, and the brain becomes more sensitive to subtle realms of experience. Perceptions alter, beliefs begin to change, and if God has meaning for you, then God becomes neurologically real. For some, God may remain a primitive concept, limited to the way a young child interprets the world. But for most people, God is transformed into a symbol or metaphor representing a wide range of personal, ethical, social, and universal values. And, if you happen to be a neuroscientist, God can be one of the most fascinating of human experiences to explore.

THE SCIENCE OF GOD

For the past fifteen years I have investigated the neural mechanisms of spirituality with the same fervor that a minister contemplates God. Some religious rituals do nothing more than relax you, others help to keep you focused and alert, but a few appear to take practitioners into transcendent realms of mystical experience where their entire lives are changed.

Our research team at the University of Pennsylvania has consistently demonstrated that God is part of our consciousness and that the more you think about God, the more you will alter the neural circuitry in specific parts of your brain. That is why I say, with the utmost confidence, that God can change your brain. And it doesn't matter if you're a Christian or a Jew, a Muslim or a Hindu, or an agnostic or an atheist.

In *Why God Won't Go Away,* I demonstrated that the human brain is uniquely constructed to perceive and generate spiritual realities.[1] Yet it has no way to ascertain the accuracy of such perceptions. Instead, our brain uses logic, reason, intuition, imagination, and emotion to integrate God and the universe into a complex system of personal values, behaviors, and beliefs.

But no matter how hard we try, the ultimate nature of the universe continues to elude our brain. So the bigger questions remain. Where does life originate, where does it end, and what ultimate purpose does it serve? Is there a spiritual reality, or is it merely a fabrication of the mind? If there is a God, does such an entity reach out to us like the hand that Michelangelo painted on the ceiling of the Sistine Chapel? Or is it the other way around: Does our mind reach out to embrace a God that may or may not be real?

Neuroscience has yet to answer such questions, but it can record the effect that religious beliefs and experiences have upon the human brain. Furthermore, it can tell us how God—as an image, feeling, thought, or fact—is interpreted, reacted to, and turned into a perception that feels meaningful and real. But neuroscience cannot tell you if

God does or doesn't exist. In fact, as far as we can tell, most of the human brain does not even worry if the things we see are actually real. Instead, it only needs to know if they are useful for survival. If a belief in God provides you with a sense of comfort and security, then God will enhance your life. But if you see God as a vindictive deity who gives you justification for inflicting harm on others, such a belief can actually damage your brain as it motivates you to act in socially destructive ways.

Having an accurate perception of reality is not one of the brain's strong points. Indeed, as Mark and I pointed out in *Why We Believe What We Believe,** the human brain seems to have difficulty separating fantasies from facts.[2] It sees things that are not there, and it sometimes doesn't see things that are there. In fact, the brain doesn't even try to create a fully detailed map of the external world. Instead, it selects a handful of cues, then fills in the rest with conjecture, fantasy, and belief. Rather than being a hindrance, such neurological ambiguity allows us to imagine and create a world filled with utopian, utilitarian, and sometimes useless things—from eye protectors for chickens to electronic corneas for the blind.

Likewise, when it comes to thinking about God, our brain creates a vast range of utopian, utilitarian, and sometimes useless theologies— from complex moral value systems to the number of angels that can fit on the head of a pin. But no matter how comprehensive our theologies become, our brain is rarely satisfied with its concepts and images of God. The end result of this remarkable contemplation has been the creation of thousands of differing spiritual practices and creeds.

Indeed, the more one contemplates God, the more mysterious God becomes. Some embrace this emergent ambiguity, some are frightened by it, some ignore it, and others reject it in its entirety. But the fact remains that every human brain, from early childhood on, contemplates the possibility that spiritual realms exist. Believers like Isaac Newton, agnostics like Charles Darwin, and atheists like Richard Dawkins have all given serious consideration to humanity's fascination with God, be-

* The paperback edition is entitled *Born to Believe: God, Science, and the Origin of Ordinary and Extraordinary Beliefs* (The Free Press, 2007).

cause the moment God is introduced to the human brain, the neurological concept will not go away.

Recently there has been a spate of antireligious books—among
them, *The God Delusion,* Richard Dawkins; *The End of Faith,* Sam
Harris; and *God Is Not Great,* Christopher Hitchens—that argue that
religious beliefs are personally and societally dangerous. But the research, as we will outline throughout this book, strongly suggests otherwise. Nor do we believe that these authors represent the views of the vast
majority of scientists or atheists. For example, though I am not specifically religious, I'm open to the possibility that God may exist, whereas
Mark, my colleague and co-researcher, prefers to look at the universe
through a purely naturalistic and evidence-based perspective. Yet we
both appreciate and encourage religious and spiritual development—as
long as it does not denigrate the lives or religious beliefs of others.

For the past four years, Mark and I have been studying how different concepts of God affect the human mind. I have brain-scanned
Franciscan nuns as they immersed themselves in the presence of God,
and charted the neurological changes as Buddhist practitioners contemplated the universe. I have watched what happens in the brains of
Pentecostal practitioners who invited the Holy Spirit to speak to them
in tongues, and have seen how the brains of atheists react—and don't
react—when they meditate on a concrete image of God.[3]

Along with my research staff at the University of Pennsylvania
and the Center for Spirituality and the Mind, we are currently studying Sikhs, Sufis, yoga practitioners, and advanced meditators to map
the neurochemical changes caused by spiritual and religious practices.
Our research has led us to the following conclusions:

1. Each part of the brain constructs a different perception of
   God.
2. Every human brain assembles its perceptions of God in
   uniquely different ways, thus giving God different qualities
   of meaning and value.
3. Spiritual practices, even when stripped of religious beliefs,
   enhance the neural functioning of the brain in ways that improve physical and emotional health.

4. Intense, long-term contemplation of God and other spiritual values appears to permanently change the structure of those parts of the brain that control our moods, give rise to our conscious notions of self, and shape our sensory perceptions of the world.

5. Contemplative practices strengthen a specific neurological circuit that generates peacefulness, social awareness, and compassion for others.

Spiritual practices also can be used to enhance cognition, communication, and creativity, and over time can even change our neurological perception of reality itself. Yet, it is a reality that we cannot objectively confirm. Instead, our research has led us to conclude that three separate realities intermingle to give us a working model of the world: the reality that actually exists outside of our brain, and two internal realities—maps that our brain constructs about the world. One of these maps is subconscious and primarily concerned with survival and the biological maintenance of the body. But this map is not the world itself; it's just a guide that helps us navigate the terrain. Human beings, however, construct a second internal reality—a map that reflects our *conscious* awareness of the universe. This consciousness is very different from the subconscious map formed by our sensory and emotional circuits. We know that these two internal maps exist, but we have yet to discover if, and to what degree, these two inner realities communicate with each other.[4]

Overall, our consciousness represents a reality that is the farthest removed from the world that actually exists outside of the brain. Thus, if God does exist, there would be three separate realities to consider: the God that exists in the world, our subconscious perception of that God, and the conscious images and concepts that we construct in a very small part of our frontal, temporal, and parietal lobes. It has been my goal to show that spiritual practices may help us to bridge the chasm between these inner and outer realities, which would then bring us closer to what actually exists in the world. I still don't know if it's possible, but the health benefits associated with meditation and religious ritual cannot be denied.

ORGANIZATION OF THIS BOOK

In the first two sections we will explore the neural correlates of spiritual experiences that our research has uncovered. The third section is filled with practical exercises that anyone can use to enhance the physical, emotional, cognitive, and communication processes of the brain.

In Chapter 2—"Do You Even Need God When You Pray?"—we'll describe our recent study showing how spiritual practices improve memory, and how they can slow down neurological damage caused by growing old. Our memory study also demonstrates that if you remove the spiritual references, religious rituals will still have a beneficial effect on the brain. We'll also show you how to create and personalize your own "memory enhancement" meditation.

In Chapter 3—"What Does God Do to Your Brain?"—we'll explore the neural varieties of meditation and prayer, explaining how different parts of the brain create different perceptions of God. We'll tell you how God becomes neurologically real and show you how different neurochemicals and drugs alter your spiritual beliefs.

In Chapter 4—"What Does God Feel Like?"—we'll share with you the surprising findings from our online Survey of Spiritual Experiences. Our data suggests that God is more of a feeling than an idea, that nearly everyone's spiritual experience is unique, and that these experiences often generate long-lasting states of unity, peacefulness, and love. Furthermore, they have the power to change people's religious and spiritual orientations, as well as the way they interact with others.

In Chapter 5—"What Does God Look Like?"—we'll show you what we discovered when we compared adult drawings of God with pictures drawn by children. We'll explain why some atheists maintain childhood images, while others draw sophisticated renditions, and share with you how agnostics tend to react when they explore their notions of God. We will also explain why each of us may have a single "God" neuron or circuit that slowly expands the more we contemplate religious ideas.

In Chapter 6—"Does God Have a Heart?"—we'll describe how Americans project different personalities onto God, and how each of these perspectives affect the neural functioning of the brain. We will also explain how God culturally evolved from an authoritarian, punitive deity to become a force that is filled with compassion and love. This "mystical" element of God affects a very important part of the brain, called the anterior cingulate, which we need to nurture as we engage in a pluralistic world filled with different perceptions of the divine.

In Chapter 7—"What Happens When God Gets Mad?"—we'll delve more deeply into the neurological dangers of anger, fear, authoritarianism, and idealism. We will also explain why everyone—believers and nonbelievers alike—is born with a built-in fundamentalist framework that is deeply embedded in the neurological circuitry of the brain.

In Chapter 8—"Exercising Your Brain"—we'll tell you about the eight best ways to keep your brain physically, mentally, and spiritually tuned-up. Three of these techniques are directly related to the neurological principles underlying meditation, but I think several of them will surprise you, especially the one that we think may be most essential for maintaining a healthy brain. They are all relatively easy to do, and we will give you pointers on how to integrate them into your daily life. We'll even show you how you can arouse your precuneus—which may be the central circuit of human consciousness—in less than sixty seconds.

In Chapter 9—"Finding Serenity"—we have used the findings from our neurological research to create a personalized "brain enhancement" program that will help you reduce stress, become more attentive and alert, develop greater sensitivity and empathy, and generally improve the overall functioning of your brain. We'll explain the three key principles of meditation and guide you through twelve exercises that you can practice at home. Included are three simple techniques to defuse anger, the emotion most likely to interfere with the normal functioning of your brain.

In Chapter 10—"Compassionate Communication"—we integrate the techniques from the previous two chapters into a new exercise that can be done while you are engaged in conversation with someone else. In less than fifteen minutes a compassionate and intimate dialogue unfolds that undermines the normal defensive behaviors we usually employ in social situations. We are currently conducting brain-scan research to document the neurological benefits associated with this

"Compassionate Communication" exercise, and we will instruct you on how to practice it with family members and friends. We'll also enumerate twenty-one strategies that you can use to effectively resolve interpersonal problems.

EXPLORING THE COMPLEXITIES OF GOD

One of the main purposes of this book is to help readers expand their understanding and appreciation of spiritual practices and experiences. In fact, religious beliefs are vastly more complex and diverse than public opinion polls show. From a neurological perspective, God is a perception and an experience that is constantly changing and evolving in the human brain, and this implies that America's spiritual landscape is virtually impossible to define. You can't nail God down for good or for bad. And you can't intuit a person's innermost values based upon their creed or the church they choose to attend. If more people realized that everyone was talking about something fundamentally personal and different, perhaps a degree of distrust would fall away.

Although our studies have focused primarily on Americans, we believe that the same diversity of religious belief exists in other cultures. Even within the American fundamentalist community, it is difficult to make generalizations because many fundamentalists are loving, caring, and tolerant of other religious beliefs, contrary to what other people may lead you to believe.

Our research also disclosed that when it comes to God, there are few "true believers," for even the most devoted believers expressed some doubts about the validity of their spiritual beliefs.[5] Even the majority of young atheists that we've interviewed expressed uncertainty about their disbeliefs. Indeed, current research reflects a growing tendency of people who are unwilling to identify themselves with any single system of belief. But you have to ask enough questions. For example, if a survey only gives the respondent the choice of a few options, the results will come out black and white. Thus, we chose to give our survey participants free rein in describing their religious beliefs and spiritual experiences. Instead of coming up with a simple set of categories, we uncovered a rainbow of colorful descriptions and beliefs. In one of our questionnaires, we even found evidence showing that educated young adults are far less prejudiced than previous generations of believers. And this bodes well for the future.

Ultimately, it is a mistake to assume that any self-assigned label, category, or description of religious belief accurately captures a person's value system or morality. Furthermore, our research suggests that the more a person contemplates his or her values and beliefs, the more they are apt to change.

THE SHADOW SIDE OF GOD

The recent spate of antireligious "scholarship" that has landed on the bestseller lists should also be viewed with skepticism. Mark and I are particularly disappointed with the lack of empirical evidence that these writers have cited that even mildly suggests that religion is hazardous to your health. The psychological, sociological, and neuroscientific data simply disagree. The problem isn't religion. The problem is authoritarianism, coupled with the desire to angrily impose one's idealistic beliefs on others.

One should also remember that during the twentieth century, tens of millions of people were killed by nonreligious and antireligious regimes, while far fewer have been killed in the name of an authoritarian God. Even when it comes to suicide bombings, half of the people involved have been found to be nonreligious.[6] Instead, their acts of violence were carried out for purely political or socially motivated reasons. As we documented in our previous book, human beings have a neurological and biological propensity to act in profoundly hostile ways. On the other hand, our research shows that the majority of spiritual practices suppress the brain's ability to react with anger or fear.

There is, however, a shadow side to religious and political *organizations,* especially when their tenets stipulate that there is only one absolute and undeniable truth. When such individuals band together, they unconsciously foster an "us versus them" mentality that neurologically generates fear and hostility toward people who hold different beliefs. Neuroscience tells us that the moment we see an angry face, or hear angry words, our brain kicks into overdrive, generating stress chemicals that will make us fight or run. Anger generates anger, and the angrier a group of people get, the greater the possibility that violence will erupt.

Over the past three decades, fear-based religions and politics have grown in power and popularity, and although their numbers are beginning to decline,[7] many national leaders, politicians, and Nobel laureates consider some of these "fundamentalisms" to be genuine threats to world peace.[8] Some surveys have estimated that only 1 percent of the worldwide Christian community are willing to take violent action against those who disbelieve, but that still adds up to a lot of angry people. My question is this: What happens when those millions of angry Christians try to confront the millions of militant non-Christians in the world?

Jesus said, "Love your enemies, do good to those who hate you, bless those who curse you, pray for those who mistreat you."[9] This, indeed, is a difficult task to do, but I'm surprised how often this biblical passage is ignored by some fundamentalists, even when dealing with other Christians. When Mark asked one ultraconservative pastor about Jesus' directive to love your enemy, he responded pithily, "I can love you, but I don't have to *like* you!" Mark was shocked by such unwarranted hostility, but the question that concerned me more was whether the pastor was an exception or the norm.

So far, in our informal interviews with numerous leaders of American fundamentalist churches, we have found that most are extraordinarily friendly and civil. Many will tell you that they prefer to not associate with followers of other religions, and some will "shun" you if you choose to leave their church,[10] but there are also congregations that will accept people with different beliefs with open arms. Mark even had a group of Pentecostal ministers bless him—in tongues!—for our neuroscientific work. In other words, you can't judge people by their beliefs, but you can judge them by how they behave toward others.

Fortunately, the majority of religious leaders in America encourage interfaith dialogue and exchange, and some of the fastest-growing churches embrace a multidenominational spirituality that blends Christian, Jewish, Muslim, and Eastern religious philosophies.[11] What strikes me the most about these contemporary places of worship is the warmth and friendship extended to every participant, regardless of one's race, ethnicity, or faith. But some writers—like the aforementioned Richard Dawkins, Sam Harris, and Christopher Hitchens—make little distinction between fundamentalist and liberal theologies, arguing that religion as a whole presents a primary threat to the world. The evidence is not there, however, and in America, only a small percentage of groups use religion to foster discriminatory political agendas.[12] In fact, as we will highlight throughout this book, most research conducted in psychology and the social sciences finds religion either neutral or beneficial when it comes to physical and emotional health. The enemy is not religion; the enemy is anger, hostility, intolerance, separatism, extreme idealism, and prejudicial fear—be it secular, religious, or political.

In the relatively brief span of American history, religious movements have played critical roles in the promotion of human rights, helping to abolish slavery, establishing rights for women and children, and spearheading the civil-rights movement of the twentieth century.[13] Religious institutions feed the hungry, shelter the homeless, and protect battered women throughout the world. Episcopal churches now ordain gay and lesbian priests. Catholic, Jewish, and other religious groups fight for interreligious tolerance, and many theologians openly respect atheism and encourage agnostic discourse. And when it comes to promoting world peace, one only has to look at the number of religious leaders who have won the Nobel Peace prize: Martin Luther King, Jr., Bishop Desmond Tutu, the Dalai Lama, and Mother Teresa, to name just a few.

Our research, along with major studies conducted at other universities, points to a general decline in traditional religions that has been quietly going on for thirty years. But it has been replaced by a growing interest in spirituality, a term that describes a broad range of individual values and personal theologies that is not connected to traditional religious institutions. Thus, God is as popular as ever, but as we will describe throughout this book, it is a God that significantly differs from historical religious beliefs. Indeed, if our survey measurements are correct, each new generation is literally reinventing God in an image that points toward an acceptance and appreciation of our pluralistic world.

To survive in a pluralistic society, we must evolve our spirituality *and* our secularity, integrating religion and science in a way that can be beneficial to all. But to do this we must overhaul antiquated religious notions that interfere with the religious freedoms of others. Most important, we will need to devise innovative ways to promote peaceful cooperation between people, especially between those who hold different religious views. In this respect, scientists, psychologists, sociologists, theologians, and politicians must forge new cooperative alliances in order to improve our global interactions with others.

GOD AND THE NEUROPLASTICITY OF THE BRAIN

Contemplating God will change your brain, but I want to point out that meditating on other grand themes will also change your brain. If you contemplate the Big Bang, or immerse yourself in the study of evolution—or choose to play a musical instrument, for that matter—you'll change the neural circuitry in ways that enhance your cognitive health. But religious and spiritual contemplation changes your brain in a profoundly different way because it strengthens a unique neural circuit that specifically enhances social awareness and empathy while subduing destructive feelings and emotions. This is precisely the kind of neural change we need to make if we want to solve the conflicts that currently afflict our world. And the underlying mechanism that allows these changes to occur relates to a unique quality known as *neuroplasticity*: the ability of the human brain to structurally rearrange itself in response to a wide variety of positive and negative events.*

In the last two years, advances in neuroscience have revolutionized the way we think about the brain. Rather than seeing it as an organ that slowly matures during the first two decades of life, then withers away as we age, scientists now look at the human brain as a constantly changing mass of activity. In mammals, dendrites—the thousands of

---

* Sharon Begley's recent book, *Train Your Mind, Change Your Brain* (Ballantine, 2007), provides one of the best and easiest-to-read overviews of neuroplasticity and the brain's potential to be changed through meditation. The research she documents underlies many of the neurological hypotheses that we will be introducing in this book. However, since the field has changed dramatically in the last two years, we will be focusing primarily on these new findings.

tentaclelike receptors extending from one end of every neuron (or nerve cell)—rapidly grow and retreat in a period of a couple of weeks. In fact, recent evidence has shown that neuronal changes can take place in literally a matter of hours. "The development of particular neuro-logical connections or skills does not occur gradually over time," says Akira Yoshii, a brain researcher at the Massachusetts Institute of Technology. "Instead such changes tend to occur suddenly, appearing in short intervals after robust stimulation. It is as if there is a single important trigger and then a functional circuit rapidly comes online."[14]

The Nobel laureate Eric Kandel, who proved that neurons never stop learning, demonstrated another important dimension of neuro-plasticity. If you alter the environmental stimulus, the internal function of the nerve cells will change, causing them to grow new extentions called axons capable of sending different information to other parts of the brain.[15] In fact, every change in the environment—internal and external—will cause a rearrangement of cellular activity and growth. Even more interesting, every neuron has its own "mind," so to speak, for it can decide whether to send a signal, and if it does, how strong a signal to send.[16]

Scientists used to believe that neurons deteriorated with old age, but the mechanisms are far more complicated than that. For example, we now know that certain neurochemicals wear out, and this alters nerve cell activity and growth. Sometimes neural connections die off, and sometimes they become too active and overconnected, bringing chaos and confusion to our internal organizational maps. Our research with memory patients suggests that meditation can help maintain a healthy structural balance that will slow the aging process.

Brain-scan technology allows us to watch a living brain in action, and what we see is amazing. Each feeling and thought changes the blood flow and electrochemical activity in multiple areas of the brain, and it appears that we never repeat the exact same feeling or thought. In fact, the mere act of recalling a single memory changes its connec-tion to other neuronal circuits—another interesting example of the enormous plasticity of the brain.

How fast do the neural connections change within the brain? Imagine filming a hundred years of growth in a forest full of trees, then playing it back in fast motion. You'd see branches growing and dying off at an incredible rate. In mammalian brains, similar changes can take place over a period of several weeks, and I suspect that in humans the neural changes occur more rapidly in the frontal lobes, where many of our spiritual concepts are formed.

If we combine all of the research on neuroplasticity, we must conclude that neurons do not have fixed properties or positions.[17] Instead, they are changing all the time, triggered by competition, environmental changes, and education.[18] Learning takes place continually, and memories are being constantly revised. New ideas emerge, flow briefly into consciousness, then quickly fade away to make room for the next brief moment of awareness.

So what does neuroplasticity have to do with God? Everything, for if you contemplate something as complex or mysterious as God, you're going to have incredible bursts of neural activity firing in different parts of your brain. New dendrites will rapidly grow and old associations will disconnect as new imaginative perspectives emerge. In essence, when you think about the really big questions in life—be they religious, scientific, or psychological—your brain is going to grow.

NEUROSCIENCE 101

In this book, we'll keep the brain anatomy to a minimum. However, when it comes to understanding how God and spiritual processes affect the brain, there are six structures that we want you to keep in mind: the frontal lobe, limbic system, anterior cingulate, amygdala, thalamus, and parietal lobe. On page 44 you'll find a drawing of these structures, but I'd like to show you a simple way to envision these important parts of the brain.

First, put two imaginary almonds (without the shells) in the palm of your hand. These are the two halves of your *amygdala*, which governs your fight-or-flight response to a perceived or imagined fear. Next, place two halves of an imaginary walnut (again, no shell) into the palm of your hand. This is your *thalamus,** which sends sensory information to all the other parts of the brain. It also gives you a sense of meaning, and what reality may actually be.

---

* Actually, you have two thalami, two amygdalae, and two frontal and parietal lobes in your brain—one in each hemisphere—and each half can be involved in different neurological functions, but to keep things simple, we'll refer to them in singular tense.

Now, make a fist and bend your forearm so your knuckles are pointing to the ceiling, Your forearm is your spinal cord, and your fist (along with the almond halves and the walnut) is the *limbic system,* the oldest part of the brain that every reptile, fish, amphibian, bird, and mammal has. Your limbic system is involved with memory encoding, emotional response, and many other bodily functions.

Next, take four sheets of eight-by-ten-inch paper and place them on top of your fist. Crumple the paper up so it fits snugly, and *voilà!*—you have a human brain. Those four sheets of paper are the approximate size and thickness of your neocortex, and all the memories, beliefs, and behaviors you have learned over a lifetime are stored on them, along with all of your visual, auditory, motor, language, and cognitive processing centers of the brain. Thirty percent of that paper is your *frontal lobe,* which sits directly behind and above your eyes. It controls nearly everything you are conscious of: your logic, reason, attention, language skills, and voluntary motivation.

Notice where the crumpled paper touches your thumb. That area approximates the location of the *anterior cingulate,* which processes social awareness, intuition, and empathy. It also contains a unique type of neuron that only humans and a few primates have. These neurons have only been around for about 15 million years, whereas your amygdala (the almonds in your fist) has been happily generating fear for 450 million years. Spiritual practices specifically strengthen the anterior cingulate, and when this happens, activity in the amygdala slows down.

There's one more area that I want you to keep in mind: your *parietal lobes,* located above and slightly behind your ears. They take up less than a quarter of those sheets of paper, but provide you with a sense of yourself in relation to other objects in the world. When activity in this area decreases, you can feel at one with God, the universe, or any other concept you are consciously focusing on.

There you have it: a half billion years of neural evolution condensed into six paragraphs, and meditation teaches you how to alter the functioning of each of these parts of the brain in ways that improve your physical and emotional health. Indeed, it can even change the way your brain perceives reality.

RELIGION MAKES US MORE "HUMAN"

The neurological evolution of the brain suggests that empathy and social awareness are the most recently developed parts of our psychological anatomy. For the most part, our brain was designed to survive in an environment that used to be incredibly harsh, and it managed to make it through tens of thousands of years without the comforts of medicine, plumbing, or democracy. We lived in small groups that competed for limited amounts of property, food, and wealth, and two opposing dynamics evolved, fueled by the development of the language centers situated in the frontal lobe. The old reptilian part of our brain selfishly fought for survival, while newer, more fragile parts struggled to form cooperative alliances with others.

Mark and I believe that historical religious groups intuitively recognized this inner neural conflict between the old and new brain. Through trial and error, some traditions developed contemplative exercises that could strengthen neurological circuits involved with consciousness, empathy, and social awareness. These circuits, when activated, helped us become more cooperative and alert, and tempered our natural tendencies toward anger, fear, and distrust. Contemplative practices allowed our ancestors to envision a better world—and possible afterworlds—and the creative processes within our brain gave us the power to make some of those visions come true. But most important, contemplative practices helped us to become more sensitive and compassionate toward others.

LEARNING TO FEEL COMPASSION

Ultimately, this book is about compassion—a primary concept found in virtually every religious tradition. Compassion, as I am using it here, is similar to empathy, and it expresses our neurological capacity to *resonate* to another person's emotions. But compassion goes a step further, referring to our ability to *respond* to another person's pain. It allows us to be more tolerant of others and more accepting of our own shortcomings and faults.

Compassion appears to be an evolutionary adaptive process, and our neurological heart appears to be in the anterior cingulate, a very small structure that sits at the center of an important communication junction between the frontal lobe (which initiates our thoughts and behaviors) and the limbic system (which processes a wide range of feelings and emotions). It helps to maintain a delicate balance between our feelings and our thoughts, and is the newest part in the evolutionary history of the brain. If you have a larger or more active anterior cingulate, you may experience greater empathy, and you'll be far less likely to react with anger or fear. If the anterior cingulate malfunctions, your communication skills will be compromised and you won't be able to accurately sense what others are thinking or feeling.

The anterior cingulate appears to be crucial for empathy and compassion, and many brain-scan studies of meditation show that this part of the brain is stimulated by such practices. The neural circuits spanning the anterior cingulate and the prefrontal cortex integrate attention, working memory, motivation, and many other executive functions. Throughout this book, we'll return to the functional importance of this special part of the brain.

We can use spiritual practices to become less hostile and greedy and feel more compassionate toward others, but internal compassion is not enough to deal with the problems we must face in the world. Thus, we must find ways of bringing our spirituality into dialogue with others. But how do you *neurologically* promote peaceful cooperation between people, especially between those who hold conflicting points of view? To address this need, Mark and I created a special meditation exercise that brings compassion directly into the dialogue process itself. It is currently being tested in psychotherapy to deal with relationship conflicts, and we are demonstrating it in schools, religious communities, and businesses to teach people how to get along better with each other. And yet, no matter how hard we try to control destructive emotions, our old reptilian brain continues to interfere.

HUMANITY'S GREATEST ENEMY: ANGER

Of all the emotions we are born with, anger is the most primal and difficult one to control. No matter how discreet, anger generates anxiety, defensiveness, and aggression in the other person—the famous fight-or-flight reaction that every living organism contains. And if you respond to someone else's anger with irritability—which is the way most brains are designed to react—the problem only gets worse.

Anger interrupts the functioning of your frontal lobes. Not only do you lose the ability to be rational, you lose the awareness that you're acting in an irrational way. When your frontal lobes shut down, it's impossible to listen to the other person, let alone feel empathy or compassion. Instead, you are likely to feel self-justified and self-righteous, and when that happens the communication process falls apart. Anger also releases a cascade of neurochemicals that actually destroy those parts of the brain that control emotional reactivity.

It takes a lot of perseverance and training to respond to anger with kindness, but this is exactly what spiritual teachers have been trying to teach for centuries. When you intensely and consistently focus on your spiritual values and goals, you increase the blood flow to your frontal lobes and anterior cingulate, which causes the activity in emotional centers of the brain to decrease. Conscious intention is the key, and the more you focus on your inner values, the more you can take charge of your life. Thus, meditation—be it religious or secular—enables you to more easily accomplish your goals, which is why we've devoted three chapters to teaching you how to exercise your brain in loving and compassionate ways.

HAVING FAITH

As a neuroscientist, the more I delve into the nature of the human brain, the more I realize how mysterious we are. But if I had to pick two things that I have learned—as a doctor, a teacher, a husband, and a father—I would first say that life is sacred. Indeed, we are literally driven to live because every cell in our body fights to survive, and every neuron in our brain strives to become strong.

The second thing I've learned is that behind our drive to survive, there is another force, and the best word to describe it is faith. Faith not just in God, or in science or love, but faith in ourselves and each other. Having faith in the human spirit is what drives us to survive *and* transcend. It makes life worth living, and it gives meaning to our life. Without such hope and optimism—synonyms for what I am calling faith—the mind can easily slip into depression or despair. Faith is embedded in our neurons and in our genes, and it is one of the most important principles to honor in our lives.

Some people put their faith in God, while others put it into science, relationships, or work. But wherever you choose to place your faith, you must still confront a deeper question: What is your ultimate pursuit and dream? What do you truly desire in your life—not only for yourself, but for the world as well? And how will you begin to make that desire a reality? Having hope and faith are essential, but something more is needed: the skill and discipline to organize your brain in ways that will successfully motivate your life. Our meditation studies have provided a few basic tools that can help you achieve those goals, and if you apply them to your life, not only will you find a little more happiness, you'll bring a little more peace into the world.

2

DO YOU EVEN NEED GOD
WHEN YOU PRAY?

Meditation, Memory, and the Aging Brain

In the summer of 2006, I began a new line of research to see if meditation could have a positive effect on patients suffering from memory problems. As you know, the older we get, the more prone we are toward cognitive impairment, so we all have an investment in keeping our brain healthy, happy, and wise. Now, there are lots of things we can do to add extra years to our lives, but after we turn thirty, brain metabolism slowly begins to decline.[1] We don't notice this until our later years, but like the engine of an aging car, things begin to break down. Gaskets can leak, the transmission fluid starts to dry out, and the spark plugs begin to misfire. Bit by bit we lose the optimal balance of neuroplasticity, and this affects our memory, coordination, attention span, information processing, problem solving, and social decision-making skills.[2] Unlike a car, we can't overhaul the brain or replace the electrical wiring with new parts. But we can give it a tune-up by "exercising" it in different ways.

Pharmaceutical companies are well aware of our national obsession for staying young, which is why they have invested billions of dollars in search of a chemical fountain of youth. But I was looking for evidence that meditation and prayer could be a better, cheaper, and safer way to go, so you can imagine my delight when I received a grant from the Alzheimer's Research and Prevention Foundation. The medical director, Dr. Dharma Singh Khalsa, asked me to investigate how a specific form of meditation might affect the neural functioning of patients who suffered from memory loss.

This was very exciting for me. Our prior research showed how advanced meditators could consciously alter the normal functioning of different parts of the brain, but it did not answer the deeper question: Could meditation change our neural chemistry and circuitry in ways that enhanced our cognitive skills? And if it did, would such changes be temporary or permanent?

For years these questions have been an issue of considerable debate, and now we had an opportunity to find out. To make things more interesting, we'd be working with people who had little or no experience with meditation. We could actually watch what changes took place in the brain over time, and document them.

The practice we investigated is called Kirtan Kriya. The technique has its roots in the sixteenth-century spiritual traditions of northern India, and it became popular in the United States in the 1970s and 1980s.[3] Specifically, this form of meditation integrates three elements: breathing, sound, and movement. The first element involves the conscious regulation of one's breath, and it is the foundation of many forms of Eastern meditation. Numerous well-documented studies have demonstrated how different forms of yoga and focused breathing can effectively reduce stress, blood pressure, anxiety, and a host of other health-related problems,[4] while increasing alertness and cognitive functioning.[5] In other recent studies, breathing meditations have been shown to have an effect on the regulation of immunity, aging, and cell death.[6]

The second element of Kirtan Kriya involves the repetition of the following sounds—sa, ta, na, and ma—which can be done either silently or aloud, and is sometimes incorporated into a melody or song. Known as a mantra, it is similar to the Catholic tradition of repeating a brief prayer for a certain length of time. In Eastern traditions, there are hundreds of different mantras. Many have sacred or symbolic meanings, and others simply involve the repetition of primal sounds. Mantras are often cited in spiritual texts, and they may be assigned to an initiate by a spiritual teacher, but they are all very simple and easy to recall. Mantras and repetitive prayers like the Rosary have been shown to have a distinct, powerful, and synchronous effect on the cardiovascular rhythms of practitioners,[7] and we hoped that our brain-scan study would shed additional light on this particular type of meditation.

The third part of the meditation technique involves specific movements of the fingers. In the East, hand, face, and body gestures are called mudras, and in the Kirtan Kriya tradition, you sequentially touch your fingers with your thumb as you pronounce each of the sounds: *sa, ta, na,* and *ma.* The technique bears a similarity to the counting of prayer beads, a universal practice that can be found in Christianity, Islam, Hinduism, and Buddhism.

From a spiritual perspective, each mudra or mantra is associated with a theological or metaphysical idea,[8] but from a scientific perspective, any form of repetitive movement or sound helps to keep the mind focused.[9] This particularly interested me because the neural deterioration of aging often affects muscle coordination and verbalization skills. Thus, the Kirtan Kriya meditation seemed to be an excellent meditation with which to experiment. It was easy to learn and do, and we set up the experiment in a way that eliminated the need for the patient to embrace any specific religious belief. Best of all, our patients would only have to practice for twelve minutes a day. Other meditation studies often focus on rituals that last for much longer periods of time.

MEDITATION FOR CONSTRUCTION WORKERS?

Anyone, I thought, should be able to do this meditation with the minimal amount of instruction, but when Gus walked into my clinic, I suddenly had doubts. In all of our previous studies, our subjects had nurtured spiritual and meditative practices for years. Gus had never meditated, and he wasn't interested in religion. He just wanted his faltering brain to function better.

Gus was a relatively large man, a bit rough around the edges, but very pleasant. He seemed more like a plumber you'd meet on a construction site—you know, someone who was likely to zone out in front of the television with a couple of beers by his side. He didn't seem to be a meditation type of guy. Indeed, when I described the exercise to him,

Gus clearly looked unhappy, but after we explained the purpose of the study, his enthusiasm returned.

"When should I do it?" he asked.

"First thing in the morning, just after you get up." I said.

He thought for a moment, then replied, "The instructions said to 'sing out' during the meditation,* but I'm usually up around five A.M., getting ready for work. I'm afraid I'll wake up everyone in the building!" Gus, it turns out, was an industrial mechanic.

I knew what he meant because I had tried the mantra a couple of times and felt very self-conscious. After all, it does seem somewhat strange to be loudly chanting, "*sa ta na ma,*" especially if you live in a crowded apartment complex in downtown Philadelphia. I told him that he could do it a little later, or, if he preferred, he could say it quietly.

Still, he seemed concerned. He wanted to do it "right" because he felt that his mental health was at stake, so I reassured him that it would not diminish the success of the practice. He felt satisfied with my response, and we proceeded to give him a series of tests to evaluate his cognitive abilities.

Then I took the first of four brain scans. The first one is called a baseline scan, during which he simply sat quietly for ten minutes listening to an intellectual description of the meditation practice. The images I recorded would serve as a marker, to be compared to later scans that measured the activity in his brain at the end of the eight-week training program.

Next, I described the meditation in detail and played him a video that demonstrated the technique. I asked him to practice it by following along with the person on the video, and then we took the second scan so we could see what was happening in his "untrained" brain during the meditation. We do this by injecting a radioactive tracer through an intravenous tube in his arm during the last few minutes of the meditation. The tracer marks the cerebral blood flow activity by leaving a

---

* The term "Kirtan" refers to a North Indian style of devotional singing, and so the mantra is spoken lyrically, not chanted. You can read more about Kirtan Kriya and listen to the version we used in our study at www.alzheimersprevention.org.

temporary residue in the brain. Then, when the meditation is complete, we can casually walk down to the room where we take the scans. The cameras would pick up the activity that was deposited during the peak moment of the meditation.

I sent him home with the CD so that he could practice every day, and we called him every two weeks to monitor his progress and answer any questions he might have. Each time we called, he replied that he was doing it faithfully and that everything was going well. Eight weeks later he returned to our lab for further testing and brain scans.

"I really enjoyed it!" he said. "It was great, and I plan to keep doing it." We got a similar response from our other subjects, who, like Gus, were complaining of memory problems. They too were everyday people who had never done any substantial meditation in their lives. Personally, I was amazed, yet pleased, at their willingness and eagerness to practice regularly. Obviously, they wanted to gain the maximum effect, and they knew we would be tracking them in order to assess the long-term improvements in cognition.

Of course, the big question was: *Did it work?* Would we find any significant changes in the brain, and would there be any improvement of memory? Our other studies had shown *how* the brain changes during intense meditation and prayer, but our prior subjects had at least ten years of intense daily practice lasting forty-five minutes or longer. Our memory patients would have only eight weeks of a twelve-minute practice. That's a big difference, and so our study would help identify how long it might actually take to make significant neurological changes. Such information might also help identify the degree of neuroplasticity that remains when we enter the final decades of life.

We know that if you do cardiovascular exercise, you enhance your physical and emotional health, but there is only a small body of evidence supporting the notion that meditation can enhance your cognitive health. Then there's the problem of complexity. The brain has a hundred billion neurons that connect to others in trillions upon trillions of ways, and no two people have the exact same configuration of connections. As things currently stand in the field of neuroscience, we only have a vague map of a small percentage of the neural circuits that control our emotions, behaviors, and thoughts. Still, the slowly accumulating evidence points to the very real possibility that meditation is an excellent exercise for maintaining a healthy brain.

PROTECTING AND STRENGTHENING YOUR AGING BRAIN

Returning to Gus: Did he alter the normal function of his brain after eight weeks of practice? Yes, he did! I took our second resting scan, and we discovered that there was a significant increase of neural activity in the prefrontal cortex, an area heavily involved in helping an individual maintain a clear, focused attention upon a task. The anterior cingulate was also activated, a structure that is involved with emotional regulation, learning, and memory,[10] and is particularly vulnerable to the aging process.[11] The anterior cingulate plays a major role in lowering anxiety and irritability, and also enhances social awareness, a feature that tends to deteriorate with age. Throughout this book, we will often return to the importance of this structure in the brain and the ways in which it is stimulated by a variety of meditative practices.

Not only does activation in the prefrontal cortex and anterior cingulate improve memory and cognition, it also counters the effects of depression, a common symptom in age-related disorders.[12] Parkinson's and Alzheimer's patients also show reduced metabolic activity in the anterior cingulate,[13] and this suggests to us that the meditation technique should slow down the deterioration caused by these diseases.

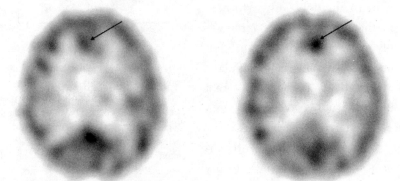

Scans before and after eight weeks of Kirtan Kriya practice showing increased activity in the anterior cingulate (arrow). The fuzziness is due to the type of technology used and rendering a color scan in black-and-white.

Personal religious practices and higher levels of spirituality are also associated with slower progression of Alzheimer's disease.[14]

Other meditation studies have shown similar benefits. In 2007, researchers at Emory University found that Zen meditation had "neuroprotective effects and reduced the cognitive decline associated with normal aging."[15] Overall, the evidence clearly demonstrates that most forms of contemplative meditation and yoga will exercise your brain in ways that maintain and promote cognitive health and vitality.

Brief prayer, however, has not yet been shown to have a direct effect upon cognition, and it even appears to increase depression in older individuals who are not religiously affiliated.[16] However, when prayer is incorporated into longer forms of intense meditation, or practiced within the context of weekly religious activity, many health benefits have been found, including greater length of life.[17] Prayer is also associated with a sense of connection to others,[18] but the reason it may have little effect on cognition has to do with the length of time it is performed. Prayer is generally conducted for only a few minutes at a time, and we believe that it is the intense, ongoing focus on a specific object, goal, or idea that stimulates the cognitive circuits in the brain.

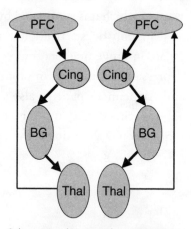

Our brain-scan study showed that the meditation Gus performed strengthens a specific circuit—involving the prefrontal and orbital-frontal lobe, the anterior cingulate, basal ganglia, and thalamus—that would otherwise deteriorate with age.[19] This circuit governs a wide variety of activities involved with consciousness, clarity of mind, reality formation, error detection, empathy, compassion, emotional balance, and the suppression of anger and fear.

Schematic showing the circuit activated by Kirtan Kriya: the prefrontal cortex (PFC), anterior cingulate (Cing), basal ganglia (BG), and thalamus (Thal). During meditation, we become more focused and alert (PFC), more empathic and socially aware (Cing), and can better control our body movements and emotions (BG). This affects our sensory perception of the world (Thal), and this information is relayed to other parts of the brain.

When this particular circuit malfunctions or deteriorates, it contributes to the formation of depression, anxiety, obsessive-compulsive behavior, and schizophrenia. We can keep this circuit healthy, and even improve it, by incorporating meditation into our daily activities and rituals, regardless of our beliefs.

THE AMAZING PLASTICITY OF THE BRAIN

Next, we asked Gus to perform his meditation in our lab. We again injected him with the tracer, as we had eight weeks before, and we took another scan. We wanted to see if his brain responded differently to the meditation than when he first tried it, and we discovered that toward the end of the twelve-minute practice there was decreased activity in the parietal lobe, a part of the cortex involved with constructing our sense of self.

In our brain-scan studies of nuns and Buddhists, we also found decreased activity in the parietal lobe. When this happens, one's sense of self begins to dissolve, allowing the person to feel unified with the object of contemplation or intention. For the nuns, their goal was to come closer to God. For the Buddhists, it was to experience pure consciousness and awareness. But for Gus, he became unified with his goal of improving memory. We don't fully understand the reason for it, but it appears that a loss of self-consciousness enhances one's intention to reach specific goals. A loss of one's sense of self also appears to improve one's ability to perform a variety of tasks, with greater pleasure.[20] In sports it's called being "in the zone," and in psychology, this state of optimal experience is called "flow."[21]

Gus's scans showed that it takes less than two months to alter the overall neural functioning of the brain. This is amazing because it demonstrates that we have the power to consciously change our brains, and improve our neural functioning, in far less time than scientists used to think. As noted in Chapter 1, we can see permanent changes in single neurons in a matter of days, and as other studies have shown, most forms of meditation will create subtle but significant changes in a couple of months. Will they be permanent? It's too early to tell concerning cognitive enhancement, but we know from our own studies that advanced meditators who have practiced for years show substantial differences in their brain when compared to nonmeditators. These differences can even be seen when the person is not meditating, but again, we don't know if the brain would return to "normal" if the meditation practice were given up. It's probably similar to exercise: the more the better, but if you stop doing it, the benefits will fade away.

As we mentioned earlier, we found significant increases in the prefrontal cortex and the anterior cingulate, areas essential for keeping one's attention focused on a task. Other types of meditation and yoga practice stimulate these same areas, but with our memory patients, we also found a significant increase in the cerebellum, which plays an important role in integrating conscious movements of the body. This makes sense since the hand movements of the meditation would necessarily involve the motor coordination areas in the brain.

Gus also showed increased activity in his basal ganglia, lying deep within the center of the brain. The basal ganglia helps control voluntary movements, posture, and motor sequencing, but it also plays an important role in memory formation, behavioral control, and cognitive flexibility.[22] Abnormal functioning in this area is associated with normal aging[23] and movement disorders[24] like Parkinson's, Alzheimer's, Tourette's, and Huntington's disease.[25] This suggests to us that movement-based meditations, more so than passive meditations, should strengthen the neural functioning of those parts of the brain susceptible to many age-related diseases. However, other forms of meditation, such as Zen, also improve cognition by strengthening different circuits of the brain that normally decline with age.[26]

TESTING GUS'S COGNITIVE SKILLS

After we took the second set of scans, we readministered our cognitive measurement tests to see if his memory had improved. We were astonished. On one of the tests, he showed almost a 50 percent improvement. Known as the Trails Test,[27] it's like an advanced connect-the-dots game. The test has been used for decades to assess a wide range of cognitive functions because it requires visual scanning, visual-motor coordination, and visual-spatial ability. Before the meditation practice, Gus took 107 seconds to complete the task. After following the Kirtan Kriya program, he completed the task in 68 seconds.

Some of our other subjects showed less improvement, but all of them showed enhanced abilities in memory recall, concentration, and verbal fluency. The overall improvement averaged between 10 and 20 percent. This is very impressive, because eight weeks, as we mentioned, is a very short time to measure these kinds of changes. Since we plan to follow our patients over a period of several years, we expect to see continuing improvement in a variety of cognitive skills. However, as other cognitive studies have shown, you need to exercise your brain daily to maintain the benefits achieved.[28]

MEDITATION WITHOUT GOD

This was our first real evidence that a meditation practice, even when removed from its spiritual and religious framework, can substantially improve memory in people suffering from cognitive problems. This is good news for millions of aging Americans, because it is easy to get into the habit of meditating twelve minutes a day.

Our study also shows that meditation can be separated from its spiritual roots and still remain a valuable tool for cognitive enhancement. Thus, different types of meditation can be introduced into our public school systems to improve our children's academic performance. In a longitudinal study completed in 2007, students showed "decreased test anxiety, nervousness, self-doubt, and concentration loss" simply by using a deep-breathing technique.[29] In another study, supported in part by a grant from the National Institutes of Health, researchers at the Medical College of Georgia found that African-American adolescents who were trained in a simple meditation (involving relaxation, breathing, and the repetition of a sound) showed a significant decline in "absenteeism, school rule infractions, and suspension days."[30] Students who took up tai chi (a gentle movement exercise) at Boston Public Middle School reported enhanced personal well-being and social awareness.[31] And for a group of young teens who attended a yoga camp, their spatial memory scores improved by 43 percent.[32] What parent, when shown this evidence, would not want to teach their children how to meditate, breathe, and relax?

GUS'S LEGACY: THE POWER OF SELECTIVE ATTENTION

Gus symbolizes the brain's remarkable capacity to heal itself and change, especially in the areas that make us uniquely human: our frontal lobes. Here we find the neurological roots of our imagination and creativity, our capacity to reason and communicate with others, and our ability to become more peaceful, compassionate, and motivated.

Our frontal lobe holds the secret for making our dreams come true. That secret can be summarized in two words—*selective attention*—the ability to voluntarily choose, from millions of pieces of data, which ones seem most relevant to your life. Daily meditation enhances our ability to focus our attention on virtually any goal we wish to achieve, and selective attention improves the memory functions of the brain. Specifically, meditation helps to maintain working memory—the information we need to make any conscious decision—and it does this by discarding irrelevant and distracting data.[33] Our study specifically showed changes in those parts of the brain related directly to the structures that are part of the working-memory circuit.[34]

Spiritual experiences, and the techniques we use to evoke them, involve a complex network of interconnecting neural functions that are equally influenced by our thoughts, feelings, memories, physical conditions, genetic predispositions, and the personal experiences we've had throughout our lives. But the key to meditation—and thus our ability to change our brain—can be reduced to a handful of specific steps. Thus, Gus's memory improved for the following reasons:

1. He *wanted* to improve.
2. He stayed *focused* on his intention and goal.
3. He consciously *regulated* his breathing, posture, and body movements.
4. He *practiced* the skill over a period of time.

The first step begins with a desire—the *conscious* wish to change. Once that decision is made, you must train yourself to remain focused on your goal. This takes practice, but our experiments suggest that this happens rapidly. Focused attention begins to build new neuronal circuits that, once established, will automatically activate those parts of the brain that involve motivational activity. And the more that activity is repeated, the stronger those neural circuits become. This mechanism is known as Hebbian learning—often stated as "cells that fire together, wire together"—and it is the primary mechanism by which all living organisms gain new knowledge about the world. Repeating a new task, such as meditation or prayer, changes the synaptic activity at the end of a neuron and will eventually change the structure of the cell.[35] Such changes affect the way information is relayed to other parts of the brain.

Desire and focus is enough to permanently alter the brain, but spiritual devotees have discovered additional ways to improve neural functioning. Regulated breathing will affect mechanisms that control emotions and sensory perception, but if you do it too deeply, you can evoke hallucinogenic visions and sounds. Slower regulated breathing has a calming effect on both your body and mind, and it also decreases metabolic activity in different parts of the brain. This is very important because our frontal lobe tends to be overly active. It uses up a lot of energy that is needed to efficiently run other neural mechanisms, and so we need to give this part of the brain a rest. Thinking uses up a lot of neural energy, but slow, deep breathing replenishes it. We'll discuss this in greater depth in later chapters.

The *sa-ta-na-ma* meditation, like other spiritual practices, allows your brain to rest while maintaining an acute awareness of the environment, which is a very useful skill to develop. By adding repetitious hand movements and speech to your meditation, you further enhance the motor and coordination centers in your brain. Thus, by increasing efficiency throughout the brain, more neural and metabolic energy is conserved. This, in turn, enhances memory formation and retrieval.

Gus wanted to improve his memory, and so he did. But other people, using similar meditation techniques, have achieved other significant goals. Some have created lasting states of tranquility and peace, while others have become more productive at work. When you intensely meditate on a specific goal over an extended period of time, your brain begins to relate to your idea as if it were an actual object in the world by increasing activity in the thalamus, part of the reality-making process of the brain. The concept begins to feel more obtainable and real, and this is the first step in motivating other parts of the brain to take deliberate action in the world.

HAVING FAITH IN REACHING YOUR GOALS

Underlying these four steps—desire, focus, regulated body control, and practice—is a fifth process, one that is essential for obtaining your desire or goal. We call it "expectation," a term, much like faith, that reflects our neurological propensity to believe that we can, and will, accomplish our goals. Expectation is different from hope because it gives you the inner conviction that your goal is attainable, even if it seems irrational. It is one of the underlying principles of optimism, and it also governs the neurological mechanism known as the "placebo effect." If you strongly believe in something—in other words, if you have enough faith in yourself—you will stimulate both your immune system and your motivational system into action.[36]

This is not a magical process, nor something that quantum physics validates, as some self-help books like to claim. Rather, it is simply the brain doing what millions of years of evolution have led it to do: accomplish goals that we set our minds to. The same is true for religious pursuits. If you set your mind on reaching a spiritual goal, you'll neurologically enhance your sense that a spiritual reality can be experienced. One can argue that Abraham, Moses, Mohammed, Jesus, and the Buddha all reached spiritual enlightenment because they devoted years to intense meditation and prayer. And we believe that cognitively impaired patients like Gus can similarly reach their goals of memory enhancement through the practice of daily meditation.

PROTECTING THE AGING BRAIN

The evidence clearly shows that most forms of contemplative practice will improve cognition, but how do you decide which technique to use? More to the point: Is the meditation that Gus used better than other spiritual practices? It will take a long time before we have a definitive answer, but we do have several working hypotheses supported by the years of research that we and others have done.

We believe that this meditation is more likely to show improvement in memory and cognition because it incorporates six different neural-altering techniques: relaxation, breathing, chanting (mantra/word/sound repetition), coordinated finger movements, background music, and intense concentration. Many other meditations only use one or two of these methods. We'll talk more about the benefits of relaxation, breathing, and concentration in Chapter 9, but for now we'll take a few moments to review the effects that repetitive movements, sounds, and music have on the brain.

Numerous studies have shown that the mere repetition of a sound, phrase, or finger movement over a period of time significantly reduces symptoms of stress, anxiety, depression, and anger, while improving the practitioner's perception of quality-of-life and spiritual well-being.[37] In fact, the addition of movement to any meditation should significantly enhance the cognitive performance of the brain.[38] Repeated, skilled finger movements also appear to improve the central and peripheral nervous systems, offsetting the age-related loss of hand control.[39] In one study, musicians who used repeated finger movements had lower rates of dementia,[40] and in another, early musical training with children resulted in the "long-term enhancement of visual-spatial, verbal, and mathematical performance."[41] In fact, it is fair to consider any musical training a form of cognitive meditation because it involves intense concentration, repetition of instructional techniques, body coordination, and motivational attention.

There is even considerable evidence documenting the effects of pleasant music on the brain. It deepens emotional experience,[42] enhances visual and auditory processing,[43] and improves attention and the processing of emotions.[44] Thus, we recommend that you play some classical or melodic music in the background when you meditate or pray. And if you "sing" your mantra or prayer, as is done in the Kirtan Kriya tradition, you'll increase your cognitive performance.[45]

We also want to point out that there is considerable interplay between the brain mechanisms that regulate anxiety, stress, and memory.[46] For example, high levels of stress lead to memory decline and increase the risk of developing Alzheimer's disease.[47] Again, most of the meditations discussed in this book will trigger the body's relaxation response and thereby lower stress. And as most people know, stress is the number one killer in America because it damages nearly every organ in the body—especially your brain.

EXERCISING YOUR DENDRITES

Our current understanding of the human brain shows that subtle deterioration in any part of a neuron—in its coating, synapses, or the way it responds to neurochemicals—will impede cognitive function.[48] But the real key to understanding cognitive enhancement and deterioration may lie in the microscopic dendrites that are on the receiving ends of neurons. In fact, they may even harbor the secret to why humans—and only humans—contemplate the nature of God.

A single neuron can have as many as ten thousand little tentacle-like branches that reach out toward the signaling ends of other neurons. Picture, if you will, the roots of a giant tree: These are the dendrites, collecting information and sending it up into the body of the neuron (the tree trunk), which then decides what other dendrites to stimulate through the axon terminals (the leaves) that grow out of the ends of one of the neuron's "branches."

Mild, short-term, or chronic stress impairs memory by disrupting dendritic activity.[49] Researchers working with rats (whose brain functions are remarkably similar to humans) found that it took only one week of mild stress to cause significant alterations in dendrite organization and growth.[50] If the situation that is causing the stress is removed, function is restored.[51] But not completely, for nearly one-third of the damaged dendrites were permanently lost if the stress was later repeated.[52]

Dendrite loss in the prefrontal cortex has also been found in aging humans.[53] For example, we have known for decades that Alzheimer's patients suffer this kind of loss.[54] However, increased neural activity,

Structure of a Typical Neuron

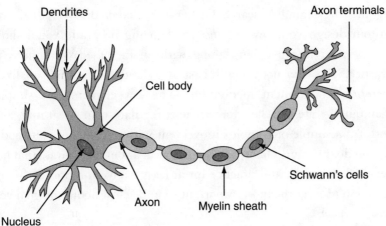

In this simplified drawing, dendrites receive signals from other neurons and pass the information to the axon terminals, which will release neurotransmitter signals to other neurons.[55]

which occurs in the prefrontal cortex and other parts of the brain when we meditate, tempers the effects of the loss.[56] This is why we believe that meditation will help maintain dendrite function: It lowers the overall levels of stress while simultaneously stimulating cognitive alertness. In fact, evidence now suggests that the more you exercise your brain, the more you can slow dendrite deterioration, and thus preserve your memory and cognitive skills.

DESIGNING A PERSONAL
MEMORY-ENHANCEMENT MEDITATION

For years, scientists have known that simple memory exercises—for example, playing mahjong or memorizing random lists of numbers or names—can enhance a variety of cognitive functions, especially for people who are older than fifty.[57] But as we will explain throughout this book, meditation appears to be more effective when it comes to strengthening the neural circuits in your brain.

In essence, the more you exercise your brain—mentally, physically,

socially, and contemplatively—the healthier it becomes. Even more interesting, as researchers at the Stockholm Gerontology Research Center and the Aging Research Center in Sweden discovered, if you
custom design your own memory-enhancing program, you'll show
even greater improvement, along with an increased willingness to
practice.[58] So why not apply this strategy and create a personalized
memory-enhancement meditation? The key elements are simple:
Maintain a state of relaxed awareness, regulate your breathing, and
perform a simple or complex movement with any part of your body.
As you do this, sing, chant, or silently repeat a sound or phrase that has
personal meaning, and practice for at least twelve minutes each day.
And don't forget the most important step: Be clear about the goal you
wish to reach.

Make the meditation as simple or as complex as you like, and feel
free to vary it from week to week. However, the more complex your
meditation becomes, and the longer you do it, the more you will
strengthen the neural circuits that tend to deteriorate with age. You
can even meditate while you're walking, jogging, or doing calisthenics,
for the more parts of your body you move, the more parts of your brain
will be stimulated.

How long will it take to make an improvement? Technically
speaking, overnight, but if you want to see measurable improvements,
you have to practice daily. As one recent study demonstrated, just four-
teen days of daily mental and physical exercise, stress reduction, and a
healthy diet, was enough to improve cognition and brain function for
people between the ages of thirty-five and sixty-nine.[59]

Other meditation studies infer that the greatest improvements are
achieved when you practice thirty minutes to an hour each day. Simply
put, the longer you practice, the greater the reward. After a few weeks
you should notice improvement in your attitude and emotional well-
being, and if you integrate meditation with psychotherapy or cogni-
tive-behavioral classes, you will find that you can maintain low degrees
of depression and anxiety long after your therapy ends—but again,
only if you continue the meditation practice of staying relaxed, alert,
and focused.[60]

TAKE A COFFEE, TEA, AND COGNITION BREAK

Meditation is great for your brain, but when it comes to needing an instant boost of cognitive powers, it is hard to beat a couple of freshly brewed cups of java.[61] Coffee may even lower your risk of diabetes, gout, Parkinson's disease, and certain types of cancer.[62]

When the U.S. Army Research Institute investigated the effects of coffee on Navy SEAL trainees, they concluded that "even in the most adverse circumstances, moderate doses of caffeine can improve cognitive function, including vigilance, learning, memory, and mood state."[63] In fact, they found that for people exposed to severe stress, coffee provided a significant advantage when cognitive performance was critical. They found that the optimal dose was two cups of coffee (200 mg of caffeine).

Caffeine may even lengthen your life,[64] but there are studies showing that more than two cups may have a variety of side effects. It may cause migraines for chronic users,[65] and it appears to weaken bone structure due to the fact that caffeine leaches calcium from your body.[66] Caffeine tablets can also be toxic, and although rare, a caffeine overdose can kill you.[67]

For those who don't like coffee, green and black tea will also improve your cognition and mental health.[68] It has most of the physiological benefits associated with coffee, plus the added benefit of lowering blood pressure.[69] It also has another ingredient, theanine, that enhances neural cognition.[70]

Finally, don't forget about water. Drink plenty of it, especially if you are exercising, because dehydration appears to impair cognition, motor coordination, and mood.[71] However, other evidence suggests that any changes—positive or negative—caused by moderate water deprivation are minor.[72]

Before we close this chapter, I want to bring up an important but often overlooked point. What you choose to meditate upon, or pray for, can do more than change your brain. You can damage it, especially if you choose to focus on something that makes you frightened or angry. In psychology this is called "rumination," and it is clearly hazardous to your health.[73] In a Stanford brain-scan study, people who focused on negative aspects of themselves, or on a negative interpretation of life, had increased activity in their amygdala. This generated waves of fear, releasing a torrent of destructive neurochemicals into the brain.

Fortunately, meditation is the opposite of rumination and, in some ways, is similar to the psychoanalytic model of free association created by Freud. In meditation, as in therapy, we learn to watch our negativity and not react to it. In the process, we train the brain to remain calm, even in the face of adversity. Thus, meditation becomes an exemplary way to reevaluate life's difficulties and mysteries. But perhaps most important, it trains the mind to become less attached to its own desires, attachments, and beliefs. When this happens, the way we see ourselves and the world will change.

3

WHAT DOES GOD DO
TO YOUR BRAIN?

The Neural Varieties of Spiritual Practice

The moment we encounter God, or the idea of God, our brain begins to change. For most American children this occurs in the first year of life when they come face-to-face with holiday religious symbolism. Brightly colored Christmas trees and Easter baskets rivet a child's attention, and this imprints a permanent image into memory. Later, when they are introduced to parental concepts of God, these ideas become neurologically connected to earlier memories and thoughts. Images build upon images, and concepts build upon concepts, until a complex neurological circuit emerges that represents a primitive system of religious belief.

Storytelling may deepen a child's fantasy about God, but rituals give personal meaning to theological ideas. That is why religious parents ask their children to pray, and why they expose them to religious ceremonies and events. We take them to our temples, churches, and mosques on the high holidays, where their senses are saturated with the sights, sounds, and smells of our spiritual heritage and beliefs. They gaze through stained-glass windows, sing hymns in foreign tongues, light candles, bow down in prayer, and sample sacramental foods. They literally enter another world. God becomes even more grand and mysterious—and sometimes frightening—and new parts of the brain light up like a fireworks display.

Rituals add substance to our beliefs, and the more intense the ritual, the more likely we are to have a religious or spiritual epiphany. Thus, spiritual practice is the key to making God personally meaningful and real. But for a researcher like myself, even the simplest ritual is hard to study because there are so many variables to consider. Take, for example, the act of going to church. We know that religious involvement is correlated with health and longevity,[1] but it is difficult to figure out why. Does it have to do with the length of time you spend in church, or how often you go? Does it matter which denomination you attend? Going to church might involve confession, communion, singing, chanting, praying, tithing, talking with other members, reading sacred scriptures, or volunteering in charitable work. Which activity has an impact on the brain? Some of them, all of them, or a specific combination of pursuits? Few studies have been able to isolate which aspects contribute to one's health, but we are beginning to discover that each one can change the way you think and feel about God.

Different religious activities have different effects on specific parts of the brain, but this does not make the results any easier to interpret. For example, praying silently affects one part of the brain, while praying out loud affects another part. And if you repeat the same prayer over and over, one part of the brain may be activated in the first few minutes, another part might quiet down ten minutes later, while other brain functions will change after forty or fifty minutes of intense prayer.

To make matters even more complicated, a single structure in the brain can be simultaneously involved in dozens of different functions, some of which specifically relate to the religious ritual and others of which do not. For example, the anterior cingulate cortex, which plays a crucial role in spiritual practices, is involved with learning, memory, focused attention, emotional regulation, motor coordination, heart rate, error detection, reward anticipation, conflict monitoring, moral evaluation, strategy planning, and empathy.[2] To understand how this single structure influences religious experience, you have to distill the information gathered in hundreds of seemingly unrelated studies. But when you connect the dots, a picture emerges that allows us to catch a glimpse of the neural reality of God.

This chapter, and the four chapters that follow, outline a general model that explains how different concepts of God affect your brain, and how your brain constructs specific impressions of God. The chart on the accompanying pages summarizes how specific parts of the brain generate different experiences of God.

THE "GOD" CIRCUITS IN YOUR BRAIN

From early childhood on, God exists in every person's brain as a combination of ideas, images, feelings, sensations, and self/other relationships. Here is a thumbnail sketch of key neural structures and circuits that shape our perception of God:

OCCIPITAL-PARIETAL CIRCUIT	Identifies God as an object that exists in the world. Young children see God as a face because their brains cannot process abstract spiritual concepts.
PARIETAL-FRONTAL CIRCUIT	Establishes a relationship between the two objects known as "you" and "God." It places God in space and allows you to experience God's presence. If you decrease activity in your parietal lobe through meditation or intense prayer, the boundaries between you and God dissolve. You feel a sense of unity with the object of contemplation and your spiritual beliefs.
FRONTAL LOBE	Creates and integrates all of your ideas about God—positive or negative—including the logic you use to evaluate your religious and spiritual beliefs. It predicts your future in relationship to God and attempts to intellectually answer all the "why, what, and where" questions raised by spiritual issues.
THALAMUS	Gives emotional meaning to your concepts of God. The thalamus gives you a holistic sense of the world and appears to be the key organ that makes God feel objectively real.
AMYGDALA	When overly stimulated, the amygdala creates the emotional impression of a frightening, authoritative, and punitive God, and it suppresses the frontal lobe's ability to logically think about God.
STRIATUM	Inhibits activity in the amygdala, allowing you to feel safe in the presence of God, or of whatever object or concept you are contemplating.

(sidebar continues)

ANTERIOR CINGULATE   Allows you to experience God as loving and compassionate. It decreases religious anxiety, guilt, fear, and anger by suppressing activity in the amygdala.

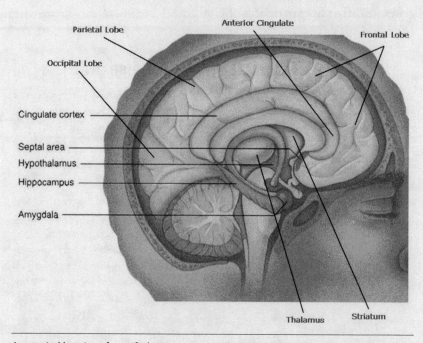

Anatomical location of specific brain structures. The limbic system consists of the amygdala, hippocampus, hypothalamus, and thalamus, in addition to other regions not shown.

CAN YOU SEPARATE SPIRITUALITY FROM GOD?

In the past, our research focused on individuals who were deeply committed to their religious and spiritual beliefs, and we could not separate them from the specific practices they used. As far as we could tell, each neurologically reinforced the other. The practitioners began with a specific goal associated with their religious beliefs and engaged in a ritual activity that strengthened that belief. If you removed the rituals, you might be left with little more than an intellectual understanding of God.

But we discovered that you could take God out of the ritual and still influence the brain. This is what our memory research demonstrated. Our patients were taught a traditional Eastern meditation, using sounds and movements that had deep religious meaning, but we did not emphasize the spiritual dimensions of the ritual. No one reported having a spiritual experience, and no one mentioned God.

If you improve your cognition by 10 percent, as our memory patients did, your age-related anxieties will decrease and you'll be pleased, but I don't know how excited you'll feel. If you change your perception of God by 10 percent, however, that can be a very big deal, especially to people who have maintained their childhood images and beliefs. As you will see in the following chapter, people who alter their concepts of God often feel as if their entire life has been transformed.

Spiritual practices are designed to stimulate dramatic experiences, but you can also transfer nearly any religious ideology from one spiritual practice to another and still receive the same neurological benefits from the experience. Herbert Benson first demonstrated this at Harvard in the early 1970s, when he extracted several key elements from Buddhist meditation and turned them into the now-famous relaxation response. Through dozens of well-designed studies, he demonstrated that you could consciously reduce stress and tension throughout your body by breathing slowly and repeating a word or phrase that gives you a sense of comfort (God, om, peace, etc.).

Today, Benson's "relaxation response" has been incorporated into many aspects of medicine and psychotherapy because it effectively treats hypertension, cardiac arrhythmias, chronic pain, PMS, insomnia, anxiety, depression, hostility, and infertility. It even lessens the side effects caused by cancer treatments and AIDS.[3] This simple meditation also improves cognition in healthy aging adults.[4]

Benson also discovered that the same benefits could be elicited by different forms of meditation and relaxation, including yoga, Zen, hypnosis, and progressive muscle relaxation (see Table 1). All of these techniques utilize breathing and relaxation while the mind stays focused and alert.

TABLE 1.

	OXYGEN CONSUMPTION	RESPIRATORY RATE	HEART RATE	BLOOD PRESSURE
Progressive Muscle Relaxation	Decreases	Decreases	Decreases	Decreases
Zen and Yoga	Decreases	Decreases	Decreases	Decreases
Relaxation Phase of Hypnosis	Decreases	Decreases	Decreases	Inconclusive
Transcendental Meditation	Decreases	Decreases	Decreases	Decreases

EASTERN MEDITATION AND WESTERN PRAYER

In the 1970s, as a result of the societal problems centered around the Vietnam war and civil rights, many young adults became disenchanted with the traditional values of America. Two-thirds of this "baby boom" generation turned away from the religious activities of their parents to seek a more personal spiritual connection.[5] Many turned to the philosophies of the East, in part because those traditions provided techniques that gave them direct experiences of peace.

In response to the 50 percent drop in church attendance, many Christian denominations reinvented themselves, introducing contemporary music and a vast array of social incentives. This joyful celebration of religion made evangelical churches the second most popular religious movement in America. Meditation, however, was shunned, primarily because of its association with Hindu, Zen, and Buddhist philosophies.

Although there are approximately twenty references to meditation in the Bible,[6] most people are unaware of Christianity's rich history of contemplative practice. In Genesis, "Isaac went out to meditate in the field," and in Joshua, followers are commanded by law to "meditate day and night." Such intense meditation may have been the catalyst for many of the spiritual epiphanies described by biblical prophets and saints.

Formal Christian meditation was developed by early monastic orders. In the twelfth century, Guigo II, a Carthusian monk, categorized four levels of practice: *lectio* (slowly reading biblical passages), *meditatio* (pondering the deeper meaning of the text), *oratio* (spontaneous prayer), and *contemplatio* (wordlessly focusing on God's love).

In the sixteenth century, St. Ignatius developed a series of spiritual exercises, including one that asked the individual to visualize scenes from the life of Jesus. His writings influenced other saints, including Teresa of Avila, who emphasized the importance of maintaining an unwavering concentration on one's spiritual goals.

In the mid-twentieth century, many Christian theologians, like Thomas Merton, were influenced by Eastern philosophies, and their books encouraged others to embrace a contemporary contemplative path. Others directly incorporated Eastern practices into the Christian tradition. For example, Friar John Main emphasized the repetition of a phrase from the Bible until the presence of God filled one's heart.[7] The ultimate goal was to be "transformed" by one's meditation, a condition synonymous with the Hindu and Buddhist notions of enlightenment.

Some theologians "rediscovered" the mystical practices of early Christianity and brought them back to life. For example, in the 1970s, Friar Thomas Keating, along with two other Trappist monks, modified a contemplative tradition first described in the fourteenth century text, *The Cloud of Unknowing.*[8] According to Keating:

> It brings us into the presence of God and thus fosters the contemplative attitudes of listening and receptivity. It is not contemplation in the strict sense, which in Catholic tradition has always been regarded as a pure gift of the Spirit, but rather it is a preparation for contemplation by reducing the obstacles caused by the hyperactivity of our minds and of our lives.[9]

Keating called his simple meditation the Centering Prayer, and it has been introduced to thousands of American Catholics and Christians.[10] You choose a word that has a sacred meaning and focus on it for twenty minutes or longer as you sit comfortably with eyes closed. When distracting thoughts or feelings intervene, you gently return to your sacred word, a practice that closely mirrors Benson's relaxation technique. (In Chapter 9 we'll discuss a "generic" version of the Centering Prayer that you can incorporate into your spiritual or secular life.)

COMPARING THE CENTERING PRAYER
TO BUDDHIST MEDITATION

In the summer of 1999, I had the opportunity to study a group of nuns who had been practicing the Centering Prayer for a minimum of fifteen years. This was the first brain-scan study of Christian contemplative practitioners, and we discovered that the neurological changes were significant and very different from how the human brain normally functions.[11] Even more surprising, the neurological changes were nearly the same as those we recorded from a group of Buddhist practitioners, who obviously nurtured very different beliefs.[12] This evidence confirmed our hypothesis that the benefits gleaned from prayer and meditation may have less to do with a specific theology than with the ritual techniques of breathing, staying relaxed, and focusing one's attention upon a concept that evokes comfort, compassion, or a spiritual sense of peace. Of course, the more you believe in what you are meditating or praying about, the stronger the response will be.

MEDITATION AND PRAYER: ARE THEY REALLY THE SAME?

Most dictionaries define prayer as the act of communicating with a deity, especially in the form of a request or a petition for help. Meditation, however, is commonly defined as a contemplative reflection or mental exercise designed to bring about a heightened level of spiritual awareness, trigger a spiritual or religious experience, or train the mind in a specific way. We consider prayer to be a specialized form of meditation, in which the practitioner makes a specific request to a spiritual entity or presence. We also view guided imagery, hypnosis, and the psychoanalytic technique of free association as forms of contemplative activity.

Both prayer and meditation can include the use of religious texts, songs, or movement rituals, but meditation usually refers to a longer, more intensive activity. Neurologically, we have found that the longer one prays or meditates, the more changes occur in the brain. Five minutes of prayer once a week may have little effect, but forty minutes of daily practice, over a period of years, will bring permanent changes to the brain.

However, we have discovered that other forms of religious practice have very different neurological effects. In 2003, I brought in members from a Pentecostal church and scanned them while they engaged in the practice of speaking in tongues. To those unfamiliar with this practice, it may sound like a foreign language or babble, but I have heard renditions that reminded me of medieval Italian liturgies and ancient Assyrian poems. For the Pentecostal practitioner, it is an energizing state, filled with profound spiritual meaning and joy.

"Glossolalia," as it is academically called, is not a form of contemplative meditation. Rather, it is a type of spontaneous verbal monologue that may or may not be accompanied by body gyrations and shaking, similar to the ecstatic trances found in various spiritual and shamanic traditions. Instead of focusing one's attention on a specific phrase or ideal, which increases activity in the frontal lobe, the practitioner surrenders voluntary control—and thus a significant degree of ordinary consciousness—by deliberately slowing down frontal lobe activity. This, in turn, allows the limbic areas of the brain to become more active, which neurologically increases the emotional intensity of the experience. With the nuns and Buddhists, the opposite experience occurs. Frontal lobe activity increases, limbic activity decreases, and the combination generates a peaceful and serene state of consciousness. Interestingly, both the nuns and Pentecostalists felt that our study demonstrated that God could intervene and directly influence the brain.

THE NEURAL CONSTRUCTION OF GOD

When we analyzed the research from all of our studies, we found that different parts of the brain produced different experiences that affected the way we perceive or think about God, the universe, our mind, and our lives. For example, our frontal lobes (the newest part of the human brain) provide us with a logical concept of a rational, deliberate, and loving God, while our limbic system (the oldest part of the brain) creates an emotionally meaningful experience of God. If either part of the brain malfunctions, unusual thoughts and perceptions can occur. Some people with neural damage can become obsessed with God, while others can lose all interest in religion. A person with an overly active limbic system might ruminate day after day on original sin, while a person with an overly active frontal lobe might become absorbed in

mathematically proving the ontological existence of God, as Kurt
Gödel attempted to do.[13]

An overly active limbic system, which generates our emotional
states, is physically and psychologically dangerous, but we now have
evidence, gathered from our recent study on yoga, that a twelve-week
training program (that includes various postures, movements, stretches,
and meditations) lowers activity in the amygdala, the key organ in
the limbic system that generates anxiety and fear. Mindfulness-based
meditation, which includes the act of consciously labeling one's moment-
to-moment feelings, also reduces amygdala activity.[14]

At the other end of the neurological spectrum, if both the frontal
cortex and the emotional centers of the brain remain inactive when a
person contemplates God, God will hold little meaning or value. This
is what we believe happens in the brains of nonreligious individuals,
and our preliminary brain-scan studies with atheists points in this direction.[15]

In order to have a positive perception or experience of God, you
need to have just the "right" balance of frontal and limbic activity.
However, the neurological literature makes it clear that every medita-

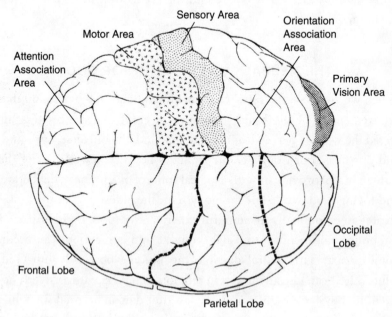

Anatomical location of major lobes and brain regions.

tive experience is somewhat unique and stimulates different parts of the brain to different degrees. Perhaps this explains why each person's experience of God is unique. Even in the Pentecostal tradition of speaking in tongues, each message is highly original and rarely repeats itself to the practitioner.

Other parts of the brain are associated with different notions and experiences of God. For example, the occipital cortex, which is at the back of the brain, helps us to envision an anthropomorphic God, while the temporal lobes (situated above the ear but below the parietal area) allow some individuals to hear God's voice. If these areas are injured, some patients begin to see or hear all sorts of phenomena that they interpret as religious, mystical, or demonic.[16]

The parietal lobe, when active, gives us a sense of our self in relation to time, space, and other objects in the world. This allows us to imagine a God that is separate from ourselves, existing beyond the boundaries of our personal being. Our brain-scan studies of contemplative forms of Buddhist and Christian meditation show that when activity in the parietal areas decreases, a sense of timelessness and spacelessness emerges. This allows the meditator to feel at one with the

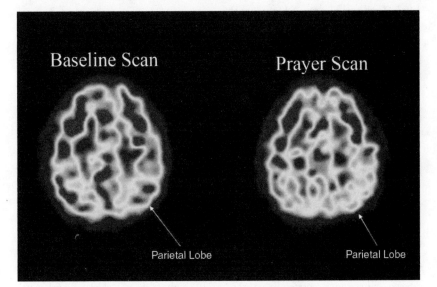

Brain scan of a nun at rest and during prayer showing decreased activity in the parietal lobe that may be associated with the loss of the sense of self.

object of contemplation: with God, the universe, peacefulness, or any other object upon which he or she focuses.

However, when Pentecostals speak in tongues, parietal activity increases. This gives them the sense that a separate entity is communicating with them. Thus, they do not report the experience of feeling at one with God. Since the parietal area also plays a role in language formation and articulation,[17] it makes sense that we would see this type of activity during the Pentecostal experience. Yet, when our memory patients sang *sa-ta-na-ma* during their meditation, parietal activity decreased, just as with the Buddhists and nuns. We don't fully understand this phenomenon, but we suspect that one would need to maintain a strong sense of self in order to maintain an internal dialogue with God. A repetitious chant may interrupt the brain's propensity to create a self/other relationship with the words.

We also found that advanced meditators had a higher level of parietal activity when they were not meditating. This suggests that meditation, over time, strengthens one's sense of self in relationship to the world, as well as to the spiritual dimensions of life. It also suggests that conscious manipulation of parietal activity strengthens this part of the brain in the same way that intellectual activity strengthens the frontal lobe. Indeed, increased parietal activity is associated with increased consciousness, alertness, and the ability to resonate to other people's feelings and thoughts.

ENHANCING COMPASSION AND SOCIAL AWARENESS

Many forms of meditation stimulate another important part of the brain: the anterior cingulate cortex.[18] The anterior cingulate is situated between the frontal lobe and the limbic system, acting as a mediator between our feelings and our thoughts.* It is involved in social awareness and intuition, and is larger in women than in men.[19] This may explain why women generally are more empathic, socially skilled, and more

---

* Some neuroscientists consider the anterior cingulate a part of the frontal lobe and prefrontal cortex; others see it as part of the limbic and paralimbic system. We, and others, view it as both part of, yet distinct from, the dorsolateral prefrontal cortex.

reactive to fear-inducing stimuli. However, largeness does not mean "better." For example, men who have difficulties expressing their feelings, or recognizing the feelings of others, have a larger anterior cingulate area in the right half of their brain.[20] Thus, they may have a greater capacity to shut down feelings by reducing fear-arousing activity in the amygdala. Such men simply experience less emotion, unless they are strongly provoked. Other studies have shown that insensitive men have *less* activity in the anterior cingulate, suggesting that they may still feel negative emotions but are unaware of them.[21]

Contemplative practices stimulate activity in the anterior cingulate, thus helping a person to become more sensitive to the feelings of others. Indeed, meditating on any form of love, including God's love, appears to strengthen the same neurological circuits that allow us to feel compassion toward others.[22]

In contrast, religious activities that focus on fear may damage the anterior cingulate, and when this happens, a person will often lose interest in other people's concerns or act aggressively against them.[23] We suspect that fear-based religions may even create symptoms that mirror post-traumatic stress disorder.[24] Brain-scan studies have shown that once you anticipate a future negative event, activity in the amygdala is turned up and activity in the anterior cingulate turned down. This generates higher levels of neuroticism and anxiety.[25] Highly anxious individuals may be attracted to fundamentalist religions because they offer a highly structured belief system that reduces feelings of uncertainty. In this respect, membership in a strict religious order can reduce feelings of anger, anxiety, and fear. And, once you are accepted as a member, you will be joyously embraced by the entire congregation. This, we believe, will have a positive effect on the anterior cingulate in the development of compassionate feelings toward oneself and other members of the group. However, if the community emphasizes disdain toward members of other groups, this will ultimately inhibit the functioning of the anterior cingulate.

If you want to maintain a healthy anterior cingulate cortex, frontal cortex, and limbic system, by all means meditate and pray, but only on those concepts that bring you a sense of love, joy, optimism, and hope. We believe that meditation is particularly important for the brain because it counteracts our biological propensity to react to dangerous situations with animosity or fear. However, it also appears to make us more sensitive to the suffering of others, which may explain why those traditions that emphasize meditation are often involved in community charities and peacekeeping ventures.

WHAT PART OF THE BRAIN MAKES GOD REAL?

One of the most unusual findings in our brain-scan studies involves the thalamus, a walnut-shaped structure that sits on top of the limbic system in the center of your brain (there are actually two of them—a pair—with one half sitting in each hemisphere). The thalamus is the Grand Central Station of sensory processing: Every sensation, mood, and thought passes through it as the information is relayed to other parts of the brain. If the thalamus ceases to function, you would, for all intents and purposes, be considered comatose. Even minimal damage will hinder the performance of other parts of the brain.[26]

In nearly all of our subjects who had meditated for over ten years, we found asymmetric activity between the left and right half of the thalamus when they were *not* engaged in any contemplative activity. In other words, one side was more active than the other side. In the general population, both sides are typically equal in activity, especially when you are at rest.

What could this mean? You occasionally find such asymmetry in epileptics and schizophrenics, but our subjects had no such symptoms. The thalamus plays a crucial role in identifying what is and isn't real, and it gives a sense of emotional meaning to the thoughts

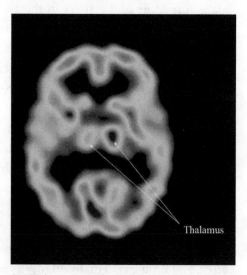

Thalamus

SPECT brain scan of an individual with more than fifteen years of meditation experience showing asymmetry in the activity in the thalamus.

that emerge in the frontal lobe. In most animals the thalamus primarily sends one-way messages to the frontal cortex, but in humans an enormous neural dialogue takes place.

We would argue that the more you meditate on a specific object—be it God, or peace, or financial success—the more active your thalamus becomes, until it reaches a point of stimulation where it perceives thoughts in the same way that other sensations are perceived. And if you exercise an idea over and over, your brain will begin to respond as though the idea was a real object in the world. This, we believe, is what may cause thalamic asymmetry in advanced meditators. Thus, the more you focus on God, the more God will be sensed as real. But it will not be a "symmetrical" reality. Instead, it will be perceived "asymmetrically," meaning that the reality will appear different from one's normal perception of the world. For advanced meditators, the asymmetric reality becomes their normal state of awareness. God, tranquility, and unity become an integral part of their lives, no longer a thought but a palpable experience, as real as the book you are holding in your hand.

The thalamus makes no distinction between inner and outer realities, and thus any idea, if contemplated long enough, will take on a semblance of reality. Your belief becomes neurologically real, and your brain will respond accordingly. But for someone else, who has meditated on a different set of beliefs or goals, a different reality will seem true.

THE CHEMICAL NATURE OF GOD

Spiritual practices also have an effect upon your neurotransmitters, the chemicals that make your brain and body work. For example, a 65 percent increase in dopamine was found when individuals practiced yoga nidra,[27] a form of meditation in which a person maintains conscious awareness while remaining in a state of complete relaxation. Dopamine heightens sensory imagery, generates pleasurable experiences, stimulates positive thoughts, increases your sense of well-being, and allows you to feel safe in the world. Even the high that results from cocaine is related directly to the sudden increase of dopamine in the brain. This may explain why some people equate spiritual experiences with drug experiences, since both share common pathways in the brain.

Indeed, the ability to believe in spiritual realms may be dependent upon the amount of dopamine that is released in the frontal lobes, and too little dopamine may bias a person toward skepticism and disbelief. On the other hand, high levels of dopamine may bias a person to foster paranormal beliefs.[28] Other research has suggested that the balance of activity between the brain's left and right hemispheres could regulate a person's predisposition to spirituality or atheism.[29]

During intense forms of meditation (mindfulness, vipassana, insight, and Transcendental Meditation), serotonin levels in the blood are altered. In some studies it increases, in others it decreases, and many question whether the effects are beneficial or harmful.[30] Some argue that meditation evokes small epileptic-like seizures, but to my knowledge not a single case of epilepsy has ever been directly tied to spiritual practices. There is, however, anecdotal evidence that people with unstable personalities could have their symptoms temporarily increased. But since there has been such widespread use of meditation in psychotherapy—where it has been proven to be especially effective in the treatment of severe depression—the evidence shows that it is a very effective treatment for mood disorders.[31] The serotonin released during meditation may also be responsible for the enhanced visual imagery and sensory experiences often reported during intense spiritual practice.

Research has shown that spiritual practices affect other important neurochemicals in the brain. For example, gentle forms of yoga that involve breathing and stretching have been shown to increase gamma-aminobutyric acid (GABA) levels in the brain by as much as 27 percent, which is associated with lower levels of depression and anxiety.[32] Transcendental Meditation (which is a simple combination of relaxation, breathing, and the repetition of a symbolic sound) also lowers the stress molecules, epinephrine and norepinephrine, which explains why contemplative practices leave you pleasurably relaxed.[33] By altering the neurochemistry of the brain, spiritual practices bestow a sense of peace, happiness, and security, while decreasing symptoms of anxiety, depression, and stress.

CAN YOU FIND GOD BY SWALLOWING A PILL?

What about drug-induced spiritual experiences? Can they help you find God? For centuries hallucinogenic plants like peyote and ayahuasca have been used as a means to interact with spiritual entities and forces. When LSD became popular in the 1960s, proponents of the drug believed they had found a fast way to reach spiritual and psychological enlightenment. But it was extraordinarily unpredictable, and psychologists soon realized that people with unstable personalities could plummet into a "bad trip"—a nightmare reality that might last for days, weeks, or months.

Experts in nearly every field of psychology and religion believe that drug-induced spiritual experiences do little to create a spiritual foundation from which to live one's life.[34] But some researchers disagree. They believe that certain drugs can stimulate profoundly meaningful experiences by disrupting malfunctioning neurological circuits. For example, marijuana alters the human cerebellar clock,[35] which may aid in slowing down hyperactivity.[36] However, as four new studies conducted in 2008 found, marijuana use tends to impair many cognitive functions,[37] and the same is true for MDMA, the popular drug known as Ecstasy.[38] Meditation enhances cognition, memory, and the ability to concentrate on specific tasks without creating any health risks to your brain.

Hallucinogenic substances like peyote, mescaline, ayahuasca, and LSD stimulate many centers of the brain, producing visions and perceptual phenomena that occasionally have religious connotations. In a recent cross-cultural study comparing psychedelic drug users to marijuana and alcohol users, psychedelic users scored significantly higher on mystical beliefs, spiritual life values, and the ability to feel empathy toward others. In addition, the researchers found that "users of nonpsychedelic illegal drugs scored significantly lower on a measure of coping ability."[39]

Another study found that users of psychedelic drugs were more imaginative and empathic. They tended to fantasize more, but were more likely to act out their feelings and possess more unconscious hostility than nondrug users.[40] Whereas meditation mildly increases activity in the frontal lobes while reducing activity in the emotional centers, psychedelics create excessive stimulation throughout the brain, similar to what is found when people experience acute psychotic episodes.[41] Thus, it is far more difficult to incorporate drug-induced experiences in a practical or meaningful way.

However, a highly publicized study conducted at Johns Hopkins University School of Medicine challenged this perspective.[42] Thirty-six subjects who had never taken psychedelics were given two different drugs on separate occasions: psilocybin (the active ingredient found in psychedelic mushrooms), and Ritalin, the stimulant prescription drug used to treat attention-deficit disorders. They were not told what they were given. With psilocybin, subjects reported significant increases in their feelings of unity, sacredness, intuitive knowledge, and ineffability. Two months later the participants continued to associate the experience with increased feelings of altruism, positive emotions, and constructive behavior. In fact, over 70 percent of the respondents stated that it was one of the top ten experiences in their lives. Approximately one-third said it was the single most spiritually significant experience in their life, and another third stated that it was in their top five.

Ritalin, however, generated little meaning or value, even though a couple of people did report mystical experiences. But before you go off in search of mushroom enlightenment, consider this: A number of subjects had increased feelings of anxiety, and 10 percent said they never wanted to have such an experience again. Furthermore, if you abuse psychedelic drugs, you'll have an increased risk of lifetime panic attacks.[43] We still have much to learn about how and why certain drugs influence our spiritual and religious beliefs, but the fact remains that meditation is safer.

REINVENTING GOD

All experiences, be they religious or secular, must be viewed as lying along a continuum. For one person a specific experience will be intense, yet for another the same experience may barely elicit a neuropsychological response. For some people, the word "God" evokes a negative neurological response; for others, the word neurologically stimulates a sense of happiness and peace.

Even among atheists, the notion of God evokes a wide range of reactions. When we asked Kevin, a long-term meditator and atheist, to focus on an image of God, one side of his frontal lobe became more active, while the metabolic activity in the other side decreased. In our last book, we described this as a form of cognitive dissonance.[44] Thus, when people focus on a belief that they strongly reject, their brain will experience some degree of emotional conflict and intellectual confusion. Others will not. When we scanned the brain of another atheist while she meditated on God, we found no significant changes in neural activity. We suspect that atheism comes in as many flavors as theism and that different nonbelievers reach their conclusions through different neurological paths of logic, experience, emotion, and social influence. Thus, we expect that each atheist will show a different pattern of neural activity when he or she contemplates God.

Since concepts of God vary from person to person, one would expect to find hundreds of different neurological "fingerprints," which is what our research has found so far. Children, however, demonstrate a more consistent view of spiritual and religious ideas,[45] which suggests that we all form a similar notion of a supernatural reality in the first few years of life, one that usually involves a face or a person who lives in the sky. This notion is rooted in the

A "STROKE" OF ENLIGHTENMENT

In her recent book, *My Stroke of Insight*, neuroscientist Jill Bolte Taylor describes her extraordinary experience when, at the age of thirty-seven, she had a stroke. It caused substantial neurological damage to the left side of her brain, but it also resulted in an incredibly euphoric experience in which she felt intimately and profoundly connected with everything. She argued that the right side of the brain, when freed from the abstract reductionistic thinking of the left hemisphere, allows a person to experience the deeply compassionate and spiritual part of our human nature. Fully recovered, Dr. Taylor says she can now easily shift between the scientific and transcendent sides of her brain. Her experience supports the notion that each of us has an inner capability to access these wonderful parts of who we are—a notion supported by our brain-scan research at the University of Pennsylvania.

neural shortcomings of a child's brain, and is deeply influenced by what adults choose to believe in and teach. (In Chapter 5, we'll explore in detail how children and adults envision God.)

To summarize, the neural varieties of religious experience are just that—varieties. There is no "God spot," nor is there any simple way to categorize religious beliefs. The data points to an endless variety of ways in which spiritual practices can affect the cognitive, emotional, and experiential processes of the brain, and each one of these experiences will lead to a different notion about God.

IS GOING TO CHURCH GOOD FOR YOU?

Even going to church will change your brain and your health, but only if you go frequently, or for many years.[46] Studies have also found that regular attendance at religious activities will lower your blood pressure, but it may not be enough to lower one's risk of a heart attack or stroke. For example, in a large national survey, those who attended religious services weekly had blood pressures that were 1.46 millimeters lower than nonattendees, and those who went more than fifty-two times a year registered 3.03 mm. lower.[47] For a person with a systolic pressure of 150, it doesn't reduce one's health risk if they lower it to 147. Of course, the optimist will argue that every little bit helps, and we would have to agree. But as skeptic and Claremont Graduate University professor Michael Shermer points out:

> In several studies on the relationship between religiosity and mortality (religious people allegedly live longer), a number of religious variables were used, but only those with significant correlations were reported. Meanwhile, other studies using the same religiosity variables found different correlations and, of course, only reported those. The rest were filed away in the drawer of nonsignificant findings. When all variables are factored in together, religiosity and mortality show no relationship.[48]

Critics of religion will point to the vast amount of research showing that health improvements are only slightly above chance.[49] But the fact that it has an effect at all is very important and should not be dismissed, as some researchers try to do. No matter how you want to interpret the findings, the evidence is clear that religious involvement has little down side and very often has a beneficial effect, especially when one feels positive about his or her religious beliefs. And sometimes the benefits are spectacular. For example, a national sampling found that those who go to church at least once a month have a 30 to 35 percent reduced risk of death.[50] The numbers are equally consistent for Caucasians, African Americans, and Mexican Americans, and for older individuals religious activity is even more beneficial.[51] Those who attend weekly are significantly less likely to have a stroke, but religious involvement didn't have an effect on diabetes or heart attacks.[52] I suppose it is fair to say that God is good for your brain, but not necessarily your heart!

These, by the way, are long-term longitudinal studies following individuals for up to thirty years, and those who infrequently attended religious services had higher rates of death from circulatory, digestive, and respiratory disorders.[53] In fact, the more you attend, the less you'll smoke,[54] and it doesn't matter what religious denomination you are.[55]

Now, one can argue that the beneficial effects are attributable to any form of social group interaction, be it secular or religious. This is an important point because no one has yet been able to factor out other variables to see if religiousness itself improves health. But religions are, by their very nature, designed to touch upon every aspect of a person's life. Religious traditions encourage certain habits and discourage others. They provide social involvement as well as a sense of purpose and meaning, variables that are essential for everyone's psychological health.

But this does not mean that you should force reluctant individuals to attend religious services more often. In one of the few studies to examine the potential health risks of religion, university researchers Kenneth Pargament and Harold Koenig found that religious *struggle*—defined as people who feel that they are being punished by God, possessed by demons, or who experience religious and spiritual discontent—significantly shortened one's life span.[56] Furthermore, if you find yourself ruminating on guilt and fear, or harboring negative attitudes toward God, clergy, and other church members, you will also be inclined toward poorer health and depression.[57] People who have anger at God have more medical problems and poorer recovery rates from illnesses and hospitalization,[58] and patients who struggle with religious issues over time are particularly at risk for health.[59]

These studies support our argument that fear-based religions can be hazardous to one's health. It's too bad that the Surgeon General can't place a warning sign on certain passages from the Bible or Koran, especially those that encourage violence toward people who hold different beliefs.

THE ELEMENT OF TIME

If you analyze the data collected from meditation studies, one of the most influential factors is time. The longer and more frequently you meditate, the more changes you'll notice in the brain. Beginning meditators show little or no change in brain function after one or two practice sessions. However, most studies, like ours, have found small but significant changes in brain activity after only eight weeks of daily practice.

Those who practice daily for thirty minutes or longer, and for many years, show the greatest differences in neural activity,[60] not only when they are meditating, but when they are also at rest. Richard Davidson, who is the head of the Waisman Laboratory for Functional Brain Imaging and Behavior at the University of Wisconsin, has been working with some of the most advanced meditators in the world. He and his team have found that these gifted individuals have extraordinary skills in manipulating specific parts of the brain that control thoughts and emotions,[61] including the capacity to generate compassion in situations that virtually no one else can obtain.[62]

Davidson's findings also demonstrate that the neuroplasticity of the brain is greater than we have imagined.[63] Another important study, recently released by the Psychiatric Neuroimaging Research Program at Massachusetts General Hospital, also showed that meditation enhanced the brain's thickness and neuroplasticity.[64] Normally when we age, our cerebral cortex thins.

IN SUMMARY

Our neurological findings have shown that different types of meditation and prayer affect different parts of the brain in different ways, and each one appears to have a beneficial effect on our neurological functioning and physical and emotional health. Some techniques increase blood flow to the frontal, parietal, temporal, and limbic areas of the brain, while others decrease metabolic activity in these areas. Intensive meditation may also trigger an unusual form of neural activity—deafferentation—in which one part of the brain ignores the information being sent to it by other parts. When this happens, we radically alter our everyday perceptions of the world.

By manipulating our breath, body, awareness, feelings, and thoughts, we can decrease tension and stress. We can evoke or suppress specific emotions and focus our thoughts in ways that biologically influence other parts of the brain. From a neuroscientific perspective, this is astonishing because it upsets the traditional view that we cannot voluntarily influence nonconscious areas in the brain. Only human beings can think themselves into happiness or despair, without any influence from the outside world. Thus, the more we engage in spiritual practices, the more control we gain over our body, mind, and fate.

NEURAL EVOLUTION AND GOD

The imagination is one of the highest prerogatives of man. By this faculty he unites former images and ideas, independently of the will, and thus creates brilliant and novel results. . . . The value of the products of our imagination depends of course on the number, accuracy, and clearness of our impressions, on our judgment and taste in selecting or rejecting the involuntary combinations, and to a certain extent on our power of voluntarily combining them.

—CHARLES DARWIN, *THE DESCENT OF MAN*

4

WHAT DOES GOD
FEEL LIKE?

The Varieties of Spiritual Experience

What *does* God feel like?

When I ask people this question, their reaction is often the same. They pause for a very long time. This means something special to a neuroscientist, namely that a great deal of neurological activity is taking place as different parts of the brain attempt to put into words a concept that defies the parameters of language for many people. Indeed, for most believers, God is much more than an idea. God is a deeply valued experience that goes far beyond any theological definition of the word, which is why most people responded with a version of, "Wow! What a question . . . it's really hard to say."

Even the atheists I queried gave pause. Some laughed, and many responded by saying that God didn't feel like anything. For these individuals, God was nothing more than an abstract idea. However, one of my nonbelieving friends, who doesn't even like to discuss religious issues, replied in all sincerity that God felt "warm and fuzzy." It was the same answer that an evangelical colleague had given me the previous day.

"But you do not believe in God," I said to my atheist friend.

"No, but I do believe in transcendent experiences—you know, those moments that reveal a deeper dimension of life." His answer reminded me that spiritual experiences can be defined in either religious or secular terms.

Only two people responded to my informal survey in less than five seconds, and both were Catholics who felt abused by their religious upbringing. For them, thinking about God brought back disturbing memories they preferred to avoid. Traumatic memories are retained longer and are rapidly recalled, which would explain why my two interviewees responded so quickly with negativity.[1] And when the brain records a traumatic experience, neural circuits will be connected to related memories as well. Let's say, for example, that you tripped on the steps of a church and broke your hip. Although the event had nothing to do with your religious feelings, your concept of God could become neurologically fused with your pain.

A large percentage of the people I queried said that God felt like love. But when I asked them what love felt like, they again paused for a long time.* Love may even be more difficult to describe because it can be used as either a noun or a verb. The brain processes each of these semantic expressions in different ways, but studies have shown that ambiguous words like "love" involve greater neurological activity—and thus more time to process—than simple nouns and verbs.[2] Thus, if you think about God as a feeling, as opposed to an entity that exists in the universe, it will take more neural time and energy to process. It also suggests that people who spend a great amount of time contemplating God are more likely to perceive God in more sophisticated ways.

It is easy to describe the qualities of a concrete object like a table or tree, but for many people, God is as real as anything else you can see or feel in the world. Why, then, is God so difficult to describe? If you search through the volumes of religion surveys, theological texts, and psychological theories, you'll find enough definitions of God to fill a book. Different believers see God as a friend, guide, teacher, father, mother, creator, or judge. Some envision God as a lawgiver, miracle worker, or a distant observer of humanity's fate. Others refer to God as spirit, hope, inspiration, life, love, or truth. Others equate God with everything, nothing, a higher power, a delusionary fantasy, or one's innermost self. In traditional psychoanalysis, God is sometimes equated

---

* In a new survey we just created, we found, in fact, that many college students do describe God and their feelings of love in remarkably similar ways.

as a symbolic projection of one's parents, a necessary illusion, or a moralistic ideal.

Most people have multiple meanings and perceptions of God, but if you simply ask average Americans if they believe in God, more than three-quarters will say "yes."[3] However, if you tie yourself to a stricter definition, and a specific group of people, as Edward Larson and Larry Witham did when they queried a thousand randomly selected members of the National Academy of Science, you will come up with very different results. They defined God as an entity that engaged "in intellectual and affective communication with humankind, i.e., a God to whom one may pray in expectation of receiving an answer," and found that only 40 percent expressed a belief in such a deity.[4]

So if you want to know what people believe, you have to ask the question in different ways. This is what Mark and I set out to do using several innovative approaches. We were interested in how people defined God and spirituality, and we were specifically interested to see if there was a difference between people's religious ideas and their personal spiritual experiences. When we integrated our findings with other polls conducted over the past two decades, we discovered that a gradual shift is taking place in America, where the importance of God's physical characteristics is declining, while an interest in spiritual values is increasing.

SURVEY OF SPIRITUAL EXPERIENCES

In 2005, I created an online questionnaire called the Survey of Spiritual Experiences, collecting data on people's religious orientation and their belief systems.* Specifically, I was interested in analyzing first-person descriptions of their spiritual experiences and relating them to people's social, religious, and personal backgrounds.

We chose to do our survey online because research has shown that respondents are more open, honest, and less biased when they are not confronted by an interviewer.[5] By the end of 2007 we had gathered

---

* To review the questions we asked or participate in the study, go to www.neurotheology.net.

information from almost 1,000 people, of which over 300 have de-scribed specific spiritual experiences in detail. Most reside in the United States, but approximately 15 percent live abroad. Thus, we had representatives from Canada, the United Kingdom, Spain, Australia, Nigeria, Brazil, Denmark, Qatar, Israel, Pakistan, India, Myanmar, Finland, and the Congo.

In our survey, we included several established questionnaires to measure religious background, spiritual activities, and the individ-ual's degree of religiosity, particularly as it related to marriage, drug use, and psychological health. I also wanted to know how tolerant people were when they encountered individuals with different reli-gious beliefs, and so we developed our own survey that we called the "Belief Acceptance Scale." The results were surprising—and some-what disheartening—because we discovered that nearly 30 percent of those queried had difficulty accepting others who held different reli-gious beliefs. In fact, more people were willing to marry someone of a different race or ethnic background (85 percent) than someone with a different religious orientation (72 percent).

BELIEF ACCEPTANCE SCALE

RESPONSES TO THE FOLLOWING QUESTIONS ROUNDED TO NEAREST PERCENTAGE	DEFINITELY AGREE	TEND TO AGREE	TEND TO DISAGREE	DEFINITELY DISAGREE
Are other religions correct, even though they differ from my own?	30%	39%	16%	15%
Would you marry someone outside your religion or spiritual belief system?	43	29	17	11
Would you marry someone who does not share your racial or ethnic heritage?	59	26	10	6

SEARCHING FOR THE REALITY OF GOD

It is easy to analyze facts about a person's religious beliefs and activities, but very difficult to gather data about experiences that have the capacity to transform an individual's perception of reality. This is why we encouraged online participants to describe, in their own words and in as much detail as possible, those experiences they believed had a profound and lasting effect on their lives. Even if they didn't have such an experience, we encouraged them to write about how their religious or spiritual perspectives had affected or changed their lives. Finally, we asked them the following two questions:

1. When you had the experience, how did it compare to your usual sense of reality?
2. In hindsight, how real does it seem now?

These questions were important to me because I have argued throughout my career that spiritual experiences neurologically alter one's perception of reality. However, as we mentioned in Chapter 1, it is very possible that our *perceptual sense* of reality is different from our *conscious awareness* of reality, since each type of reality is assembled through different neurological circuits that do not communicate with each other.[6] We believe that consciousness represents a limited and somewhat fragmented view of reality that is discrepant from the holistic view generated by nonconscious processes in the brain. Perhaps this explains why people intuitively know that reality is more than what they consciously understand, and why some equate that reality with God. By combining our neurological research on meditation with the subjective reports gathered through our survey, we hoped to expand our understanding of how spiritual experiences alter the brain, and why no two people see eye-to-eye when it comes to religious and spiritual beliefs.

But how do you analyze personal narrative descriptions of spiritual experience? The technique we used is called "content analysis," which categorizes how often certain words or groups of words are used. For example, if I wanted to know how many people experienced a feeling of unity with God or the universe, then words such as *unity, oneness,* or *wholeness* could be grouped together and then compared to other people's words such as *separate, distant,* or *alone* to describe their spiritual experiences. Basically, we were searching for the commonalities of religious and spiritual experience. In fact, we didn't find any, which was a very significant discovery.

PERSONAL VARIETIES OF SPIRITUAL EXPERIENCE

Of the nearly 5,500 words that people used to describe their experiences, no common terminology emerged.* Even the words *experience* and *spirituality,* which you would expect to be high in a survey that specifically addressed spiritual experiences, logged in at only 23 and 17 percent, respectively. *God* was only mentioned 18 percent of the time, and *Jesus* less than 4 percent. Barely 10 percent of the respondents mentioned *love,* and only 6 percent talked about *peace.* Less than 5 percent referred to *faith, consciousness,* or *truth*—words that I expected would be used far more often when describing spiritual and religious experiences. Here are the top six words, and the approximate percentage of people who used them:

Experience	23.0%
God	18.0
Feeling	17.0 (includes feels, feelings, and felt)
Spirituality	16.7 (includes spiritual)
Life	14.9
Belief	13.8 (includes believe and beliefs)

To give you a clearer picture of the commonality—or lack—of usage, when we printed the entire list of words used by our participants, we ended up with a hundred pages, with 57 words per page. The words on page 2 were used, on average, 6 percent of the time, page 3 dropped to 5 percent, page 10 was below 2 percent, and every word on the remaining eighty pages was used less than 1 percent of the time. In essence, hardly anyone used the same words, phrases, or expressions to describe his or her personal encounter with the divine. Truly religious and spiritual experiences are unique, at least when it comes to our ability to describe them in words.

* Words like *a, and, the, out,* etc., were excluded from our analysis of this data.

This is astonishing, especially since many researchers in psychology and religion have argued for the universal nature of spiritual phenomena—the "perennial philosophy," as it has been called.[7] The only common denominator we found was not in the description, but in the positive effect that such experiences had on the participants' lives. In fact, 89 percent of the respondents felt a deeper sense of spirituality. Only 10 percent felt that their spirituality was unchanged by their experiences, while 1 percent said their sense of spirituality was adversely affected by their experience. Even more important, 79 percent said they felt more purpose in their lives, compared to 4 percent who felt less purpose.

When we asked our participants about how spiritual experiences affected their religiosity, we kept the definition of that term purposely vague to see how they would answer without any prompting. About half said they felt more religious, a third said their religiosity didn't change, and 11 percent said they felt less religious. Numerous respondents said that their spiritual experiences were not adequately addressed by religions in which they were raised, and so they turned away from them to engage in more individualized pursuits. In a new survey we have just begun, we are finding that college students express very strong interests in Eastern spiritual philosophies, especially when compared to Western religious traditions. These results support the idea that America is gradually becoming less religious but more spiritual and that the quality that governs this shift is influenced by the use of spiritual practices that integrate meditation and prayer into one's daily life.

In our online survey, 60 percent of the respondents felt that their family relationships improved as a result of their spiritual experiences, and 8 percent felt they got worse. This may reflect increased friction with parents who embrace stricter religious beliefs.

Fifty-three percent also felt that their health was enhanced, while only 3 percent felt their health declined. Interestingly, this suggests that individual spiritual pursuits may have similar health improvements as those found in people who regularly attend church. On a psychological level, 76 percent said they now felt less fear about death, while only 2 percent felt more. In general, other studies have found that religiosity lessens death anxiety, but often the correlation is weak.[8] Thus, our finding suggests the possibility that spiritual experiences may be the key element that lessens a person's fear of death. This resonates to the Buddhist belief that meditative experiences can reduce one's anxiety about death.

Finally, I found confirmation that spiritual experiences alter one's sense of reality in a significant way. At the time of the experience, 63 percent said that it was more real than their normal experience of reality, and 7 percent said it felt less real. Looking back, only 46 percent said the experience felt more real. It appears that the impressions left by altered states of reality can dissipate over time. Unfortunately, since we did not ask our respondents for their definitions of reality, they may have answered our questions with something else in mind. This is an inherent problem associated with research questionnaires.

The sense of realness at the time of the experience and in retrospect broke down this way:

	REAL AT TIME	REAL LOOKING BACK
More real	63.2%	46.0%
Same	23.6	44.0
Less real	6.8	5.2

Still, I believe it's safe to assume that spiritual experiences have a unique quality that make them feel very different from our everyday sense of reality and that this is true for the majority of people who have them. Furthermore, it appears that some relatively universal sensory elements make these experiences what they are, even though they are described in vastly different ways. Cognitive processes turn God into an idea, but sensory processes turn God into a generalized feeling that changes the way we perceive the world.

IS GOD PRIMARILY A FEELING OR AN IDEA?

Returning to our analysis of the survey participants' descriptions, we began to group different words into different types of categories. By far the largest category included words that reflected strong emotional content. Nearly a third described their experiences as being intense, using words like *ecstatic, exciting, great, strong, powerful, exhilarating,* and *profound.* Nearly one-half described their experiences using words that expressed calmness, serenity, and contentment. This correlates well with our neurological model suggesting that spiritual experiences simultaneously stimulate the sympathetic (arousing) and parasympathetic (calming) nervous systems. Generally speaking, it is rare that an experience both arouses and calms, which is one of the reasons why we think spiritual experiences stimulate the brain in a unique way.

Our data demonstrates that spiritual experiences, when they occur, are feeling states, not abstract forms of intellectualism. In fact, words like *feel, felt,* and *feeling* were used as often as words that referred to God. Does that mean that "God" is more of a feeling than an idea? Apparently not, because most of our respondents used the term in a historical, comparative, or philosophical context, as the following examples demonstrate:

"I do believe in Spinoza's God."
"I don't believe in God in a traditional way."
"God is too big to fit into one religion."
"My thought is that God is the name of the collective unconscious."

In fact, of the 1,000 references made about God, only 42 related to direct personal experiences, while 99 percent used the term in a highly abstract way. We found it surprising that only 1 percent of our respondents felt that they had a direct, personal encounter with God. Instead, God was typically used to intellectually explain the source of the spiritual experience.

Based upon what we know about the brain's processing of sensations and the conscious recognition of experiences, we believe that a person's spiritual experience (such as being born again) precedes cognitive awareness by approximately a half second. Then, to translate that awareness into language, the brain must engage in dozens of unrelated activities to turn that experience into words. This takes additional neurological time, so the gap widens between the actual experience and the expression of it through language. The experience may be common to many people, but the words used to describe it will inevitably vary from person to person. Thus, it is possible that different spiritual texts are describing a universal experience but using language that is idiosyncratic to the culture and denomination in which it was written.

For the person who has not had some level of a spiritual experience, God will remain an intellectual idea—a promise or a possibility of something that may or may not exist. For these people, faith becomes the essential key for maintaining religious beliefs. But for the person who has had a powerful spiritual experience, God is both a feeling and an idea. And as far as the brain is concerned, if you give an experience a label (in this case, "God") and imbue it with meaning, it will be perceived as something that actually exists in the world.

So why do people call this experience "God"? For the simple reason that the brain must affix a name onto anything it experiences in order to file it into memory. Vague experiences stimulate many parts of the brain, generating uncertainty and anxiety, and so for survival reasons the brain will consolidate and reduce a feeling into an identifiable category. If you consciously interrupt the labeling process that naturally occurs in your frontal lobe, you will interfere with your ability to communicate the experience to others. Religious practitioners who do this are often considered mystics because they refuse to define their experiences in unambiguous ways.

GOD FEELS LIKE LOVE AND EVOKES PEACE

Our content analysis showed that most people who have had spiritual experiences will talk about God in the context of a positive *felt* experience. The two words used most often to describe the experience and its aftereffects were love and peace, and for most people, love was often associated with God. Here's how one respondent put it:

> The experience changed my life. Over time, old feelings have been wiped clean from me and I no longer react or behave the way I used to. I see life from a much clearer perspective based on love. But even the word "love" doesn't really convey the magnitude of which I

speak. I'm speaking about the kind of self-love and acceptance that the energy of God recognizes in all of us.

For many of our respondents, God became a symbol for love and peace. For others, God symbolized light or truth. Many people also experienced God as a way of connecting to the universe, to nature, and with others. Overall, they saw their spiritual experiences as learning experiences, but not on a mundane level of day-to-day living. For example, few people said that their experiences touched upon issues like work, vacation plans, or what things they need to shop for. Their experiences were almost always associated with deep philosophical and fundamental issues.

RELEASING THE DEMONS

Spiritual experiences aren't always positive, and nearly 10 percent of our respondents said that they experienced negative emotions such as depression, anxiety, and fear. The reasons could include: discomfort with having old beliefs shattered, concern about how friends and family members might react, and the fact that spiritual awakenings may occasionally unleash disturbing unconscious material, especially for people who are very sensitive or suffer from emotional disorders.

In one dramatic case, reported in the *Journal of Transpersonal Psychology,*[9] a young professional woman had been attending a kundalini meditation group when, without warning, she began to wildly hallucinate. She tore off her clothes, ran from the ashram, and admitted herself to a psychiatric hospital, where she was sedated for several days. Afterward, she had dreams in which she found herself in hell, having sexual relations with her father. In therapy, she recalled numerous incidents of emotional abuse, memories she had tried to suppress for decades. With the aid of her therapist, she came to understand how certain types of meditation can break down psychological resistance, leaving a person vulnerable to extraordinary feelings and thoughts. She later became involved in the Catholic tradition of her youth, where she found tranquility and a deeper purpose to life.

Such occurrences, though uncommon, are now acknowledged by

the American Psychiatric Association as a temporary state of crisis involving a "loss or questioning of faith, problems associated with conversion to a new faith, or questioning of other spiritual values which may not necessarily be related to an organized church or religious institution."[10] As more Americans experiment with different religious values, health-care professionals need to become aware of this type of psychospiritual problem.

SPIRITUAL EXPERIENCES ADD NEW DIMENSIONS TO LIFE

Of the more than three hundred respondents to our survey who described their spiritual experiences in detail, 80 percent said that they had some form of sensory, visual, or auditory experience. People described seeing light, colors, or auras; hearing sounds like humming or ringing; or hearing voices. These sensations greatly enhanced the power and meaning of their experience. Interestingly, such experiences translated into more permanent perceptual abilities. Some people said that their everyday senses were heightened, and 60 percent felt they actually developed new abilities that allowed them to interpret information in different and more meaningful ways. One person stated that "God gave me a vision of who I am." Another found that she could, at times, "hear angelic music and see shadows or people who would speak to me." For one scientist, his experience led him to accept the reality, validity, and utility of intuitional insight:

> I have been meditating for several years on and off, but one day, while not involved in any formal meditation, everything in life seemed to click. I had this clarity and it was as if I was looking at life from the inside out. It was almost as if my intuition from somewhere "deeper" had offered some sort of direct experience that validated my scientific need for proof. It is actually hard to put into words because it was not merely a "logical" linear experience and many common words cannot really do it the justice it deserves.

Again we see the difficulty people have when describing spiritual experiences. But even when the experience defies description, many people felt that it transformed their orientation to life. As one respondent wrote, "The world became more three-dimensional. More rich, intense, and pleasurable." Spiritual experiences also have the power to alter one's sense of self, as seen in the following dramatic descriptions:

I felt my "self" (as a process, not a thing) go quiet, and became aware of an implicit silence, darkness, and emptiness within me and surrounding me. Within this silence, I felt an abyss or void full of possibilities, hope, creativity. It also seemed a lot like a mirror—that is, that my consciousness was "pure" consciousness without subject or object, that Reality was myself in macrocosm and that I was Reality in microcosm. I also felt an openness, positive feeling, gratitude, unconditional regard, etc., for all things and people. As though I encountered the Golden Rule, love of neighbor as myself, concretely within this moment. These feelings or instances of awareness were intuitive and implicit—that is, they seemed to come without actual thoughts or words.

During meditation, I have had the experience of feeling like a disembodied consciousness suspended in infinite space. I have also had the experience of unity with all that is. I experienced a spiritual presence, and I have come to know that the presence I experienced was not other than myself.

I felt a great, unconceivable exterior/interior energy full of power, love, and clarity. There is not anything superior to this in my entire life.

These descriptions are very similar to those recorded a century ago by the American psychologist William James,[11] which reinforces the popular conception that spiritual experiences have remained relatively consistent throughout history. It also highlights my premise that for thousands of years the human brain has spontaneously generated spiritual and mystical experiences. The universality of this neurological phenomenon is critical for helping us understand the fundamental similarities and origins of religious and spiritual traditions. Yet within this universality, our inability to linguistically express these experiences with any degree of accuracy has led to the great diversity of religious ideas and theologies.

SPIRITUAL EXPERIENCES CHANGE YOUR OLD BELIEFS

In our survey, many people reported that their spiritual experiences altered their beliefs, and as I mentioned above, "belief" was the sixth most common word used. We also found evidence to support the notion that spiritual experiences alter one's traditional ideas about God. For many people, God lost its biblical sense of otherness and became a force that resided inside:

> Since that moment [of mystical experience] I am sure God cannot get a name. God is something, not someone, and it is not something independent of me. But I use the word "God" simply to express an idea, not a specific character.

> These experiences, when I have had them, do not seem to be "personal" insofar as I do not feel I am encountering a larger Person. I guess the idea of God simply as a person seems like an anthropomorphism to me; making God in our own image.

Such notions contradict many traditional doctrines, which may explain why people who see themselves as spiritual are often less willing to attend church or identify themselves with their religious past. Our data found that half of the people changed their religious orientation as a result of such experiences. They were more willing to marry outside of their religious belief system, yet changing religion did not make them more willing to accept the "correctness" of other religious beliefs.

A related study at the University of California, Los Angeles, found that the trend toward exploring alternative forms of spirituality is growing. In 1982 less than 20 percent of the student population indicated no religious preference. In 2004, 31 percent of the incoming freshman students claimed no religious affiliation, yet over three-quarters said that they were "on a spiritual quest." One-third of the students also felt it was important to use college as a place to encourage their "personal expression of spirituality."[12] Other surveys on religion and spirituality reflect similar changes in beliefs. Ironically, as spiritual interests increase, church attendance declines.[13]

BECOMING ONE WITH GOD,
THE UNIVERSE, AND OURSELVES

The bottom line in understanding the phenomenology of subjective religious experience is this: Nearly every spiritual experience, in some small way, changes our sense of reality and the relationship we have with the world. Generally, it increases our sense of unity and wholeness, not just in a metaphoric sense, but in the way we conduct our lives. In fact, almost three-quarters of our respondents indicated that they felt a sense of oneness with the universe or a unity with all of life. These feelings are also associated with a greater sense of purpose and meaning in one's life.

Such experiences involve a degree of self-transcendence and a suspension of personal egotism. In those moments, one no longer feels the need to control the external environment, because everything seems fine just the way it is. Past and future are suspended, and a sense of living in the present pervades one's consciousness. In such a state, some believe they are in the presence of God, while others may simply feel the suspension of negative moods. All is as it should be, for believer and disbeliever alike. As one of our survey participants described it, "I feel that every person is a spark of Oneness, doing what he or she is supposed to do."

Religion and spirituality operate on different levels, but they ultimately affect each other. Religion creates a template for spiritual practice, and spiritual experiences alter one's conception of religion.

WHAT MAKES A PERSON MORE TOLERANT OF OTHER RELIGIONS?

People who score higher on our belief acceptance scale have less religious prejudice than those who score lower. Those engaged in Eastern spiritual practices were more accepting of other religious beliefs than those who adhered to Western monotheistic traditions. Women were more comfortable with other belief systems and also more likely to participate in other religious practices. High socioeconomic status, when compared to low socioeconomic status, also predicts greater tolerance, but one's level of education was the greatest predictor that encouraged people to be more accepting of others. Interestingly, people who had unity experiences were also more accepting of other people's beliefs.

Thus as long as people have experiences they equate with spirituality, religious beliefs will change.

THE FUTURE OF GOD

All of the research that we and others have accumulated allows us to make a prediction about the future of God. Clearly, God is not going to go away, but it won't necessarily be the God depicted in our sacred texts. According to a recent Barna survey, the biblical views of an all-powerful, all-knowing creator is waning.[14] What will take its place? If our survey sheds any light on the question, it will be a God that maintains its mystery, a very intimate experience that cannot be captured by words. And if the trend toward personal spirituality continues, we should see a world where many notions of God coexist. Hopefully, this will inspire greater tolerance between people of different religious faiths as they realize the underlying unity and diversity of these experiences.

How will traditional religious institutions respond? In the same way they have in the past—reinventing themselves to meet the needs of the next generation of seekers. Mainstream churches are liberalizing their theologies. Evangelicals are moving away from the rhetoric of fundamentalism, and New Age churches are growing throughout the country. Even in Muslim countries, support for extremist politics and beliefs is beginning to decline.[15]

Religion and spirituality are constantly changing and evolving, and this is a good thing, for both society and the human brain. New ideas challenge us to think more deeply about personal values and survival, and the more you think about the mysteries of human nature, the more likely it is that you'll have an epiphany that can improve the inner quality of your life. For most Americans, that is what spirituality is about.

5

WHAT DOES GOD
LOOK LIKE?

*Imagination, Creativity, and the Visual
Representation of Spirituality*

God is both a feeling and an idea, but which comes first? Spiritual experiences appear to emerge spontaneously in human brains, but as far we can tell, they rarely occur in early childhood. Instead, young children are introduced to the *idea* of God by their parents. Through storytelling and simple religious rituals like prayer, a child begins to grasp the concept of God and what it represents. This becomes our neurological basis for future religious beliefs, and they will color our spiritual experiences for the rest of our lives.

As far as the mechanical functioning of the brain is concerned, it doesn't matter whether God is physically, mentally, or spiritually real. It only matters whether the concept is useful for survival, and since notions of spiritual realms have permeated cultural history, this suggests that religion has played an important role in helping people cope with their lives. As the biologist and anthropologist David Sloan Wilson points out, religious belief "is intimately connected to reality by motivating behaviors that are adaptive in the real world."[1]

DRAWING PICTURES OF GOD

All conscious thoughts and images have a neurological impact on the brain, but certain words emotionally affect a person more than others.[2]

Even *yes* and *no* are processed emotionally, and in different areas of the brain.[3] It actually takes a person longer to respond to *no,* which suggests that the brain does not take kindly to having its behavior interrupted. In fact, it takes years to train a child's mind to understand the concept of "no."

But what about the word *God?* We believe that this concept has a specifically unique effect upon the brain, because the evidence shows that children begin with a simple concrete image of God that slowly becomes more abstract and emotionally arousing in either a positive or negative way. Indeed, *God* may be one of the most powerful words that a person encounters in childhood.

In order to give you a personal sense of the neurological power of a single word, I want you to get a pencil or pen and a blank piece of paper and *draw a picture of God.* Be spontaneous and draw whatever comes to mind, without worrying about the quality of your art, but you must complete the drawing in two minutes. Also, pay attention to the first reaction you had when I asked you to draw a picture of God. When you finish your drawing, write a brief description of its meaning below the picture.

We've been conducting this experiment for several years with different groups of religious and nonreligious people, and if you're like most of the adults who have participated, the question probably caught you off guard. Nearly everyone pauses for a long time—even longer than when we asked, "What does God feel like?"—which tells us there is increased activity occurring in many parts of the brain, especially in the visual, motor, association, cognitive, and emotional centers.[4] Indeed, the question appears to be so neurologically challenging and psychologically provocative that some people simply refuse to draw anything. Children, however, have no difficulty with the request, and delight in drawing their impressions of God.

For sixty years researchers have been asking children to draw pictures in order to explore their religious concepts and beliefs. Young children, in particular, do not have the language to articulate religious concepts well, but their pictures give great insight into their feelings and thoughts. In general, children live their religious lives through imaginative daydreams and symbolism, rather than through words.

For example, in 1986 psychologist David Heller interviewed forty children using drawings, doll play, and innovative forms of dialogue.[5] He found that Catholic children associated God with family. Jewish children talked about God in relationship to suffering. For Baptist children, God was controlling, providing order, organization, and structure to one's life. Hindu children identified their gods with community. For them, a divine being symbolized energy or a force in the universe, not a person.

One might assume from this that different religions generate different images of God, even among different Christian sects, but a recent study compared the drawings of children from Unitarian and Baptist backgrounds and found no significant differences.[6] This suggests that religious denomination has little to do with a child's physical image of God.

Interestingly, no researcher has collected data on what adults render when asked to draw a picture of God. When we did, it provided fascinating evidence about the neurological "evolution" of religious imagery in the minds of believers and disbelievers. The evidence even suggests that atheists contemplate God with as much depth and sincerity as a religiously committed believer. But before we address how adults envision God, let's take a look at the children's research.

A CHILD'S IMAGE OF GOD

Four major studies have analyzed children's pictures of God.[7] The first was conducted in 1944 by the American sociologist Ernest Harms, who amassed 4,000 pictures from children between the ages of three and eighteen. In 1980 the German religious educator Hermann Siegenthaler collected 350 pictures from children five to sixteen years of age. And in 1996, Helmut Hanisch, a professor of religious education at the University of Leipzig, gathered more than 2,500 pictures from children aged seven to sixteen. A fourth study, conducted in 1998 by three American university professors, analyzed 968 drawings made by children between the ages of three and eighteen.

Each researcher used somewhat subjective criteria to analyze the pictures, but together, certain common themes emerged that corresponded to the child's age and the religious affiliation of their parents and teachers. For example, children below the age of six usually drew faces, while children between the ages of six and ten mostly drew faces and people. God was seen as a protector or a king, sometimes living in a palace or in the clouds. Occasionally, angels or biblical scenes would be depicted, but as children grew older, faces and people were replaced by more symbolic images such as crosses, hearts, open hands, or an eye hovering in the sky. The oldest children often represented God as the sun or as radiating spirals and light. In all studies, the use of symbols increased with age.

Hanisch took the research to another level. He gathered 1,471 pictures from West German children who attended Christian-oriented schools. Then he collected 1,187 drawings from children who attended schools in East Germany, where an official antireligious doctrine had governed the country.

In the religious group, children between the ages of seven and nine represented God as a face or person more than 90 percent of the time, but as we saw in the earlier studies, there was a gradual decline as the children grew older. By the time they reached sixteen, only 20 percent drew pictures of faces or people. Instead, they preferred symbols like suns, circles, and spirals. Commentaries from the older children reflected a loving perception of God.

This did not happen in the artwork collected from the nonreligious students. By age sixteen, 80 percent of the nonreligious children

Drawings of God from a seven-year-old girl (left) and a fourteen-year-old boy (right). Both children attended Sunday school.

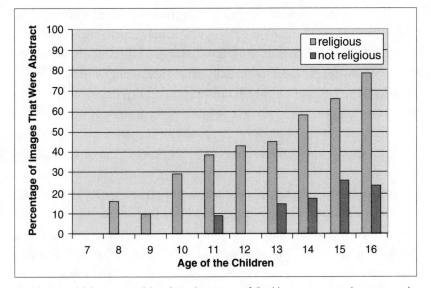

As religious children grow older, their depictions of God become more abstract, reaching 80 percent by the age of sixteen. Only 20 percent of the pictures drawn by older non-religious children were abstract; 80 percent remained anthropomorphic. (Chart modified after Hanisch.)

still used people to symbolize God. Their comments were generally negative, referring to God as powerless and weak, and often included references to war, misery, suffering, and poverty. As one twelve-year-old girl wrote, "I don't understand why God is allowing all this. Therefore I don't believe in God."

IMAGINING GOD

Young children do not have the cognitive skills to articulate abstract concepts of God, but they can use their visual imagination to comprehend spiritual realms. Even in the adult brain, ideas appear to be associated with internal visual processes, and mathematicians often think in pictures when they describe the invisible forces of the universe. Even when we imagine the distant past or future events, we activate the visual-spatial circuits in the brain.[8] In fact, if you cannot see, hear, touch, taste, or smell something, the brain's first impulse is to assume that it doesn't really exist. Thus, for anyone, the brain's first response is to assign an image to the concept of God.

Without this capacity for visual imagination, we would barely be able to think. Even when we sleep, our visual representations of the universe remain active, albeit in unusual ways. Children, however, do not have the neural capacity to easily separate fantasy from fact, and so they form beliefs that blur the boundaries of reality. They easily believe that their nightmares are real, while adults have advanced neural processes to help them analyze perceptual discrepancies.

The imaginations of children run wild, and this makes it easy for them to define God with simple pictures and words. Furthermore, the ways they hear adults talk about God will also contribute to the images they form. If you tell a child that God can see you, or listen to your prayers, then the child's imagination will associate those qualities with the eyes and ears of a face. If you tell that same child that God gets angry, the brain will generate images of frowns, gritted teeth, or perhaps fists banging against a wall—visual constructions that represent how a child perceives anger in other human beings. If you tell your child that God can perform miracles, then the internal imagery takes on superhuman traits. For example, one boy drew God with a cape and a large S on his chest.

Girls, by the way, draw somewhat different pictures than boys. They tended to use more symbolic and abstract representations, and in Hanisch's study, a small percentage of seven-year-olds drew female representations of God. Neurologically, we know that males and females process emotional words in different ways and in different parts of the brain, and this may explain the subtle differences.[9]

Slowly, a concept of an anthropomorphic deity evolves in the child's brain. As the brain begins to make the neural connections needed for abstract reasoning, religious images become more abstract. Yet abstract concepts will still be visually processed. Thus, a notion like love or compassion—which has no physical form in the world—might be "seen" as a heart or a hand reaching out to another. Happiness may be drawn as a smile, guilt or shame may be represented through the use of dark colors, and an all-powerful benevolence might be drawn as a sun radiating down on the Earth. But when it comes to our most primal sense of God, it all begins with a face.

GOD IS A NOUN

We are born with a neurological mechanism to identify objects, and the first objects infants learn to identify are their family and caretakers. With each new object that a child learns to recognize, the brain labels it, the first of many steps that turn an image into a concept and a word. Thus, the first words infants speak are those that identify the people they see.[10] But the only part of the person that an infant recognizes is the face.

Young children can only grasp the simplest concepts because the neurological capacity to comprehend abstract concepts won't mature until adolescence.[11] The easiest type of word for children to learn is a concrete noun, because it refers to something the child can see, touch, or taste.[12] Young children cannot understand words like "peace" or "democracy" because these are highly sophisticated ideas, and the places in the brain where abstract nouns are processed remain poorly developed for many years. A young child's brain has no choice but to visualize God as a face that is located somewhere in the seeable physical world, and this is what we find when we analyze the pictures drawn by children younger than ten.

Brain-scan studies show that nouns are linked primarily to visual object-processing regions.[13] Furthermore, each time a novel idea is introduced, the brain responds with increased activity in specific parts of the right hemisphere,[14] in the same areas that construct our visual representations of reality. Thus, when a child is introduced to a spiritual concept, the brain automatically gives it a sense of realness and personal meaning. Children who continue religious education will be introduced to new ways of conceptualizing God, and each time that happens, the brain will revise its "spiritual" map, so it is not surprising to see children's pictures becoming more complex as they mature.

God is a noun, and nouns stimulate the "where" and "what" part of the brain, specifically regions in the parietal lobe.[15] This region is responsible for identifying and integrating shapes it perceives in the world,[16] and from what we know about how the brain processes visual objects, we can assume that a child's parietal lobe is very active when thinking about the nature of God. Thus, the brain attempts to place

God somewhere within the physically observed universe. As a result, it might be less likely that children can purposefully feel a sense of unity with God. As our brain-scan research has shown, only advanced meditators can willfully suppress activity in the parietal area.

However, older children may be able to alter the brain by shifting neurological attention from the visual centers to the frontal regions where abstract thinking takes place. Brain-scan studies show that this occurs when adults focus on complex ideas, and when this happens, we neurologically disconnect from our visual orientation. This would allow God to lose his gender, face, and position in relationship to ourselves, and thus the boundaries "God" and "self" begin to blur or merge. As we will describe in the next few sections, some adult believers represented this spiritual experience by drawing mirrors to symbolize God and oneself as being the same.

Mature frontal lobe processes are also responsible for the greater imagination, creativity, and originality adults use when they attempt to describe the immaterial qualities of God. If these new ideas are repeated, old memory circuits can be permanently altered and changed. Still, our childhood notions of God will continue to influence our thoughts. This too is seen in adult pictures of God.

EXAMINING ADULT PICTURES OF GOD

Based upon the changes reflected in children's pictures of God, we reasoned that adult drawings should reflect similar developmental patterns. After all, neurological growth continues well into middle age—shouldn't our concepts of God also mature?

To test this assumption, we set up our experiment to address several issues. First, we presumed that adults who regularly attended church or engaged in spiritual activities would produce more abstract drawings than children. Second, we presumed that the abstract drawings would be different in content and meaning from those done by children. Third, we presumed that most of the drawings made by nonreligious adults and atheists would be anthropomorphic, reflecting little maturity or change. Our first two presumptions were right, but our presumption about atheists was wrong.

Participants included congregational members from four different Religious Science churches, congregants from a Unitarian church, students from a community college, and members of a California Free-Thought/Atheist society. For our preliminary evaluation, we collected 256 pictures. Most of the college students were between the ages of eighteen and twenty-four, whereas the average age in the other groups was between forty and seventy, so we certainly had a wide range of adults we could analyze. Nearly half of these individuals had spent at least four decades seriously contemplating God, in both positive and negative ways.

ADULT CHURCH ATTENDEES

Of our survey participants, 160 were members of the Church of Religious Science (not to be confused with Christian Science),* and most had been members for many decades. This spiritual group was founded in the early twentieth century by Ernest Holmes, and they subscribe to a New Thought philosophy that sees God, the universe, the mind, and one's personal self as interconnected. As stated in the philosophical tenets of the United Church of Religious Science:

> The Science of Mind is built on the theory that there is One Infinite Mind which of necessity includes all that is, whether it be the intelligence in man, the life in the animal, or the invisible Presence which is God. In it we learn to have a spiritual sense of things.[17]

In the tenets of Religious Science International (another of several institutes based on the principles established by Ernest Holmes), an emphasis is also placed on the value found in other religious traditions and sects:

> Religious Scientists believe, very simply, that the Universe is fundamentally spiritual—it has intelligence, purpose, beauty and order.

---

* In 2008, in response to a growing dislike in American culture toward religion and church organizations, many of these groups dropped the words "Religious Science" and "Church," and referred to themselves as various centers for "Spiritual Living."

Whether we call it God, spirit, energy, or Universal Intelligence, every person, place and thing emanates from this spiritual universe. We believe this Universal Intelligence is within us, as well as around us, and that we are conscious of it. Our beliefs are in harmony with the basic tenets of all the world's great religions.[18]

As a group, I have found these congregations to be particularly optimistic about life, and they place great emphasis on the power of positive thinking to bring both spiritual and material prosperity into one's life. In addition to embracing contemporary psychological principles, they also attempt to integrate modern science and physics into their principles and beliefs.

As part of a workshop program that we have been introducing to religious institutes and public schools, we handed out a survey form on which we asked them to draw a picture of God. As we expected, faces and people appeared only 14 percent of the time, which was even less than the 20 percent found in Hanisch's religious sixteen-year-olds. This suggested to us that old anthropomorphic images continue to be neurologically revised as a person's religious involvement continues. Eighty-six percent drew a wide range of abstract designs, which, factoring out the gender differences, was nearly the same as Hanisch's group. Similar to the findings in all of the other studies, nearly half of the abstract drawings were composed of suns, spirals, and radiating

Drawing from a twenty-two-year-old Religious Science woman who was raised Catholic (left), and a seventy-two-year-old man (right) who had been affiliated with Religious Science for forty years.

light. Approximately 10 percent drew nature scenes, 10 percent drew clouds, and 6 percent drew hearts, themes that were also common among the children of the earlier research studies. Unlike the children, there wasn't a single representation of a biblical theme, perhaps reflecting the nonbiblical theology of the church.

There was also a greater variety and complexity of abstract representations. Some people mixed animals with stars and crosses and suns, some drew arrows pointing in different directions, and a few represented God by drawing the symbol for infinity or an atom, with electrons spinning around its core. Several members drew mirrors to capture the notion that God and self were reflections of each other, a belief integral to the teachings of Religious Science.

The words chosen to describe their pictures represented highly positive abstract concepts that few children used. For these people, God was energy, peace, freedom, and awareness—a blend of intellectual concepts and experiential senses similar to the descriptions we found in our online Survey of Spiritual Experiences.

Another unique quality of "drawing" was captured, for 8 percent of the participants handed in pages that were left completely blank. Often they would add a comment stating that their picture symbolized "all," "everything," or "pure spirit." With the exception of a few eighteen-year-olds, no children, to my knowledge, deliberately left their picture blank, nor did any child refer to God in similar abstract terms. These findings support our hypothesis that as the brain matures, the more abstract and mysterious one's concept of God becomes.

For these members of the Church of Religious Science, God is a symbol for a transcendent level of consciousness. When this occurs, both words and pictures fail to capture the quality of the experience. The "reality" of God remains, but the concept becomes a metaphor for other personal and spiritual qualities of life. Such drawings also lend support for James Fowler's model of faith development. His book, *Stages of Faith,*[19] is one of the most comprehensive models describing a person's spiritual development over the course of a lifetime. He argued that if we deeply contemplate life's meaning, our notions of God will evolve from concrete ideas to mythical beliefs, and from there toward more universal values of social responsibility.

Three of the Religious Science groups we surveyed were 90 percent Caucasian, living in middle- to upper-class neighborhoods. The fourth congregation was 90 percent black, and the church was situated in a poorer inner-city neighborhood. However, the percentages of the different styles of drawing were the same, which meant that racial and socio-economic differences did not change the way these people envision God.

UNITARIAN PICTURES OF GOD

Unitarianism, first established in sixteenth century Europe with the explicit purpose of demonstrating tolerance toward different religions, attracts individuals from many faiths and backgrounds, including a large percentage of agnostics and atheists. Unitarian belief systems emphasize humanitarian principles of justice, equal rights, co-existence with others, and a willingness to integrate scientific evidence in the search for truth, meaning, and democratic freedom.[20]

When we gave one Unitarian congregation a range of categories by which they could identify themselves, 75 percent circled "freethinker," 75 percent circled "humanist," 40 percent circled "agnostic," and 11 percent circled "atheist" (most respondents circled multiple categories—again, a reminder that many Americans prefer not to label their religious orientations). Like the members of the Church of Religious Science, Unitarian "pictures of God" reflected a wide variety of positive, abstract, symbolic, and nature-oriented imagery. Indeed, they had the lowest percentage of faces and people—less than 1 percent—compared to any other group, a visual demonstration that they have distanced themselves from a biblical interpretation of God. Fifty percent of their "God" drawings were highly abstract, 26 percent reflected scenes from nature, 20 percent drew suns, planets, stars, or radiating spirals, but less than 1 percent left their pages blank—far fewer than the other adult groups we've surveyed. Their commentaries about God also reflected their tolerance and open-mindedness toward people who hold different religious and philosophical beliefs.

COLLEGE STUDENTS

The community college students in our study presented a very different profile, which was reflected in the ways they envisioned God. When asked what their current religious or spiritual orientation was, half wrote down that they were either religious or spiritual, but few were affiliated with an organization. The other half said they were either nonreligious, agnostic, or atheist.

But then we asked a variety of questions designed to more accurately ascertain their degree of belief and disbelief concerning God. We discovered that many of the religious and spiritual students also considered themselves agnostic, nonreligious, interfaith, or freethinker. Even those who considered themselves nonreligious would often select additional terms that could easily be interpreted as spiritual or religious. As we have pointed out before, it is very difficult to ascertain what a person's religious beliefs are, and we believe that if you ask enough questions, you'll find that most people simultaneously hold a multiplicity of seemingly discrepant beliefs. This was certainly true of our college student sample.

In fact, of all the categories chosen, the majority of students—both religious and nonreligious—identified themselves (as the Unitarians did) as freethinkers. Usually, the term is used by atheists and agnostics who reject all forms of institutionalized religious belief, but an informal query showed that these individuals did not like to identify themselves with any particular belief, especially those represented by older members in society. In the literal sense, they saw themselves as thinking "freely," willing to change their belief systems as they saw fit.

Does this imply that adolescents as a group are less religious than adults? Yes. We know, for example, that religious interests rapidly decline during adolescence[21] and that many teens will reject their parents' values as they attempt to redefine their spiritual beliefs.[22] Indeed, for many people religiosity continues to decline through the rest of life,[23] a trend that has continued since 1970.[24]

For the entire group, 20 percent drew faces and people, but only half of these people associated themselves with a denominational faith. The other half were agnostic. In fact, only one atheist drew a face, and even she said that she sometimes believes in God. Once again we see a gradual decline in anthropomorphic representations, even among those who are disinclined to believe. In Hanisch's study, 80 percent of the sixteen-year-old atheists continued to draw faces and people, but we found much lower representations among atheist college students. One reason for this discrepancy is obvious. Hanisch's children were raised in an antireligious culture that would not tolerate acceptance. American children are exposed to an extraordinary variety of mostly positive religious beliefs, and we know that variety stimulates neurological activity. Thus, American children are unconsciously encouraged to envision many possibilities of both God and godlessness.

Of the college students who drew faces and people, many said their pictures represented the images they had as children. One Catholic-turned-Wiccan even drew a baby, saying, "When I was younger, I viewed God as a child, like me— we were toys." We also noted a high propensity of anthropomorphic representations from religious Catholics, but we'll need to collect more data to see if this observation holds up.

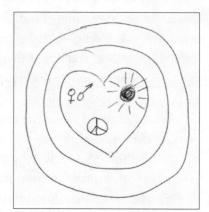

Sixty-three percent of the entire group of students used a wide range of nature-based and abstract drawings: fields, trees, flowers, animals, suns, stars, planets, spirals, and other abstract forms. Some were particularly creative. For ex-

Drawing by an agnostic nineteen-year-old female college student who saw God as a natural loving energy that was both male and female and that permeated the universe.

ample, one person used musical notes to describe her uplifting feelings when she practiced yoga and meditation. A "questing" Catholic drew three overlapping faces—a man, woman, and a cat—to reflect the "multifaceted nature of God," and a self-proclaimed deist drew a clock to symbolize the timelessness of a spiritual universe. Again, this supports our argument that neurological development correlates with evolving abstract conceptualizations of God.

We also had a high percentage (17 percent) of blank pages. Unlike the members of our church study, most of these students were nonreligious or agnostic. Many simply said that if God doesn't exist, you can't draw a picture of God. Only a few people left the page blank to symbolize a mystical presence.

We asked our participants to write a brief description of their drawing, and most of the comments made by these "freethinking" students were positive. Many were neutral, but as the person moved closer to disbelief or atheism, negative comments increased. Those who expressed the strongest degrees of disbelief often used sarcasm in their drawings and commentaries. For example, one atheist said that God was Morgan Freeman, from the movie *Bruce Almighty*. Another drew a picture of the McDonald's golden arches and wrote "Over One Billion Served." Then he crossed out "Served" and wrote in "Saved." Such cynicism might be expected, since considerable research shows that older adolescents enter a period where they question and doubt religious beliefs.[25] Couple that with the usual irreverent tone of teenagers, and it is easy to see why such sarcasm might arise.

When we asked them about their initial reactions to drawing a picture of God, most expressed surprise. One student said, "I can't believe we're being asked this in a public school!" Another said, "I knew it!" And one Catholic, who described her spiritual orientation as "lazy," actually shouted out, "Oh my God!" Many students said they didn't have a clue what to do, but those who strongly disbelieved were either shocked or humored by the experiment. Interestingly, the more religious students had less resistance and negativity than the agnostics.

Perhaps most surprising, nearly everyone in the student survey expressed varying degrees of doubt concerning the existence of God, and even those who said they were atheist—which represented 12 percent of the sample—expressed doubts concerning their disbelief. In fact, 60 percent of those who circled "atheist" on the form to describe their orientation also circled "agnostic." Yet when they were asked the question, "Describe your current religious or spiritual orientation," many wrote down "unsure," "disinterested," or other ambiguous terms.

I point this out to cast doubt on national polls showing that 70 to 80 percent of Americans are religious. Most surveys ask narrow questions or give limited choices, and this can taint the pollster's conclusions. Thus, I recommend that you take all survey findings—ours included—as suggestive, not definitive. With that caveat, I would say that our survey showed a much higher degree of agnosticism, at least among college students, than other studies. Of those who considered themselves atheist (12 percent, by the way, is much higher than the reported 1 to 3 percent found in various American polls), only 1 percent said they were certain that God did not exist.

If these young agnostics and ambivalent atheists hold on to these perspectives as they grow older—and prior research has shown that they will—we may soon have a nation where most of the population will be questioning virtually every dimension of traditional religious belief. Given such a scenario, I can barely imagine what types of spiritual communities will be born. But given the history of American religion, I'm sure it will rise to the task.

Current evidence supports the notion that changes in the spiritual beliefs of young adults will dramatically alter the spiritual landscape of America. Why? Because young Americans appear to be very critical of religious organizations, and in particular, mainstream Christianity. For example, research shows that only 20 percent of "churched" teens remain spiritually active by the time they reach age 30,[26] and although most consider themselves Christian, it is in name only. According to research conducted by the Barna Group, a *nouveau Christianity* is emerging, filled with rootless values: "While young Americans have adopted values such as goodness, kindness and tolerance, they remain skeptical of the Bible, church traditions, and rules or behaviors based upon religious teaching."[27] David Kinnaman, president of the Barna Group, found that these young Americans see present-day Christianity as judgmental, hypocritical, old-fashioned, boring, overly political, anti-homosexual, insensitive toward others, and out of touch with reality.[28]

Similar sentiments are voiced by the distinguished Oregon State University professor of religion and culture, Marcus Borg. He found that many of his students view Christians as "literalistic, anti-intellectual, self-righteous, judgmental, and bigoted."[29] Furthermore, as we will explain in the following chapter, we see evidence that many Americans are rapidly moving toward religious and spiritual beliefs that embrace interfaith tolerance and acceptance, along with a more loving and mystical conception of God.

ADULT NONBELIEVERS

Here's where the real surprise came in. Of the twenty-three members of the Freethinker society, only 20 percent drew people and faces, far less than those drawn by the "freethinking" college students and the

East German children described above. In fact, the quantity of anthropomorphic representations of God was only 5 to 7 percent higher than what we found in the members from the Church of Religious Science.

Fifty percent of adult atheists left their pictures blank, compared with 8 percent of the Religious Science church attendants and 17 percent of the agnostic college students (only one atheist student left her picture blank). In addition, 50 percent of the adult nonbelievers refused to make any comments about God in the space provided on the form. And yet there was far less hostility than what we found with our atheist/agnostic college students, or what Hanisch found with his East German children. Instead, the comments were mostly neutral and civil. A few intimated that God was equivalent to beauty, energy, and the unknown, but most saw God as an outdated idea reflecting biblical notions of a powerful immortal being. For these individuals, God imbued no personal meaning to their lives.

THE PICTORIAL MEANING OF GOD

Our ongoing research continues to demonstrate that all human beings develop multiple images of God, many of which are largely hidden from consciousness. Yet these images affect the way we think and feel. We also believe that asking people to "draw a picture of God" encourages children and adults to articulate spiritual values and concerns that are often difficult to convey. It's a fun exercise to do in classrooms, churches, and family gatherings, and it generates the kinds of conversations that help people of all persuasions to appreciate the wide differences of religious and spiritual beliefs.

Drawing is a form of communication that is neurologically distinct from writing and speech.[30] Where writing involves the abstract functioning of language centers in the left hemisphere, drawing involves the language centers of the right hemisphere, where meaning is ultimately processed.[31] In essence, words and pictures are two integrated elements of language, and most words, as I mentioned earlier, have an "image" quality associated with them.[32] If the right hemisphere is injured, words and pictures lose their meaning. Thus, to have a comprehensive concept of God, the brain needs to integrate abstract associations with image-associated metaphors and feelings. Words are not enough to describe a spiritual experience, but the combination of words and pictures may actually come closer to representing one's individual relationship with God.

Overall, we found that atheists were either highly creative or highly unimaginative when it came to drawing pictures of God. For those who simply lost interest in God, only childhood images were recalled—usually the old man with a beard—but those who seriously contemplated their doubts often used sophisticated symbolism to represent their feelings and thoughts. For example, a leader of a national freethinker group sent me a beautiful four-color mandala made out of concentric circles within circles. Although she does not believe in God, she wrote that her drawing reflected the elements of nature, which she worshipped as a religious person worships God. For her, nature was a source of revelation in much the same way the universe was a source of revelation for Einstein.[33]

Another leader of an atheist/human-rights organization sent me a picture of a famous optical illusion, similar to the drawings made by the illustrator M. C. Escher, to express her view of religious beliefs. This eighty-year-old woman wrote: "When you first look at it, it seems to make sense, but when you examine it closely, it makes no sense at all. It has no real-world application."

Drawing by a forty-year-old male atheist who reported having spontaneous mystical and transcendent experiences at various times in his life.

In a drawing by a male atheist who regularly meditates, he used overlapping circles to represent the transcendent nature of a universe governed by the laws of time, space, and relativity. He used black circles to represent different religious traditions, intersecting lines to symbolize human consciousness, and a small white circle near the center to represent "man's conception of God." For this individual, God was much smaller than the forces that govern a "non-self creating universe."

Circles and spirals, as I noted earlier, are one of the most common themes used to represent spirituality by religious adolescents and adults. Interestingly, intersecting circles, lines, and triangles were also used by abstract painters like Kandinsky to represent the spiritual nature of the world:

> Every man who steeps himself in the spiritual possibilities of his art is a valuable helper in the building of the spiritual pyramid which will some day reach to heaven. . . . A yellow triangle, a blue circle, a green square, or a green triangle, a yellow circle, a blue square—all these are different and have different spiritual values.[34]

In every child, and perhaps every adult, there is an artist that is capable of reaching out beyond the confines of a limited human mind to touch some deeper essence of life. So wherever you turn, and whomever you ask, it appears as though everyone has some image of God, even if it is represented by nothing other than a blank sheet of paper. To a neuroscientist this suggests that believers and disbelievers may harbor a "God neuron" or a "God circuit" somewhere inside the brain. For one individual, such a neuron might connect with feelings of pleasure and awe, but for another, to feelings of disappointment or pain. There may even be people who lack the neural circuitry to construct either a positive or negative image of God. Instead, they must find meaning and purpose somewhere else.

IS THERE A GOD NEURON IN *YOUR* BRAIN?

In a recent neuroimaging study published in *Nature,* researchers demonstrated that a single neuron in an individual's brain would only fire when the person was shown a well-recognized face.[35] They implanted electrodes in several epileptic patients' brains prior to surgery, and each was shown a large number of photographs of people, places, and objects. For one patient, a single neuron fired to images of Jennifer

Aniston and nothing else. For another, a neuron responded when the patient was shown a picture or a drawing of Halle Berry, the actress who played the role of Catwoman in a Hollywood film.

In a previous study, the same team found an individual who had a single neuron that would fire to Bill Clinton. Another patient's neuron responded to images of the Beatles. The researchers also discovered that individual neurons will fire selectively to images of animals, buildings, or scenes. Thus, it is possible for some people to have a single neuron that will only fire when they see a familiar image of Jesus, a sitting Buddha, or the Jewish star of David. That neuron could represent the cornerstone of their religious training and belief.

Is it possible that some people could have a neuron, or specific set of neurons, that would fire when they are asked to envision God? Yes, but it would probably be associated with the image they were introduced to in early childhood. For many people, that neuron might be associated with one of the most famous paintings in the world: the image portrayed by Michelangelo on the ceiling of the Sistine Chapel (which, by the way, is similar to ancient pictures of Zeus). This God—that wise, compassionate, and powerful man with the long white beard and flowing robe—is the image that remains imprinted in my mind.

Today, my memory circuits of God have entwined themselves with my neurological research and childhood beliefs. And the same thing happens in every person's brain. We all begin with a simple neural circuit that captures our earliest impressions of God, and as we associate new meanings and qualities, these circuits interconnect, becoming larger and more complex over time.

As brain-scan technology becomes more refined, I suspect we will see that each human being has a unique neural fingerprint that represents his or her image of God. The East German students were not encouraged to contemplate religious beliefs, so their neurological sense of God included little more than a primitive image of a face, one that was fused with the negative messages they were taught. But Religious Science congregants transformed their childhood images in ways that attempted to include the totality of life. For them, God, thoughts, the universe, and an optimistic view of oneself have all been fused together into a vast interconnecting web of neurons that can influence nearly every aspect of one's life. And for people who choose to meditate, they create a different neural network based upon the images and thoughts they contemplate and experience.

ENVISIONING TRANSCENDENCE

For the genuine mystic, God transcends every concept the brain can possibly generate. But what happens in such a brain? What happens when you go against your biological propensity to turn God into an image? At first your brain rebels. It doesn't like uncertainty, and when it encounters a problem that appears to be impossible to solve, it releases a lot of neurotransmitters, which put you on alert. You'll feel an odd combination of anxiety, curiosity, irritability, frustration, and excitement—feelings that stress chemicals trigger in your brain. And if you don't find a solution, you could easily end up depressed. In religious circles this is called the dark night of the soul.

Yet those who embrace a mystical vision of God rarely suffer psychological angst for extended periods of time. Instead, they find new ways to make sense out of the unimaginable realms to which they feel drawn. This indeed is a creative process, which means they have interrupted habitual patterns of thinking. Like children, they allow their minds to fantasize and speculate, and in the process new neural connections are made that allow them to integrate old and new perspectives. Artists, inventors, and theoretical scientists do this all the time, and so do theologians. And for these people, there is nothing more gratifying than looking at the world with new eyes. New images are formed, and if they prove useful in life, the old images will be dismissed.

Based upon the research we have accumulated, we believe that the more you examine your spiritual beliefs, the more your experience of God will change. And if you cannot change your image of God, you may have trouble tolerating people who hold different images of God, and that may threaten our planet's survival. In the words of the religious philosopher Martin Buber:

> Time after time, the images must be broken . . . [for it] is the human
> soul which rebels against having an image that can no longer be be-

lieved in, elevated above the heads of humanity as a thing that demands to be worshipped. In our longing for a god, we try again and
again to set up a greater, more genuine and more just image, which
is intended to be more glorious than the last and only proves more un-
satisfactory. The commandment, "Thou shalt not make unto thee an
image," means at the same time, "Thou canst not make an image."
This does not, of course, refer merely to sculptured or painted images,
but to our fantasy, to all the power of our imagination as well. But we
are forced time and again to make images and forced to destroy them
when we realize that we have not succeeded. The images topple, but
the voice is never silenced.[36]

From a neurological perspective, images of God are unavoidable,
but from many theological perspectives, there is no true image of God.
Thus, if you cling to your childhood perceptions, you will limit your
perception of truth. This is the drawback to any religion that insists
upon a literal, biblical image of God. If you limit your vision, you
might feel threatened by those who are driven to explore new spiritual
values and truths—people who one day might turn out to be our future
leaders and saints.

THE SELF-EVOLVING BRAIN

The neural evolution of God is unavoidable in most human beings, but
not in the Darwinian sense of the word. Human beliefs are not tied to
the principles that govern genetic evolution,[37] and thus we are free to
reinvent ourselves, and our spirituality, with every new generation.

What makes human beings unique is the extraordinary impermanence of their ideas, and this impermanence is reflected in our extraordinary neuroplasticity. Neurons do not have fixed properties. Instead,
they are changing all the time.[38] It takes less than two weeks for a neuron to grow new axons and dendrites,[39] and in some cases the change
occurs suddenly.[40] Competitive behavior,[41] environmental influences,[42]
education,[43] or even a rousing sermon can trigger a rapid rewiring of
circuits. In essence, evolution gave us a nervous system that actively
participates in its own neural construction, something we do not see in
other animal brains.

It even appears that our brain has a mutant strand of DNA that contributes to our creativity, inventiveness, and individual uniqueness. These "jumping genes," as scientists are fond of calling them, can cause cells to change their functioning as we grow.[44] This explains why identical twins are not really identical, why one family member can be brilliant at math, while another excels at sports, or why one relative ends up struggling with a serious mental illness when no other family member has any semblance of a problem. No two people perceive the world, or God, in the same way, because no two human brains begin with the same genetic code.

Terrance Deacon, the esteemed professor of anthropology and neuroscience at the University of California in Berkeley, describes the human brain as an "evolutionary anomaly" because human beings have unparalleled cognitive abilities to imagine the unimaginable:

> We think differently from all other creatures on earth, and we can share those thoughts with one another in ways that no other species even approaches. . . . We alone brood about what didn't happen, and spend a large part of each day musing about the way things could have been if events had transpired differently. And we alone ponder what it will be like not to be. . . . No other species on earth seems able to follow us into this miraculous place.[45]

We live most of our lives in a world that is filled with imaginative thoughts, and as we age, we continually modify our beliefs. We are born anew, as the evangelicals like to say, and we can do it as often as we like. We can change our religion, we can change our moral code, and we can change our pictures of God, thanks to the evolution of a truly unusual brain.

6

DOES GOD HAVE A HEART?

Compassion, Mysticism, and the Spiritual
Personalities of the Brain

What is God's personality?

When a team of sociologists at Baylor University asked a nationally representative sample of Americans to describe which qualities symbolized their impression of God, they discovered that four distinct personalities emerged.[1] These personalities not only tell us a great deal about our religious landscape, they also illuminate the inner neurological landscape of the American soul. In the Baylor study, which was cofacilitated by the Gallup organization, 34 percent of the participants were evangelical Protestants, 22 percent were mainline Protestants, 21 percent were Catholics, 5 percent were associated with black Protestant congregations, and 2.5 percent identified themselves as Jews. Approximately 5 percent associated themselves with other religions such as Buddhist, Christian Science, Mormon, Hindu, Jehovah's Witnesses, Muslim, Christian Orthodox, and Unitarian. Another 10 percent considered themselves unaffiliated with a specific denomination or creed. Responders were spread over all ages, from eighteen on up, and represented a variety of levels of education, socioeconomic status, and locations throughout the United States.

Before I share the Baylor findings with you, take a few minutes to think about God. What type of qualities come to mind? Is God loving, or critical, or both? Does God seem friendly or frightening, motherly or fatherly, forgiving or punitive, gentle or severe? How much does God care about the world? Do you see God as distant observer, or as a force that actively interacts in the world?

Whether we are conscious of it or not, we all assign a personality to God, which appears to be neurologically based on the nature of our own personality and beliefs. Different people have different ways of imagining God, and these preferences deeply influence the way we see the world.

THE FOUR GODS OF AMERICA

Many people use the word "God" to express what they feel is a universally understood concept, but when you look more closely, the definition of God becomes extraordinarily diverse. According to the Baylor research, some see God as kindly and loving, but twice as many Americans see God as punitive and stern. Some see God as distant and unconcerned, but many experience God as being actively involved in their lives. In fact, 20 percent even believe that God favors a specific political party. For example, during the 2004 presidential campaign, 30 percent were convinced that God looked favorably on George W. Bush.

When they put the data together, the Baylor researchers concluded that the Americans sampled tended to embrace one of four different personalities of God: authoritarian, critical, distant, or benevolent. But these four categories could not be easily assigned to any specific denomination or sect. For example, some evangelicals embraced a benevolent God, most saw God primarily as an authoritarian, and a few saw God as a distant entity who does not involve himself in human affairs.

THE AUTHORITARIAN GOD

Those who believe in an authoritarian God represent 32 percent of America. They believe that God is very angry and willing to punish anyone who is unfaithful or who acts in an ungodly way. They may even believe that God causes earthquakes and human disasters as a wake-up call about the sinful behavior of people.

This God is highly involved in world events and the personal lives of individuals, and the people who embrace an authoritarian God want our government to be run according to Christian-based values. One might suspect that the majority of these people would be very negative toward members of non-Christian sects, yet only 22 percent believed it was important to convert others to their belief.

Over half of evangelical and black Protestants assign to God an authoritarian personality. They attend church more often (51 percent go weekly), and nearly half believe in the literal truth of the Bible. This helps to reinforce the image of a wrathful, punitive God. These findings are similar to a University of Rochester study that found that more than 60 percent of American born-again Christians and Catholics believe they will "suffer negative consequences if they disobey their religion."[2]

THE CRITICAL GOD

Another 16 percent of Americans believe that God is critical but will neither punish nor comfort his flock. This God has an unfavorable view of society. He does not intervene with the world, but he will cast judgment on people in the afterlife.

Interestingly, every religious category had close to the same proportion of people who saw God as a critical entity. Catholics and Protestants were only a few percentage points higher than evangelicals, Jews, and those unaffiliated with religious groups.

Only 4 percent of this group felt that it was important to convert others to their religious belief, far less than those who embrace an authoritarian God. Religious observance took low priority, and only 10 percent attended church weekly. After all, if God shows little interest in you, why should you care about God?

Interestingly, when it comes to protecting the environment, this group takes the strongest stance, although I want to point out that the other groups also favored environmental protection. Believers in a critical God were also more likely to favor the equal distribution of wealth and Affirmative Action programs, but again, the percentages were only slightly higher than the other groups. Perhaps if you believe that God is uncaring, this places greater responsibility on society, and on one's own shoulders, to manage the affairs of the world.

The Four Personalities of God

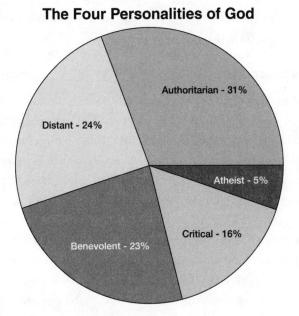

The different perspectives on God obtained in the Baylor University survey.

When combined with the first group of believers, nearly 50 percent of all Americans embrace a God that is cold, critical, and harsh. This, to me, reflects an underlying pessimism about the human condition and the moral state of the world.

THE DISTANT GOD

The second largest group, comprising 24 percent of the American population, sees God as distant and uninvolved. He does not hold opinions about the world or about personal behavior; thus we are left to our own free will to decide what is right and wrong. This God is less of a person and more like a cosmic force that set the laws of nature into motion.

Those who perceive God as distant have higher levels of income and education than any other group. Almost half never go to church, and 38 percent never pray. In contrast, only 2 percent of those who believe in an authoritarian God never pray. It makes one wonder: Does a fear of God make one want to pray more often?

Approximately a third of all Catholics, Protestants, and Jews believe in a distant God, yet this group is more open-minded when it comes to gay rights, abortion, and premarital sex. Within this group, many people question the existence of God.

THE BENEVOLENT GOD

In contrast to 72 percent of Americans who believe in an authoritarian, critical, or distant God, only 23 percent see God as gentle, forgiving, and less likely to respond with wrath. Like those who believe in an authoritarian God, believers in a benevolent God think he is very active in their lives. He listens, responds to prayers, and cares deeply about the suffering of others, but he sometimes causes suffering and pain.

Only a quarter of Catholics, mainline Protestants, and evangelicals embrace a loving God, whereas less than 14 percent of black Protestants and Jews see God as a benevolent force. And of those who are unaffiliated, only 5 percent see God in a kindly way. Since most of the Old Testament describes a wrathful God, this may be the primary reason why so few people see God as a symbol of eternal love. To see God as primarily loving, a person must embrace a liberal interpretation of the Bible, ignoring or rejecting the vindictive passages.

Only half of those who believe in a benevolent God strongly advocate Christian values for the rest of the country and the world, while the other half believes in exercising tolerance toward people who hold different religious views. Thus, believing in a loving God is not enough to sway many believers toward accepting a pluralistic nation or world.

THE NEURAL PERSONALITY OF GOD

The personality you assign to God has distinct neural patterns that correlate with your own emotional styles of behavior. For example, according to the Baylor study, most of those who embrace an authoritarian God tend to favor the death penalty, want to spend more money on the military, want to give the government more power to fight terrorism, and insist that prayer should be allowed in public schools.

Envisioning an authoritarian or critical entity—be it another person or God—will activate the limbic areas of the brain that generate fear and anger. Thus, the brain is primed to fight, and so it should come as no surprise that the strongest advocates of an authoritarian God often call themselves "God's warriors."

However, when you perceive God as a benevolent force, a different part of the brain is stimulated in the prefrontal cortex. Loving, compassionate images, faces, or thoughts activate a circuit that involves a tiny area in the front part of your brain called the anterior cingulate. It conveniently sits between the limbic and prefrontal structures, and when stimulated, it suppresses the impulse to get angry or frightened. It also helps generate feelings of empathy toward others who are suffering or hurt.*

We suggest that the anterior cingulate is the true "heart" of your neurological soul, and when this part of the brain is activated, you will feel greater tolerance and acceptance toward others who hold different beliefs. The God of the limbic system is a frightening God, but the God of the anterior cingulate is loving.

Anything that you value will also stimulate different structures in your limbic system, but if the emotional circuits in your brain are weakly stimulated, then God will have little meaning in your life. This is what we think we saw in the brain scans we've taken of atheists. Frontal lobe activity went up, signifying that they were thinking about God in an abstract way, but we saw little activation in the areas that generate meaning, value, pleasure, or discomfort. This suggests that people who perceive God as distant are not emotionally stimulated by the idea. Neurologically, such a God would feel less real, or more distant, and would incline an individual toward agnosticism or disbelief.

In the four personalities described in the Baylor study, God maintains an "otherness" in the mind of the believer. Neurologically, activity in the parietal lobe is responsible for maintaining this quality of otherness about God. The parietal lobe makes God an object that has a

---

* As we discussed in earlier chapters, the anterior cingulate performs many essential functions related to assessing social situations. It detects when people lie, and it helps orchestrate strategies for handling conflicts. It reduces anxiety, fear, guilt, and anger, and is involved in learning, memory, and focused attention. The anterior cingulate is strengthened by meditation, which explains why meditation is effective in generating greater social awareness and compassion.

specific location in the universe, separate from yourself. You see this most clearly in children's drawings: God is "up there" in heaven, and we are "down here" on earth.

The religious philosopher Martin Buber believed that one must maintain an "I-Thou" separateness and otherness in order to have a personal interaction with God,[3] and this makes perfect neurological sense. For example, when we brain-scanned Pentecostals while they were speaking in tongues, activity in their parietal lobes increased as they experienced the Holy Spirit talking to them. Other forms of contemplative meditation decrease parietal activity, which allows the practitioner to feel more unified with God. God, then, appears to be everywhere and nowhere, a formless energy, both universal and unique. This God was frequently identified in our studies and surveys, but was not reflected in the Baylor study.

THE MYSTICAL PERSONALITY OF GOD

Our Survey of Spiritual Experiences, which we described in Chapter 4, illuminated a fifth personality of God that we think the Baylor study missed. The Baylor researchers provided a checklist of qualities one might associate with God, but they did not include terms that could reflect unitary spiritual experiences in which God transcends the biblical image of a heavenly powerful deity. Instead, their list of "personality" terms was biased toward the otherness of God. For example, they chose words that are easily associated with human traits, like *motherly, fatherly, kingly,* etc. Other questions also reinforced an anthropomorphic image by asking if the respondent saw God as angry, concerned, involved, or uninvolved in one's affairs. Only one question allowed the participant to describe God as a "cosmic force in the universe."

In contrast, when we asked our survey participants to describe their spiritual experiences, many talked about God as an emotional presence, using words like *peace, energy, tranquility,* or *bliss.* God was not a separate entity, but rather a force that permeated everything. God didn't create the universe, God *was* the universe, a radiance that extended throughout time and space. God was light, God was freedom, and for many people God was consciousness itself. For them, a mystical God often cannot be described with words.

A mystical God is neither "he" nor "she," nor is it punitive, critical, or distant. People who embrace this type of God are often attracted to religious groups that fall outside of mainstream denominations, and often see different religions as reflections of a single underlying spiritual truth. They are more accepting of religious differences and more willing to sample other spiritual traditions and beliefs. Others join nondenominational spiritual groups that liberally apply teachings from different religions and philosophical views. According to sociologist Robert Wuthnow, there are approximately three million active, small spiritual groups in America,[4] and most are not mentioned in public opinion polls.

Based upon national surveys conducted by the Barna Group, 11 percent of Americans believe that God is "a state of higher consciousness that a person may reach." Eight percent define God as "the total realization of personal, human potential," and 3 percent believe that each person is God.[5] Overall, it's fair to estimate that a quarter to one-third of all Americans believe in a nontraditional mystical God that is neither authoritarian, critical, nor distant.

In fact, the percentages may even be higher because there are many members of traditional religious groups who also embrace a unitary vision of God. And if you include the spiritual practices of Hinduism,

GENERATION "WHY"

Generation Y is a loosely defined term for people born between 1978 and 1989. Many of these Y'ers are in college today, and when we gave them a broader list of "God" qualities to choose from, we found evidence to dispute the Baylor study. Most of these students, as we reported in Chapter 5, see themselves as freethinkers and agnostics. They are actively involved in questioning every aspect of religion, which is why I'm calling them Generation "Why." In the survey we handed out, some of the most commonly selected words were *mysterious*, *indescribable*, and *unknowable*, qualities we associate with a mystical God. Other popular choices included: *everywhere*, *nowhere*, *transcendent*, *nothing*, *everything*, and *metaphoric*. However, many of these people also selected a wide range of contradictory terms—*punishing*, *caring*, even *illusionary*—again suggesting that young adults see a multidimensional God that cannot be easily categorized. However, those who strongly disbelieved tended to see God in primarily negative terms.

Buddhism, Taoism, Sikhism, Jainism, Sufism, Bahá'í, Shinto, and others, the mystical God emerges as the primary spiritual belief system in the world, with over two billion followers and believers. In non-Western cultures, supreme deities are seen as enormously loving and rarely depicted as being angry, critical, or distant.

THE 99 ATTRIBUTES OF ALLAH

In Islam, the various personalities of God are named, to be meditated upon in silence. Some are loving, some are cruel, and others are unique to the Muslim and Sufi traditions. Allah is: compassionate, merciful, sovereign, holy, bestower of peace, grantor of security, guardian, mighty, irresistible, majestic, creator, organizer of all, perceiver, illustrious, all inclusive, everlasting, all able, determiner, expediter, delayer, the first, the last, victorious, hidden, patron, supreme, kind and righteous, relenting, avenger, pardoner, pitying, owner of all, majestic, equitable, unifier, all rich, emancipator, defender, harmful, benefactor, light, guide, incomparable, immutable, inheritor of all, teacher, timeless, fashioner of forms, forgiver, subduer, bestower, provider, victory giver, all knowing, abaser, exalter, giver of honor, giver of dishonor, all hearing, all seeing, arbitrator, just, kind, all aware, indulgent, infinite, all forgiving, grateful, sublime, great, preserver, nourisher, reckoner, majestic, generous, watchful, responsive, vast, wise, loving, glorious, raiser of the dead, the witness, truth, dependable, strong, steadfast, friend and helper, praiseworthy, originator, producer, the restorer, giver of life, bringer of death, ever living . . . and the ninety-ninth name of God is sustainer.

Although many people may believe in a mystical God, we suspect that less than half—or far fewer—have had a personal mystical experience. Usually, such experiences happen either spontaneously or after many years of intense spiritual practice. Our research supports the idea that our brain is built in such a way that we can have occasional mystical experiences, but we suspect that the more intensely you meditate or pray, the more likely you are to experience a mystical or transcendental state.

THE NEURAL EVOLUTION OF GOD

In practice, most people maintain multiple images of God. But just as human personalities evolve, so does one's concept of God. I'm going to suggest that the different personalities of God—authoritarian, critical, distant, benevolent, and mystical—correlate to the neurological evolution and development of the brain.

I'm also going to go a step further and argue that authoritarian gods are associated with the oldest, most primitive structures of the brain, whereas a benevolent or mystical God is experienced through the most recently evolved parts of the brain, structures that appear to be unique in human beings. This developmental view, by the way, roughly parallels the cultural evolution of religious traditions throughout the world. For example, the mythological gods of nearly every tribal community had nasty personalities. Zeus was an arrogant bully, Huitzilopochtli—the bloodthirsty god of the Aztecs—needed a steady diet of human sacrifices, killing everyone in her path, and the God of the early Hebrews wiped out nearly every living creature with forty days of rain. But as societies and religions developed, you tend to see the emergence of kinder deities and gods.

In Eastern cultures a similar development can be seen. Hinduism, one of the oldest religions in the world, is filled with every sort of deity imaginable, but as Asian culture evolved, the gods of love dominated the popular literature in India, China, and Japan. Buddhism went a step further, rejecting religious hierarchies, and its evolution showed a gradual movement toward a neutral or mystical spirituality. Of course, you'll still find remnants of hostile deities in the folk religions of the East—for example, the demons portrayed in Tibetan Buddhist art—but they are viewed as metaphorical reflections of our inner weaknesses and faults.

Something happened in the brains of our ancestors that gave us the power to tame this authoritarian God. No one knows exactly when or how it happened, but the neural structures that evolved enhanced our ability to cooperate with others. They gave us the ability to construct language and to consciously think in logical and reasonable ways. Our research shows that they are the same structures stimulated when we meditate and pray, which is what allows us to consciously envision a loving and compassionate God. Without these new neural connections, humans would be limited in their ability to develop an inner moral code or a societal system of ethics.

A hundred thousand years ago the consciousness embedded in our frontal lobes began to dominate human behavior, and this, we believe, is when humanity first developed a primitive conception of God. We formed communities that were partly governed by supernatural beliefs, and we built primitive temples to symbolize the power of these unseen forces of the universe. When we eventually learned to write and sculpt, we carved our deities into the surfaces of the temple walls.

As a species, we have overly active frontal lobes that continue to create, imagine, and rearrange a seemingly endless variety of ways to envision and change the world. As far as we can tell, no other living species has a brain that is capable of manipulating inner and outer worlds.

THE CULTURAL EVOLUTION OF GOD

Today, our frontal lobes continue to envision spiritual realities, along with new ideas and definitions of God. Archeological records suggest that the earliest public structures were temples, and even the artwork found in prehistoric caves suggests that humans drew pictures of their gods. But different brains, in different parts of the world, create different religious beliefs.

Yet, for most of human history, religion and society were inseparable. Thus, from a cultural perspective, our earliest images of God were inextricably tied to the rules and punishments that dictated social behavior and morality—realms that clearly reflect the authoritarian personality of God. As Albert Einstein noted:

> The Jewish scriptures admirably illustrate the development from the religion of fear to moral religion, a development continued in the New Testament. The religions of all civilized peoples, especially the peoples of the Orient, are primarily moral religions. The development from a religion of fear to moral religion is a great step in people's lives. And yet, that primitive religions are based entirely on fear and the religions of civilized peoples purely on morality is a prejudice against which we must be on our guard. The truth is that all religions are a varying blend of both types, with this differentiation:

that on the higher levels of social life the religion of morality pre-
dominates.[6]

In Western culture, the authoritarian notion of God dominated
human thought until the 1400s, when a series of events undermined
the power of the church. The Black Plague wiped out half the population of Europe, which helped to undermine religious authority. Science
gained favor, and God retreated farther into the heavens. In a minority
of Jewish, Islamic, and Christian texts, God's wrath also declined, to be
replaced by images of a more benevolent and mystical force.

For the next two hundred years, Europe experienced a series of
conflicts between competing Christian theologies. The Catholic Church
splintered as people pulled up their roots in their search for a more personal God. And where did they seek the freedom to practice religion as
they saw fit? In the colonies along the North American coast.

GLIMMERS OF AMERICAN MYSTICISM

Many of the people who first came to America were religiously perse-
cuted in Europe, and yet they continued to embrace an authoritarian
God. In the 1500s, Protestant England found a toehold along the
northeastern seaboard, but times were harsh, and this too was reflected
in the Puritan vision of God.

Slowly, Puritan severity gave way to more moderate Anglican
parishes, which under English law was the only sanctioned religion allowed. But by the early 1700s the Anglican establishment was challenged by the Presbyterians, Baptists, and Methodists. These Protestant
dissenters shared an evangelical fondness that made God more personal and joyful. Compared to earlier religious traditions, early American evangelism represented a true liberation from a state-controlled
religious authority.

Still, the founders of our country continued to battle over issues of
religious freedom. Eventually, the then-vague notion of church/state
separation won out, and people were free to envision God in any way
they saw fit. America became the first world nation to encourage reli-

gious pluralism, and for the most part American religious ideology was liberal, antislavery, antiwar, and supportive of women's involvement with the church. On the other side of the religious coin, many hell-and-brimstone preachers continued to flame the images of a wrathful God.

Then something unusual occurred in the mid-1800s. Small groups of people—many of them wealthy, educated, and culturally sophisticated—became enamored of various esoteric, spiritualistic, and transcendental philosophies imported from Europe and Asia. These were the people who introduced the notion of a truly mystical God, and the movement captured the imagination of America. One could argue that the "spirit" of Christianity was reborn, and it spawned new sects across the country. For example, Christian Science practitioners embraced the notion that God was entirely good and perfect and that, through divine love, all forms of sickness could be healed. Evil was simply an absence of truth.

The Unity School of Christianity went a step further. Founded in 1889 by Charles and Myrtle Fillmore, it transformed the idea of God into a benevolent presence that lives within each person. Thus, all people are spiritual beings who can shape their lives through the use of affirmative positive thoughts and prayer.

These "New Thought" churches changed the religious landscape of America by taking the authority of God completely out of the hands of the clergy and giving it to their congregants. Suddenly, God was no longer a distant heavenly power, but an internally active force that anyone could directly experience and use. Evangelical revivalism swept through the nation as tens of thousands of people were touched by gifts of the Holy Spirit.* The mystical God had arrived.[7]

DOES GOD HAVE A WALLET?

Spiritual optimism and the belief in personal transformation became so widespread that they flowed beyond the walls of the church and into

---

* The evolution of religious beliefs is not as linear as I describe it. For example, few people today realize that having direct access to the Holy Spirit dates back to the Quaker movement of the seventeenth century.

the business and secular communities. God took up residence on Wall Street, and many authors promoted the notion that faith in oneself was enough to bring both spiritual and material wealth. Here is an example of what one could call secular spirituality, written in 1901 by William Atkinson, editor of the popular magazine *New Thought*:

> I believe that the mind of Man contains the greatest of all forces— that Thought is one of the greatest manifestations of energy . . . that not only is one's body subject to the control of the mind, but that, also, one may change environment, "luck," circumstances, by positive thought taking the place of negative. . . . I believe that Man is rapidly growing into a new plane of consciousness, in which he will know himself as he is—will recognize the I AM—the Something Within. I believe that there is an Infinite Power in, and of, all things. I believe that, although today we have but the faintest idea of that Power, still we will steadily grow to comprehend it more fully—will get in closer touch with it. Even now we have momentary glimpses of its existence—a momentary consciousness of Oneness with the Absolute.[8]

Atkinson placed this spiritual power in the human brain, and his ideas ignited a flurry of books on the powers of positive thinking and power to manifest wealth. Others, like Ernest Holmes, used similar ideas to create the Church of Religious Science, founded in 1926. In this evolution of New Thought theology, God, oneself, and the universe are interconnected, creating new doorways to happiness and success.

Along with the Unitarians, Unity Churches, and Quakers, the Church of Religious Science developed philosophies of greater open-mindedness by proclaiming the inner divinity of the human being and extending kindness to every person regardless of their religious orientation or belief. In these churches, God, consciousness, morality, and science are melded into a universal *human* spirit that is simultaneously mystical and materialistically pragmatic. In many ways these modern churches reflect the same deist philosophy that had captured the imagination of the eighteenth-century leaders of the Enlightenment. God had fallen out of heaven and taken up residence in the mind.

OLD GODS NEVER DIE

In reaction to these new, liberal, and modernistic theologies, Milton and Lyman Steward produced a twelve-volume set of books in 1910 called *The Fundamentals*.[9] Their basic tenets insisted on the inerrancy of the scriptures, the virgin birth and the deity of Jesus, the doctrine of atonement solely through faith and God's grace, the bodily resurrection of Jesus, the authenticity of Christ's miracles, and his imminent return. But the books went much further, specifically attacking Catholicism, socialism, New Thought philosophy, atheism, Christian Science, Mormonism, Spiritualism, and evolution. For many decades the movement was small, but after World War II, and with the rise of "televangelism," fundamentalist churches burst forth on the American scene, waging war against what they saw as a rampant immorality throughout the world. The authoritarian God became a genuine political force, and it landed on the White House steps. But a question remains: How *dangerous* is the belief in an authoritarian God?

> **WHAT DOES GOD READ?**
>
> The Baylor study found that the more people attend church, the less likely they are to read *The Da Vinci Code* by Dan Brown. Those affiliated with non-Judeo-Christian religions were three times more likely to read the book than Evangelicals.

THE WAR BETWEEN THE AMERICAN GODS

Of all the hate crimes conducted in America, victims of religion are ranked as second, although well below those related to race. According to the FBI, 68 percent of the religious hate crimes were against Jews and 13 percent were against Muslims.[10] So the question naturally arises: How tolerant are we as a nation? It is difficult to tell. On the average, there are 1,400 religious hate crimes carried out each year, compared to 800,000 violent crimes. But is 1,400 an "acceptable" number? Not for a country that was founded on the principles of religious tolerance, especially considering that underneath these statistics a larger problem looms: *religious prejudice.*

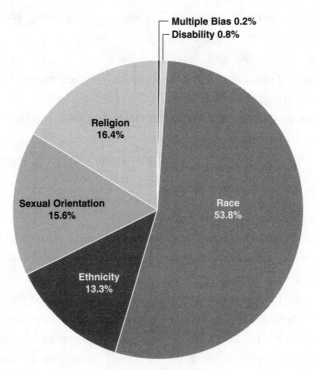

Percentage of hate crimes reported by the FBI in 2004.[11]

According to the Baylor study, more than half of Americans are intolerant of non-Christian values, which is not surprising considering that half of those surveyed embraced an authoritarian or critical God. This may also explain the constant Supreme Court battles we see concerning the attempts to introduce religious values (such as prayer and Intelligent Design) into the public school system, or attempts to insert the Ten Commandments and references to God into government activities and facilities.

In our survey, of the people who reported spiritual experiences, only one-third said they were uncomfortable with those who held different religious beliefs. Still, that represents as many as 100 million Americans. Two other studies conducted in 2002 also showed high degrees of intolerance.[12] They found that 17 to 18 percent of Americans—50 million people—believed that their religion should be the only true religion in the world. Seventy-one percent said that we should not try to convert people of other religious faiths, but that still leaves close to

60 million Christians who want to convert every Muslim, Jew, Hindu, and Buddhist to their religion. Interestingly, our online survey found that people who took up Eastern spiritual practices were more tolerant and accepting of other religions than those who were involved in Western monotheistic traditions.

If you put all the surveys together, there appears to be a slow decline in religious intolerance, especially over the last five years, and many religious leaders are speaking out about the need to embrace a different perception of God. Marcus J. Borg, professor of religion and culture at Oregon State University, points out that the emerging paradigm of tolerance creates a new but difficult vision for traditional Christian followers.[13] If you see the Bible as metaphorical, it becomes an inspirational text, not a literal document by which you should govern your life. This transforms Christianity into a tool through which people can transform their lives in the here-and-now. Religion becomes a guideline, not a truth, and this allows people to see different traditions as paths that also lead to personal and spiritual growth.

Similar sentiments have been recently voiced by leaders of the Catholic, Protestant, Buddhist, Hindu, and Muslim communities. For example, the Episcopalian bishop John Spong believes that Christianity must reinvent itself, and that "theism, as a way of defining God, is dead." He argues that a "new way to speak of God must be found."[14] Spong's message reflects a strong rebellion against religious conservatism, a view that is mirrored by many recent surveys and polls. According to one study, within the evangelical community, a quarter of its young members feel that their religion has lost touch with the basic teachings of Jesus.[15] The study noted that in each new generation, more Americans shift their allegiance from Christianity to other faiths or systems of belief. Some embrace agnosticism and atheism, and as our college student survey showed, many prefer to see themselves as spiritually inclined but unaffiliated with any religious group. As a recent Gallup survey found, Americans may maintain their belief in God, but in general, Protestantism has been slowly declining since 1965.[16]

Fundamentalists will continue to argue for a return to biblical orthodoxy, but Americans seem bent on reinventing Atkinson's creed. Consider the phenomenal success of Rhonda Byrne's *The Secret* after endorsements from Oprah and Larry King.[17] The funny thing is that the philosophy behind New Thought religion and materialism comes very close to several fundamental neurological truths:

- Your thoughts clearly affect the neurological functioning of your body.
- Optimism is essential for maintaining a healthy brain.
- Positive thoughts neurologically suppress negative thoughts.
- When you change the way you think, you begin to change your outward circumstances.
- Consciousness, reality, your mind, and your spiritual beliefs are profoundly interconnected and inseparable from the functioning of your brain.

Today, for many people, God has become a metaphor for our search for ultimate truths and our ability to imagine a better future for all. And, as a recent UCLA study found, this search for meaning is usually viewed as a spiritual pursuit, not a religious one.[18]

The cultural evolution of God follows the neurological evolution of the brain. The circuits that generate images of a wrathful God are closely tied to the oldest structures in the brain, and the circuits that allow us to envision a compassionate and mystical God are in the newest part of our brain. We can't get rid of our old limbic God, which means that anger and fear will always be part of our neural and spiritual personality. However, we can train the newer structures in our brain to suppress our biological tendency to react with anger and fear.

EXERCISING YOUR COMPASSIONATE NEURONS

The emotional circuits of our limbic brain have less plasticity than the frontal lobe.[19] For example, we all get angry or frightened in the same way, but everyone experiences love in surprisingly different ways.[20]

Still, it's not fair to call our reptilian brain primitive, for it too has co-evolved with the frontal lobe and now has the ability to adapt and respond with increased appropriateness to new situations and stress.[21] Other primates do not exhibit this adaptive skill. Unexpected changes frustrate them and they often lash out because the limbic structures in their brain are less flexible, with far fewer connections with their frontal lobe.

To bridge this gap between our "old" and "new" brains, a special structure appears to have recently evolved—the anterior cingulate.[22] As I mentioned earlier, it connects our emotions with our cognitive skills, playing a crucial role in emotional self-control, focused problem-solving, and error recognition. Most important, it integrates the activity of different parts of the brain in a way that allows self-consciousness to emerge, especially as it applies to how we see ourselves in relation to the world.[23]

Since meditation stimulates this circuit, we believe there is also a coevolution of spirituality and consciousness, engaging specific neural circuits that allow us to envision a benevolent, interconnecting relationship between the universe, God, and ourselves. The circuit that extends from the frontal lobe to the limbic system has a rich interconnection of neurons centered in the anterior cingulate cortex, which is activated whenever we see someone who is suffering, and this allows us to feel empathy and compassion.[24] If you can't resonate to other people's pain, then you are less likely to come to their aid. The anterior cingulate is a delicate structure, and damage to this area can change your personality in unpleasant ways.[25] You can become depressed and lose your ability to be empathetic and sensitive to the feelings of those around you.

The anterior cingulate also contains a class of spindle-shaped cells called von Economo neurons, which are found only in humans, great apes, and certain whales.[26] These neurons have an extensive array of connections with other parts of the brain and are believed to be intimately involved in the development of social awareness skills by integrating our thoughts, feelings, and behaviors. They guide us toward positive emotions and away from negative ones.[27] But they are also disrupted by stress. If you expose yourself to ongoing stress, their functioning is reduced, but if you place yourself in an enriched environment—with a lot of love, communication, and sensory and intellectual stimulation—you strengthen the effectiveness of the von Economo neurons and the anterior cingulate.[28] Since meditation simultaneously reduces stress while stimulating activity in the anterior cingulate, this supports our premise that spiritual practices enhance social awareness and compassion.

We also know that the von Economo neurons are especially vulnerable to degeneration in patients who suffer from Alzheimer's disease and other aging disorders.[29] As we saw in Chapter 2, patients with cognitive disabilities improved their memory by meditating for only twelve minutes a day, which suggests that spiritual practices may indeed enhance the functioning of this rare primate neuron.

The best way to describe the relationship between your emotional limbic system, your frontal lobe, and the anterior cingulate is to visualize an imaginary seesaw:

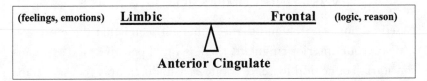

The anterior cingulate acts as a kind of fulcrum that controls and balances the activity between the frontal lobes and limbic system.

In this example, the emotional limbic system, which includes the fear-producing amygdala, has a reciprocal relationship with your frontal lobe and your ability to use logic, reason, and language. The anterior cingulate, which sits right on the boundary between the limbic system and the frontal lobe, acts like a fulcrum, balancing your feelings and thoughts. If you get too emotional, blood flows into the limbic system, stimulating alertness, defensiveness, and fear in the amygdala. Just like a seesaw, as activity goes up in the limbic area, activity goes down in the frontal lobe. Thus, when you're angry or anxious, you stop being logical or reasonable, and your cognitive skills are suppressed.

When the amygdala becomes active, the anterior cingulate shuts down, which allows your reptilian brain to run the show. Empathy and intuition decline, and you lose your ability to accurately assess how other people feel.

On the other hand, if your frontal lobe becomes active, you stimulate the anterior cingulate, which slows down activity in the amygdala. Thus, logic and reason subdue anger and fear. It's that simple. When one side of the imaginary seesaw goes up, the other side goes down. But if the anterior cingulate is damaged—through a stroke, a lesion, or even too much anger—everything becomes unbalanced. Thus, it is essential that you nurture that inner negotiator, which is what meditation and spiritual practices do. They strengthen the frontal lobe—which stimulates the anterior cingulate—and this allows you to pursue your conscious goals in life with greater purpose and serenity. A strong frontal–anterior cingulate circuit also inhibits anxiety, depression, and rage.

EMBRACING COMPASSION AND PEACE

Based on our research and that of others, it seems that the more you activate your anterior cingulate, the less you'll perceive God as an authoritarian or critical force. It's quite easy to do. Simply focus on compassion or an image of peace as you breathe deeply and relax. Hold this thought for at least twelve minutes a day, and in a matter of a few months you'll begin to build and strengthen new neural circuits of compassion, and these will interrupt the neurological tendency to shy away from people who appear to be different than you.

Of course, you don't need to believe in God to establish empathy and serenity; you simply need to absorb yourself in memories associated with the feelings of kindness and love. If you consciously interrupt pessimistic thoughts and feelings with optimistic beliefs—even if they are based on fantasies rather than reality—you'll stimulate your anterior cingulate. Fear, anxiety, and irritability will decrease, and a sense of peacefulness will slowly take its place. However, if you obsess on your doubts and worries, your emotional limbic system will slow down those parts of the frontal lobe that generate logic, empathy, and pleasure. Again, it's a simple seesaw effect. Love goes up, and fear goes down. Anger goes up, and compassion goes down. If you focus on a benevolent God, the authoritarian God recedes. The choice is entirely yours—that's how easy it is to control nonconscious circuits in your brain.

But meditation, prayer, and a belief in a loving God may not be enough to eradicate the limbic system's tendency to distrust people who appear to look or think differently. Instead, you'll need to bring your spiritual practice into your social interactions with others. We'll show you how to do this in Chapter 10.

Social interaction strengthens the anterior cingulate's ability to respond to others with less stress,[30] and so we encourage you to interact with as many different people as you can. Attend social events that include different cultures and ethnicities, and visit different churches. Experiment with unfamiliar forms of meditation and prayer, and share your experiences with others who are on a spiritual path.

THE ELUSIVE MYSTICAL GOD

It is easy to embrace the notion of a benevolent God, but far more difficult to experience the qualities associated with mysticism. As our Survey of Spiritual Experiences showed, unitary experiences that transform God into a virtually indescribable sensation appear to happen spontaneously. This is true for advanced meditators as well. Nearly everyone will feel more peaceful and relaxed as they experience deeper levels of awareness, but only a small percentage will report intense altered states of consciousness that rapidly transform their spiritual beliefs. Time and the length of practice clearly influence one's ability to experience mystical states, but as many Eastern teachers have said, there is no promise of enlightenment.

If you consciously want to explore mystical spirituality, our research suggests that you may need to engage in a daily practice that lasts from twenty minutes to an hour. In Chapter 9 we'll take you through the basic steps of setting up a meditation practice. You might not reach enlightenment, but you will find yourself in a more peaceful and happy frame of mind.

Practitioners from every religious tradition have succeeded in reaching mystical states, but they all seem to concur on one point: God can never be fully known by the mind. The experience is simply too grand, too awesome, and too profound to describe with pictures or words. God becomes the totality of life, and a force that is absolutely and irreducibly real. But it is a God that does not fit neatly into the tenets of traditional religious beliefs. Einstein called it a "cosmic religious feeling," and he considered it to be "the strongest and noblest motive for scientific research."[31]

Intense meditation appears to be the most direct route to experiencing mystical states. Are there any side effects? During meditation, activity in the amygdala temporarily declines, but we found that the brains of advanced meditators had mildly higher amygdala activity when they were resting. One would expect the opposite, so what might this mean? Is a mystical God frightening? In a certain sense, yes, because many parts of the brain want to clearly identify and label anything it perceives. Your brain just doesn't like mysteries, and people who are overly sensitive to uncertainty might prefer to embrace a more traditional notion of God.

It is also possible that those who are attracted to meditation may have higher initial levels of anxiety, compared to the general population. Therefore, they meditate because it is an effective way to become more serene. However, if meditation makes them more sensitive and aware, it may also make them more emotionally vulnerable when they are around others who are anxious or mad.

Overall, however, the benefits of intense meditation outweigh the risks. For example, in one recent study, advanced meditators were shown to have superior skills at discerning subtle changes in the environment,[32] which, from an evolutionary perspective, has significant survival value. The majority of studies also have found that even brief periods of meditation significantly improve your ability to cope with a wide variety of psychological problems and physical disease. Perhaps this explains why the practice of meditation has increased in popularity in recent years. In 1993, five million people said they meditated. By

2003, the numbers soared to ten million,[33] and in 2007, fifteen million.[34] Church involvement in America is declining, but spiritual practices are on the rise.

THE FUTURE OF GOD

If our description of the neural evolution of religious belief is correct, it might be possible to predict the future of God. Historically, the notion of God has been reinvented a thousand times over, evolving from an authoritarian image toward a symbol of unity and love. Will a mystical God come to dominate the spirituality of the twenty-first century? Perhaps, but history tells us that such a change will be both psychologically and neurologically difficult to achieve. Rather, I think we will see a very slow acceptance of pluralism, in which believers of different faiths struggle to incorporate the disparate spiritualities that populate our world. But as one study reported, this may lead to lower levels of religiosity.[35] However, the research we've reported on suggests that spiritual interests will continue to prosper and grow.

The God of the future would have to fill many roles and transcend many interpretations of historical religious texts. But as I have always argued, if God is truly infinite, then God must have infinite manifestations. Each person can only see a very limited version of whatever God or the universe might be. It is like the old story of the blind men who are asked to describe an elephant. The one who touches the trunk says that it is long, flexible, and wet. The one who touches the foot says it is short, stout, and rough. And the one who handles the tusk disagrees with the other two, saying that it is slender, smooth, and hard. They are all correct but will not be able to grasp what an elephant is until they put all the parts together. Perhaps, in a similar way, if we bring together all of our descriptions of human nature, reality, spirituality, and the universe, we might achieve a fuller understanding of what God is.

The enemy of a pluralistic God would reflect selfishness, anxiety, fear, anger, and racism—in other words, all the qualities that manifest themselves in an "us versus them" mentality. But you can't pluck out your amygdala, that neural fundamentalist in your brain. Instead, you must tame it, through education, contemplation, and love. That's what your frontal cortex and anterior cingulate are designed to do. They can imagine a better future, and they can manipulate the world to make those dreams come true. And as long as there are unanswered questions about ourselves, the universe, or the meaning of life, our brains will constantly invent new spiritual frameworks to make sense out of an incomprehensibly complex world.

7

WHAT HAPPENS WHEN
GOD GETS MAD?

Anger, Fear, and the
Fundamentalist in Our Brain

As we have argued throughout this book, most Americans have greatly benefited from their personal relationships with religion, spirituality, and God. But when it comes to sharing our religious beliefs with others, certain problems may arise, especially if we want them to embrace our spiritual points of view. If we use our powers of persuasion to reach a general consensus of belief—which, from an evolutionary point of view, is essential for social cooperation—we are bound to create conflicts with those who hold different religious beliefs.

The culprit is not religion per se, but what our brain is biologically inclined to do when we encounter people who embrace different visions of "truth." One part wants to reject opposing ideas, while another part tries to understand, cooperate, and compromise. In essence, we all have two brains—one selfish and suspicious, another open-minded and kind. Since we live in a world filled with uncertainties, both brains are constantly on the alert.

THE TWO WOLVES

Once upon a time, or so the Cherokee legend goes, a young Indian boy received a beautiful drum as a gift. When his best friend saw it, he asked if he could play with it, but the boy felt torn. He didn't want to share his new present, so he angrily told his friend, "No!" His friend ran away, and the boy sat down on a rock by the stream to contemplate his dilemma. He hated the fact that he had hurt his friend's feelings, but the drum was too precious to share. In his quandary, he went to his grandfather for advice.

The elder listened quietly and then replied. "I often feel as though there are two wolves fighting inside me. One is mean and greedy and full of arrogance and pride, but the other is peaceful and generous. All the time they are struggling, and you, my boy, have those same two wolves inside of you."

"Which one will win?" asked the boy.

The elder smiled and said, "The one you feed."

We all harbor a pack of neurological wolves in our brain. The old ones reside in the limbic system, and they are filled with aggression and fear. They're fast, efficient, and potentially deadly, and they've been running the show for 150 million years. The younger ones reside in our frontal lobes and anterior cingulate, where empathy, reason, logic, and compassion reside. These pups are playful and imaginative, but they are also neurologically vulnerable and slow when compared to the activity in the emotional parts of the brain.

So, when it comes to making sophisticated moral decisions, which one will win? The selfish brain or the cooperative one? Again, as with the two wolves, it depends on the one you feed. If you allow anger and fear to dominate, you will lose the neurological ability to think logically and act compassionately toward others. In fact, it is nearly impossible to find peace and serenity if your mind is preoccupied by negative, anxious, or hateful thoughts.

Excessive anger or fear can permanently disrupt many structures and functions in both your body and your brain. These destructive emotions interfere with memory storage and cognitive accuracy, which, in turn, will disrupt our ability to properly evaluate and respond to social situations.[1] Anger makes people indiscriminately punitive, blameful, pessimistic, and unilaterally careless in their logic and reasoning skills.[2] Furthermore, anger encourages your brain to defend your beliefs—be they right or wrong—and when this happens, you'll be more likely to feel prejudice toward others.[3] You'll inaccurately per-

ceive anger in other people's faces,[4] and this will increase your own distrust and fear. It's an insidious process that feeds on itself, and it can influence your behavior for very long periods of time.[5] Eventually, it will
even damage important structures in your brain.

Nor is it good for your heart. Regardless of your age, gender, or
ethnicity—anger, cynicism, hostility, and defensiveness will increase
your risk of cardiovascular disease and cerebrovascular problems.[6]
What makes anger particularly dangerous is that it blinds you to the
fact that you're even angry; thus, it gives you a false sense of certainty,
confidence, and optimism.[7]

When people use their religion or politics—or even humor or
teasing[8]—as a weapon to aggressively disparage others who embrace
different beliefs, they unwittingly stimulate the other person's brain to
retaliate with similar aggression. Aggression and hostility shut down
activity in the anterior cingulate and striatum—the two key areas of
the brain that control anger and fear—and when this occurs, the amygdala takes over, generating a "fight or flight" response that is spread
through every other part of the brain.[9]

In fact, brain-scan evidence suggests that you won't even be able to
read this chapter without having some of your "limbic buttons" pushed,
because the moment the brain hears or sees words that have a negative
meaning, your amygdala goes on the alert.[10] Words like *anger, fear, selfish, danger,* and *punish*—which are used more than fifty times in this
chapter—are neurologically unpleasant, whereas emotionally positive
words like *love, compassion,* and *trust* activate the striatum and other
parts of the brain that are related to pleasure, happiness, peace, and
the sense of impending reward.[11] In this chapter, we'll be addressing
the positive and negative aspects of "fundamentalism," but because the
word has become so closely associated with authoritarianism, right-
wing conservatism, and terrorism, it is virtually impossible to talk about
this important societal issue without stirring up feelings of discomfort.

SELFISHNESS AND MORALITY

As we reported in detail in our previous book, a tremendous amount of
research points to the fact that we are born with a selfish brain and that,

when given a choice, we have a biological tendency to act in self-serving ways, especially if no one is watching.[12] Children do not know how to behave morally because their brain has not developed the cognitive skills to comprehend abstract ethical principles. And as every parent has learned, different degrees of punishment are needed to train young brains to follow societal rules. In fact, from the perspective of evolutionary biology, it appears that social forms of mild punishment enhance most people's propensity to behave in altruistic ways.[13]

Not only are we neurologically inclined to act selfishly, but we are also neurologically equipped to detect acts of selfishness and deceit in others.[14] When we do, we unconsciously react in a punitive, authoritarian manner. Even when adults play games, if they sense that their partner is being overly aggressive or unfair, they will react more punitively, with less compassion.[15] Indeed, a balanced combination of punishment and reward tends to foster cooperation between individuals and groups. As a recent article in *Science* explains:

> Research indicates that strong reciprocity—the combination of altruistic punishment and altruistic rewarding—has been crucial in the evolution of human cooperation. People often reward others for cooperative, norm-abiding behaviors, and they punish violations of social norms. For thousands of years, human societies did not have the modern institutions of law enforcement—impartial police and impartial judges that ensure the punishment of norm violations such as cheating in an economic exchange, for example. Thus, social norms had to be enforced by other measures.[16]

One such measure was the institutionalization of religion, which, for centuries, has struggled with ways to promote group coherence by demoting socially destructive behaviors. Thus, it is not surprising to find that the "Two Wolves" tale has been used as a metaphor by different religious groups.[17] For example, a young Southern Baptist pastor named John Bisagno used it to describe a spiritual struggle that went on in the heart of a Native American who had been converted to Christianity:

> At the instant of conversion God places into our being an entirely new nature, His own nature. Now we possess two natures—the old

and the new, the carnal and the spiritual, the flesh and the spirit. . . .
An old missionary returned to the home of a convert among the Mo-
hawk Indians. When the missionary asked him how he was doing,
old Joe said, "Well, it seems that I have a black dog and a white dog
inside of me and they are always fighting." The missionary asked
him, "Which one wins?" and Joe said, "The one I feed the most."
Our daily fellowship with God is determined by which nature we
feed the most.[18]

The tale illuminates a person's inner struggle between spiritual
and physical pleasures, and Billy Graham used a version to portray
"the inner warfare that comes into the life of a person who is born
again."[19] Bisagno and Graham intuitively identified the neurological
struggle that exists any time we attempt to embrace higher ethical
principles and ideals. However, if a person dwells obsessively on the
inner warfare, he or she can do as much damage to the brain as a lifetime of alcoholism or drugs.[20]

TAMING YOUR SELFISH BRAIN

We all begin life with a biological propensity for selfishness, and evidence shows that we rarely, if ever, completely abandon these traits.
We may suspend them temporarily in order to get along with others,
but even then, altruism frequently appears to be a by-product of mutu-
ally satisfying each individual's personal desires.[21] In one intriguing experiment, subjects were asked to assign two jobs, one to themselves,
and another to a participant whom they could not see. One task was interesting and offered a financial incentive, but the other was boring
and offered no reward. Most individuals chose the beneficial task for
themselves. Another set of participants were told they could flip a coin
to help with the decision-making process. Half used the coin, but the
majority still assigned themselves the more enjoyable job, even when
the coin toss went against them. However, when a mirror was placed in
front of those making the assignment, they acted more fairly.[22]

Perhaps they did so out of guilt, or because they were reminded
that another real person was involved. Interestingly, when researchers
at the University of British Columbia introduced the concept of God

during a simulated competition or "trust" game, participants—whether they were religious or not—acted far more generously toward their opponent.[23] Clearly, spiritual incentives can induce people to act morally, but the researchers found that thoughts or images of police or civic authorities also increased generosity. This study does lend credence to the notion that authoritarian concepts can help tame the uncooperative "wolves" in society, which may explain why most ancient religions were filled with punitive gods and rules. But there is a fine line that needs to be walked, for as I mentioned earlier, too much focus on the negative can lead to anxiety, fear, and neurological distress.

Young children have a particularly difficult time with stories describing God's anger. For example, we know that nightmares are directly related to a child's reaction toward frightening images and hostile words,[24] and we know that images of a punitive and authoritarian God increase children's anxiety, not just in Christians, but in Muslim children as well. In a study conducted in the United Arab Emirates, psychiatrists explored the prevalence of fear in 340 adolescents. Of the sixty fear items listed, belief in the devil and fear of breaking a religious law evoked extremely negative reactions in 50 percent of the subjects. According to the researchers, "Nearly half of the children reported that the fear caused considerable distress and interfered with daily activities."[25]

How do we find the "right" balance between punishment and reward? It is a question that has never been satisfactorily answered from either a psychological or theological perspective. Nor has anyone been able to conclusively show that religion strengthens moral convictions. For example, one study found no relationship between honesty and religiosity,[26] while another study found that students associated with religious organizations were more academically dishonest than those who practiced spirituality on their own.[27] And although many individuals believe that their conversion to a deeper religious life helped them to abandon destructive behaviors, one study found that "saved" men were just as likely as "unsaved" men to read pornography and abuse their wives.[28]

So is there something more definitive that we can do to tame our selfish brain? Neurologically, the answer is surprisingly simple, because all we need to do is consciously exercise kindness and fairness toward others. As many studies have shown, the more compassionate we become, the more generous those around us become.[29] And when we perceive others as being sensitive to our needs, our brains respond with greater generosity, a condition known as reciprocal altruism.[30] This is the phenomenon we casually refer to as "you scratch my back, and I'll scratch yours." Thus, when we treat others with kindness and respect, even those who hold different beliefs will respond in kind. An upward spiral is created that stimulates the anterior cingulate, a crucial part of the true heart and soul of the brain. As neuroscientists at the University of California in Los Angeles point out, activation of the anterior cingulate and prefrontal cortex "reflect the active suppression of unwanted racial biases."[31]

We live in a pluralistic society, and this is enough to trigger a biological response toward prejudice, but research has shown that those who consciously strive toward embracing pluralism and a diversity of beliefs tend to treat others with greater equality, fairness, and generosity.[32] In fact, many studies have demonstrated that the more friendly contact you have with members of different religious, cultural, ethnic, and racial groups, the less prejudice you will harbor in your brain.[33]

Research has also shown that when people embrace egalitarian beliefs, they become less authoritarian in behavior.[34] It even appears that human beings have a biological and evolutionary drive toward creating equality between competing groups and individuals,[35] and when equality is established, cooperation improves.[36] This, indeed, provides a foundation of hope when dealing with the overwhelming number of conflicts that currently involve many nations throughout the world.

AN "US VERSUS THEM" MENTALITY

Although we can train ourselves to be less prejudiced and more accepting of others, we will still harbor elements of an exclusivist mentality deep within our brain, dismissing the relevance of other people's beliefs. In fact, we are all biased toward perceiving our own beliefs as true, even when the evidence clearly contradicts our points of view. For example, in a study assessing how religious and nonreligious students evaluate the beliefs of the other group, both groups tended to see the other side as illogical, yet failed to see the illogic in their own perspectives and beliefs.[37] In other words, our minds are always biased toward seeing evidence that only supports our point of view. To put it another way, our brain has a preference for consistency, and this is what helps us to maintain our systems of belief.

Our brain automatically places objects and people into separate, distinguishable groups, and then we select a preference for one group over the other. We will root for our favorite baseball team and disparage the challenging team, and we will tend to distrust whatever the opposing political party says. The same holds true for anyone we perceive as being a member of a "different" group—be it religious, political, or ethnic—and when we do this, the tendency is to treat the other group unfairly. As many studies have confirmed, the "in" group will always orchestrate scenarios that are less than favorable for any "out" group.[38] In-group morality is also associated with intergroup conflict.[39]

An "us versus them" mentality exists even when the division is arbitrarily assigned in an experiment or game. When individuals were randomly placed into different groups, they felt stronger about their own group and tended to feel negatively about other groups, even when issues of religion, sexual identity, and culture were factored out.[40] In other words, simply being a part of a group results in feelings of ill will toward others, and this evokes the desire to isolate oneself from them.

But there is a simple solution. As Princeton University professor Susan Fiske explains, if you want to decrease your natural tendency toward prejudice and out-group bias, don't "categorize" yourself. People, she states, can get beyond—and even prevent—"their automatic use of category-driven impression formation and decision making."[41] You'll do your brain, and society, a lot of good if you don't identify yourself as a Christian, Muslim, Jew, or atheist. Even labels like Democrat, Republican, or American can trigger an unconscious "us versus them" mentality in your brain.

Brain-scan studies have helped document the inherent biology of exclusive thinking as it relates to the balance of the limbic system and frontal lobes. One study showed that when we see someone who is a member of a different racial group, our brain reacts with fear in a matter of seconds.[42] Fortunately, we can train ourselves to override this prejudicial nature of the brain, but it again requires a conscious commitment to show tolerance and compassion for others.[43]

Thus, we always have a choice. We can be driven by our negative emotions of the limbic system, or tilt the balance toward the compassion of the anterior cingulate and frontal lobes. Children too have the beginnings of both wolves, and therefore have a biological propensity to exclude other children who fall into a minority group. However, when they are placed in a mixed cultural group and given a project that requires everyone's assistance, prejudices fall away, hostility fades, and group cooperation flourishes.[44]

FUNDAMENTALISM AND ANGER

Although nearly one-third of Americans consider themselves Christian fundamentalists,[45] it is probably the least understood form of religiosity, even by those who are members of fundamentalist congregations. Nor is there a simple definition of fundamentalism. To address the many dimensions of the world's fundamentalisms, University of Chicago professors Martin Marty and Scott Appleby directed a multiyear interdisciplinary study, called the Fundamentalism Project, that culminated in the publication of five encyclopedic books on the topic.[46] As a way of generalizing the numerous forms of fundamentalisms and fundamentalist-like movements, the hundreds of experts considered that fundamentalists rely on strict interpretations of their sacred texts. Fundamentalisms usually emerge from conservative, traditional, or orthodox religious cultures, and people in such cultures usually feel threatened by what they see as the modern erosion of traditional values and beliefs. In addition, they sometimes feel they must take vigorous action against those who disagree.

Other scholars have pointed out that fundamentalism is not a unitary religious tradition and that there is a wide range of interpretations within fundamentalist traditions. Some are peaceful and serene, while others are hostile and militant. Thus, there are both positive and negative sides to fundamentalism, but overall, it represents a very personal and complex meaning system for the believer.[47]

On an individual level, strong religious identification appears to have a beneficial effect on one's health, for as several studies have shown, as religious convictions increase, anxiety and depression tend to decrease.[48] In Iran too, higher degrees of religiosity among medical students are associated with lower degrees of anxiety.[49] People feel comforted by strong beliefs because it gives them an unambiguous understanding of the world. And within the fundamentalist community, there exists a strong sense of social support. However, family emotional support in general has been shown to be more effective than religion in helping individuals cope with anxiety.[50]

On the other hand, religious and nonreligious fundamentalists (especially men) appear to have higher levels of trait anxiety,[51] which tends to generate distrust toward others in positions of power. Unfortunately, this creates a double bind, for the more we pathologize individuals who distrust us, the more we validate their reasons for distrust.[52] Thus, the only alternative is to counter suspicion with understanding and compassion.

As we see it, the neurological problem of fundamentalism does not lie in the firm adherence to a specific set of beliefs. Rather, the problem arises when individuals use their religion to justify angry feelings toward others. Specifically, expressing or listening to angry thoughts can disturb the normal neural functioning of many parts of the brain. In fact, just reading emotionally evocative words stimulates the amygdala and hippocampus in ways that resemble the encoding of traumatic memories.[53]

When you listen to angry speech—in a congregation or political forum—specific parts of your brain begin to mirror the angry content of the speaker.[54] All you have to do is see a harsh, angry, or contemptuous face in a picture, and the same neural reaction will be triggered[55] because the circuits involving the human amygdala are particularly responsive to the emotional expressions on other people's faces.[56] And the stronger the expression, the stronger your emotional reaction will be.[57]

Even watching violence on the news, or taking in a violent movie, will make you feel more angry, aggressive, negative, and powerless.[58] And the same thing happens in your brain when you listen to songs with hostile lyrics,[59] even if they are presented in a humorous way.[60] Furthermore, a meta-analytic review of video-game research found that "violent video games increase aggressive behavior in children and young adults."[61] According to University of Iowa researcher Craig Anderson, "the deleterious effects on behavior, cognition, and affect" are directly linked to "serious, real-world types of aggression."[62] No matter how you look at it, exposure to, or expression of, any form of anger is hazardous, not only to the health of the individual, but to society as well.

Unfortunately, as far as the brain is concerned, negative speech has a stronger effect than positive speech.[63] Negative remarks and memories are more strongly encoded in the brain, and they are the most difficult memories to eradicate. In fact, simply being around negative people will make you more prejudiced, because listening to negative opinions can easily undermine your positive opinions about virtually anything.[64]

In essence, our brains are designed to mimic the emotional expressions of others.[65] Not only does this allow us to feel what others feel, but it causes what is known as "emotional contagion," a universal neurological process whereby subjective feelings are transferred to other people and spread through social groups.[66] So how fast does it take the brain to react to another person's emotion? When you see an angry expression, it takes less than one second for your brain to respond with fear.[67]

RESPONDING TO ANGER WITH COMPASSION

So how do we deal with someone who persistently uses angry rhetoric to try to change our beliefs? One solution is to walk away, the other is to try compassion. The closest I came to being in such a situation was when I was dating a girl in high school whose family were strong fundamentalists. The family believed in the literal interpretation of the Bible, and since I did not follow their doctrines, I was going to end up in hell. They continuously bombarded me with statements and arguments about why they were right and I was wrong. Sometimes the exchanges became quite heated, and even though we strongly disagreed with each other, we did try to keep the dialogue going.

As an impressionable teenager, I found this experience fascinating, but disturbing. I tried to challenge their beliefs—to no avail—but I was always respectful, and in the process, I learned a great deal about my own personal values and beliefs. I once asked them how they would respond if an alien family from another world came to visit Earth. "If they looked at every religion," I said, "they would find that each one had its own sacred books, sacred songs, and sacred truths. How would they know what religion to choose?" My girlfriend's family acknowledged that the alien would have a very tough time—that it was ultimately a leap of faith. And perhaps that is something we all need to remember. No matter what our beliefs are, our brain is making a leap of faith.

Because I showed an openness to their ideas, they treated me with respect, and I came away from the experience knowing that this was an essential element when dealing with people who hold fundamentally different beliefs. I also wondered whether it was ever possible to easily alter someone's way of thinking, especially if he or she was a "true" believer. It is a question I have pondered for decades, and the short answer is, "No." From a neurological perspective, the more we immerse ourselves in a specific ideology, the more the brain responds to that belief as if it were objectively real. Thus, there is no simple technique, or drug, that will change a person's fundamental beliefs.

WILL SKEPTICISM HURT YOUR BRAIN?

No, but cynicism will. Skepticism implies open-mindedness and the willingness to suspend judgment until both sides of an argument are considered, and this enhances neural functioning, particularly in the frontal lobes. A cynic, however, is a person who has taken their disbelief to a point of emotional distrust and rejection that borders on hostility toward the other point of view. This "limbic" personality is pessimistic and is so neurologically dangerous it can even shorten your life.

The same holds true when dealing with angry people. It is difficult to do, but if we can show compassion for their underlying suffering and pain, their brains will resonate to our kindness. In fact, research has shown that highly empathic people are more likely to respond to an angry expression by smiling.[68] Angry people, however, do not have this ability. In fact, highly aggressive people automatically assume that other people will react to them with anger, and thus they will become even more aggressive, even though no hostility was shown toward them.[69]

In the battle between two wolves, the one who refuses to fight will often walk away unscathed. And as considerable meditation research has shown, people who maintain a mindful state of acceptance tend to have better relationships with others.[70] Thus, when we train ourselves to be empathic, interpersonal animosity declines.[71] We will explore this principle in greater depth in Chapters 9 and 10.

I believe that the best manner for dealing with strong fundamentalists is through education and exposure to other ideas. Our research has shown that the more you hear, read, and think about different ideas, the more those ideas take root. Over time, distrust toward those who hold different beliefs begins to decline. This was recently demonstrated on a large scale in California's "Bible Belt." The Modesto public school system created a mandatory course on world religions for freshman high school students.[72] The program was accepted by an advisory council of Modesto's religious leaders, and when the students were tested after taking the course, their general respect for religious liberty increased. The students were less willing to express disrespectful opinions toward other religious members, especially Muslims. In addition, they felt greater comfort with their own religious identity and came away with increased understanding and appreciation of the similarities between major religions.

"NOBLE" IDEOLOGIES

The problem, as we see it, is not religious fundamentalism but authoritarianism and the impulse to impose one's ideals on as many people as possible. In fact, as Philip Zimbardo demonstrated in a famous experiment at Stanford University, it is socially and neurologically dangerous to place oneself in a position of open-ended authority.[73] He randomly divided a healthy group of adults into "prisoners" and authoritarian "guards," then put them into a make-believe prison. All the guards were told to do was maintain discipline and control over the prisoners. In less than twenty-four hours the experiment spun out of control. Prisoners were punished, humiliated, and degraded, and it soon mirrored the same type of behavior that U.S. soldiers doled out at Abu Ghraib, the American military detention prison in Iraq. Zimbardo pointed out that behind every form of religious and political abuse, you'll find "noble ideologies that allow the worst possible destructions, because you could always say, 'I did it for God.' "[74]

Sarah Mancuso, at Oberlin College, also discovered that the ideology itself propels an individual toward violence.[75] Ideological rigidity—be it religious or political—leads to less openness toward change. Furthermore, religious and political idealists tend to be dogmatic, closed-minded, and intolerant of ambiguity.[76] They have a pessimistic view of others and perceive anyone who holds a different ideology as a threat to their own existence. Furthermore, the more extreme the ideologies become, the greater the degree of intolerance, especially toward those who hold different beliefs.

Mainstream conservatism—be it religious or political—does not reflect the kind of cognitive rigidity that I am describing here.[77] In fact, the number of American religious groups that are outwardly hateful is relatively small when compared to the general population. Thus, when it comes to fundamentalism, religion is not the problem. Even the authoritarian ideologies that lie behind them are not the source of the problems we see in the world today. Anger is the problem. And when anger is married to a specific ideology and organized into an institution—be it religious or political—then there is a real danger that individual hostilities will feed upon each other until an emotional tipping point is reached. At that moment, destructive irrational behaviors can more easily be expressed in the world. This is the underlying neurological basis for violence, and it all begins with the primitive fundamentalist traits that exist within the limbic brain.

WHEN GOD GETS ANGRY WITH YOU

Some people struggle so deeply with their inner wolves that they reach a point where they feel that God may be punishing them for the way they have led their lives. As a physician, I have often seen this in people who are dealing with certain types of disease, especially cancer and substance abuse. They first ask the question, "Why me?" They wonder if God is angry at them, and they often ruminate on guilt, asking, "Why did I get this problem when I have always tried to be good?" In the cases where young children are involved, I sometimes hear the parents lament, "Why would God allow this to happen to such an innocent being?" This is tantamount to the question about why bad things happen to good people, a theme that has occupied the minds of theologians for several thousand years.

When things don't go the way we think they should, the brain will wonder what went wrong. If you blame the world or God, you've relinquished self-responsibility, and that certainly won't solve the problem. But if you blame yourself, guilt can shut your frontal lobes down. If that happens, you lose your ability to analyze the situation, and the longer you stay focused on negative self-beliefs, the more likely you are to become depressed.[78]

In hospital situations most patients don't understand the medical reasons for their illness, and many blame themselves in a variety of creative ways: "I didn't eat right, or exercise, or properly pray." And if you're religious, you may wonder if you have sinned. If not, you might blame your subconscious mind. Sometimes these individuals don't even try to get better—they don't want to. They won't take their medications, they won't try abstinence programs, and they don't try to rework their lives. It's a very difficult cycle to break, especially for those who hold deep religious beliefs. Research has shown that religious fear and guilt can evoke feelings of depression and thoughts of suicide, particularly for people who believe they have committed an unforgivable sin.[79]

Often, logic and medical reasoning has little effect on these patients. However, most university hospitals have come to realize that for many patients, the problem is as much a spiritual issue as a medical one. Thus, our medical facility, like many others, has added spiritual counseling and pastoral care for those who wish to use it. As doctors, we have come to realize that people need to deal with their spiritual pathology in addition to their physical and mental concerns. In this context, I am reminded of the biblical story of Job, who suffers terribly, even though he lives a virtuous life. His friends believe that he is a sinner and is being punished by God. Job questions God, but God declines to answer, until he finally says, "Where were you when I created the world?" The implication, at least for me, is that we can never know the mystery that is God. Nor should we be so arrogant as to think that we truly understand how the world works. This is where faith comes in, be it in ourselves, in medicine, in science, or in God. Faith tempers our anxiety and fears, and it may even temper one's belief in an angry God. The beauty of Job's story is that it reminds the suffering believer that God is ultimately compassionate. And from the perspective of medicine and neuroscience, compassion can heal the body as well as the soul.

In the evidence we've cited throughout this book, it is obvious that most forms of spiritual contemplation lead to a healthier brain, and most likely to a healthier society as well. But you must exercise that brain by exposing yourself to new ideas. Think about God and spirituality in different ways, as deeply as you can, and you will learn to appreciate the diversity, fallibility, and mystery of human beliefs.

But no matter how open-minded you become, and no matter how tolerant or compassionate you think you are, there will always remain the remnants of a neurological exclusiveness and fundamentalism in your brain—a wolf that will respond with fear and anger to all that is different and new. The struggle between good and bad, between tolerance and intolerance, between love and hate, is the personal responsibility of every individual on this planet. The question remains: Which wolf will you feed, and which wolf will you tame?

THREE

TRANSFORMING YOUR INNER REALITY

A UNIVERSAL SERENITY PRAYER

*May I find the serenity of mind
to accept the things about myself
that can't be changed,
the strength to change the things
that can be changed,
and the wisdom to know the difference.*

8

EXERCISING YOUR BRAIN

*Eight Ways to Enhance Your Physical,
Mental, and Spiritual Health*

Throughout this book we have emphasized that many forms of spiritual practice affect your brain in fundamentally healthy ways. It doesn't matter how you believe in God, and there is considerable evidence that such practices work even if you don't believe. Part of the reason for this is that spirituality is often defined in terms of personal values and the search for meaning and truth, and thus, spiritual practices can take on many forms.

If you take the most conservative assessment of the hundreds of medical, neurological, psychological, and sociological studies on religion, two conclusions are evident.

First, involvement with religious and spiritual activities generally does no harm, unless, as we described in the last chapter, you focus on an authoritarian God who fills you with anger and fear. And as we reported earlier in the book, even minimal religious participation is correlated with enhancing longevity and personal health.

The second conclusion is this: Activities involving meditation and intensive prayer permanently strengthen neural functioning in specific parts of the brain that are involved with lowering anxiety and depression, enhancing social awareness and empathy, and improving cognitive and intellectual functioning. The neural circuits activated by meditation buffer you from the deleterious effects of aging and stress and give you better control over your emotions. At the very least, such practices help you remain calm, serene, peaceful, and alert. And for nearly everyone, it gives you a positive and optimistic outlook on life.

However, when we looked closely at the neurological principles underlying most spiritual practices, we discovered that the health benefits associated with prayer and meditation can be achieved through activities that are unrelated to religion. Meditation is certainly *one* of the best ways enhance the neural functioning of your brain, but there are seven other "techniques" that you should consider incorporating into your life.

You won't find drugs or supplements on this list because, as a medical researcher, I am not convinced that they are any better at enhancing neural functioning than the methods I'm about to describe. Furthermore, most drugs can have potentially significant side effects.* Diet is also not included, not because it doesn't affect brain function— it does, in very important ways—but because it is nearly impossible to isolate how the component nutrients influence neural metabolism and health. It would require a separate book, and it would be far more controversial than the suggestions that follow. Suffice it to say that a generally healthful diet is always good for your brain.

Sleep also did not make it to our list, but not because it is unimportant to cognitive functioning. It is. In fact, sleep is so important to the brain that we cannot survive without it. Like other body parts, it needs time to rejuvenate and strengthen the connections between nerve cells. This process, called "consolidation," enables nerve cells to strengthen their connections. If the brain does not rest, those circuits will be damaged. And if you *chronically* sleep less than five hours a night, cognition significantly declines.[1] The problem is, a "good" night's sleep is dependent upon many variables, especially the amount of stress you've experienced while awake. In fact, even a single exposure to a stressful situation can disturb your normal pattern of sleep.[2] Any form of stress exhausts our neural capacity to function optimally, and nearly every-

---

* An interesting exception is the serotonin-enhancing antidepressants. They appear to improve neural and synaptic plasticity, especially in areas related to memory storage and recall, and may even cause new growth in the hippocampus and amygdala.

thing we do is stressful, to one degree or another. Take driving, for example. With every hour we spend on the road, our alertness decreases, and the resulting fatigue impairs cognitive functioning.[3] So the problem is stress-induced fatigue, and the cure is adequate rest.

Sleep deprivation will disrupt normal neural functioning,[4] but it's hard to assess to what degree, and in what ways, given all the variables involved in an individual's constitution and lifestyle. For example, nearly every form of cognitive and physical disturbance will disrupt your sleep.[5] Sleeping pills won't help either because many of them disrupt REM sleep and dreaming, which are essential components for maintaining a healthy brain. Deprive a rat, which normally lives two or three years, of REM sleep, and the poor thing will survive for about five weeks.[6] Sleep *disturbance* is the problem, but an increased *quantity* is not necessarily a cure.

Neuroscientific evidence has governed our choice in selecting the eight best ways to maintain a healthy brain, but it wouldn't surprise me if we left out a few strategies that are equally effective in terms of promoting neurological health. Still, I think several items on our list will surprise you. None are based on any religious orientation, but you can easily integrate them into any spiritual tradition you favor. In fact, we believe that in addition to helping your brain, they can all be used to strengthen your ethical behavior. They will also transform your inner reality, and when that happens, your perception of the world will change. Your spirituality will change, and so will your notions of God.

THE EIGHTH BEST WAY TO EXERCISE YOUR BRAIN

Smile. Even if you don't feel like it, the mere act of smiling repetitively helps to interrupt mood disorders and strengthen the brain's neural ability to maintain a positive outlook on life.[7] And even if you fake a smile, other people will respond to you with greater generosity and kindness. To my knowledge, the only religion to incorporate smiling into a spiritual practice is Buddhism. For example, Thich Nhat Hanh suggests that we do "smiling meditation" whenever we have a spare moment during the day. Smile when you're going up in the elevator or when standing in line at the supermarket, and you will notice that the people around you calm down. You'll feel better, you'll exude empathy, and people will respond with kindness. As Thich Nhat Hanh wrote, "If we are not able to smile, then the world will not have peace."[8] Smiles, by the way, are neurologically contagious in every culture, and women are more susceptible than men.[9]

Smiling stimulates brain circuits that enhance social interaction,[10] empathy,[11] and mood.[12] In fact, smiling has such a powerful effect on the brain that if you just see a picture of a smiling face, you will involuntarily feel happier and more secure.[13] Conversely, frowning (or looking at frowning faces) stimulates feelings of anger, disgust, and dislike. In one controversial study, Botox injections into frown lines appeared to alleviate subjective feelings of depression.[14]

Laughing, however, stimulates different neural paths.[15] Laughing and humor did not make it onto our list because part of the mechanisms involved are associated with surprise and the perception of incongruity.[16] Laughter and humor can stimulate the amygdala, suggesting that these feelings are sometimes related to discomfort and fear.[17] This helps explain why many people laugh when watching videos where others do foolish things and are hurt, for it may be a way of quickly releasing anxiety (an alternative explanation would be that some people experience an inherent sadistic pleasure when others make mistakes).

There is some evidence to suggest that laughter may help lower stress and boost the immune system, even turning on various genes that are related to fighting cancer, diabetes, and AIDS.[18] But the changes appear to be temporary, and the studies fail to demonstrate if any appreciable improvements in health are gained.

Nurturing a laughing personality may be beneficial, but until someone takes a group of test subjects and asks them to arbitrarily laugh for fifteen minutes per day, then scans them again in eight weeks, we won't know if the neural circuits stimulated are related to anxiety, pleasure, sadism, or peace.

However, we do recommend that you listen to "happy" music (yes, your brain organizes sound into a range of emotions). It can stimulate a smile response and improve your mood,[19] and it is particularly effective in helping your brain when you are dealing with a chronic or serious disease.[20]

THE SEVENTH BEST WAY TO EXERCISE YOUR BRAIN

Stay intellectually active. This should be (if you will pardon the pun) a no-brainer. When it comes to the dendrites and axons that connect one neuron to thousands of others, if you don't use it, you will lose it.[21] Intellectual and cognitive stimulation strengthens the neural connections throughout your frontal lobe,[22] and this, in turn, improves your ability to communicate, solve problems, and make rational decisions concerning your behavior. Nearly every age-related cognitive disability is related to the functioning of your frontal lobe, so it's particularly important to exercise this specific part of your cortex, which, by the way, has more neural interconnections than any other lobe. A highly functioning frontal lobe also makes it easier to diet, exercise, and avoid tempting activities that have health risks.[23]

Memory and mnemonic exercises, strategy-based games like chess or mahjong, and other forms of visual/spatial exercises or games can significantly improve cognitive functioning, especially in older adults.[24] And the more intense and frequent the game playing, the greater the cognitive gain. Furthermore, intellectual stimulation, in nearly any form, lowers your propensity to react with anger or fear. Imagination even improves the motor coordination of your body, and if you rehearse a dance step or a golf swing in your mind, you'll actually perform the task better. The same is true for attaining personal goals. The more often you imagine what you want, the more likely you are to achieve it.

Try to spend as many hours a day engaged in the most intellectually challenging activities you can dream up, and solve as many complex problems as quickly as you can, because speedy intellectual reasoning helps you maintain a healthy brain.[25] Read books (fiction or nonfiction, it doesn't matter) or listen to books on tape. Watch the education and science channels on TV, take a class, attend a lecture, go to a museum, play chess, or write in your diary. However, doing math exercises and crossword puzzles apparently doesn't help,[26] and performance pressure can even interfere with memory functioning.[27] So be sure to make your intellectual pursuits enjoyable. The research also suggests that you must engage in a wide variety of sophisticated, challenging cognitive activities in order to keep your neurons and dendrites well connected.

Engaging in religious and spiritual issues and problems will also stimulate brain function. Reading scriptures, reflecting on meaning, discussing issues with friends, and seriously thinking about the deepest issues facing humanity are outstanding ways of activating complex circuits in your brain.[28] In fact, religious and spiritual issues are among the most challenging we face today. Focusing your mind on such problems, grappling with them, exploring different perspectives—all of these help expand and enhance your brain's activity.

There is one mental activity that I suggest you be wary of: videogame playing. The more you do it, the more aggressive you *may* become and the more your coping skills are reduced.[29] Frontal lobe functioning declines, exasperating attention deficit problems,[30] dependency issues,[31] and addictive behavior in children and adolescents.[32] And, as we mentioned in the previous chapter, violent video games clearly stimulate aggressive behavior.[33] However, there is no convincing evidence to suggest that *nonviolent* video gaming causes permanent neurological or behavioral damage.[34]

But what about computer-based cognitive training programs? Can they improve brain function? Recently, there's been a great deal of publicity about different brain stimulation programs, but there's also been considerable controversy and doubt in the scientific and academic communities. Cognitive-based computer games appear to improve neural functioning, at least for people with cognitive problems, but no one has yet created an effective way to compare one type of exercise to another.[35] One learning program, developed a few years ago to aid children in language and reading development, showed initial promise, especially when dealing with serious learning problems, but the improvements have been so small as to have little practical benefit.[36] Newer "brain fitness" programs that claim to reduce neurological deterioration have also been heavily publicized, and although the research looks promising,[37] we won't know for many years how practical they might actually be, especially for the average aging individual.

THE SIXTH BEST WAY TO EXERCISE YOUR BRAIN

Consciously relax. I'm not talking about taking a nap, or assuming the position of a couch potato in front of a television set. I'm talking about deliberately scanning each part of your body to reduce muscle tension and physical fatigue. And if you add pleasant music, your body will relax more quickly.[38] Calming music, by the way, has been shown to sharpen your cognitive skills[39] and improve your sense of spiritual well-being.[40]

Simple, repetitive activities that are pleasurable and meaningful can also take you into a deep state of relaxation. In one of my most recent studies, we found that the ritual practice of counting rosaries lowers tension, stress, and anxiety. Many other religious and spiritual practices calm the mind and allow the brain to rejuvenate, and even activities like knitting will have a similar relaxing effect.

In the next chapter we'll explore several techniques that will help you experience a very deep state of relaxation, which turns out to be the first essential step in any meditation practice. But relaxation does much more than relieve bodily tension. It interrupts the brain's release of stress-stimulating neurochemicals, and stress is the number one killer in America. Lowering stress reduces heart disease, high blood pressure, and pain. And one of the keys to reducing stress involves conscious focusing on the breath. However, when it comes to relaxation, a dozen deep breaths is not as effective as you might think. There's a much faster way to simultaneously relax *and* raise consciousness, and it comes next on our list.

THE FIFTH BEST WAY TO EXERCISE YOUR BRAIN

Yawn. Go ahead: Laugh if you want (though you'll benefit your brain more if you smile), but in my professional opinion, yawning is one of the best-kept secrets in neuroscience. Even my colleagues who are researching meditation, relaxation, and stress reduction at other universities have overlooked this powerful neural-enhancing tool. However, yawning has been used for many decades in voice therapy as an effective means for reducing performance anxiety and hypertension in the throat.[41]

Several recent brain-scan studies have shown that yawning evokes a unique neural activity in the areas of the brain that are directly involved in generating social awareness and creating feelings of empathy.[42] One of those areas is the precuneus, a tiny structure hidden within the folds of the parietal lobe. According to researchers at the Institute of Neurology in London, the precuneus appears to play a central role in consciousness, self-reflection, and memory retrieval.[43] The precuneus is also stimulated by yogic breathing, which helps explain why different forms of meditation contribute to an increased sense of self-awareness.[44] It is also one of the areas hardest hit by age-related diseases and attention deficit problems,[45] so it's possible that deliberate yawning may actually strengthen this important part of the brain.

For these reasons we believe that yawning should be integrated into exercise and stress reduction programs, cognitive and memory enhancement training, psychotherapy, and contemplative spiritual practice. And, because the precuneus has recently been associated with the mirror-neuron system in the brain (which allows us to resonate to the feelings and behaviors of others), yawning may even help us to enhance social awareness, compassion, and effective communication with others.[46]

Yawning is so effective and important to the functioning of your brain that I'm going to ask you to review for yourself the thirty-four yawn-related studies I've cited in the endnotes (you can read the abstracts and several papers by going to pubmed.gov). Why am I so insistent? Because if I were to ask you to put this book down right now and yawn ten times to experience this fabulous technique, you probably won't do it. Even at seminars, after presenting the overwhelmingly positive evidence, when I ask people to yawn, half of the audience will hesitate. I have to coax them so they can feel the immediate relaxing effects. There's an unexplained stigma in our society implying that it's rude to yawn, and most of us were taught this when we were young.

As a young medical student, I was once "caught" yawning and actually scolded by my professor. He said that it was inappropriate to appear tired in front of patients, even though I was actually standing in a hallway outside of the patient's room. Indeed, yawning does increase when you're tired, and it may be the brain's way of gently telling you that a little rejuvenating sleep is needed.[47] On the other hand, exposure to light will also make you yawn, suggesting that it is part of the process of waking up.[48]

But yawning doesn't just relax you—it quickly brings you into a heightened state of cognitive awareness.[49] Students yawn in class, not because the teacher is boring (although that will make you yawn as well, as you try to stay focused on the monotonous speech), but because it rids the brain of sleepiness, thus helping you stay focused on important concepts and ideas. It regulates consciousness and our sense of self, and helps us become more introspective and self-aware.[50] Of course, if you happen to find yourself trapped in a room with a dull, boring, monotonous teacher, yawning will help keep you awake.

Yawning will relax you and bring you into a state of alertness faster than any other meditation technique I know of, and because it is neurologically contagious,[51] it's particularly easy to teach in a group setting. One of my former students used yawning to bring her argumentative board of directors back to order in less than sixty seconds. Why? Because it helps people synchronize their behavior with others.[52]

Yawning, as a mechanism for alertness, begins within the first twenty weeks after conception.[53] It helps regulate the circadian rhythms of newborns,[54] and this adds to the evidence that yawning is involved in the regulation of wakefulness and sleep.[55] Since circadian rhythms become asynchronous when a person's normal sleep cycle is disturbed, yawning should help the late-night partygoer reset the brain's internal clock. Yawning may also ward off the effects of jet lag and ease the discomfort caused by high altitudes.

So what is the underlying mechanism that makes yawning such an essential tool? Besides activating the precuneus, it regulates the temperature and metabolism of your brain.[56] It takes a lot of neural energy to stay consciously alert, and as you work your way up the evolutionary ladder, brains become less energy efficient. Yawning probably evolved as a way to cool down the overly active mammalian brain, especially in the areas of the frontal lobe. Some have even argued that it is a primitive form of empathy.[57] Most vertebrates yawn, but it is only contagious among humans, great apes, macaque monkeys,[58] and chimpanzees.[59]

In fact, it's so contagious for humans that even reading about it will cause a person to yawn.[60]

Dogs yawn before attacking, Olympic athletes yawn before performing, and fish yawn before they change activities.[61] Evidence even exists that yawning helps individuals on military assignment perform their tasks with greater accuracy and ease.[62] Indeed, yawning may be one of the most important mechanisms for regulating the survival-related behaviors in mammals.[63] So if you want to maintain an optimally healthy brain, it is essential that you yawn. However, excessive yawning can be a sign that an underlying neurological disorder (such as migraine, multiple sclerosis, stroke, or drug reaction) is occurring.[64] However, we and other researchers suspect that yawning may be the brain's attempt to eliminate symptoms by readjusting neural functioning.

Numerous neurochemicals are involved in the yawning experience, including dopamine,[65] which activates oxytocin production in your hypothalamus and hippocampus,[66] areas essential for memory recall, voluntary control, and temperature regulation. These neurotransmitters regulate pleasure, sensuality, and relationship bonding between individuals, so if you want to enhance your intimacy and stay together, then yawn together. Other neurochemicals and molecules involved with yawning include acetylcholine, nitric oxide, glutamate, GABA, serotonin, ACTH, MSH, sexual hormones, and opium derivate peptides.[67] In fact, it's hard to find another activity that positively influences so many functions of the brain.

12 ESSENTIAL REASONS TO YAWN

1. Stimulates alertness and concentration
2. Optimizes brain activity and metabolism
3. Improves cognitive function
4. Increases memory recall
5. Enhances consciousness and introspection
6. Lowers stress
7. Relaxes every part of your body
8. Improves voluntary muscle control
9. Enhances athletic skills
10. Fine-tunes your sense of time
11. Increases empathy and social awareness
12. Enhances pleasure and sensuality

Our advice is simple. Yawn as many times a day as possible: when you wake up, when you're confronting a difficult problem at work, when you prepare to go to sleep, and whenever you feel anger, anxiety, or stress. Yawn before giving an important talk, yawn before you take a test, and yawn while you meditate or pray because it will intensify your spiritual experience.

Conscious yawning takes a little practice and discipline to get over the unconscious social inhibitions, but people often come up with three other excuses not to yawn: "I don't feel like it," "I'm not tired," and my favorite, "I can't." Of course you can. All you have to do to trigger a deep yawn is to fake it six or seven times. Try it right now, and you should discover by the fifth false yawn, a real one will begin to emerge. But don't stop there, because by the tenth or twelfth yawn, you'll feel the power of this seductive little trick. Your eyes may start watering and your nose may begin to run, but you'll also feel utterly present, incredibly relaxed, and highly alert. Not bad for something that takes less than a minute to do. And if you find that you can't stop yawning—I've seen some people yawn for thirty minutes—you'll know that you've been depriving yourself of an important neurological treat.

THE FOURTH BEST WAY TO EXERCISE YOUR BRAIN

Meditate. I wish I could say that meditation and intensive prayer were number one, because that's where our research has been focused, but being number four is nothing to sneeze at (no, sneezing doesn't help the brain and may even be a symptom of a rare cerebellar disorder[68]). And when it comes to enhancing spiritual experiences, it certainly takes first place. If you stay in a contemplative state for twenty minutes to an hour, your experiences will tend to feel more real, affecting your nervous system in ways that enhance physical and emotional health. Antistress hormones and neurochemicals are released throughout the body, as well as pleasure-enhancing and depression-decreasing neurotransmitters like dopamine and serotonin. Even ten to fifteen minutes of meditation appears to have significantly positive effects on cognition, relaxation, and psychological health, and it has been shown to reduce smoking and binge-drinking behavior.[69]

There's even solid evidence that meditating before taking a test will significantly improve your score. When researchers at the University of Kentucky taught students a forty-minute relaxation and concentration technique, they did better than those who exercised or took a nap.[70] Caffeine helped, but not as much. And of course, don't forget to yawn.

Visualization, guided imagery, and self-hypnosis are specific variations of meditation and are equally effective in maintaining a healthy brain. In the next chapter, we'll guide you through the basic steps for establishing a meditation practice that you can integrate into your personal or spiritual life.

THE THIRD BEST WAY TO EXERCISE YOUR BRAIN

Aerobic exercise. Vigorous exercise strengthens every part of the brain, as well as what it is connected to—the body. If you're between the ages of eighteen and ninety, exercise is going to lengthen your life.[71] How much should you experience? In general, the more intense the better. For example, running is better than walking, and walking is better than stretching,[72] but it is important to find the "right" amount of exercise that feels the best for you. Certain health conditions will also affect the type and length of exercise you can do, so creating a personalized program is a complex but important issue to address.

Exercise can even be viewed as a form of meditation because it involves sustained concentration and a deliberate regulation of body movements and breathing. Studies have even shown that it enhances relaxation[73] and spiritual well-being.[74]

Vigorous stretching, such as yoga, also does wonders for both your body and your brain. Yoga has similar cognitive benefits to other forms of contemplative meditation, and in a recent meta-analysis of 813 meditation studies, the researchers stated that yoga was as beneficial as exercise.[75] It can lower the risk of cardiovascular disease,[76] help control the symptoms of diabetes,[77] lessen the severity of menopausal symptoms,[78] reduce chronic back pain,[79] and prevent the onslaught of migraine headaches.[80]

In a study conducted in 2007, researchers at the Boston University School of Medicine found that levels of the neurotransmitter GABA increase after a single sixty-minute yoga session.[81] Since people who suffer from depression and anxiety disorders have low levels of GABA, yoga exercise is a valid modality for improving psychological mood. It's even been found to reduce the symptoms of schizophrenia.[82] Research has also shown that a few weeks of yoga training enhances a wide range of cognitive skills in children and adults.[83]

All forms of exercise enhance neural performance[84] and rebuild damaged circuits caused by brain lesions and strokes.[85] Exercise improves cognition and academic performance.[86] It repairs and protects you from the neurological damage caused by stress.[87] It enhances brain plasticity.[88] It boosts immune function.[89] It reduces anxiety.[90] It can be used to treat clinical depression,[91] and it is just as effective as antidepressants.[92] In fact, for older patients, exercise is equivalent to twelve sessions of psychodynamic psychotherapy.[93] It slows down the loss of brain tissue as you age,[94] protects you from Alzheimer's disease,[95] and reduces your vulnerability to chronic illness.[96] Need I say anything more to convince you of the importance of exercise?

A forty-minute cardiovascular workout every other day is enough to keep your brain healthy, but why limit yourself to just one modality? When you look at all the techniques that have proven effective in treating physical and emotional problems, you'll find that most treatments use a combination of approaches. For example, when Dean Ornish created his famous program to reverse heart disease, he combined exercise with meditation, breath awareness, relaxation, and a low-fat vegetarian diet.[97]

Combined strategies are always more effective, so why not assemble all of the above techniques into a cardiovascular meditation? Warm up with a dozen yoga stretches and yawns, then put on your running shoes and smile. And, since there's no reason why you can't contemplate God or focus on developing inner peace as you strengthen your muscles, bones, heart, and brain, why not pick a spiritual or personal goal that you want to accomplish in your life? You can literally sprint to success. Get together with a small group of spiritually minded friends and sponsor an interfaith marathon with your church. Become a cardiovascular Christian. Do isotonics for Islam. Jog for Judaism. Bike for Buddhism. Eat plenty of vegetables and be as healthy as a Hindu. And don't forget to yawn. You'll open your heart and your mind, in both a spiritual and literal way.

If you think this sounds silly, let me tell you about an experiment conducted with nineteen churches in Baltimore, Maryland.[98] Five hundred twenty-six Baptist, Holiness, Catholic, and Methodist African-American women spent a year integrating spirituality and exercise. They did aerobics to gospel music, and chanted religious praises during a cardiovascular dance. They also received scripture-based messages encouraging physical activity and healthy eating. Participants had significant improvements in dietary energy and blood pressure, weight and waist reduction, total fat reduction, and lower sodium intake. Church involvement specifically contributed to the program's success, but the addition of spirituality did not significantly improve outcomes. Still, it does point out the potential power that religious groups have in fostering physical and emotional health.

THE SECOND BEST WAY TO EXERCISE YOUR BRAIN

Dialogue with others. Language and the human brain coevolved with each other,[99] allowing us to excel over many of the physical and mental skills of other mammals and primates. And if we don't exercise our language skills, large portions of the brain will not effectively interconnect with other neural structures. Dialogue requires social interaction, and the more social ties we have, the less our cognitive abilities will decline.[100] In fact, any form of social isolation will damage important mechanisms in the brain leading to aggression, depression, and various neuropsychiatric disorders.[101] Without dialogue, we would not be able to cooperate with others, and without cooperation, human behavior rapidly deteriorates into conflict. We can either talk our way out of a problem or fight our way out, and dialogue is certainly the more civilized solution for attaining and maintaining global peace.

But don't just talk about the weather or gossip about the neighbors. These forms of dialogue are more like monologues, and they won't engage the brain as much as a deeper conversation. Talk about abstract ideals like harmony and peace. Ask what your neighbor thinks about evolution and the Big Bang. Talk about what the twenty-third century might look like, and by all means talk about God—but with one caveat: Don't get entrapped in an angry dialogue. As we made clear in the previous chapter, irritable conversations will do considerable damage to your brain.

Since religion is central to many of the world's conflicts, we need to create empathic communication strategies to bridge spiritual differences. Unfortunately, communication skills are rarely taught in schools or in religious groups. To address this issue, we have taken the principles of meditation and adapted them to create a unique dialogue experience that you can do with anyone: with your partner, kids, friends, business associates, or even a complete stranger. It will create deep intimacy between any two people in less than fifteen minutes, and it only takes a few minutes to learn. We'll teach you how to practice Compassionate Communication in Chapter 10, but first, it's time to share with you the most essential component for maintaining a healthy brain.

THE NUMBER ONE BEST WAY TO EXERCISE YOUR BRAIN

Faith. No matter what choice we make concerning our physical, emotional, and spiritual health, we'll never know for certain if we are absolutely correct in our beliefs. We can make educated guesses about the world, but some degree of uncertainty will always remain. This is true for medicine and science, and it's certainly true when it comes to our religious beliefs.

Still, we have to trust our beliefs, and this is a matter of faith. But it's always unsettling to realize that we can't be a hundred percent sure about anything. We can't even trust our eyes when it comes to something as obvious as color, because color doesn't exist in the world. Light waves exist, but we can't see them at all. We only know they exist through the instruments we construct and the mathematical formulas that underpin our experiments. Color is a product of our imagination, and so is our perception of the world.

The same can be said about God. We can take surveys, or scan people's brains as they contemplate God, but this will tell us more about the brain and nothing about the true nature of the universe.

To be spiritually inclined, you have to rely on faith. Those who don't believe in such realms will use different criteria to govern their decisions and ideas, but they too must rely upon their intuition and faith to guide them through the unknown aspects of life. None of us can be certain if we've made the "right" decision, especially when it comes to dealing with abstract concepts like justice, fairness, or moral ideals. If we don't have faith that we're making the best decision we can, then we will be swallowed up in doubt. And doubt, at least as far as your brain is concerned, is a precarious state in which to live.

Faith is equivalent with hope, optimism, and the belief that a positive future awaits us. Faith can also be defined as the ability to trust our beliefs, even when we have no proof that such beliefs are accurate or true. The psychiatrist Vicktor Frankl, who was imprisoned in a Nazi death camp until the end of World War II, said that the single most important thing that kept a survivor alive was faith. If a prisoner lost faith in the future, he was doomed, because the will to live seldom returned.[102]

Similarly, Mark and I are convinced that for many people, if their faith in God was weakened, they could suffer deeply. Clearly this happened to many Jews, who came away from the Holocaust with the nearly unbearable question, "God, how could you let such a tragedy occur?" Many abandoned their faith in God, but they maintained their faith in humanity, and in their cultural heritage as Jews. More important, many chose to fight for the religious and civil rights of others.

To me, it doesn't matter if God is an illusion or fact, because even as a metaphor, God represents all we are capable of becoming, an ideal that offers hope to millions of people throughout the world, especially for those who may have little to fall back on other than their religious ties. Faith in an optimistic future may be a placebo, but it's important to remember that placebos can cure, on average, 30 percent of most physical and emotional diseases. Even an irrational belief in a cure that has been proven *not* to work can significantly boost the body's immune system when dealing with a deadly disease.[103]

Recently, a team of National Institutes of Health researchers concluded that "a moderate optimistic illusion" appears to be neurologically essential for maintaining motivation and good mental health.[104] They also found that highly optimistic people had greater activation in the same parts of the anterior cingulate that are stimulated by meditation. If you recall from previous chapters, the anterior cingulate plays a crucial role in controlling anxiety, depression, and rage, as well as fostering social awareness and compassion.

Even the medical researchers at the Mayo Clinic stress the importance of optimistic thinking for maintaining optimal health. They found that positive thinking decreases stress, helps you resist catching the common cold, reduces your risk of coronary artery disease, eases breathing if you have certain respiratory diseases, and improves your coping skills during hardships.[105] An optimistic attitude specifically reduces the stress-eliciting cortisol levels in your body,[106] and many other studies have demonstrated how optimism improves behavioral coping in a variety of physical illnesses.[107] In a forty-year follow-up conducted at Duke University, optimists had increased longevity when compared to pessimistic individuals.[108] Indeed, the role of optimism is so important in maintaining psychological health that the University of Pennsylvania has an entire institute—the Positive Psychology Center, headed by Martin Seligman—dedicated to this research.[109]

Faith is essential for maintaining a healthy brain, but if you exclude exercise and companionship, you are going to cripple your health. So my advice is to nurture all three. And if religion is high on your list, then I suggest that you include meditation, since it appears to be the best way to make spiritual values neurologically real. For those who don't value religion, meditating on hope, optimism, and a positive future will have similar neurological benefits.* Best of all, meditation undermines the everyday doubts and anxiety we all harbor when we reach for new goals and ideals. In other words, meditation will strengthen your faith—in yourself, in people, and in God.

THE PRINCIPLES OF AFFIRMATION

Before I close this chapter, I want to briefly address the widespread popularity of the "power of positive thinking," especially as it relates to

---

* Neither religion nor a belief in God made it to our "Top Eight" list because religious beliefs, in and of themselves, have no specific effect on the brain, especially if they hold little meaning or value for the individual. But because religion is often a combination of social dialogue, intellectual stimulation, and faith, it can be a powerful mechanism for exercising your brain and optimizing the brain's functions. On the other hand, negative religious beliefs can have a harmful effect on neural functioning, especially if they are ruminated on for extended periods of time.

the notion that you can use your thoughts to attain anything you want in the materialistic world. Overly simplistic books and CDs like *The Secret* have been turned into million-dollar best-sellers when they're touted by television talk-show hosts, but do they really work? From a neuroscientific perspective, the answer is yes, but not in the magical ways implied.

In fact, nurturing a fantasy is the first step in the neural process of achieving success in the world. It begins with creative imagination, a process that takes place in your frontal lobe, the area in your brain that has the unrelenting capacity to dream up virtually anything. If you can't imagine a specific goal, you won't make it to second base, which is figuring out *how* to make your dream come true.

Now, as I have emphasized throughout this book, truth can only be approximated by the brain. Instead, what the brain does best is calculate the odds of success. Here is where faith kicks in, because it is essential to remain optimistic about your chances of reaching your goals.

So what do you do when all of the subtle, and not so subtle, self-doubts kick in? You can do several things: suppress them, evaluate them, or ruminate on them. Neurologically, it's actually easier to suppress them, because the more you keep your mind focused on your optimistic belief of success, the more you will inhibit the functioning of your limbic system, which generates doubt and fear. However, anxious individuals have a more difficult time suppressing negative thoughts,[110] and often get caught up in the repetitive process of rumination. This, unfortunately, strengthens the neural circuits that generate anxiety and embed the information into long-term memory banks.[111] We recommend that such people engage in a more intensive meditation regime, as we will describe in the next chapter.

But suppression of negative thoughts is not enough to make any dream come true. At some point you may have to evaluate the practicality of your goal. For example, practitioners of Transcendental Meditation used to believe that if they concentrated hard enough, they would eventually be able to levitate. Known as "yogic flying," some students spent thousands of dollars for training, but so far all anyone has been able to do is hop. It may be an ecstatic, enlightened hop, but it isn't levitation. Well, the same holds true for obtaining wealth. If you concentrate hard enough, I do not doubt that your income will rise, but don't be surprised if doesn't reach the moon.

Concentration is essential to set your goal in motion, and the suppression of self-doubt is critical, but more is necessary to achieve success. You have to become motivated to do something about it. You have to take action, you have to tell others about your dream, and you need something to offer them to make them participate in your success.

In other words, you can't do it alone. And you can't depend on the universe to oblige your every whim, as some of these books suggest. There's no clear evidence that there is a quantum force that emanates from any part of you that influences the cosmos to do your bidding. Quantum properties do appear to be involved in the synaptic activity between neurons,[112] and we can use quantum dots to track peptides in cells,[113] but this does not clearly translate into any observable phenomena inside or beyond your body.[114] Even if quantum physics could be shown to influence your life, it would more likely do so on the quantum level, meaning that you'd experience a *subatomic* increase in personal wealth. Dream about a million bucks, and you'll be a penny richer! Certainly we can all do better than that.

The magic comes when other people *feel* and *see* your optimism and excitement about your project, which makes similar circuits in their brain resonate to yours. If they have the time, energy, and mutual interest, they will be neurologically inclined to join forces with you, or at least support you and give you helpful advice.

The longer you focus (i.e., meditate) on your goal, the more real it begins to feel, and if you stay focused long enough, you'll alter the neural circuitry in your brain. The same is true for any principle or belief. Focus on God long enough, and God becomes neurologically real. Focus on peace, and your body will become relaxed and serene. And if you intensely focus on wealth, monetary issues will permeate your mind and influence your behavior in the world.

Goal achievement begins with the belief that you *can* succeed, but it is equally important to establish *what* goal you truly desire. This too is easy to do. Chris and Janet Attwood, authors of *The Passion Test,* describe a useful technique of making a list of your desires and goals to meditate on and review throughout your life.[115] They also suggest that you create a "vision board" that contains pictures and images associated with your goal. From a neuroscientific perspective, this makes a lot of sense because, as we explained in Chapter 5, the visualization process makes it easier for the brain to translate ideas into concrete attainable goals.

When you meditate on what you desire, immerse yourself in positive images associated with your goal. For example, try to envision meeting important people who can help you on your quest. Then take action. Call up everyone you know—not with trepidation, but with the knowledge that people are neurologically inclined to help—and ask them for the name of someone they know who might help you to achieve your goal. In very little time you'll connect with the right individuals. Networking is the fastest way to success, especially when it concerns relationships and work. And that's exactly what your neurons are genetically designed to do: network with each other.

ARE THERE ANY DRAWBACKS TO UNREALISTIC OPTIMISM?

Skeptics might argue that maintaining an illusory optimism is problematic, but the evidence points in the opposite direction. Researchers at the University of California found that people who have self-enhancing illusions exhibit lower cardiovascular responses to stress, more rapid cardiovascular recovery, and lower baseline cortisol levels.[116] In fact, an unrealistically optimistic belief about the future appears to be health protective, even when dealing with a disease as serious as AIDS.[117]

Simply put, faith and optimism will add months or years to your life,[118] and the only drawback—and a potentially serious one—is a decreased perception of risk.[119] It will increase your resistance to common colds and flu viruses, though bias you toward underestimating the severity of your symptoms.[120] Optimism leads people to underestimate their risk of getting divorced and to overestimate their prospects for success in the marketplace. Thus optimism can be taken to an extreme, especially if you choose to ignore realistic concerns. For example, optimistic smokers underestimate their chances of getting ill,[121] and this is indeed a dangerous form of faith. All forms of optimism are associated with a less realistic view of the world.[122] But then again, so is pessimism.[123] Thus the question we must face is this: Are we using our optimistic beliefs to maintain a destructive behavior or belief? If so, then a healthy dollop of reality testing should be added to your recipe for health.

If the human brain did not have a bias toward optimism, we would be prone to increased anxiety and depression.[124] Pessimism, however, has few benefits, and it leaves the person more at risk to depression, anxiety, sleeping problems, obsessive-compulsive behavior, and impaired social functioning.[125] In a thirty-year longitudinal study conducted by the Mayo Clinic, pessimism was significantly associated with a shorter life span and poorer mental functioning.[126]

Evolution has given us the biological ability to be optimistic and hopeful about the future, even when there is no concrete evidence to support our beliefs. This too is one of the functions of our frontal lobes, but we need to exercise it daily, having faith in humanity, and especially in ourselves.

9

FINDING SERENITY

Meditation, Intention, Relaxation,
and Awareness

God can change your brain. This much we have shown. But now our meditation research has brought us to a turning point, for we can distill from the world's spiritual practices a set of simple exercises that will enhance the neural functioning of the brain. When we do so, we improve our physical, emotional, and cognitive health, adding years of greater happiness to our lives.

As a doctor, I must emphasize that these techniques do not, in any way, replace the appropriate use of current medical practice,* but if you add them to your daily repertoire of activities, you will find that they can have a very powerful effect on your life. They will boost the responsiveness of your immune system, sharpen your productivity at work, and enrich the quality of your relationships—not just with family and friends, but with strangers whom you might casually meet. Empathy and compassion will be enhanced, and you'll even find it easier to interact with those who hold beliefs that differ from your own.

---

* There is little evidence suggesting that gentle forms of meditation have any negative health effects. Although several researchers have hypothesized that the neurological changes associated with meditation may increase the possibility of triggering an epileptic seizure in people prone to this disease, no reports of seizures have been documented. Anecdotal psychological evidence also suggests that people with certain personality disorders should be carefully evaluated and monitored before engaging in intense spiritual practices.

That's a lot to promise, but we feel that the thirty-plus years of research into the underlying mechanics of spiritual practice is so conclusive that we are planning to incorporate these exercises into various programs at the University of Pennsylvania's Center for Spirituality and the Mind.*

INTENTION

The exercises in this chapter center on three main interconnecting principles: intention, relaxation, and awareness. *Intention* refers to the goal you want to manifest in your life, for everything we do has an underlying intention, whether we are conscious of it or not. We use our intention to determine what we want to focus on, and the goal can be anything you choose: money, power, peace, insight, romance, or a closer connection to God. Before you sit down to practice any of the following exercises, clarify what your intention is. Better yet, write it out on a slip of paper and keep it posted in a prominent place. When you clearly articulate your intention or goal in writing and speech, your frontal lobes can more efficiently direct your motor cortex to carry out your desire as you actively engage with others in the world.

It's an extraordinary process: You begin with a goal-oriented thought, and the more you focus on it, the more your brain begins to plot out strategies to carry that thought into the world. Other animals, even primates, can barely do this because they have far fewer neural connections that run from the frontal lobe to other parts of the brain.

RELAXATION

Relaxation is the second principle, and it is found in most contemplative practices and stress-reduction programs. Thus, one begins the intention by consciously relaxing the body. Usually this involves focusing on

---

* The center brings together an interdisciplinary group of faculty from all of the university schools to develop, organize, and coordinate research, scholarship, education, and dialogue, both locally and globally, that focuses on the relationship between spirituality and the brain. By establishing courses, teaching materials, public and academic lecture programs, and local and Internet outreach programs, the center's resources will be available for all individuals interested in topics related to the intersection of religion and science.

the breath, but as we mentioned in the previous chapter, yawning may be a faster way to achieve deep relaxation and alertness.

Breath awareness serves another function, because it trains your mind to stay focused on a natural—and essential—body process. By focusing your conscious intention on your breath, you begin to slow down mental "busy-ness." Your thoughts become fewer and more integrated, and your body begins to relax. In an fMRI* experiment we just completed, when we compared a breath-based meditation to a meditation that focuses on a word or phrase, we discovered that breathing awareness increases activity in the limbic system while activity in the frontal lobe decreases. Thoughts recede, but the emotional intensity of the experience increases.

Relaxation is a key element in meditation—for keeping your body and brain tuned up—but for many people, focusing on one's breath will not achieve the deep state of relaxation associated with neurological health. That is why we've included several different kinds of relaxation exercises, and I strongly recommend that you try them all. Use the ones that feel best, but it's also a good idea to alternate between them. Over time you'll realize that the same technique affects your body in different ways.

AWARENESS

Once a deep state of relaxation is reached, the next step involves becoming aware of your body in relation to the world. Focused breathing enhances self-awareness by increasing activity in the precuneus, an important circuit that regulates consciousness in the brain.[1] But in mindfulness practices, this is only the first step in generating greater awareness and attentiveness. For example, you might be asked to observe a simple activity like eating or walking. Usually, you will do it in slow motion, paying attention to every tiny movement you make. If you put some food in your mouth, you'll pay attention to every muscle that is used when chewing, noting the subtle qualities of smell, flavor,

---

* An MRI brain scan shows a detailed picture of the brain's activity, whereas an fMRI (*functional* magnetic resonance image) scan is more like a motion picture. We can watch moment-to-moment changes in the brain as the test subject performs different mental or physical tasks.

texture, and temperature of each bite. You'll also pay attention to every muscle needed when you lift the fork to your mouth.

You can experiment with this technique right now. Because your attention is focused on reading, you'll notice that you aren't aware of the book that you are actually holding in your hands. But the moment I bring your attention to it, other sensations become conscious. Notice how heavy the book feels. Now notice the texture of the cover. What does the smoothness feel like? Is it warm, or cool? And what about the paper on which these words are imprinted? How thick is it? How dark or light is the ink? What happens if you focus on the spaces, rather than the words? Now do one more thing: Take in ten very deep breaths and watch how your sensation of the book changes.

Each of these shifts in awareness intensifies the experience of the book, which is what meditation is designed to do. It heightens the quality of the experience and reminds you that there is so much "experience" in everything we do. Meditation broadens your scope of conscious experience, and this strengthens important circuits in your brain. Furthermore, it neurologically helps your frontal lobes become more focused and organized. Research confirms that advanced meditators have a greater cognitive ability to recognize subtle changes, not only in themselves, but in the environment as well.[2]

There is another neurological benefit, for as you become aware of your mental processes, you learn to watch them and not react. You simply observe your thoughts and feelings as they constantly flow through your mind. Some refer to this as "mindfulness." If an anxious, irritable, or depressing thought pops up, you note it, then immediately return to your breathing or relaxation, watching what the next thought or feeling will be. Frontal lobe consciousness increases to the point that it begins to neurologically suppress the emotional circuits in your brain. When this happens, feelings of anxiety, irritability, or depression subside, which has a profoundly beneficial effect on every other aspect of neural functioning.

WHAT HAPPENED TO GOD?

Even though some of the following exercises grew out of different religious traditions, the neurological benefits are primarily associated with intention, relaxation, and awareness. So, for the purposes of reaching the broadest audience, we have removed the religious inferences. However, if you incorporate your ethical, spiritual, or religious beliefs into these exercises, they can become even more meaningful and experientially rich. For example, we recently studied the religious practice known as the Rosary, which involves the repetition of specific prayers as you count a string of beads, and we found that performing it is associated with lower levels of anxiety and stress. Furthermore, you can bring many of the following techniques into your church, temple, or mosque and integrate them into the rituals of the religion. In fact, Eastern meditation has been widely adapted by many sects of Christianity.

This brings us to the question of religious involvement in general. Does it have a meaningful effect on your health? The answer, briefly put, is yes. The data on religious involvement consistently shows that those who regularly attend religious services live longer and have fewer problems with their health.* Even those who attend once a month have a 30 to 35 percent reduced risk of death.[3] The numbers are equally consistent for Caucasians, African Americans, and Mexican Americans, and for older individuals, religious activity is even more beneficial.[4] Those who attend weekly are significantly less likely to have a stroke, but interestingly, religious involvement did not have an effect on heart attacks.[5] Nor does it protect a person from abusing drugs.[6] Overall, it appears that religious activities and beliefs have only a minor effect on an individual's use of drugs.

Are there any drawbacks to religious involvement? Yes, but it mostly involves issues concerning anger and fear. As we mentioned in Chapter 7, if you see God as a punishing figure, or have negative attitudes toward the clergy or other church members, you will be inclined toward poorer health and depression.[7] And if you find yourself in conflict with your religious feelings or beliefs, your health can deteriorate and your risk of dying will increase.[8] So by all means, pick a religious system or spiritual practice that makes you feel good about yourself and others.

---

* The data, however, is largely *correlational*. This means that we do not know which part of the "equation" produces the effect. For example, it is *possible* that people who live longer may have a greater inclination to be religiously involved.

CONFRONTING THE BELLIGERENT BRAIN

The exercises we will describe can change your brain in a matter of minutes, but many people resist doing them, even when they feel an improvement in cognitive function and mood. Why? There are different explanations, but the one that makes the most neurological sense is this: After spending decades building a somewhat stable personality to handle life's tribulations, the brain is hesitant to alter its underlying beliefs. After all, even if your behavior is dysfunctional, it has helped you to survive, which is what your brain is primarily designed to do.

It took your brain decades to form these habits, and it's not easy to turn them off. Old neural circuits do not disappear, especially if they are tinged with negative or stressful memories. In fact, it takes a lot of metabolic energy to grow new dendrites and axons or rearrange synaptic connections that have been firmly established over the years. Furthermore, any disruption in old neural patterns creates a certain degree of anxiety in the brain. That old limbic system, which is largely responsible for maintaining synaptic stability, is not as flexible as the creative frontal lobes. Thus, it's easy to dream up a new idea, but exceedingly difficult to get the rest of the brain to comply. Even if you succeed in changing different aspects of your personality, don't be surprised if old patterns of behavior reassert themselves from time to time.

So what is the solution to this neural resistance to change? Mark and I recommend three things: a conscious commitment to make a small improvement every day, a good dose of social support to help you honor that commitment, and a hefty serving of optimism and faith.

Oh, and one other thing: a willingness to practice, at the very least, for a few minutes every day. With practice, you can build up to twenty to forty minutes a day, which may be the ideal range of time to enhance the neural functioning of your brain.

BEGIN WITH A SIMPLE GOAL

When learning meditation on your own, it is wise to begin with simple goals, then work your way up the ladder to more complex tasks. At that point you can even work in some of the loftier ideals of forgiveness and compassion. But if you ultimately want to promote world peace, start by generating a few minutes of peacefulness during a coffee break. Then extend it into your lunch hour. Yawn a few times and take several deep breaths when you find yourself stuck in rush-hour traffic, and send a small blessing to the driver who just cut you off. At first you'll feel some resentment, but soon you'll notice an overall lessening of frustration.

Pick a simple goal for today—right now. It doesn't matter what you choose, because if you focus on the three main principles—relaxation, focused awareness, and intention—your brain will stimulate neurological circuits to help you accomplish that goal. The key to reaching any goal is conscious commitment, and the first step required is to stay focused on the idea. Focused awareness teaches you to ignore competing goals or desires, and relaxation will teach you patience, something that is essential to help you over those moments when you think that the meditation is doing nothing at all. Whether you are aware of it or not, neuroscience demonstrates that benefits are unconsciously taking place.

Beginners often find it frustrating to stay focused on something as simple as relaxation or the breath. Irritating thoughts intrude, so if you find that you can't turn them off, shift your goal to passively watching them. I mentioned it earlier, but it bears repeating: By training yourself to observe your thoughts, you are learning to subdue the emotional reactivity that normally governs the neural activity of the brain. Sitting quietly and watching your thoughts and feelings may seem boring, but for people who ruminate on anxious or depressing thoughts, it turns out to be a profoundly therapeutic process. In fact, rumination on negative thoughts and emotions intensifies and prolongs the experience,[9] and it stimulates the amygdala to generate increased anxiety and fear.[10]

Still, if you are like most beginning meditators, it can drive you nuts to just sit there and watch your mind telling you that you're a fool to be sitting there, doing nothing. After all, your frontal lobes are inclined to induce you to do something—*anything,* for that matter. It's a powerful incentive, driven by parental and societal norms and maintained by all the beliefs you have melded together over the years. In fact, your mind can generate so many distracting thoughts and reasons to dissuade you from doing these exercises that a few good books may be needed to keep you on the mindfulness path. Meditation and relaxation CDs are particularly helpful since the instructions are easier to follow when you listen to a spoken voice. In fact, when we conduct our research with initiates, we often send them home with an audio-recorded exercise. (In Appendix C you'll find a list of recommendations for a variety of books, CDs, and training programs.)

PRACTICE, PRACTICE, PRACTICE

So how long should you practice? It's up to you. Research studies often use a specific amount of time such as an eight-week training program with up to fifty minutes of practice each day, but if you only feel comfortable meditating for five or ten minutes, once or twice a day, then trust your intuition. Obviously, the more time spent, the greater the results. I would recommend that if you want to create a formal program, try to set aside a specific time of day like the first thing in the morning after you awake, shortly after work, or the last thing in the evening before bed. A regular time trains your brain to get into the habit of being mindfully relaxed. In our studies, we have found that those who set a specific time received the greatest degree of benefit.

Here's a list of the exercises that we have included in this chapter:

1. Breathing Awareness (page 179)
2. Deep Yawning (page 182)
3. The Relaxation Response (page 184)
4. Progressive Muscle Relaxation (page 185)
5. Visualization and Guided Imagery (page 187)
6. Candle Meditation (page 192)
7. The Centering Prayer (page 193)
8. Walking Meditation (page 195)
9. Memory Enhancement (page 199)
10. Sitting with Your Demons (page 201)
11. The Imaginary Fight (page 205)
12. Sending Kindness and Forgiveness to Others (page 206)

In developing your personalized "brain enhancement" program, we recommend that you do three of these exercises each day. Nearly every meditation and stress-reduction technique begins with a breath awareness exercise, so we suggest that you begin with Exercise 1. Exercises 2 through 5 will take you into deeper states of relaxation, so you should select at least one of these to practice every day. On different days, you can switch between them, and as you become more skilled, you can vary them or combine them at will. Finally, pick one of the more formal meditations (6 through 9) to practice each day.

When you combine these breathing, relaxation, and meditation exercises, you will have created a basic brain-enhancement program to provide you with a twenty- to forty-minute daily practice. But if you don't have the time to practice this long, select one of the exercises that most closely aligns with your intention, desire, or goal. Perhaps at another time (for example, before going to bed), you'll be able to add another exercise or two.

Exercises 10 and 11 are specifically designed to use when you are dealing with anger, irritability, and frustration, and Exercise 12 focuses on forgiveness and self-love. However, you'll get the most from these meditations if you first begin with a breathing awareness and relaxation exercise.

TEST-DRIVING YOUR BRAIN ENHANCEMENT PROGRAM

As you go through the twelve exercises in this chapter, practice each one, as best you can, while you read. Then select the ones you plan to practice tomorrow. Write them on a sheet of paper, and set an alarm clock to remind you when to begin. As I mentioned earlier, your brain will neurologically provide you with an endless stream of resistances, which is one of the first things all beginning meditators discover. And don't feel bad if the resistance doesn't fade away. Even the Dalai Lama says he has trouble meditating, which is why he practices all the time.

Before we begin, I want to include a brief note about sitting positions, postures, and the use of mantras, prayers, or sounds. Different teachers will sometimes argue that one specific posture or prayer is more effective than others, but the neurological evidence disagrees. You can stand, sit on a Zen cushion, recline in your favorite chair, or lie down. What is important is that you feel comfortable and relaxed. The only drawback with lying down is that you might fall asleep.

Nor has any specific mantra or sacred word been proven to be better than another for obtaining healthy neurological results. Instead, we recommend that you choose a phrase that has meaning for you, because this will significantly enhance your practice. The brain actually "marks" these important rituals, and thus each time you perform them, your memory circuits will guide you into the desired state more quickly and with greater intensity.

EXERCISE 1: BREATHING AWARENESS

Some meditations use passive techniques in which the practitioner is instructed to simply pay attention to his or her natural breathing patterns, while others use various forms of controlled breathing: light, deep, slow, rapid, nasal, mouth, or a combination of styles. Gentler forms of breathing enhance awareness and relaxation, while vigorous styles increase emotional intensity at the expense of feeling relaxed. Research has shown that breathing exercises lower stress and anxiety, improve coping skills, help people deal with substance abuse, improve their general sense of well-being, and improve self-esteem. Breathing exercises also help people deal with problems such as panic disorder, heart disease, and lung disease.

Slow focused breathing triggers the body's relaxation response.[11] It also increases dopamine levels in different parts of the brain during the first ten minutes of meditation, which explains why the experience is pleasurable.[12]

WHAT'S SO SPIRITUAL ABOUT BREATHING?

In Western cultures, breathing would not be considered a spiritual activity, but in Eastern traditions it is the core of spiritual practice. Why? It's partially a matter of semantics. The Sanskrit word for breath is *prana*, but *prana* also means "life force" or "vital energy." In the Hindu and Taoist traditions, the breath is also a metaphor for "spirit" and "soul." Thus, by regulating your breath, you deepen your spirituality. Buddhism shifted the focus to the mind and devised breathing meditations that would give you greater control over mental and emotional states. This, it turns out, is neurologically effective. In Eastern traditions, developing consciousness and mental control are genuine spiritual pursuits, and it all begins with the breath.

Deeper breathing triggers a different neurological response and initially decreases activity in the frontal lobes. It lowers the amount of carbon dioxide in the blood, which in turn lowers blood flow in other parts of the brain and reduces cognitive activity. Simply put, it helps to calm your mind, so if you have trouble turning down your thoughts, deepen your breathing as you meditate.

Deep or rapid breathing also has a stimulating effect on the limbic system, and this can trigger a wide variety of emotional responses. If you do it for even a few minutes, it can disrupt your consciousness in unexpected and sudden ways. For this reason, we suggest you limit deep or rapid breathing to no more than thirty seconds at a time, then return to a gentler breathing rhythm.

In general, when meditating, we recommend that you breathe through your nose. Why? It turns out that nasal breathing increases the release of nitric oxide in the body, and this improves the functioning of your lungs and your circulatory system.[13] Increased nitric oxide may also assist in the lowering of anxiety, especially in socially intense situations.[14] Nasal breathing, like yawning, also serves to keep the internal temperature of the brain in balance.[15]

So let's get going with the most basic meditation practice in the world—breathing. We'll begin with you sitting in a chair, but later you may try other postures, like sitting upright on a cushion on the floor. If you have someone reading this to you, close your eyes; it will help you to concentrate better.*

1. Sit down in a comfortable chair, in a quiet place where nothing will disturb you for the duration of the exercise. Rest your hands in your lap and uncross your legs, placing your feet flat on the floor.

2. Now, do nothing more than pay attention to your breath. Breathe in slowly through your nose, and notice the cool temperature of the air.

---

* This exercise combines elements from a wide variety of breath-awareness meditations, but the underlying principle is the same: to train your mind to stay focused on your breathing and the effects it has on your body and mind.

3. Now, slowly exhale through your nose. Notice the temperature as you breathe out. How warm is it?

4. Continue to slowly breathe in and out through your nose ten times, and notice how the sensations change. Take nice, slow, deep breaths in and out. Try not to think about anything other than your breath.

5. If your mind wanders, don't get frustrated, just return to focusing on your breathing in and out. Notice too how focusing on your breathing affects your thoughts. Notice each thought or feeling, then immediately return to your breath.

6. Now, shift your focus to your chest, and feel how it rises and falls with each breath you take. Slowly breathe in to the count of five, then slowly breathe out to the count of five. Do this ten times and then return to your normal breathing. Notice how it has changed, and notice if it feels different. Are you breathing slower? Or deeper? Or more shallow? How far down into your lungs can you feel the coldness of the air? Take another five breaths and notice how the sensation in your lungs begins to change.

7. Now shift your attention to your abdomen. Take a deep breath in to the count of five, and watch how your chest and belly moves. Which moves first, your chest or your belly? Does your belly expand when you breathe in, or contract? Take ten more breaths and watch how it changes the movement in your abdomen and chest.

8. Now return to your normal breathing and listen to the sounds in the room. Do they seem more intense? Notice how many different sounds you can hear, both inside and outside your body. Once more, return your awareness to your body. Does it feel more tense or relaxed? Does it feel more warm or cool? Are there any parts of your body that seem tense or uncomfortable? Just notice the tension, and take another deep breath through your nose.

9. Now, slowly breathe through your mouth. Notice how this changes the movement of your belly and your chest. Repeat this deep breathing ten times, counting the seconds as you breathe in, and counting the seconds as you breathe out.

10. Shift your attention to your mouth and feel the cold air across your tongue as you breathe in. Now feel the warmth when you breathe out. Shift your attention to the roof of your mouth, and notice how different the temperature feels. Return to your natural pattern of breathing and notice any differences you feel. Are you more relaxed or more tense? Do you feel more tired or awake? Whatever you are feeling, don't judge it. Just notice it and accept it, and return to watching your breath.

11. Now bring this exercise to a close. Slowly look around the room, turning your head from one side to the other. Then slowly rise from your chair. Take a moment to see how you feel standing up, and consciously breathe in and out. Slowly start to walk, and see if you can continue to be mindful of your breath as you return to your daily routines.

You can do this whole exercise in just a few minutes or for as long as twenty to thirty minutes. The longer you do it, the more peaceful and relaxed you will feel. This practice trains your mind to be still, but neurologically it is in a heightened state of awareness—the perfect state in which to set about on the tasks that you need to do. As you become more familiar with breathing awareness, feel free to vary it in any way you like, combining it with any of the following exercises, or just watching how your mind responds as you consciously breathe in and out.

EXERCISE 2: DEEP YAWNING

Now that you have had the experience of "mindful" breathing, I want you to compare how yawning affects your awareness, alertness, and bodily relaxation. Even though I enticed you to yawn in the previous chapter, I'm formalizing it here because it is so important for your brain. Yawning will physiologically relax you in less than a minute, and this allows you to move more rapidly into other meditation states. Start the exercise by doing the following:

1. Find a quiet, comfortable place where you won't be disturbed by others. Stand in a place where your arms are free to swing side to side. You can sit, but standing allows you to achieve a fuller inhalation.

2. Begin by taking a very deep breath and stretching your mouth wide open. As you exhale, make a long, sighing sound. Don't worry if you don't feel like yawning or don't believe you can. Just use your memory and fake a series of yawns. Continue faking them and pause briefly after each yawn. By the fifth or sixth one you'll feel a real one coming on.

3. Pay close attention to what happens in your mouth, your throat, your chest and belly, and don't be surprised if your eyes start watering.

4. You should allow yourself about twelve to fifteen yawns with a few seconds pause between each one. The total time for this exercise should be about two minutes.

If you have trouble yawning, get together with a family member or friend. Yawning is a "contagious" activity, for if you hear and see someone else yawn, it will neurologically stimulate the same response in you.

Conscious yawning generates a deep sense of relaxation, calmness, and alertness, and as we detailed in the previous chapter, it stimulates a unique circuit in the brain that enhances self-reflective consciousness, the key to any contemplative or spiritual practice. Yawn before you tackle a difficult problem, and yawn when you find yourself in a conflict with another person. If you do aerobic exercises, yawn at various times and you may feel an immediate improvement in motor coordination. Yawning will help reduce stress, literally in a matter of minutes.

EXERCISE 3: THE RELAXATION RESPONSE

Dr. Herbert Benson at Harvard made this meditation famous thirty years ago, and it is one of the most researched techniques in the world. Today it is used in hundreds of stress reduction programs throughout the country, generating neurological and psychological states of serenity and health.[16] You simply focus on a word, phrase, or mantra—love, peace, God, om, etc.—that makes you feel happy, peaceful, or calm, and you repeat it as you breathe slowly and deeply. Or, if you prefer, you can recite a brief passage from a sacred text.

What matters is that you find it personally meaningful and relaxing, not which religious tradition you choose. In one intriguing study, equal benefits were obtained by those who used "om mani padme hum" (Buddhism), "Rama, Rama" (Hinduism), "Lord have mercy (Christianity), or "Shalom" (Judaism).[17] In fact, mere repetition of any positive phrase will reduce stress, anxiety, and anger while simultaneously improving one's quality of life.[18] This exercise has been adapted from Dr. Benson's work:

1. Find a comfortable place to sit where you won't be disturbed, and close your eyes.

2. Take several deep breaths, and as you exhale, silently, or with a whisper, say a word, phrase, or sound that gives you a feeling of serenity or joy (peace, love, slow down, relax, om, God, etc.).

3. Stay with your breathing and the repetition of your personal mantra. Repeat the mantra slowly with your breathing for about ten to twenty minutes.

4. If unwanted thoughts or feelings intrude, acknowledge them and let them go, returning to the repetition of your mantra. Don't try to achieve a particular goal or state; just keep focusing on your word for the full ten to twenty minutes.

5. When you finish, sit quietly for a few moments and then open your eyes. Notice how you feel, yawn three times, and slowly move about the room.

If you do this exercise once each day, you will notice, in just a few weeks, significant shifts in your awareness and behavior. You'll feel calmer, less anxious, and more receptive. You may even find, as Benson's research uncovered, that you lose some of your desire to smoke, drink, or overeat. Feel free to change your mantra as often as you like, paying attention to how different concepts affect your awareness in different ways.

EXERCISE 4: PROGRESSIVE MUSCLE RELAXATION

Some people have a very difficult time using their mind to relax their body, so I often recommend this technique, which was developed in the 1920s by the American physiologist Edmund Jacobson. I call it the "heavy artillery" of relaxation training because it is particularly effective with people who are unusually tense. It is useful in reducing stress and anxiety, helping with pain, fibromyalgia, heart disease, and a variety of neurological, psychological, and physical disorders.[19] It has also been effective to help people relax before operations, and it speeds up post-operative recovery.[20]

Progressive muscle relaxation was the first technique I ever tried on other people. When I was in junior high school, I did a report on progressive muscle relaxation, so I experimented on my whole class. They all loved it, and one person even fell asleep (but then, that wasn't so unusual in my school). Which reminds me: Many people report that this exercise, when practiced before going to bed, helps them fall asleep. In fact, studies have shown that progressive muscle relaxation is just as effective as taking a variety of sleep-inducing medications.[21] And if you pair it with music, the effects appear to be enhanced.[22]

Progressive muscle relaxation is easy to do. Essentially you tighten and then relax each muscle group in the body, and in between you take a nice deep breath or yawn. The exercise is best done lying down, on a thick carpet or mat, but you can do it in any large well-padded chair. I also recommend that you have someone read this to you if you are especially tense, or make or purchase a recording. But for now, try to do as many steps as possible as you read. If the deep breathing makes you dizzy, take smaller and shorter breaths.

1. First, take a deep breath, hold it as long as you can, then breathe out as much air as possible. Again, hold your breath as long as you can before inhaling. Repeat this five times.

2. Next, take a deep breath in, and as you do this, tense all the muscles in your body, from head to toe, and hold it as long as you possibly can (most people can do this for about ten to twenty seconds). Then relax everything, expelling the air from your lungs. Do this three more times. Then breathe out and relax all the muscles in your body.

3. Take another deep breath, and starting at the top of your head, tighten up all of your face, then let it go as you breathe out.

4. Breathe in deeply, scrunch up your forehead and hold it for five seconds. Then release, breathing out.

5. Breathe in, tighten your mouth and jaw, hold it for five seconds, and release as you breathe out. Now stretch your mouth open as wide as you can. Hold it for five seconds, and release. Take another deep breath and yawn, and release all of the tension in your face.

6. Take a deep breath in, pull your shoulders up toward your head, and tighten all of the muscles in your neck. Hold for five seconds, then push your shoulders way down as you exhale. Slowly roll your head from side to side as you fully and completely relax.

7. Take another deep breath in and tighten your arms and your hands. Clench your fists tightly and hold them tight for as long as you can. Breathe out and relax your arms and hands. Breathe in, push your arms into the chair or floor, hold for ten seconds, and release, breathing out. Shake out your hands and arms, then take another deep breath. Yawn, and take a few moments to sense the relaxation in your upper body and face.

8. Next, take in a breath and tighten your abdominal muscles. Hold it for a count of ten, then relax, pushing all the air out of your

lungs. Push your stomach out, pull it in, push it out again, and then let all of your tension go. Repeat the pushing and pulling ten times.

9. Take another deep breath, and tighten your buttocks. Hold it as long as you can, then breathe out and relax. Breathe in, tighten your upper legs, then quickly relax as you breathe out. Breathe in, tighten your calves, hold for five seconds, then release. Breathe in again, scrunch up your toes, hold, and release, then stretch them upward and apart as you slowly breathe out all the air in your lungs. Now shake your feet and legs as fast as you can for another ten seconds, then rest.

10. Yawn, and spend a few moments feeling the relaxation flowing through your legs. Once more, take a huge breath in, tighten your entire body, hold for ten seconds, then release as you force all the air out of your lungs.

11. Do a body scan: Feel how relaxed your face is ... then your neck ... your shoulders ... your arms ... your chest ... your abdomen ... your back ... your legs ... and finally your feet. Lie there for a few minutes and gently stretch.

12. When you feel ready, slowly stand up, and slowly walk around, feeling how each part of your body moves. But take it easy for a few minutes—you are very relaxed at this point, and your consciousness may be in an altered state of awareness.

EXERCISE 5: VISUALIZATION AND GUIDED IMAGERY

Even if you don't think you're good at visualization, your brain is built to envision virtually every thought it has. Even abstract notions like peace are first processed unconsciously within the visual centers of the cortex. As I've said before, the more you visualize a spiritual or emotional state, or a specific goal in life, the easier it will be for your brain to bring that intention into your inner and outer reality.

Guided imagery simply refers to the process of using pleasant visions and memories to induce a deep state of relaxation, and it has been proven to be very effective in reducing pain.[23] It effectively lowers anxiety and depression in people before and after they undergo a medical or surgical intervention,[24] and if you visualize a positive outcome prior to surgery, you'll have a better recovery.[25] Guided imagery and visualization will even buffer the effect of stress on the immune system, making you less susceptible to viral infections.[26]

In a recent brain-scan study I just completed, guided imagery reduced the symptoms of patients suffering from post-traumatic stress disorder by lowering activity in the emotional centers of the brain and raising activity in the areas that allow us to voluntarily control our feelings and thoughts.[27] Thus, guided imagery techniques can help individuals deal with trauma, as well as a variety of physical and mental illnesses. In fact, a recent fMRI study conducted at Yale University found that visualization and guided imagery stimulate almost the exact same areas in the brain that our meditation subjects activated when doing Buddhist, Christian, and yoga meditation techniques.[28]

To experience the benefits of visualization, choose any place—imaginary or real—that feels beautiful and relaxing: a beach, a mountaintop, a waterfall, a sailboat on a lake. Now, pretend you're watching a movie. Can you see yourself there? Can you slowly turn around and visualize the tiny details on the ground and in the sky? If you're at work and feeling especially pressured and tense, you can take a three-minute "vacation" to calm the neural dissonance in your frontal lobes by simply recalling a pleasant memory. If you wish, you can visualize a loved one, or a romantic scene. Let your fantasies take you to wherever they want to go. And, if you find that you have trouble visualizing, yawn a dozen times, because it stimulates an important part of the self-visualization process in your brain. Remember, imagination is what the brain does best, and pleasurable fantasies are like desserts, but completely calorie-free.

See how well you can visualize the following scenario, commonly used in self-hypnosis, guided-imagery therapy, and stress-relaxation programs. And remember, the slower you read, and the slower you speak, the more physiologically relaxed you'll become.

1. Find a quiet place to lie or sit down. Close your eyes and take five deep breaths, followed by four or five yawns.

2. Take another deep breath and visualize yourself lying on a warm, sunny beach. Feel the sun radiating through your skin and warming the muscles underneath. Feel yourself sinking into the warm, soft sand as you become more and more relaxed. Take another deep breath and feel yourself melting into the beach. Stay with this image for two or three minutes, and let your imagination take you wherever it wants to go.

3. Now, imagine yourself walking through a thick, humid, tropical forest. Take a deep breath and feel the warm damp air blow across your face. Visualize the path, surrounded by lush, green, tropical plants. Can you hear the birds chirping quietly in the trees? What do they sound like? What do they look like? What colors do you see?

4. As you walk down the path, you come around a bend. There, in front of you, is the most beautiful waterfall in the world. Watch how the water spills down the side of the mountain, over the rocks, and into a crystal clear pool of water.

5. Now step into the pool. Take a deep breath and feel the warm tropical water washing over your feet as you slowly step into the waterfall. Feel the clear, warm water gently flow over your head, washing away all of your tension and cares. Take three deep breaths, and with each exhalation, let the water wash all of your worries away.

6. Now feel your body melting into the pool. As you breathe in deeply, you feel yourself turning into a stream. As you and the water become one, you begin to slowly flow down the stream. Feel the sun shining overhead as you float down the river, far, far away from all of the tensions of the world. Watch where the river takes you, and continue the inner journey as far as it wants to go. When your journey is finished, notice how relaxed you feel.

When creating your personalized "vacation," or when guiding a friend through these visualizations, remember to use repetitive words and phrases that evoke relaxation: warm, soft, deep, heavy, etc. For example, tell yourself that you are "feeling *more* and *more* relaxed ... going *deeper* and *deeper* into relaxation ... arms feeling *warm* and *heavy* and *relaxed* ..." The repetition lulls you into a trancelike state of peace.

You can even use visualization and guided imagery with your children. At the pain management clinic at Children's Mercy Hospital in Kansas City, researchers found that a combination of guided imagery and progressive muscle relaxation was more effective than breath-based relaxation techniques when working with children who suffered from abdominal pain and discomfort.[29] This is why, to achieve the greatest effect, we recommend that you combine as many techniques as you feel comfortable with.

Visualization is an important aspect for setting any goal, since much of your unconscious brain is oriented around a visual construction of the world. If you want to do better in sports, many studies have confirmed that visualizing your performance actually improves your game.[30] The same is true for work. If you visualize a possible solution to a problem, the problem is more easily solved because it specifically activates cognitive circuits involved with working memory.[31]

Visualization helps us distance ourselves from a disturbing memory or problem, yet it simultaneously brings us closer to our desires. Thus, if you envision a sacred or spiritual symbol, it reinforces your religious beliefs. You can visualize yourself being a better golfer, or you can envision yourself as being a more ethical person, but in either case, your neural connections will help you actually achieve those goals.

MEDITATION AND PRAYER

The five exercises we have just described represent the core elements for remaining relaxed and alert. But we want to encourage you to go further by incorporating one or more of the following traditional meditation techniques, because they can make profound and permanent changes in your consciousness and your fundamental perceptions of the world. Our research has shown that they enhance memory, cognition, and attentiveness. Most important, they significantly lessen stress.

Three of the meditations below—Centering Prayer, Walking Meditation, and Sitting with the Demons—are variations of what are sometimes called "mindfulness-based" meditations. Mindfulness-based exercises have been widely studied and found to help people with depression, anxiety, high blood pressure, psoriasis, trauma, eating disorders, substance abuse, and a variety of psychopathological behaviors.[32]

In fact, most forms of meditation and intensive prayer practices have helped people with a wide variety of psychological and physiological problems, including attention deficit disorder, liver disease, HIV, and cancer. Obviously, meditation practices were not originally developed for these purposes. Instead, they were designed to create feelings of self-awareness, peacefulness, compassion, and spiritual enlightenment.

Research suggests that meditation consistently takes the practitioner into deep states of consciousness. When compared to everyday awareness, the brain, during meditation, is operating in an unusual way. And, since the underlying mechanics of meditation are theologically neutral, it can be integrated with any religious doctrine or creed, or used in schools to improve social cooperation and cognitive performance.*

Today, meditation comprises a huge group of practices that range from the deeply spiritual to the completely secular. Some meditation practices involve the repetitive focus on a particular object, while others involve the neutral observance of the thoughts and feelings produced by the mind. There is even a technique called "emptiness meditation," which we will go into later.

Most meditations begin by calming the mind through relaxation, breath awareness, or maintaining one's focus on a specific object or thought. Then they progress to the more complex strategies of watching one's feelings and thoughts. In advanced stages, different meditations might focus on a variety of philosophies or esoteric goals (developing

---

* Whereas prayer is not allowed in the public school system, meditation, when stripped of any religious overtones, has been introduced, but often with considerable controversy, since some people still associate it with Eastern spiritual traditions. If meditation is framed in the language of mindfulness, stress reduction, focused attention, or awareness enhancement, the church/state obstacle can be overcome.

forgiveness, enhancing sensuality, dissolving the self, merging with the cosmos, expanding consciousness, becoming one with God, etc.).

In fact, there are so many meditation techniques to choose from that the trick is to find the one that resonates best with who you are and what your specific goals might be. A meditation that is spiritually based might be great for a religious person but not an atheist. Some people might like meditations that involve movement (like yoga), while others may prefer a meditation that integrates mantras and prayers. So if you try a meditation program and don't like it, don't reject the other types. Somewhere out there is the perfect one for you. Pick one that is consistent with your personal, ethical, and spiritual beliefs, and integrate those beliefs into every exercise you do. And if you choose to work with a meditation teacher, make sure that his or her underlying philosophy is consistent with your own.

EXERCISE 6: CANDLE MEDITATION

This first exercise is considered a concentration meditation, and neurologically, it is designed to interrupt the endless stream of chaotic thinking that normally occurs in the frontal lobe. Ideally, you should do this in a darkened room, but that isn't essential.

1. Begin by placing a candle that will burn for fifteen minutes in a safe holder, on a dining room table or coffee table, close to a comfortable chair. Smells can augment meditation experiences, so a scented candle may be used. Sit down, with feet flat on the floor, with a lighter or matches in your hand.

2. Take a few deep breaths and yawn, just focusing on the unlit candle. Then, in slow motion, light the candle, and take another deep breath. Slowly put the lighter down, and sitting up straight, begin to gaze at the candle. Blink as little as possible.

3. Bring your focus to the flame. Let it fill your entire consciousness as you observe how it dances and flutters. What colors does it make? Does the flame grow taller, then retreat? Keep watching all of the qualities of the flame for three or four minutes.

4. If interruptive thoughts come into your mind, just let them be there, acknowledge them and let them go, and bring your focus back to the candle flame.

5. Now close your eyes and visualize the flame in your mind. Watch how it dances and flutters in your imagination. If the image of the flame fades, open your eyes, study the flame, then close your eyes again. Keep doing this until you hold the image of the flame in your mind for five minutes with your eyes closed.

That's it! It's simple, powerful, and enjoyable. Each time you do the meditation, try to extend the time. In some practices, you use your imagination to become one with the candle. To do this, you imagine the flame coming closer and closer to your closed eyes. Then you imagine that you're inside the flame.

In another variation, you imagine the flame burning away all of your thoughts, desires, and problems: anger, stress, impatience, greed, etc. You can also use other objects—a pretty rock or a crystal, an autumn leaf, or even the food on your plate—to immerse your attention upon. Breathing meditations teach you to become aware of your inner state and body, whereas object meditations, like this candle exercise, train your mind to become more observant of the outside world.

EXERCISE 7: THE CENTERING PRAYER

When we brain-scanned a group of Franciscan nuns, they used the Centering Prayer, a contemplative method first described in the fourteenth century text *The Cloud of Unknowing*.[33] According to Friar Thomas Keating, one of three Trappist monks who reintroduced this technique to the Christian community in the 1970s, it brings the practitioner "into the presence of God" by "reducing the obstacles caused by the hyperactivity of our minds and of our lives."[34]

This meditation is very similar to various forms of Eastern contemplation, and as we discovered in our lab, the neurological effects of the Centering Prayer are nearly identical to the mindfulness practices in Buddhism. It is also similar to Benson's relaxation response, which I described before, but the goal is different: to feel connected, immersed, and unified with the *conceptual* object of your contemplation. The nuns' goal was to feel closer to God, but the Buddhist practitioners wanted to experience pure consciousness—an intense state of awareness of the world.

In a Centering Prayer, like other forms of mindfulness meditation, you are not concentrating on a single object or thought, nor do you repeat an expression or a phrase. Instead, you allow your mind to reflect on all the qualities associated with a particular idea, and you allow the thoughts and feelings to freely flow through your mind, taking you where they will.

As you engage in this form of meditation, you don't try to analyze the experience. You just let it unfold. There is no specific goal other than observation. You don't try to make your mind blank, and you don't even aim for peace.

For the purposes of this book, I have slightly modified the Centering Prayer so it may be incorporated into any secular or spiritual tradition. The original version, as developed for Catholic practitioners, can be found at www.centeringprayer.com. Begin by finding a comfortable place to sit where you will not be disturbed for twenty minutes.

1. First, identify what your objective is (finding inner peace, experiencing compassion for others, receiving the gift of God's presence, etc.). Or, if you prefer, pick a particularly meaningful quote, poem, or passage from a book.

2. When you have found a concept or passage you wish to explore on a deeper, intuitive level, sit down in a comfortable chair. Close your eyes, breathe slowly and deeply, and make sure all of your tensions are gone.

3. Now focus your awareness on your selected object of contemplation. Do not repeat any words or expressions to yourself. Just be aware of all the thoughts, perceptions, feelings, images, and memories that your contemplation evokes.

4. Notice how you are feeling. Are you happy? Joyful? Sad? Now bring your attention back to your goal, and again watch what feelings and thoughts emerge.

5. If your mind wanders too far away, gently return your awareness by taking several deep breaths, bringing your focus back to your goal, phrase, or prayer. Again, let your thoughts take you wherever they want to go.

6. If the object of your contemplation becomes vague or disappears, simply watch what happens next. Don't "do" anything or "make" anything happen—just let the experience naturally unfold. After several minutes return again to the object of your contemplation. Do not choose to focus on a different phrase or prayer. Instead, let the contemplation work on you.

7. Continue this process for a minimum of twenty minutes. Then slowly open your eyes. Remain silent for two more minutes while you take slow, deep breaths and yawns.

It is helpful to have a muted timer to let you know when twenty minutes have passed. During long meditations, you will notice pains, itches, twitches, and periods of restlessness. Observe them the best you can, but if you feel impelled to move around or scratch, give yourself permission, then take several deep breaths and return to the meditation practice.

The worst thing you can do in meditation is to critically judge your performance—and yet you'll find that there's a critical voice inside of all of us that is constantly judging every little thing we do. Meditation practice teaches us how to be accepting of who we are, of our weaknesses as well as strengths. Remember: Self-criticism stimulates the amygdala, which releases myriad stress-provoking neurochemicals and hormones.

EXERCISE 8: WALKING MEDITATION

Another important step (literally!) of meditation is to bring your awareness and relaxation into the world through action. By walking and focusing on your breathing—along with an awareness of the world around you—you can achieve a very calm and balanced state of mind. In particular, this state allows you to actually experience the world in a very pleasant and engaging way. You'll even perceive the world more intensely than in your usual state of mind. Since walking is a well-established technique for enhancing physical fitness, walking meditation has the added benefit of providing a mild form of exercise, which may be especially beneficial for people with heart and lung disease. There is even evidence to suggest that it can enhance memory, attention, and quality of life,[35] as well as delaying the effects of age-related disorders.[36] Since we all have to walk at least a few minutes every day, why not make it a part of your daily brain-enhancement program? All you need to do is to bring attention to the act of taking a single step.

The following exercise integrates a traditional Buddhist walking meditation with Moshé Feldenkrais's "awareness through movement" techniques. Feldenkrais's work is, in essence, a mindfulness meditation, and research has shown it to be effective for reducing pain and enhancing mood, self-awareness, and overall health.[37] In fact, just imagining that your movements become more flexible significantly increases the flexibility and coordination in that part of the body you are focusing on.[38] Why? Because the motor cortex is highly interconnected with the imagination-processing centers in the frontal, occipital, and parietal lobes.[39] In other words, our thoughts and behavior are inseparably intertwined.

The exercise appears simple, but it really requires concentrated attention and awareness, so watch out for that inner critic who is always in a rush. However, if you experience any balance or coordination problems, do not try this exercise without assistance from a friend.

1. First, find a place where you can walk for about ten or twenty paces. A long hallway will do, or a lawn or open park, but try to find a quiet and pleasant spot, like a garden.

2. Stand up (you can hold this book in your hands as you follow these instructions) and gently shift your weight back and forth be-

tween each foot. But take your time. Notice at what point the heel of one foot comes off the ground, and notice how your weight shifts onto the various parts of your other foot. Do you have more weight on the balls of your feet, on the side, or on your heel? Continue to shift your weight back and forth for at least sixty seconds.

3. Now slowly shift your weight forward and backward, and notice what happens in your toes. What does your big toe do as you move? Your little toe? Repeat this for another minute.

4. Continue to shift your weight forward and backward, but turn your attention to the part of your body that makes you shift. Is it in your ankles? Your calves? Your hips? Notice how hard it is to identify where the movement comes from, and continue to rock for another minute.

5. Next, in slow motion, begin to take a single step forward. But only lift your heel a couple of inches. In which muscle does the step begin? In your foot, or leg, or knee? Raise your heel ten times.

6. Now change to the other foot and lift your heel another ten times. Notice how different it feels. Shift your attention to your knee, and notice how it feels.

7. Slowly, *very slowly,* lift your foot a few inches from the ground, and pay attention to the subtle body adjustments that must be made for balance. Lower your foot and raise the other foot two inches. Continue to alternate twenty times as you study which parts of your body are involved. What happens in your hips? How much does your body sway? How does it make you feel to move so slowly and deliberately? Notice any judgments, take a deep breath, and let them go.

8. Now begin to take slow steps forward, four steps with every breath in, four steps with every breath out. After a few minutes

take three steps with each inhalation and exhalation. Do this for another two minutes, then try taking only two steps as you slowly breathe in, and two more steps as you exhale. Practice integrating your breathing with your walking for the next five minutes, walking as slowly as you can.

9. When you reach the end of the hall or yard (or after about twenty steps), turn around in slow motion. Take two minutes to turn around, watching how your balance works, then slowly walk back to where you began.

At first, each step will feel uncoordinated, but as you become aware of how your feet, legs, hips, back, and shoulders move, your steps will become more fluid. This is an ideal exercise to do after a sitting meditation, and for many people it's so intriguing that they can do it for a half hour or more.* The longer you practice, the more you'll become aware of the texture of the ground, the colors of the grass, the sound of people talking, and the exquisite movements of your body. Whatever you perceive, focus on it, and then come back to your breathing and take another step.

And don't forget to smile while you walk. As the Buddhist teacher Thich Nhat Hanh said, "Your half-smile will bring calm and delight to your steps and your breath, and help sustain attention. After practicing for half an hour or an hour, you will find that your breath, your steps, your counting, and your half-smile all blend together in a marvelous balance of mindfulness."[40]

To fully appreciate the power of walking meditation, do it with your partner or a friend. With just a little practice, you'll find that you can take your relaxation with you anywhere. From a spiritual perspective, walking meditation also encourages you to bring your inner values into play with the world, thus helping you experience daily life with greater depth and unity.

---

* You can also order a book/CD/DVD combination by Nguyen Anh-Huong and Thich Nhat Hanh (*Sounds True,* 2006) demonstrating three different forms of walking meditation in nature and in public places.

EXERCISE 9: MEMORY ENHANCEMENT

The meditation that our memory-impaired patients used (see Chapter 2) is more of a concentration and repetition ritual than a form of mindfulness. It includes four different sounds that are sung, not said, and while this happens, you touch different fingers with each sound. The addition of movement and singing to any meditation appears to significantly enhance the brain's performance.[41] Neurologically, there are both similarities and dissimilarities to other forms of meditation, which is not surprising, considering that it uses a complex movement ritual (a mudra, in Eastern terms) that activates a variety of motor and cognition centers in the brain. Our research suggests that the more complex you make your meditation, the more you enhance additional functions in the brain. Indeed, there are some esoteric meditations, like those practiced by the Sufi whirling dervishes, that require so much skill we would expect to find very enlarged circuits in distinctive areas of the brain.

Our subjects sang the sounds *sa, ta, na,* and *ma* as they touched each of their fingers with the thumbs of each hand. Take a moment and try it now, but don't be surprised if you feel a little odd at first. I did when I first tried it, and so did some of our patients. Touch your thumb and index finger when you say *sa,* your thumb and middle finger when you say *ta,* your thumb and ring finger when you say *na,* and your thumb and pinky when you say *ma.* Now you are ready to begin.

In the Kirtan Kriya tradition, each sound has a specific meaning that relates to the overall cycle of life or existence, but when we taught our memory patients, we did not emphasize the spiritual meanings of the sounds. Based upon an overview of mantra meditation research, it is not certain if the meanings have an effect on the neural enhancement of cognition. Thus, you are free to substitute any other sound or word that has meaning to you. But for the moment we'll teach you the technique in the same way we instructed our subjects. In our study, the sounds were sung out loud to the notes of A, G, F, and G (you can find them on a piano, guitar, or other instrument). However, different spiritual traditions sing this meditation using different notes. Singing, by the way, stimulates the anterior cingulate,[42] which plays an important role in memory formation and cognition.

1. Start by finding a comfortable place where you can sit upright with good posture. Take two minutes to focus on your breathing, watching how your chest rises and falls.

2. Begin singing the sounds *sa, ta, na, ma* while you touch your fingers in succession on both hands. Continue for two minutes.

3. Next, repeat the sounds in a whisper while continuing the finger movements. You can still sing it, but just in a whisper. Do this for another two minutes.

4. Now, repeat the sounds internally. Say them silently to yourself while continuing the finger movements, and do this for four minutes.

5. Repeat the sounds in a whisper for another two minutes as you continue to touch your fingers on both hands.

6. Finally, sing the sounds out loud for the final two minutes as you touch your fingers in succession. Then rest and pay attention to how you feel.

Will your memory improve? Our research suggests that eight weeks of practice creates at least a 10 percent improvement. However, since other meditation studies have shown a wide range of cognitive enhancements, we suspect it is the underlying nature of meditation itself that works—intention, relaxation, and awareness—and the willingness to practice every day.

Since complexity is an important key to neural enhancement, we recommend that you create variations on this meditation. Mark, for example, used the basic structure to hike in the mountains. He chose four words—peace, happiness, compassion, and joy—and touched each finger as he said the words out loud as he walked. Then he took each word and spelled them out on his fingers. With *peace,* after he touched his four fingers for the first four letters, he touched his first finger again for the letter *e.* Then he spelled it again, starting with the second finger.

If you try it, you'll see that it requires intense concentration, but that too is key to making neurological changes in the brain. The point I want to make is that you may modify any meditation to suit your interest or needs, and it can still enhance the overall functioning of your brain.

EXERCISE 10: SITTING WITH YOUR DEMONS

Anger and chronic negativity are cognitively, emotionally, relationally, and spiritually destructive. In fact, no other emotion is more difficult to control, or more likely to interfere with your meditation practice, than anger. So I want to offer you several meditation and visualization techniques to help transform irritability into love.

Anger is a defense we are born with, but it is an enemy to dialogue, empathy, and trust. Until it subsides, we cannot negotiate or communicate our needs, nor resolve a conflict with ease. In relationships, anger seems to pose a double bind: If we express it openly, we stimulate defensive neural circuits in the other person. Thus, whoever gets angry first (even if it is disguised behind a false smile) will lose the argument, even if that person's position was right. The only way out of this dilemma, the experts say, is to become intimately familiar with this destructive emotion and its many hidden forms: jealousy, pessimism, prejudice, cynicism, sarcasm, criticism, selfishness, etc. We have to watch it and study it—in other words, meditate on it—if we want to uncover the feelings it may hide. As Steven Levine wrote:

> Rather than pushing [such feelings] down or spitting them out, we can let them come gently into awareness. We can start to give them space, to get a sense of their texture, of their voice, of their inclination. We begin to investigate the nature of *the* anger instead of getting lost in *my* anger.[43]

When dealing with anger and frustration, researchers have found that meditation, imagining volatile scenarios, and deliberately suppressing negative thoughts were equally effective in diffusing anger.[44] Deliberately substituting positive thoughts for negative ones is another effective strategy.[45]

If the anger is not severe, you can use mindfulness meditation to work through this destructive emotion.[46] When we meditate upon the demons within, we become more observant and relaxed, allowing us to go deeper into our emotions without losing control. Thus, we can safely acknowledge our anger with greater detachment and clarity, and without expressing it to others. It may feel good at the moment to express anger openly, but hundreds of converging studies in psychology and neuroscience now confirm that the expression of anger only generates more of the same.

The only trick is to *remember* to meditate when you are angry, because anger interferes with nearly every cognitive process in the frontal lobes. That's why we want you to try this exercise now, when you're not angry, so it will be in your memory when you find yourself caught up in irritability, self-criticism, or frustration toward someone else. As with the other exercises, find a quiet place to sit, where you will not be disturbed by others or by the phone.

1. Take ten deep breaths, even if you don't feel like it, followed by ten fake or genuine yawns.

2. Recall a time from the past when you were very, very mad at a specific person. Picture the person's face in as much detail as you can, and spend a minute thinking about the things that made you angry. Take three more deep breaths and deepen the intensity of the memory. Tighten your jaw, tighten your fists, hold them for ten seconds, and then let them relax.

3. Allow yourself to remember the feelings of anger that you felt inside. Where do you feel the anger now? In your head? Your chest? Your belly? Take a deep breath and let your emotions take you in any direction they want, watching with detachment.

4. Observe your feelings as if you were watching a movie. Notice each feeling, and label each one with a simple word or phrase: "I feel angry and hurt," or simply, "Anger . . . doubt . . . hurt." Say it

out loud, then let the feeling go and return to your breathing. Watch what the next feeling is and give it a label. Then let it go. Do this for three minutes, and after each minute of observation, note how you are feeling, then take a deep breath and yawn. The internal dialogue might sound something like this: "Anger—anger—sadness—pain—I feel like running away—I want to lash out and hit—I want to run away—I don't care that I'm angry—this meditation is stupid—I'm not getting anywhere with this—now I'm really sad—ah, the feeling is fading—no, it isn't . . ."

5. If your mind wanders to some other topic, simply take another deep breath and refocus on your angry memory. Notice if your feelings begin to change, but do not judge yourself.

6. Next, ask yourself if you have ever felt this kind of anger before, and make a mental "list" of all the times you can recall. Is there a person from kindergarten whom you can recall being angry at? Visualize that person and say his or her name aloud, if you recall it. Then do the same thing with first grade, second grade, third grade, fourth, fifth, sixth, seventh, and eighth. Then high school: How many people do you recall being angry at when you were an adolescent? Say their names, take a deep breath, and let the memories and feelings fade away.

7. Now shift your attention to your family. Recall an instance of anger toward your mother, your father, a sibling, Take another deep breath and let these memories fade away.

8. Think about the last time you got angry. With whom? About what? Remember how you reacted. How does it make you feel now? Once more, take a deep breath and let those feelings go.

9. Yawn five times and note how your feelings have changed. If the anger is still there, don't judge it, condemn it, or condone it. Just accept it as a natural feeling inside.

The next time you feel angry toward someone, set aside ten minutes and improvise on the exercise above. Visualize the person's face. Watch where in your body you experience the anger, and use your breathing to explore all the memories of anger associated with that individual. For some people this may take far longer than ten minutes, but it's important to see how deep they run. See if the anger you feel reminds you of different people in the past, and take a few minutes to make a mental list of their names.

Often your anger will subside by observing it, but sometimes negative feelings run very deep, and they will not go away by meditating on them. But that is okay, because the practice trains your mind to slowly disconnect from your feelings. Simple observation is a frontal lobe activity, and the more you activate your frontal lobe and anterior cingulate, the more you'll decrease activity in the limbic areas that generate anger and hurt.

When dealing with difficult people in your present life, you may find it helpful to set aside a few minutes every day to practice this meditation in conjunction with the forgiveness meditation you will shortly learn. If you choose to meditate on the roots of your anger by simply watching where your thoughts and feelings go, in a few days or a week you should notice a distinct difference in how you emotionally process your anger. In fact, you might find that underneath the anger are other strong feelings, like hurt. Use the same structure I just taught you and substitute the new feeling for anger.

If you find yourself stuck in anger, I recommend that you do some form of aerobic exercise—you can even run around the block—until the anger subsides. It's almost impossible to stay angry when you're exercising, because any form of cardiovascular workout strongly activates frontal lobe circuits. Indeed, it may be the best and most reliable mood enhancer in the world.[47]

But meditation does something that exercise fails to do. It trains your mind to recognize the hundreds of subconscious thoughts associated with every mood. You start to *understand* how feelings work. By passively observing your emotions, you disengage from them, and this allows for a calmer mental state to take over. As far as we can tell, only human beings have the power to use their frontal lobes to quash destructive feelings and thoughts. And that is one of the most important lessons that meditation has taught.

EXERCISE 11: THE IMAGINARY FIGHT

When dealing with anger, it helps to have an arsenal of peacekeeping weapons on your side, and research has found that having an imaginary fight will interrupt anger, and thus keep it out of your dialogue with others.[48] In fact, if you have an imaginary fight with someone you're angry at, you can discover what will and will not work, at least when it comes to getting what you want. Try this exercise the next time you feel angry at your partner, your child, or a friend, but for now—assuming you are not particularly angry with anyone—just recall an unresolved conflict from the past.

1. Visualize the person you were (or are currently) angry with. Scrunch up your face into a frown, and using your imagination, visualize the most unpleasant encounter you can: nasty expressions, a terrible fight, a screaming fit, or a cold, demeaning stare-down. Watch your visualization like a movie. Act it out in your imagination scene by scene. Imagine them insulting you, and respond by being as mean as you can. Let the spontaneous fight take over, and watch where it eventually leads. How does it end?

2. Next, think about the way you would normally confront this person. Say, in your mind, whatever comes to your mind. Yell at the person, or decide to talk in a firm tone.

3. Now imagine how that person responds. Ask yourself if that was the response you wanted to hear. If not, then repeat Step 2 by saying something different. How does your imaginary partner respond now? Keep repeating this step until you imagine how you can get the other person to respond the way you would like.

4. Finally, visualize the ideal encounter between you and the person toward whom you feel conflict. What could you say to make them relax and be open to your view? Play it out in your imagination,

and see how your imaginary partner responds. Ask yourself: "Is it possible to actually interact with this person in real life?" If the answer is no, repeat this step again.

Usually, this exercise will help you quickly find a strategy that is likely to succeed when you actually confront the person you are having a problem with. Most people, when they're angry, don't take the time to do this, but if you turn it into an imaginative exercise, logic and reason will eventually win out. Thus, by using one's imagination, you can resolve many conflicts before they actually occur.

A suggestion: Whenever you confront a person about something that bothers you, begin with a genuine compliment. Otherwise, the other person will probably be on the defensive, and if so, your strategy may fail. Also, slow your speaking down; it will significantly decrease the blood pressure and muscle tension in both your *and the other person's* body.

EXERCISE 12: SENDING KINDNESS AND FORGIVENESS TO OTHERS

After you have interrupted your anger, I want you to do one more meditation before you engage with any person who has upset you. It is simple to do, but you'll be surprised at the amount of resistance you may feel, even if you're not feeling angry. In fact, it may be the most difficult—yet most important—meditation in the world. It is part of most mindfulness training programs, and interestingly, it is also the cornerstone of every major religious tradition: the golden rule of loving your neighbors as you would love yourself.

But the Buddha and Jesus went one step further: They recommended that you practice forgiveness by loving your enemies as well. Gandhi, when counseling a Hindu whose child was killed during a religious war, suggested that the man adopt an orphan, but he was told to raise the child as a Muslim. I know few individuals who would have the fortitude to follow Gandhi's solution for alleviating religious hatred, but it does not dismiss the importance that forgiveness plays when it comes to getting along with others.

Forgiveness improves family relationships,[49] decreases depressive symptoms while enhancing empathy and life satisfaction,[50] and it can heal a wounded romantic heart.[51] Even the act of choosing to replace an unforgiving attitude with a forgiving one affects the peripheral and central nervous systems in ways that promote physical and psychological health.[52] In addition, most forms of religious involvement increase your capacity to be forgiving,[53] and so does meditation.

Take a moment to think about the person you hate the most, and imagine sending him or her love. It's not easy, is it? Most people would find it repugnant to think kindly about a psychopathic murderer, yet research has shown that victims of violent crime and war who can forgive their perpetrators have decreased anxiety and depression, while those who can't forgive are more inclined toward psychiatric disease.[54]

There are hundreds of books written on forgiveness, but the following meditation exercise stands out as my favorite.

1. Begin by sitting quietly. First, send love to yourself by repeating the following prayer ten times, out loud, or silently to yourself:

   May I be happy.
   May I be well.
   May I be filled with kindness and peace.

   Notice how it makes you feel. If you feel uncomfortable, repeat this prayer by sending love to someone whom you love—a friend, or even a pet: "May you be happy, may you be well, may you be filled with kindness and peace." Keep repeating it until you are filled with a warm, compassionate attitude toward that person.

2. Now turn that energy around and direct it to yourself: "May I be happy, may I be well, may I be filled with kindness and peace." I cannot stress strongly enough the neurological necessity of generating self-love, so if you still have difficulty with this step, make this meditation a priority in your life.

3. Next, turn your attention to the person you like the most. Smile as you visualize his or her face and repeat the prayer above. Then return the love to yourself.

4. Then move on to another person, perhaps a family member or friend, and send that person your prayer. Notice how the feelings change when you think about this person.

5. Keep enlarging your circle by generating love to as many different people as you can: colleagues, neighbors, the mail carrier, etc. Again notice how the feelings change your mood.

6. Now extend your feelings to the people you find more difficult to love or forgive. Try saying the prayer and sending a loving thought to those who have hurt you in the past. If you feel resistance, don't fight it. Just acknowledge your feelings and come back to loving yourself.

7. Pick one person whom you find it difficult to forgive. Look for one small quality that you like about them—perhaps his smile, or the way she styles her hair—and focus your entire attention on that single trait. Try to recall one kind thing he or she once did, and concentrate on that. Hold the positive thought as long as you can, then notice if your feelings have changed. Do you feel less anger? Less hurt? Even the slightest decrease is beneficial to your brain. Each time you do this exercise, extend your forgiveness to other "difficult" people and groups.

8. Finally, extend your love, kindness, and forgiveness to the world: "May everyone be happy, may everyone be well, and may everyone be filled with kindness and peace." Hold a vision in your mind of all the different people in the world, all cultures, all colors, all religions, and all political groups. Imagine everyone getting along with each other and living together in peace.

It doesn't take much effort to practice kindness and forgiveness, and if you make an internal commitment to do so a few minutes every day, you'll train your brain to suppress anger and fear. You might even grow a few new neurons in your hippocampus, which we now know humans can do, but it's important to remember that the hippocampus—which is essential for memory formation and emotional control—is the very first structure damaged by the neurochemicals of anger, anxiety, and stress.

So the next time someone cuts you off on the freeway or makes a clumsy mistake, instead of killing off some neurons in your own brain, just send them a blessing. They probably need it more than you.

Based upon research studies of different training programs developed at universities around the country, we recommend that you do a forgiveness meditation at least once a day for a minimum of six weeks.[55] When vice presidents and advisors at American Express were given a one-day forgiveness workshop, followed by four teleconference follow-ups over the following year, stress levels were reduced by 25 percent. They also generated an increase of 18 percent in gross sales, whereas those who didn't participate in the forgiveness workshop only improved their sales by 10 percent.[56] Forgiveness meditation improves not only the health of your brain and heart, but your pocketbook as well.

FINAL REFLECTIONS ON MEDITATION, RELAXATION, AND CONSCIOUSNESS

Although we have only included twelve meditation-related exercises, if you did them all together, it could take you more than two hours. This, I am certain, would turn most people off. Even a daily practice of forty minutes is more than many people are willing to do. Each person has a different capacity and willingness to engage in healthy activities, so it's kind of like going to the gym. Some people love it, some hate it. Some people can only exercise for ten minutes, and some like to spend hours working out. Doctors will tell you to spend twenty to forty minutes doing aerobics, and many patients simply won't try, even when their lives may depend on it.

The truth of the matter is this: Each person should do what feels intuitively right. Otherwise, it becomes *work*. The same holds true for spiritual and mental practices. If it becomes a chore, you'll resist and resent it. So if going to church once a month suits your nature, then enjoy it. After all, guilt will also hurt your brain. And the same applies to meditation. Remember, our memory patients practiced for only twelve minutes a day, and they improved their cognitive skills. Other studies have shown that even a few minutes can be beneficial to your health. So the amount you practice is really up to you. The more, the better, and the greater variety, the better, but that's about all we can say. After all, happiness is perhaps the ultimate ideal, but everyone will find happiness through different walks of life.

From a neurological perspective, there is some advice to give. Exercise, social interaction, and optimism all tie for first place in terms of keeping your brain healthy, and meditation comes in second. Benson's relaxation exercise, progressive muscle relaxation, and guided imagery all appear to offer equal health benefits and have been extensively researched, but between meditation techniques, there's some debate as to which are best. A wide variety of other meditations—yoga, mindfulness, Transcendental Meditation, Centering Prayer, mantra, etc.—all provide a wide range of neurological benefits. Each has specific health benefits, but they aren't the same. And, considering that there are probably close to a thousand variations of meditation, if not more, it is next to impossible to definitively analyze all of the neural mechanisms involved.

So it all comes back to intention: What is it that you really want to achieve? If you want to sleep better, then try progressive muscle relaxation. If you want to feel more calm and alert, then use any of the mindfulness techniques we've discussed. Yawning may be the fastest way to relax, but it probably carries the greatest social stigma, since most people interpret it as a sign that you are tired or bored. And if you're angry, it should be clear which of the above exercises to use.

But if you want to reach enlightenment, or feel a unity with God, then we have some specific advice for you to follow. You'll need to meditate daily, for at least thirty minutes, possibly more. And you'll need to become expert in one of the mindfulness techniques, like the Centering Prayer described in this chapter. At least, this is what the research has shown so far. Of course, there's no guarantee that you'll have a unitary or mystical experience, a fact well recognized in the meditation communities.

Advanced meditators can achieve deep states of unity and connectedness through intensive practice, and this can trigger some unusual activity in the brain. If parietal activity declines, you alter your sense of self, and if you do this often enough, you may permanently alter the structure of your thalamus, which is part of the reality-processing circuit in the brain. In these situations, the meditator may see the universe in an entirely different light.

When you consciously direct your intent on a particular object, the brain blocks out sensory and neural information that does not pertain to the object of contemplation, and it screens out anything it considers irrelevant. As your meditation progresses, this blocking becomes more intense. The end result is intense awareness of the object, and a loss of awareness of anything other than the object of meditation. If that object is God, then the meditator has the experience of becoming one with God, or the sense that God pervades all of reality. If the object of meditation disappears, as sometimes happens in the most intense mystical states, the person may experience the universe as a completely undifferentiated whole—a sense of absolute unity of all things. When this happens, you might become aware that "you" are not your thoughts, and this raises the paradoxical question of what "you" may actually be. This can happen in any of the exercises we described before, but it typically results after many months of intense meditation.

Focused awareness sometimes creates the uncanny sensation of losing your sense of self. As you begin to realize that "you" is a rather arbitrary neural construction, activity in the parietal area of the brain decreases, and your sense of self begins to dissolve. Most practitioners describe this state as being simultaneously enlightening and disturbing, because a core sense of self is one of the earliest neural constructs in the brain. However, simply shifting your focus back to your breathing turns out to be an effective way to handle such disturbances. Now you can understand why relaxation is such an important foundation, especially if your goal is to modify an unwelcome personality trait. The only people who run into trouble are those with serious underlying personality disorders.

Ultimately, all that we are asking you to do is become a little more aware of life. We want you to slow down by paying attention to your body movements and your breathing as you go about your daily activities. And we want you to learn to become more aware of how your mind produces an endless stream of unconscious feelings and thoughts. By simply becoming more aware of what you think, feel, say, and do, you train your brain to become more organized and calm. Stress diminishes, and life begins to feel more pleasant and rich. It's easy to be mindful throughout the day, and all you need to do is remind yourself to be aware. You can take a minute to "meditate" in the elevator, when you're standing in line at the grocery store, when you're stuck in rush hour traffic, or when you're gazing into the eyes of those you deeply love. This is what mindfulness is all about, and it will change your brain in beneficial ways.

DESTROYING THE ILLUSION OF THE UNIVERSE

Having a conscious intention or goal underlies nearly every form of meditation and prayer, but there is one style worth mentioning that has a very different objective. It is common in some forms of Eastern philosophies, but absent in most Western religious traditions. It involves the conscious pursuit of having no goal at all. You are attempting to achieve absolute inner silence. No emotions or thoughts—just pure awareness or consciousness of what is.

Many people have had spontaneous, momentary experiences of emptiness, but deliberately evoking such a state for more than a few seconds often takes years of practice. Those who accomplish it say that it is one of the most serenely ecstatic states they have experienced. To my knowledge, no scientist has yet to capture this neurological condition with brain-scan technology. However, one group of researchers may have come close. They found that an advanced group of Zen practitioners could reduce activity in parts of the brain that are usually stimulated by other forms of contemplative practice.[57] The result is a complete sense of unity, which is also described as absolute reality, a term that has been variously defined as pure consciousness, nonduality, the negation of physical reality, seeing the world or the mind as illusion, pure Godness, supreme spirit, or nothingness. Others have used the term to describe what is essentially unknowable, indefinable, unfathomable, immutable, unmanifest, timeless, spaceless, or formless.

I have previously identified this state in the brain as being related to a complete blocking of all information into your consciousness. Thus, the end result may be similar to the state reached through intense meditation on a single object when the awareness of the object entirely disappears. At that point the experience is often described as a complete sense of oneness with the divine.

Clearly, this can be one of the most powerful types of experiences people can have, and it lies at the heart of many great philosophical and spiritual traditions. It is associated with a deep sense of realness, so real that our everyday reality seems like it is nothing more than an illusion.

Such experiences might be the ultimate goal of religious or spiritual practices, but the exercises presented here are not likely to get you to such a state. Instead, they will help you achieve a greater sense of relaxation, enhance your cognitive skills, and foster a greater engagement and awareness of yourself and the world in which you live.

10

COMPASSIONATE COMMUNICATION

Dialogue, Intimacy, and Conflict
Transformation

Meditation is good for your brain, and it can bring you closer to God. But we discovered that it can also be used to rapidly establish intimacy with others. "Intimacy," as we are using it here, does not refer to sexual closeness, but to those qualities associated with friendship, trust, and compassion. When we feel intimate toward another, we willingly suspend self-protective attitudes that we normally use when closely interacting with others. Intimacy fosters acceptance, and greater degrees of intimacy are correlated with greater personal health.[1]

In this chapter we'll discuss how you can build on the meditation exercises in the previous chapter and apply them directly to the process of communication with family members and friends. The technique that Mark and I designed was specifically created for working with spouses and partners, but we will show you how to adapt the exercise when interacting with colleagues, distant acquaintances, and even strangers. When you do so, you can turn an ordinary conversation into an extraordinary event in less than fifteen minutes, because it will neurologically undermine defensive behaviors inherent in any dialogue. This creates an environment in which conflicts can be more easily resolved.

You can even use this meditation technique to teach groups of people with opposing perspectives how to be more accepting of each other's systems of beliefs. We call this exercise "Compassionate Communication" because it helps individuals express vulnerable thoughts while maintaining mutual sensitivity and respect for each other. Here, we define compassion as the neurological ability to resonate to the emotional feelings of others, to share their suffering and their joy. Our ability to be compassionate is part of our biological makeup, but every human brain has a different degree of emotional sensitivity when it comes to reading the inner feelings of others.[2] From the research we've accumulated, we believe that anyone can strengthen his or her neurological capacity to feel greater compassion toward others.

In fact, we view the overall concept of compassionate communication as essential to all forms of interpersonal exchange. Compassion is a fundamental tenet of nearly every spiritual tradition, and it is especially critical when considering the larger issues of interfaith dialogue, discussions between atheists and religious individuals, and communication within the science and religion debates.

Compassion also implies the neurological ability to express kindness, empathy, and forgiveness.[3] Like intimacy, compassion is associated with greater emotional and psychological health.[4] From a neurological perspective, it is generated and regulated by the anterior cingulate,[5] and as we have explained in prior chapters, this unique part of the human brain enhances social awareness, recognizes the feeling states of others, and decreases our propensity to express anger and react with fear. The anterior cingulate is also one of the core neural mechanisms responsible for our deepest feelings of romantic love.[6] It allows us to feel emotionally connected and attached, but if it functions poorly, a person's ability to resonate to the feelings of someone else will be impaired.[7]

P254: MEDITATION, COMPASSION, AND MIRROR-NEURON THEORY

In psychological, anthropological, and neuroscientific communities, there is much excitement about the potential discovery of a human mirror-neuron system that would explain how our brains come to "know" what is going on in the brains of other human beings. These unique neurons are located in areas directly affected by meditation and appear to be intimately involved in the processes of facial recognition, compassion, communication, and self/other consciousness. The rapidly ex-

(sidebar continues)

panding research in this area suggests that mindfulness-based spiritual practices may be ideally suited for enhancing social empathy and communication with others. For an excellent overview of how meditation affects the mirror-neuron system of the brain (which, in turn, helps us to become more emotionally attuned to others), see Daniel Siegel's *The Mindful Brain*.

PRACTICING COMPASSIONATE COMMUNICATION WITH STRANGERS

Mark first introduced a version of Compassionate Communication to members of the Association for Transpersonal Psychology in 1992,[8] but we recently modified the technique so we could monitor the neurological changes taking place in the brain. In conjunction with Stephanie Newberg, a licensed clinical social worker and assistant director at the Council for Relationships in Philadelphia (the oldest counseling center in America), we are currently training therapists to use this exercise to improve dialogue and intimacy with conflicted couples. Research also shows that when therapists practice awareness-based and mindfulness-based meditations, they have better results with their patients.[9]

We are expanding the program to include other university counseling centers and conflict-resolution organizations around the country, and have begun conducting research in churches and public schools to measure the improvements made according to various empathy and intimacy scales. The results so far are surprising and positive.

When we introduce Compassionate Communication in a group setting, we ask participants to pair themselves up with a person they do not know. We specifically request that couples and spouses do not work together because, in a group situation, couples converse with greater defensiveness than when they practice Compassionate Communication with a stranger. At first this may sound counterintuitive, but many long-term studies have shown that the complex demands of marriage increase the degree of stress between couples.[10] An intimate conversation can easily bump up against unaddressed conflicts, so a natural reaction is to avoid those issues—and specifically, those conversations—that may threaten marital attachment. However, when you experiment with Compassionate Communication in a group situation, where there is less at stake, participants can take the positive experiences home with them, where they can practice with greater willingness and comfort.

Let's return to our workshop participants. After they paired up with a stranger, we gave them a modified version of the Miller Social Intimacy Scale—a well-established tool for measuring social friendship, closeness, and defensiveness[11]—and asked them to respond to the questions as they related to the person they were sitting with. Then we guided them through a seven-minute exercise (which I'll introduce to you shortly) that used a combination of the relaxation exercises we described in Chapter 9.

Next, we asked them to hold a compassionate thought about the person with whom they were sitting. This turns out to be an important step, and it reflects the principles in the forgiveness meditation we discussed in the previous chapter. We instructed them to *imagine* an intimate conversation with the stranger they were sitting with because visualization enables the brain to more easily put into practice whatever goal one wishes to accomplish. In this case, the goal was to stimulate the neural circuits involved with empathy, social awareness, and communication.

Finally, we asked the participants to smile and make eye contact* with their partners as they continued to imagine the possibility of an ensuing compassionate dialogue. They were given seven minutes to talk to each other, but had to stay focused on their breathing and only speak briefly, taking turns talking about whatever came to mind, without censoring anything. They were specifically instructed *not* to make a conversation happen; instead, they were to simply allow a spontaneous dialogue to flow wherever it wanted to go. When we do this in workshop situations, it's not surprising to see many pairs sharing personal stories they would normally reserve for a close friend.

Participants were invited to share their experiences with the group, and after the exchange, we asked them to pair themselves up with a

---

* Substantial neurological and psychological research has demonstrated the necessity of eye contact and intentional gazing for generating empathy and social responsiveness. Mutual eye contact stimulates the same circuits as meditation and is considered integral to human mirror-neuron theory.

new partner—again, with someone they did not know. They practiced Compassionate Communication for another five to ten minutes, and then we paired them with another person. But this time we didn't have them talk. Instead, we again gave them the modified Miller Social Intimacy Scale to see if there was any change in their willingness to feel empathy or affection toward a stranger.

When we analyzed the data, we found an 11 percent improvement on the intimacy scale. Now, 11 percent might not sound like much, but in scientific research it's an impressive change, especially considering the brief amount of time that was spent. Certain areas of intimacy had even greater changes. For example, there was a 20 percent increase in participants' willingness to feel close and spend time with an unfamiliar individual. We also found that men showed as much improvement as women and that race did not play a factor in creating intimacy with others. People over the age of forty showed a slightly greater improvement in their willingness to be open toward others, which suggests that compassion, empathy, and intimacy improves with greater life experiences and maturity.

We were also able to measure the "baseline" intimacy levels of the participants before they practiced Compassionate Communication. Although women had slightly higher levels, the difference between women and men was not statistically significant, thus contradicting the popular opinion that women have a greater capacity for closeness. Other studies also show mixed results when searching for gender differences. For example, women may exhibit greater degrees of empathy, but men tend to be more forgiving.[12] On the other hand, women tend to express more compassion than men toward people who have treated them unfairly.[13] Overall, the research suggests that we must be cautious when comparing men's and women's capacities for closeness.

After practicing Compassionate Communication with strangers, both men and women were more likely to share personal information and were more willing to listen to personal disclosures. They felt closer to each other and were more willing to be emotionally supportive and socially affectionate. Thus, Compassionate Communication appears to be an effective strategy for generating interpersonal understanding and peace.

COMPASSIONATE COMMUNICATION WITH COUPLES

The therapists we're training are introducing the technique to selected couples who are struggling with different levels of conflict in their relationship. The patients take a battery of tests to evaluate their psychological state and level of intimacy, and in the first counseling session are guided through the steps of the meditation by the therapist. Then, with minimal supervision—which is usually a reminder to speak briefly and return to focusing on one's inner state of relaxation—they practice the exercise by allowing a spontaneous conversation to emerge. Later, when they become more proficient, they'll use the exercise to address specific issues and problems.

We send them home with a CD that guides them through the instructions, and we ask them to practice with each other for approximately fifteen minutes each day. From week to week the therapists observe the changes in their intimacy level, and at the end of four weeks the participants are again given a battery of tests.

Compassionate Communication integrates an awareness-based meditation directly into the dialogue process, something that to our knowledge has not been researched or tested until now. In fact, at a recent conference on spirituality and health, I spoke with several well-known scholars who were lamenting that there were no meditation programs that actively engaged people in dialogue. They were surprised and excited when I told them about the research we'd begun, and we are currently working on developing protocols with several universities. Over the next few years we plan to initiate a number of interdisciplinary studies to expand upon the data we are currently collecting.

Evidence from university research has demonstrated that couples who use a mindfulness-based meditation separately are more likely to respond empathically toward each other.[14] In another study, those who practiced mindfulness meditation showed "improved levels of relationship happiness, relationship stress, stress-coping efficacy, and overall stress."[15] Other awareness and mindfulness-based meditations have been integrated into psychotherapy to foster relationship empathy[16] and improve parenting skills.[17]

But all of these meditations are conducted in privacy and silence. This is why the Compassionate Communication technique can be so effective. It builds on the existing evidence that meditation enhances interpersonal relationships, but adds the component of actively engaging two individuals in a dialogue. Our preliminary evidence also suggests that Compassionate Communication helps deepen spiritual bonds within relationships, which is why we are training ministers and their congregations in ways that integrate dialogue into their religious rituals and beliefs.

Bringing meditation into any conversation is surprisingly simple. All you have to do is maintain consistent eye contact and stay physically relaxed and mindful of your responses as you participate in a flow of spontaneous conversation. You say a few sentences slowly, then return to your breathing awareness while the other person responds. The unstructured conversation that follows will quickly move into surprisingly intimate areas. And, like the walking meditation we discussed in the previous chapter, the more you practice, the easier it becomes.

Soon you'll find yourself bringing serenity and awareness into every conversation you have—even with those who do not engage in contemplative or spiritual practices. After all, it doesn't matter if the other person is consciously meditating with you, because your own state of awareness and relaxation will influence the other person's mood. Human brains are designed to resonate to the inner emotional states of others, so as long as one of you maintains a posture of openness and serenity, the other person will unconsciously respond in kind. It might not be as much as you desire, but when it comes to something as complicated as personal relationships, every little bit helps.

CHANGING OUTER GOALS INTO INNER VALUES

During the summer of 2007, while Mark was collecting data from congregants of a Church of Religious Science, we accidentally discovered that Compassionate Communication could change a person's values, desires, and goals. At that time, a very popular video called *The Secret*[18] had become the focal point at many of these churches, mainly because the concept—that you can obtain whatever you desire by asking the universe to provide—closely coincided with the basic teachings of the organization.*

On the survey scale we handed out, Mark decided to add the following question: "What is your 'secret' desire?" It turned out to be a fortuitous measure of how meditation can change your relationship with the world. Before doing the exercise, most people responded with a materialistic goal: more money, a better job, a nicer house, a new relationship, a vacation, improved health, etc. But at the end of the hour-long exercise, when asked the same question again, most people changed their desire to a broader range of intrinsic values. Peace, happiness, and contentment were often cited, but here's a sample of changes made by specific individuals:

DESIRE *BEFORE* PRACTICING	DESIRE *AFTER* ONE HOUR OF PRACTICE
Sell my paintings	Become self-accepting
Be a megamillionaire	Live in grace and harmony
Financial independence	Be spiritually fulfilled
Have a happy marriage	Serve humanity

My favorite response came from a woman who initially put down the desire to be a writer, but after practicing Compassionate Communication with people she barely knew, she changed her goal to wanting to "run with giraffes."

We conducted a content analysis, as we did with our online Survey of Spiritual Experiences, and found that after the meditation experience, an interest in financial concerns dropped from 34 to 14 percent. There was a 60 percent increase in a desire for peace, while desires for self-love and interpersonal love nearly tripled.[19]

The shift in responses confirms my intuition that spiritual practices—even when stripped from their religious components and applied to secular situations—take people inward, where they often re-

* For example, the central theme of Science of Mind philosophy is that "there is power within you" that "can lift your life to its highest level . . . change illness into health . . . bring peace amid turmoil . . . bring success out of failure, victory out of defeat," and "bring companionship and happiness out of loneliness." In the writings and sermons, Religious Science followers see God, the universe, and consciousness as essentially interconnected with their inner selves.

alize the importance of compassionate values and humanitarian ideals, qualities that are found at the heart of most religious traditions.

HOW TO PRACTICE COMPASSIONATE COMMUNICATION

Human communication is one of the most complex neural processes in the brain. It involves face and voice recognition, language processing, memory recall, speech coordination, concept recognition, imagery mapping, emotional regulation, deceit and fairness evaluation, strategic planning, and the activation of neural circuits governing volitional activities and behavior.

Any degree of stress will interfere with the integration of these internal processes, so the first step in effective communication—with anyone, friend or foe—is to remain calm and relaxed. But most people do not view conscious relaxation as a social event. Instead, it's something you usually do alone, or with a good bottle of wine and a couple of friends. Yet all of the research we've collected points to the fact that relaxation is an essential key to virtually every aspect of social interaction. If you integrate breathing, awareness, observation, optimism, and emotional neutrality into your conversation, a far more meaningful and constructive dialogue will emerge.

Relaxation heightens our visual and auditory skills, which means we can listen more carefully to others and better ascertain the subtle facial cues that are indispensable to the communication process. Increased attentiveness will positively affect your partner, and this will encourage a greater willingness for him or her to disclose more intimate feelings and thoughts.

But intimacy brings with it vulnerability, and if the other person reacts with anxiety, the conversation will be derailed. Relaxation lowers the neural reactivity in your brain. In addition, when the circuits relating to social awareness and compassion are stimulated, pleasure-enhancing neurochemicals are released, and these also decrease the risk of reacting with anger or fear.

Compassionate Communication is easy to learn. All you need is a willing partner or friend, but you can also do the exercise alone, using your imagination to envision a caring person. You'll receive all the benefits that traditional meditations bestow, and then, when you enter a conversation with another person, you can internally practice the technique. For example, before you speak to someone, take a slow deep breath and consciously relax all of the muscles in your body. Then speak slowly and briefly, letting the other person respond. While he or she talks, stay quietly focused on your state of relaxation. When the other person stops, take a subtle breath and respond.

You might think that your slower talking will attract undue attention, but when you try it, you'll discover that other people will experience your slowness as being more attentive and receptive. If you ask them, they'll probably tell you that they felt you were deeply interested in what they said. And then, if you tell them what you were doing, you'll have the pleasure of passing on a valued technique that someone else can use.

Of course, if you know you'll be walking into a conflict-ridden situation, you should take ten minutes beforehand to rehearse the Compassionate Communication instructions in your imagination. Ideally, both parties would benefit if they practiced this technique together, but we live in a world that is far from ideal.

The instructions that follow are what we use in our workshops and couples therapy, but feel free to modify them to suit your situation. As you read the instructions, perform as many steps as possible in your imagination. Later you can read them to a friend or your partner, guiding the person through each step. Speak slow and gently, using your voice to lull your partner into a state of deep relaxation. Thanks to the innate capacity of human brains to resonate to each other's emotional condition, you will find yourself relaxing as well. If not, ask your friend to read the instructions back to you before you begin the conversation. He or she should be extremely relaxed, which will facilitate the process of creating a deep, shared meditative experience.

If you can, record the instructions, because listening to them makes them easier to follow than reading them. You can also go to markrobertwaldman.com to order a prerecorded CD (see Appendix A for additional information). If you make your own CD, insert the sound of a bell at each place you see an asterisk in the instructions. The bell is used as a reminder to focus on your breathing and relaxation.

We suggest that you do Compassionate Communication once a day, alone or with someone else. You can even try it over the telephone, as some of our patients have. The relaxation induction takes about seven minutes, depending on how slow or fast you read (we recommend slow). On the CD, the induction is followed by another seven minutes of silence, during which you practice with a partner. Every thirty seconds the silence is punctuated by the gentle sound of a bell to remind both people to talk less and relax.

When you are alone, after you have done the relaxation induction, try to have an *imaginary* conversation with someone about a topic that is causing you concern. Like the "Imaginary Fight" exercise in the previous chapter, this can be an effective way to exercise your tactfulness and predict how another person might respond.

So let's begin. In this first trial run, imagine you are sitting in a chair, opposite someone you like. Later you can practice with a person with whom you feel comfortable, and still later, you can try it with someone with whom you are having difficulty. Read slowly, and each time you see an asterisk, stop for five seconds and take a very deep breath. Obviously, you can ignore, for the moment, the suggestion to close your eyes!

> Sit down on two chairs placed close together and face your partner. If you are comfortable enough, your knees or hands can touch each other. Close your eyes and take a few deep breaths, relaxing all the muscles in your face. Let your forehead relax, and then let the muscles around your eyes relax. Take another deep breath and relax your jaw. Now relax all the muscles in your neck. Take a deep breath and relax your shoulders, and take another breath as you relax the muscles in your arms and your hands. Feel your shoulders drop and relax some more. Each time you hear a bell,* it is a reminder to pause, relax, and breathe. Take another breath, and feel all of the tension draining out of your body as you become more and more relaxed. Now relax all the muscles in your back. Feel your legs relax as they melt into the cushion of your chair. Now relax your feet. Scan your entire body for any excess tension in your muscles, then take a deep breath and let that tension go.*

Now, yawn ten times, because it will make you extraordinarily relaxed and alert. It doesn't matter if you fake it, just try to yawn; by the fourth or fifth one, they'll begin to feel real, and you'll feel yourself becoming more and more relaxed. Yawn again, and listen to your partner yawn, and feel how relaxed you become. Once more, take another deep breath and yawn.*

Still keeping your eyes closed, smile and visualize your partner sitting across from you and smiling. Stay aware of your breathing as you hold a compassionate image or loving thought in mind. Think about something you like about that person, or recall a memory that brought you pleasure or peace. Take a deep breath and continue to relax.*

Imagine having an intimate conversation with your partner. It's a beautiful conversation, filled with compassion and respect. In this conversation, you take turns as each one of you speaks slowly and briefly, less than thirty seconds, saying only a sentence or two—only ten or twenty words. Then stop. After each sentence, come back to your breath, and let all your thoughts melt away, staying present, staying in the moment, and focusing on your relaxation and breath.*

Imagine hearing your partner talk slowly, and no matter what your partner says, you will stay relaxed, smiling and holding a compassionate thought in your mind. As you listen, all your defenses fall away. Remember, all you have to do is talk . . . breathe . . . listen . . . breathe . . . and relax.*

The conversation that emerges in your imagination is slow, spontaneous, and relaxed. There is no need to rush. All you need to do is talk softly, breathe, listen, breathe, and relax. In your mind let the conversation take any direction it wants. Don't control it. Don't try to make a point, and don't worry if the subject changes. Just stay relaxed as you imagine having a compassionate dialogue: talking, listening, breathing, and relaxing.*

Take one more yawn, and open your eyes. Gaze compassionately into your partner's eyes as you hold a loving thought, and continue to do this for ten seconds. Smile warmly as you hold that thought in your mind.*

In a moment you will begin your conversation by opening up with a compliment and listening to a compliment from your partner.

It does not matter if the compliment feels forced at the beginning, because the other person will still respond in a positive way.*

Keep your eyes focused on each other as you let a spontaneous conversation emerge. Speak only a sentence or two, as slowly as you can, for no longer than thirty seconds, and then let your partner speak. Continue for the next five minutes, breathing, talking, breathing, listening, and staying as relaxed as you can.*

After five minutes take the conversation a little deeper by sharing a more intimate thought. Then, after another three minutes have passed, close the conversation by giving each other a compliment.*

Research, by the way, has shown that a person needs to hear five compliments before he or she can listen nondefensively to a criticism. So I highly recommend that you train yourself to deliberately give compliments to different people throughout the day. If you keep a list, you may even notice that after a few weeks more people will compliment you.

RESISTANCE

Many people feel awkward when they first think about trying Compassionate Communication, so don't be surprised if your friend or partner puts up some defense at first. Even people from our workshops have told us how powerful the experience was, but they still had resistance to practicing it with their partners. However, one woman in her sixties went home and asked her husband (who was unwilling to go to the workshop) if he would do the exercise with her. When it came to the compliment part, he said, "You're really beautiful." After they dialogued, she asked him if he'd meant it. He said, "Of course!" In their forty years of marriage, he had never told her she was pretty.

But if you and your partner are fighting, you'll both need to make a serious commitment to cooperate with each other, at least throughout the exercise. If you see your partner frown, it may be a sign that he or she has had a strong emotional reaction to something you said, and the defensiveness that follows shuts down the brain's ability to remain consciously attuned.

Another level of resistance comes from a mild discomfort at engaging in an artificially constructed dialogue. "It just doesn't feel real," some people will say. And of course it's not real. It's training. Whether it's sports, education, or communication, you have to practice a new skill before it feels natural to your body or your mind.

Another problem often arises concerning the limitation of speech. Most people aren't used to it, but in Compassionate Communication it is very important to talk for thirty seconds or less. Why? Because your brain is only capable of consciously holding a handful of concepts—approximately four to seven "chunks" of information[20]—in its working memory, and it can only hold them for twenty to thirty seconds. If each person takes turns talking for no more than thirty seconds, both individuals will be able to follow every aspect of the communication process and respond to it in a comprehensive way.

In "normal" conversation, most people talk longer than that, so it's not surprising to find out that your partner can only recall—and respond to—the last few things you said. If you engage in an intellectual dialogue for longer than thirty seconds, your frontal lobes may begin to disconnect from the emotional centers in your brain. You'll find yourself getting lost in your words, and that further breaks the empathic bond between you and your partner. Even when you stop talking, your frontal lobes are inclined to keep racing along, and this is where breathing and yawning is needed. It slows down the internal monologue.

For many people, thirty seconds doesn't feel like enough time to articulate a complex feeling or thought, so they forget about the "rule" and continue to talk. That's where the bell on the CD helps. At first it is hard to understand how brief exchanges in dialogue can lead to a meaningful experience, but neurologically, the nonverbal parts of each person's brain are learning how to resonate to each other. This creates a sense of connectedness, and when this state is established, conversations begin to flow more smoothly. And with practice, the slow, limited speech will teach your brain, and your conscious mind, to be more selective with your words. Talking becomes more mindful and direct.

In Compassionate Communication, the purpose is *not* to make a point. Rather, the goal is to train the mind to watch where a spontaneous conversation leads. If you don't force the conversation in a specific direction, your brain will automatically focus on underlying issues that are often difficult to put in words. This is the true beauty of Compassionate Communication. Like other forms of mindfulness meditation, it quickly takes you into uncharted territories of feelings and thoughts while you remain relaxed and alert.

As you become comfortable with the exercise, which may take two or three practice sessions, you'll find that you can shift the dialogue to a specific issue or problem. As long as you remember to stay relaxed, you'll be able to resolve many issues in less than an hour. That is what we see in the counseling room, but obviously there's a third person present to help you stay on track. When you do this outside of counseling, you and your partner should agree to help each other stay on track. For example, one of you can signal the other to take a deep breath by gently touching him or her on the hand.

In marriages, it's important to have your knees or hands touching. The closeness and the touch is often enough to undermine unconscious defensiveness. Furthermore, a few minutes of partner contact lowers blood pressure, cardiovascular reactivity, and levels of cortisol and norepinephrine (our stress chemicals) while raising levels of oxytocin, the brain's "cuddle" chemical.[21] But if you find it uncomfortable, I suggest that you make that the topic of conversation while you practice the Compassionate Communication exercise. With friends or colleagues, touching may be uncalled for. Instead, the two of you should consciously decide what the "right" distance should be. Even a conversation on this topic can stimulate deeper intimacy.

Once you become proficient at Compassionate Communication, you can relax the "rules" and allow a more normal dialogue to ensue. However, if you remain in a "dialogical" meditative state for thirty minutes or longer, activity in your parietal lobe will probably decrease, and that can lead to a revelatory experience. When parietal activity goes down, the neurological boundaries between "I" and "you" begin to blur and you'll feel more united with each other. Egotism and narcissism will subside, to be replaced by a sense of mutual connection and trust. "You" and "I" turn into "we," which is an ideal state to nurture cooperation and interpersonal peace.

COMPASSIONATE COMMUNICATION
AND CORPORATE MINDFULNESS

When interacting with colleagues or distant acquaintances, you can privately use the steps we have outlined above to bring Compassionate Communication into every conversation you have. The other person doesn't even need to know that you are "practicing," for as we have outlined in previous chapters, human brains are designed to resonate to the cognitive and emotional states of each other.

The next time you are called on to participate in a business conference, try the following experiment. Before the meeting, take five minutes to deeply relax, and then use your imagination to fantasize your "ideal" interaction. Visualize the smiling face of each person with whom you will interact (even if he or she is grump) and spend a minute holding a compassionate thought. Then go into your meeting. Greet everyone with a smile, and then—quietly, to yourself—take a slow breath and deeply relax your arms, legs, and face. When you speak, talk slowly and briefly, and allow the other person to respond. But keep coming back to an awareness of your own state of relaxation. I'm willing to bet that after a couple of times, the people you talk with will begin to respond with greater empathy.

ACCEPTANCE

Awareness-based meditations like Compassionate Communication do something different from other forms of therapeutic interventions. They teach you how to *accept* your underlying faults. The therapeutic importance of acceptance was not recognized until recently, because most people, when addressing a problem, expect to make a change. We go to a doctor because we want to eliminate a symptom, and we consult a counselor to improve the quality of our life. For most people, acceptance is rarely a goal. Change is the goal, along with achievement and success. Acceptance, in fact, is often equated with failure—failure to succeed, failure to improve, and failure to transcend one's old self.

But acceptance is not the same as failure. As we are using it here, it implies an overall trust that things are "good enough." It also implies tolerance and the ability to respond nonjudgmentally to others or toward ourselves. Thus, when we face a problem, the first step, before changing it, is to watch it. We simply allow the problem to exist for the moment, and in that moment we become more aware of what the problem is. We observe it, we notice it, and we tolerate it as we remain in a calm state of relaxation. Acceptance and mindfulness clearly go hand in hand.

Acceptance is particularly important when dealing with serious emotional problems, and in this sense, acceptance simply means that we lower our expectations. If we don't, perfectionism will take its toll by increasing our sense of failure. If you want to quit smoking but only succeed in reducing a three-pack-a-day habit to one pack, you've made a significant improvement. And improvement is good enough for the brain.

The same is true for love. If our expectations are too high, we'll always end up disappointed. And disappointment will undermine our capacity to think clearly, communicate effectively, and stay emotionally grounded and relaxed.

The solution is found by creating a balance between acceptance and change. This was a big discovery in psychotherapy, and it turns out that acceptance-based therapies provide an excellent solution for dealing with emotional problems.[22] By simply observing destructive thoughts and feelings, people feel less anxious about what they feel they can't control, and this actually allows them to have more control over their lives.

When meditation was incorporated into psychotherapy, the results were so successful that they generated a whole new category of treatments, including mindfulness-based cognitive behavioral therapy, acceptance and commitment therapy, and dialectical behavioral therapy.[23] They have been used to treat depression, anxiety, anger, grief, and a variety of stress-related disorders.[24] Mindfulness has even been used to help schizophrenics lower anxiety,[25] and acceptance-based therapies are particularly effective in dealing with chronic pain and addictive behavior.[26] Because academic and professional interests in these new therapies have burgeoned in recent years, we've included numerous references in the endnotes for those who are interested in looking more closely at the research.

MOVING FROM ACCEPTANCE TO COMPASSION

When we accept ourselves for who we are—as people filled with strengths and weaknesses—it's easier to accept the flaws we find in others. Acceptance makes it easier to tolerate differences, and this allows for greater cooperation. Meditation, as we have seen, specifically strengthens the key neural circuit that connects our cognitive skills with our social skills and our emotions, and the end result of a well-functioning brain is the generation of deep compassion and love. And, unlike other animals, we appear to have the only brain that can show compassion toward every living thing on the planet. That, truly, is an amazing neurological feat.

So tomorrow, after you drive home at the end of the day, take a few minutes to relax before you get out of the car. Imagine the people you will soon see, and generate a compassionate thought. Yawn a few times, and think of a compliment you can give. It doesn't have to be large, just genuine, and a small one will do just fine. Even saying something simple, like, "It's good to be home," can open the doors of compassion. Then, mindfully walk to the front door with a smile on your face, remaining conscious of every step and sound. Even if you say nothing when you stroll through the door, you'll feel better, and that emotional state will resonate in everyone else's brain. By speaking and behaving mindfully toward others, you will have made your relationship an integral part of your personal and spiritual path.

TWENTY-ONE STRATEGIES FOR KEEPING THE PEACE

Compassion sets the stage for conflict resolution, but once a compassionate dialogue begins, other skills are needed to ensure that the conversation stays on track. To help you accomplish this, we're going to suggest twenty-one strategies that have been consolidated from hundreds of studies in the fields of psychology, business management, divorce mediation, and political peace-making strategies. And it all begins with a cardinal rule: When it comes to dialoguing with others, anger *never* works. This is the consensus of nearly all psychologists, consultants, spiritual leaders, and neuroscientists throughout the world. Anger, hostility, and even a demanding attitude expressed in a dialogue is enough to trigger the release of numerous stress hormones throughout your body and brain.[27]

Anger may be an unavoidable facet in conflicted relationships, but it always derails the communication process by interrupting the frontal lobe processes of language, logic, and cooperative interaction. Even hearing an underlying angry tone in the other person's voice is enough to shut down a constructive discussion.[28] Conflicting emotional cues can also disrupt other cognitive functions.[29]

Even if the other person disguises a contemptuous feeling behind a smile, the anterior cingulate in your brain can register the discrepancy, letting you know that he or she is being deceitful. Human brains may not be very good at discerning truth, but they are superb at picking out lies. So if you are feeling irritable, it is best to first use the meditation techniques described in Chapter 9 that specifically deal with anger.

First, I recommend that you go over the following strategies with your partner. Do you each agree to each item? If not, revise them to suit your mutual needs. If you want to help keep things on track, sign a piece of paper stating that you will consciously *try* to adhere to the agreed-upon rules and that you'll *compassionately* remind each other when one of you has fallen off track.

I've marked the most important strategies with an asterisk, but there are two nonnegotiable items that are essential when dealing with strong emotional issues.

First, *confrontations are by appointment only.* You can't just barge into a room and expect that your partner (or your employee or boss) will be ready to discuss your issue. Both parties must feel prepared, a process that could take several hours or days. Briefly describe your problem, then ask your partner to pick a time to talk. In some spiritual communities, both partners make a verbal commitment to spend a few days privately reflecting on the problem before they sit down to discuss disturbing issues. Then, when they do talk, they try their best to apply the spiritual principles they most deeply believe in and trust.

There is another nonnegotiable rule: During the conversation, either person may call for a time-out at any time he or she chooses. This is essential for keeping destructive emotions, like anger and fear, in check. If your partner's buttons are pushed, he or she must take all the time that is needed to return to a compassionate state. Otherwise, progress won't be made. A time-out can last for a few minutes or several hours—perhaps even days—but it is the responsibility of the person who calls for the break to suggest a specific time to reconvene.

The strategies fall into four general categories:

• Three Strategies for Beginning a Constructive Dialogue
• Six Strategies to Contain Disruptive Emotions
• Six Strategies to Improve Communication
• Six Strategies for Finding Creative Solutions.

And don't forget the golden rule of neuroscience, which I cannot emphasize enough: *Anger never works.* It might make you feel good for the moment, but it will seriously disrupt the communication process and damage important parts of your brain.

Again, the asterisks highlight the most essential strategies to adhere to: picking the right time, opening with kindness, avoiding provocative language, softening the tone of your voice, suspending blame, respecting your partner's point of view, equally "sharing" the conversation, closing with kindness, and getting a follow-up progress report.

THREE STRATEGIES FOR BEGINNING A CONSTRUCTIVE DIALOGUE

* 1. *Pick the right time.* Make an appointment—the first of the two non-negotiable rules—to sit down and talk, and decide how long both of you are willing to set aside. Make sure you give yourself some additional "free" time to reflect on the conversation you will have. But before you request an appointment, ask yourself the following question: "Can my partner hear me and respond to me at this

time?" If not, consider waiting for a better time. It's okay to spend several days, or even weeks, waiting for the right moment when your partner can truly listen without judgment. Avoid discussing difficult issues when you first wake up, at meals, before going to work or right afterward, and certainly not before going to sleep.

2. *Find the best location.* Agree to meet in a place where the two of you won't be disturbed by telephones, business, or kids. Avoid confrontations in the bedroom; always reserve that room for peacefulness and rest. Consider having your discussion in the most beautiful, quiet place you can find, perhaps in a garden or at your favorite park. Walking while you talk often takes the edge off particularly sensitive issues. If you think your partner may get angry, you might consider meeting in a restaurant or other public place.

* 3. *Open your dialogue with kindness.* Begin any confrontation with an expression of respect by giving a compliment, a small gift, or a tender embrace. This is essential because it lets your partner know you are entering the dispute with a willingness to protect the underlying love that you share. You can even hold each other's hand—this makes it difficult for many people to get defensive. And as far as your anterior cingulate is concerned, kindness is its favorite synaptic treat!

SIX STRATEGIES TO CONTAIN DISRUPTIVE EMOTIONS

* 1. *Avoid provocative language.* No insults. No accusations. No denunciations. No condemnations. No character assassinations. No sarcasm. No swearing. No threats. No yelling. And be careful about using the word "No." Brain scans show that even seeing this word can stimulate a defensive response. Ask your partner to tell you if your communication feels like an attack—you'll be surprised how often the other person will feel defensive by a communication style you're not even aware of.

* 2. *Soften the tone of your voice.* Pay close attention to your voice as you speak. Hostility can be communicated through tone as well as

words. Your communication will be more effective if you speak slowly, with warmth. Soothing, gentle speech goes a long way in getting your message across. And slow down; fast talking makes it more difficult for the other person to take things in.

* 3. *Don't blame.* Instead, talk about yourself: Begin sentences as often as possible with "I feel . . ." rather than "You are . . ." Don't make the mistake of thinking that you "know" what the other person's problem is; you wouldn't like it either. Talk about what's going on inside you, but be specific: Avoid over-generalities and vague descriptions. For example, instead of saying "I feel hurt when I'm criticized," identify the specific event and the feelings they brought up for you at the moment: "When I'm told I'm a slob, it makes me feel bad, but it doesn't help us find a solution. Maybe you can ask me instead to clean up my mess."

4. *Be aware of nonverbal communication.* Feelings and emotions can be communicated nonverbally through facial expressions and body movements. Looking away, frowning, an exaggerated smile, or rolling your eyes can be easily interpreted as anger, hostility, sarcasm, or disbelief. These cues can stimulate an unwanted reaction from your partner, so ask him or her for feedback about any nonverbal message you may send. Work out a system (raising a finger, for example) where each of you can let the other person know when communication is breaking down.

5. *Monitor your anger and recognize the danger zone.* If you find yourself getting more upset as you talk or listen, take a few minutes to calm down. Close your eyes, yawn, take deep breaths, and stretch your arms and legs. Ask your mate for help—the contact of your partner's hand will have

THE REFEREE IN A BOX

One of the best ways to reduce anger in a conversation is to turn on a tape recorder while you talk. Just the presence of the tape is enough to suppress anger, and if it does erupt, you and your partner can review it to see what triggered the emotional reaction.

a soothing effect. Monitor your pulse rate; if it rises, take a twenty-minute break. Shakiness, increased perspiration, clamminess of the skin, muscle tension, a tight jaw, chest pressure, clenched arms or fists, exaggerated facial expressions, and other intimidating body motions are signs that you may soon lose emotional control. Ask your partner to point out any warning signs that you may fail to notice, and then take a break.

6. *Call for a time-out.* If you feel stuck or overwhelmed, call for a five- to thirty-minute break—but don't just walk away or suddenly hang up the phone. An abrupt interruption can upset your partner because you have not given her or him enough time to prepare for your time-out. Take a minute to explain why you need to take a break, and then set a time to resume. During the time-out, practice relaxation and the Compassionate Communication exercise in your imagination. If communication breaks down again, consider rescheduling for the next day, or later in the week. Remember: This is a nonnegotiable rule. Time-outs are essential if either one of you loses the ability to compassionately listen or talk.

SIX STRATEGIES TO IMPROVE COMMUNICATION

1. *Be specific.* Make a list of the issues you want to address, but focus on one problem at a time. If you're talking about a hurtful statement your partner recently made, for example, don't bring up other events from the past. Stay focused on the specific event that occurred. Provide concrete details and complete explanations of the problem and ways in which it can be resolved.

* 2. *Show respect for your partner's point of view.* It is important to acknowledge your partner's perspectives and criticisms, even if you don't agree, for no two people see a problem in exactly the same way. Let your partner know that you appreciate hearing what he or she thinks: "I really want to know what you think and how you feel about this problem." Or: "It really helps me understand you better when you explain your perspective."

3. *Take equal responsibility.* Learn to think about conflicts as a conjoint problem. Rarely is the problem simply "yours" or "mine."

* 4. *Don't monopolize the conversation.* Talk briefly, then let your partner talk. In Compassionate Communication, you deliberately limit your dialogue to thirty-second segments, but in conflict resolution it is sometimes necessary to spend one or two minutes to express a complex idea. But be forewarned, the neurological evidence clearly shows that the other person will have difficulty absorbing the information. If you feel you need more time to talk, ask your partner if he or she would be willing to listen for an extended period. Then make sure you ask for feedback. In specific, ask your partner to summarize what you just said. If he or she can't, assume it was your problem and briefly summarize your points.

5. *Ask for clarification.* If you're unclear about what your partner is saying, ask him or her to restate the issue: "I'm not sure if I really understand. Can you tell me again, or in a different way?" Ask for more specific details so your partner can illuminate the important points. But do so in a compassionate way.

6. *Avoid mind-reading.* Don't presume that you know what your partner thinks or feels. Ask questions instead. Rather than saying, "You always get defensive when we have company over," which is an example of mind-reading, turn it into a question: "When we have company over, do you get defensive?" Questions are less threatening than statements. In fact, you can have a profoundly intimate exchange if you continue to inquire deeply about your partner's feelings and thoughts. But beware of questions that are really criticisms: "Can't you see that you're being defensive?" is in fact a critical "you" statement in disguise.

SIX STRATEGIES FOR FINDING CREATIVE SOLUTIONS

1. *Search for constructive ideas.* Offer specific suggestions and ask your partner for alternative ideas. Write them down on a sheet of

paper and talk about them. Search for solutions that include the other person's ideas in your plan.

2. *Try brainstorming.* Turn on your creativity. Take turns dreaming up the most ridiculous solutions you can: "Let's adopt a pet elephant and bring him with us when we visit my parents." Be silly and use your imagination, writing down every notion that pops up. When you've done this a dozen times, often an idea is touched upon that works. Half of the products that exist in the world (computers, the Internet, cell phones, new car designs, atomic bombs, even the book you're reading right now) came out of brainstorming sessions, and the technique works just as well when solving personal conflicts.

3. *Sit with your problem for a week.* If an effective solution is not found, sit with it for a few days or longer. Don't try to solve it. Instead, use the mindfulness technique of watching your feelings and thoughts. Just be aware that, often by week's end, a new solution will suddenly pop into your mind. If not, ask your friends for some additional ideas and discuss them with your mate.

4. *Implement your plan.* Play with different solutions: "If we did A, then B could happen, possibly leading us to C . . ." When you "test-drive" your plans in this way, using your imagination, you can often identify and resolve unrecognized difficulties before they occur. Work out a step-by-step solution to your problem— who will do what, when, where, and how—and write it down.

* 5. *Close with kindness.* Give supportive remarks ("I really appreciate your willingness to go through this process—I know how hard it is") and give each other a hug, doing everything possible to generate kindness before your conversation ends.

* 6. *Get a progress report.* Keep checking in with your partner over the next few days and weeks, requesting feedback: "How do you feel about our plan?" "Do you think we are making progress?" Then evaluate your problem-solving skills: "What did you like the most about the process, and what did you like least?" "What would you do differently the next time a problem occurs?" And, if the two of you fail to resolve the problem, don't wallow in criticism. Instead, meditate on acceptance and the fact that life is beautiful just as it is.

DON'T WAIT: GET STARTED NOW

Twenty-one strategies—plus the first commandment: *Thou shalt not get angry when you talk.* It's a lot to remember, and you'll certainly need your partner to help you stay on track, but the rewards are great. I recommend that you post these strategies on your refrigerator and review them once a week.

The best time to practice these techniques is *before* a serious problem erupts. If you wait until underlying irritations build up, it may be too late, because the brain literally can become entrapped by its own production of anger. Remember, ongoing resentment can injure the very mechanisms in the brain that control destructive emotions.[30] Fortunately, compassion and forgiveness can heal those damaged structures in the brain.[31]

So by all means, make meditation, compassion, and acceptance a part of your relational and marital life. It will make you feel more connected, closer, optimistic, and more tolerant of the differences that exist.[32] And when you train yourself to be present, attentive, and conscientiously sensitive to your inner states of awareness, as well as to those of your partner, you will enhance the neural functioning of both of your brains.

PAY IT FORWARD

In closing this chapter, I would like to make one further suggestion, inspired by the book and movie *Pay It Forward*.[33] In the novel, a high school teacher gives the following assignment to his class: "Think of an idea for world change, and put it into action." One boy came up with the notion of doing a good deed for three people. In exchange for the help he gave, he asked that each one do a good deed for another three people. He believed that doing something helpful for others would eventually spread throughout the world.

Will such a concept work? I can't say for certain, but similar "pay it forward" strategies have worked. For example, a pastor at a Kansas City Unity Church came up with the idea of encouraging people to go twenty-one days without complaining.[34] You wear a rubber bracelet to remind you of your goal, but each time you complain, you have to put the bracelet on the other wrist and begin your twenty-one days anew. The exercise is essentially an acceptance-and-compassion-based meditation, and it may sound easy, but it takes most people four to eight months to go twenty-one days without complaining. To date, more than five million individuals—including children—have participated in the experiment, and that, by any measure, is a positive step toward undermining irritability in the world.

Mark and I would like to ask you to "pay it forward" with Compassionate Communication. Introduce the exercise to three people, and practice it with them for fifteen minutes. That's just forty-five minutes of your time. Try it with a friend, your kid, or a colleague at work, and then ask him or her to pass it along to three others. At the very least, photocopy the instructions and hand them out to a dozen people, asking them to do the same—a legal, compassionate chain letter, so to speak. If you succeed, you will have introduced a little more relaxation, peace, and intimacy into the world. Or create your own exercise to enhance human kindness and acceptance and share it with as many people as you can.

P.S.: You get extra credit if you teach three people to arouse their precuneus by having them yawn ten times in a row. But be forewarned: It's harder than you might expect to get someone to consciously yawn, even though it's one of the most relaxing things you can do.

IS GOD REAL?

A Personal Reflection

Throughout this book Mark and I have attempted to speak to you with a united voice, liberally substituting *I* and *we* as a literary device. Some of the personal anecdotes were mine, and some were Mark's, but we chose ones that reflected our research and mutual beliefs. In closing, however, I wanted to spend a few pages sharing with you my personal journey and the ways that God has changed my brain.

God, for me, is a very personal concept, one that has preoccupied my thoughts since childhood, and I often just sit back and watch where my mind wants to go. One day, I was thinking about God, and I had the startling revelation that the relationship was strangely analogous to my relationship with my dog. I do not mean this in a literal sense, but more as a metaphor. It occurred to me that when it comes to communication, God is to man as man is to dog.

I played with this idea for a while, contemplating the enormous differences between species. Our lives are thousands of times more complex than that of a dog. We have so many more relationships, so many different ways of behaving and responding to others, and so many different thoughts and feelings when compared to the life of a pet. We understand our pets, or at least we think we do, but I am certain that dogs have little understanding of us. They cannot comprehend what we do at work, how we drive the car, or how we know when and what to feed them. Dogs clearly have emotions and thoughts, but these are extremely limited when compared to the average human being.

Even if dogs could begin to understand what we were thinking, it would be impossible to explain it to them since they have only a minimal understanding of our language. For the most part, all they usually understand are their name and a limited number of commands such as "Sit," "Stay," and "Fetch." We may like to think they understand us, but what they probably hear is "Blah blah blah, *Rover,* blah blah *food.*" There is no way to explain to them why work is difficult, why you feel frustrated with one of your friends, or why you're excited to be going away over the weekend with just your wife. Fortunately, they do understand basic behaviors. They can tell if you like them, or whether they have done something wrong. But this is usually the limit of their understanding of us. Everything else we do is essentially a mystery to them.

My thoughts then turned to our relationship with God. For many people, God is generally regarded as an infinite, all-powerful, and all-knowing being. In contrast, we are finite and fairly weak and limited, even though we think we know more than we actually do. How can we ever hope to comprehend the infinitude that is God? It is probably a million times more difficult than a dog's ability to understand us, but the analogy seems to fit. We cannot understand what God does at work, whether God has any "friends," what God looks like, or what God's personality actually is. These are human characteristics, and they are unlikely to be applicable to God.

Of course, there are those who believe they have received the word of God, either directly or through the scriptures. But even the Bible cannot fully capture the reality of God. Our understanding will always come up short, no matter how perfect the words may be.

To me, it seems rather arrogant to believe that we fully comprehend what God is, or how God wants us to live. Even the Ten Commandments strikes me as a very limited version of what God must want us to understand, and it reminds me of the way we give simplistic commands to our pets. Instead of "Don't bite," "No barking," and "Heel," we are told "Don't lie," "Don't kill," and "Honor the Sabbath."

Dogs often fail to carry out our commands, and people often fail to honor God's commands. Please understand that I am not in any way trying to belittle the holiness of God. I am merely pointing out that as incredible as God is, we can only hope to understand the smallest aspect of God. It's like the story of the blind men and the elephant. Each touches only a small part, and that is what they know. And when it comes to God, we are all partially blind.

This brings me to a final point in this allegorical comparison. Even though dogs can barely understand who we are and what we say, they are extremely compatible with us. If we show them love, they return it tenfold because they faithfully depend on us for their safety. Similarly, if we believe in God, we express great love and devotion and we hope that God will do the same. And even though we can barely understand God, many people faithfully depend on God for ultimate security and strength.

Faith steps in where understanding falls short. As a physician, I might not be certain if a cancer treatment will work, but I sincerely hope that it will. And I have faith that a patient's beliefs in the treatment will improve the odds of recovery. Physicists and astronomers do the same when they consider the universe in its entirety. They realize the incredible limitations of the mind to comprehend its truths, and yet they have faith in their hypotheses and beliefs. Scientists and theologians never give up the search.

Still, how do we ever know if our beliefs about the universe or about God are accurate or true? Wouldn't we have to experience and evaluate every possible perspective? And when it comes to spiritual truths, is there anyone who has fully read the sacred texts of every religion on Earth, or engaged in all of the rituals? Of course not! Even if we could test every religious belief and spiritual practice, each of us has a brain that will interpret the data and experiences in very different ways. There may be a universal or ultimate truth, but I doubt whether the limitations of the human mind will ever allow us to accurately perceive it or find any common ground, especially when it comes to the reality of God.

Admittedly, I find this conclusion somewhat disconcerting, but I try to stay focused on my optimism, believing there may be some way of getting to the answers of the really big questions in life. And as Mark and I have often stated, our faith is our strongest asset.

THE ULTIMATE METAPHOR

In looking at the positive side of our ability to understand our universe, I like to think of God as a metaphor for each person's search for ultimate meaning and truth. Financial and relationship stability may be a major goal for most people, but I believe that within each of us there is a primal drive to reach for something higher. We want to understand *why* we're here and what our purpose *should* be. We want to understand where we came from, and where we will eventually go. And we want to understand what reality actually is. With that understanding, we are then compelled to act in a more intuitively rational way.

Immanuel Kant called this the "categorical imperative," the notion that we are essentially driven by reason to follow an intrinsic moral law. This concept was quickly adapted by other philosophers to reflect a divine voice that guided the human spirit into consciousness. But I see the human spirit as being driven by a *cognitive* imperative, and from the moment we are born, we strive to learn as much as we can about the world. That philosophical drive is biologically embedded in our brain.

Sometimes I think that my dog, Rock, may be a philosopher too, but only to the extent that he wonders where I am. He does not think about what it means to be a dog or how he should act according to the natural "dogginess" inside of him. He does not wonder how he is guided through his life. But I think all human beings ponder what it means to be *human,* and I believe that most people try to act according to the natural humanity inside of them. Yet that humanity is often a challenge to maintain because of the selfish and negative tendencies generated by our brain. Thus, many people, beginning in childhood, conceive the possibility that there is someone, or something, that is guiding them through life in a positive direction. But the human brain does not rest. Instead, it wants to know where God might be. At that moment, the philosopher brain becomes a theologian.

However, we are not born with either a philosophical or theological mind, but only the potential for it. As children, our neural connections are so incomplete that we are utterly dependent on others for direction on what to believe. We're too young to invent or discover God, yet we are surrounded by others who actively proclaim God's existence. For better or worse, we start out life with our parents' and society's religious beliefs.

At this vague stage of awareness, God remains an uncertainty. But the human brain doesn't like ambiguity, so it tries to give God a shape, starting with a face. Why? Because faces tell us about the inner emotional states of others. With this information, the brain can determine if the person or being is a friend or a foe, something that is essential for a young child to grasp. In fact, most children will shy away from a doll that has an angry or fearful expression on its face.

For the first few years of life children can only construct the world using concrete images in the mind, so in all cultures, spiritual concepts are first embedded in familiar objects that exist on the physical plane. And then, at around the age of ten, something happens in the child's brain. The more he or she thinks about God, the more God becomes an abstract or supernatural force. This is because the neural connections that govern abstract reasoning are growing at a stupendously rapid pace.

When adolescence hits, most neural connections are almost complete, and the human brain, having access to greater knowledge and cognition, begins to reevaluate its old beliefs. In this biological quest for independence, the skeptical brain is born, and so most teenagers start to question nearly every aspect of life: values, morals, and especially religious beliefs. Some want to believe, but can't, and those who do believe develop doubts. Some like the idea of a loving, protective God, but most despise the image of an angry, authoritative God.

At this stage of human development, many adolescents are burdened by the emergence of an agnostic brain. For some, God may be real, but distant. For others, science and spirituality may appear incompatible. And for a few, negative religious experiences may cause internal conflict and pain. But for those who remain open-minded, or experiment with different religious rituals, something happens in the brain that can tip the scale toward an acceptance of spiritual truths. For some people, God takes on a living reality. For others, God becomes a metaphor for inner values. And for a few, old notions may give way to a transcendent perception of the world. Such experiences can be so profound that it changes a person's career.

For those who embark on a spiritual journey, God becomes a metaphor reflecting their personal search for truth. It is a journey inward toward self-awareness, salvation, or enlightenment, and for those who are touched by this mystical experience, life becomes more meaningful and rich.

Personally, I believe there has to be an absolute truth about the universe. I don't know what it is, but I am driven to seek it, using science, philosophy, and spirituality as my guide. Mark, however, takes a more skeptical view:

> Personally, I find science more satisfying *and* mysterious than philosophy or theology. So for me, God is a metaphor, not a fact. Yet I consider a person's search for God a noble quest, and the questioning of God's existence is an essential part of that quest. I'm utterly fascinated by the stories people tell me about their spiritual journeys, be they fundamentalists, atheists, agnostics, or mystics. I see truths and values in people's beliefs *and* disbeliefs, so I suppose this makes me a humanist and a pluralist. But even these terms fail to capture who I am or what I really believe. In fact, I dislike all categories and labels because they create arbitrary lines of separation between people.
>
> Personally, it really doesn't matter if one chooses to believe or disbelieve in God. What matters more, at least to me, is how one behaves toward others. If you use your belief in God to practice charity, compassion, and acceptance, that's great. But if you use your beliefs to generate any level of discrimination, then I personally have a problem with that. Still, I have faith in human beings, and I believe that each of us can be held responsible for creating an ethical life that allows us to get along with others, irrespective of one's religious or political beliefs. If we can do a good job at that, everything else will hopefully fall into place.

Unlike Mark, I harbor the hope and feeling that God or some ultimate reality, in whatever form it may take, actually exists. I don't know if my intuition is true, but I am quite comfortable with my uncertainty.

Indeed, it allows me to appreciate both sides of any argument or debate. I have my father to thank for this, for I spent many adolescent hours debating everything under the sun, including God. My father is a true agnostic, with a law degree, so whatever side I took, he could brilliantly argue—and win—the opposing point of view. But he did it with immeasurable love, so I grew up with the belief that every perspective is neither right nor wrong and that both sides reflect valid points of view coming from a limited brain trying to understand a limitless universe.

Mark can attest to this quality of mine, because every time he tries to pin me down to a position, I involuntarily argue the other side. I would even say that it reflects a basic spiritual truth that borders on the mystical, a view that is captured in the following Sufi tale:

> The Mulla Nasrudin [a whimsical character who appears in numerous Middle-Eastern teaching stories] was sitting court one day. A husband and wife came in to settle the matter of who should be in charge of the education of their son. The wife argued that she should be given sole custody, giving many fine reasons to support her view. The Mulla said, "You are absolutely correct!" Then the husband spoke to defend his position. In response, the Mulla again exclaimed, "You are absolutely correct!" Immediately, a cleric in the back of the court stood up and cried out, "Nasrudin, they both can't be right!" To which the Mulla replied, "You are absolutely correct!"

I must admit that I am like the Mulla, and this allows me to see some truth in everything. I only wish that more religious believers felt the same. Atheists, agnostics, and theologians have all made substantial contributions to humanity, morality, and the quest for ultimate truth.

I don't know what that ultimate reality or truth may be, but as far as I can tell, no one does. This brings every one of us back to our inner beliefs and the faith we must rely upon as we strive to comprehend the world. Contemplating God brings us face-to-face with such ultimate issues, while lesser concepts (like money) won't take you to those deeper questions. For some people, science will raise such questions, but I have also argued that science, by itself, is not enough to understand the underlying meanings of life.

DON'T TAKE THE EASY WAY OUT

People often ask me if I believe in God. A simple answer like "Yes" or "No" can't do justice to such a profoundly personal belief, so I used to answer with a rather long-winded discussion about the complex nature of God, science, and religion. Now I respond by asking for that person's definition of God. It's not easy to do, and again, as our surveys have disclosed, nearly everyone's definition is unique. Depending on what the individual says, I might agree with some aspects of their definition while rejecting others. But the moment someone tries to confine the definition of God, I immediately know that it can't be true. One cannot limit what is infinite, and thus science—as wonderful as it is—cannot hope to untangle this knotty problem of God's existence by itself. Science can't find God because we don't even know what to look for. And if we did find God scientifically, we might not even realize it.

Science, however, can help expose some of the ways we think and feel about God, and this can help us broaden our personal beliefs. This is also why I think it becomes necessary to help science along by studying the concept of God on a personal, subjective, and theological level. By combining the goals and perspectives of science and religion, I think we stand a chance at answering the God question. Both science and religion, by themselves, face too many limitations and difficulties. This is the true nature of the journey—challenging ourselves to push our minds and brains to the limit. Then, and only then, can we begin to change the world.

But don't take the easy way out. Work hard to explore the nature of the world, and share your uncertainties with others. If you let your curiosity and compassion play with all the possibilities, then you'll enrich your life, and hopefully improve the world. And by all means, go deeply into your contemplation of God, because you'll eventually discover yourself.

This, for me, is how God and science, when the two come together in the brain, can affect and transform your life.

COMPASSIONATE COMMUNICATION

CDs, Workshops, and Online Research

As described in Chapter 10, Compassionate Communication is a fifteen-minute exercise designed to neurologically undermine defensive behaviors that are inherent in normal dialogue and conversation. When practiced with another person, the technique enhances empathy and social awareness, thus creating an environment in which conflicts can be easily resolved. When practiced daily, it reduces stress, anxiety, and anger while improving the cognitive and emotional functioning of the brain.

In conjunction with Stephanie Newberg, LCSW, who is an assistant director at the Council for Relationships in Philadelphia, we are currently training individuals in the therapeutic use of Compassionate Communication. Under the direction of Andrew Newberg, MD, selected patients are participating in a brain-scan study at the University of Pennsylvania to track the neurological changes associated with the practice. Under the direction of Mark Waldman, Associate Fellow at the University of Pennsylvania's Center for Spirituality and the Mind, we are presenting Compassionate Communication workshops at religious institutions, public schools, and community groups to track improvements in social empathy. Our preliminary evidence also suggests that the exercise helps to deepen a person's spiritual and ethical values.

In Chapter 10 we describe the steps of this unique meditation, but it is easier to do when listening to a recording of the exercise. If you would like to obtain a CD version of Compassionate Communication, you will find ordering information at www.markrobertwaldman.com.

The forty-six-minute CD also includes three lectures on developing intimate dialogues, dealing with anger, and creating effective strategies for handling relationship problems. At the website, you will also find materials to help you track your progress, along with a link that will allow you to participate in an online research project. If you would like Mark to present a Compassionate Communication workshop to your organization, business, school, or religious group, please send an e-mail to markwaldman@sbcglobal.net.

HOW TO PARTICIPATE IN OUR
RESEARCH STUDIES

We invite you to participate in our online Survey of Spiritual Experiences, which we reported on in Chapter 4. You will be helping us gather comprehensive information on the varieties of spiritual and religious experiences that people throughout the world have had, and how they have shaped their personal beliefs. Go to www.neurotheology.net, which will direct you to the survey site (please note: only the suffix *.net* will take you to the correct location, whereas *.org* and *.com* take you to an unrelated site).

We are also continuing to gather data concerning adult drawings and conceptions of God, as we described in Chapter 5. The questionnaire and exercise is fun and simple to do, and takes about 10 to 15 minutes to conduct with any size group. It encourages people to think more deeply about their religious and personal beliefs, and the information we gather helps us to track the diversity of spiritual beliefs among various groups, cultures, and societies. If you would like to facilitate a "Draw a Picture of God" survey with your religious, secular, or community group or school, please e-mail Mark Waldman at markwaldman@sbcglobal.net for instructions and survey forms.

MEDITATION AND MINDFULNESS

Books, CDs, and Resources

Today, "mindfulness" refers to the art and practice of bringing increased awareness to the daily activities in our lives. Originally, mindfulness-based meditations were derived from Eastern spiritual practices, but for the past thirty years they have become secularly integrated into Western medicine and psychotherapy.

Creating a personalized meditation and relaxation program is easy to do, and there are many fine books, CDs, and organizations that can guide you through the beginning steps. The following resources have been helpful to many of our readers, students, and patients.

BOOKS

Introductory meditation books include a variety of exercises ranging in length from five to fifty minutes, and the authors often describe many of the problems that a beginning practitioner encounters. We recommend that you look at three or four different books (or use Amazon.com's "search inside" browser) before purchasing, so you can sample the author's style and orientation. For example, Jon Kabat-Zinn's books and CDs tend to be more secular, focusing primarily on personal awareness and health, whereas books and CDs by Jack Kornfield and Sharon Salzberg reflect elements from Buddhist and Eastern traditions. If you wish to find a meditative practice that reflects your personal spiritual beliefs, many religious institutions can provide you with appropriate recommendations and books. However, it is also very easy to adapt the meditation techniques from one tradition to another without losing any of the beneficial health effects.

For beginners, we recommend Kabat-Zinn's *Full Catastrophe Living* or Kornfield's *A Path with Heart.* Dr. Herbert Benson's original book, *The Relaxation Response,* is also a good resource, and if you are struggling with depression or chronic unhappiness, try *The Mindful Way Through Depression,* by Williams, Teasdale, Segal, and Kabat-Zinn. It includes a CD that guides you through the stress-reduction training program developed at the University of Massachusetts Medical School. The exercises in these books are the ones that have been most thoroughly researched in the scientific community.

For professionals interested in how meditation has been integrated into psychotherapy, see *Mindfulness and Acceptance,* edited by Hayes, Follette, and Linehan, *Mindfulness-Based Cognitive Therapy for Depression,* by Segal, Williams, and Teasdale, and *Mindfulness-Based Treatment Approaches,* edited by Baer.

CDS

Since it is often difficult to "read" your way through a meditation, we recommend that you purchase a few CDs to guide you through the basic forms of practice. Check out Kabat-Zinn's *Guided Mindfulness Meditation* (three CDs), Kornfield's *Meditation for Beginners* (two CDs), or Kornfield's two-CD collection, *Guided Meditation.* Nguyen Anh-Huong's and Thich Nhat Hanh's book, *Walking Meditation,* includes a CD with five guided meditations and an instructional DVD. *Contemplative Prayer,* by Thomas Keating, guides you through the Christian-oriented Centering Prayer, which we described in Chapter 9, and *Meditation for Christians,* by James Finley, will introduce you to a simple contemplative practice that focuses on Jesus and God.

All of these recordings are produced by Sounds True (sounds true.com) and can be ordered online or from bookstores. On your computer, you can also listen to five introductory meditations created by

Diana Winston at the UCLA Mindful Awareness Research Center: http://marc.ucla.edu.

PROGRAMS, CENTERS, AND ACADEMIC RESOURCES

Many academic centers have ongoing research programs focusing on meditation, relaxation, and stress reduction. There are also a growing number of centers throughout the country that specifically integrate spirituality and health—for example, the Center for Spirituality and the Mind at the University of Pennsylvania; the Duke Center for Spirituality, Theology, and Health; the Center for Spirituality and Health at the University of Florida; the Center for Spirituality and Healing at the University of Minnesota; and the Institute for Religion and Health, which is associated with the Texas Medical Center. Many of these centers offer classes and events that can provide support for developing your own spiritually oriented health program.

Mindfulness-based stress reduction courses and therapy programs can be located at universities throughout the world. These centers offer workshops, classes, retreats, and professional training to address a wide variety of health issues. See, for example: University of Pennsylvania Stress Management Program, Stanford Center for Integrative Medicine, Center for Mindfulness at the University of Massachusetts, University of California San Diego Center for Mindfulness, University of Virginia Mindfulness Center, Mindfulness Practice Center at the University of Missouri, Duke University Integrative Medicine, Center for Spirituality and Healing at the University of Minnesota, Center for Health and Meditation at SUNY University Hospital, plus dozens of other university/hospital programs throughout the United States. For further resources, visit the Consortium of Academic Health Centers for Integrative Medicine website at www.imconsortium.org.

ACKNOWLEDGMENTS

All books represent a collaboration of many voices, and this book is no exception, so there are many people we would like to thank—our friends, families, colleagues, students, and patients—for they provide us with the inspiration to do the work we do. We especially want to extend our gratitude to our agent, Jim Levine, and to our editors, Caroline Sutton and Marnie Cochran, who helped shape and refine many parts of this book.

At the University of Pennsylvania, our deepest gratitude goes to the faculty members and staff who have been supportive of our research and work. Special thanks to R. Nick Bryan, Gail Morrison, Abass Alavi, Michael Baime, Ralph Ciampa, John Ehman, Joe Maffei, Nancy Wintering, and Arthur Rubenstein.

At the Council for Relationships, we want to thank Stephanie Newberg and Stephen Treat for their contributions to our Compassionate Communication research. For research assistance at Moorpark College, our thanks to John Baker, Paul Mattson, Janice Daurio, and Jerrold Caplan. For our Compassionate Communication workshop and research assistance, we want to thank Pam and Patrick Geagan, Molly Rockey, Arthur Chang, Maria Flannigan, Jymme Taylor, Sue Rubin, James Lockard, and the many wonderful volunteers and religious leaders who contributed their talents, time, and infectious optimism to making our programs come alive. We also want to express our appreciation for the technical support, feedback, and contributions made by Andrew Davidson, Grace Boyett, Janet and Chris Attwood, and Jeremy Tarcher.

Finally, we wish to thank all of the people who participated in our studies and workshops. You have helped to redefine contemporary American religion and spirituality for the twenty-first century, and without you this book could never have been written.

—ANDY NEWBERG AND MARK WALDMAN

ENDNOTES

CHAPTER 1. WHO CARES ABOUT GOD? (PAGES 3–21)

1. Newberg A, d'Aquili E. *Why God Won't Go Away.* Ballantine, 2002.
2. Newberg A, Waldman M. *Why We Believe What We Believe.* The Free Press, 2006.
3. Newberg A, Waldman M. *Born to Believe.* The Free Press, 2007.

   Newberg AB, Wintering NA, Morgan D, Waldman MR. The measurement of regional cerebral blood flow during glossolalia: a preliminary SPECT study. Psychiatry Res. 2006 Nov 22;148(1):67–71.

   Newberg A, Pourdehnad M, Alavi A, d'Aquili EG. Cerebral blood flow during meditative prayer: preliminary findings and methodological issues. Percept Mot Skills. 2003 Oct;97(2):625–30.

   Newberg AB, Iversen J. The neural basis of the complex mental task of meditation: neurotransmitter and neurochemical considerations. Med Hypotheses. 2003 Aug;61(2):282–91.

   Newberg A, Alavi A, Baime M, Pourdehnad M, Santanna J, d'Aquili E. The measurement of regional cerebral blood flow during the complex cognitive task of meditation: a preliminary SPECT study. Psychiatry Res. 2001 Apr 10;106(2):113–22.

4. The nature of human consciousness is a hotly debated topic in science, and the reality-formation mechanisms of the brain are poorly understood. To draw the hypothesis that two inner maps of reality coexist, Mark and I have combined two important theories—put forth by Nobel laureates Francis

Crick and Eric Kandel—with a recent MRI study I just completed showing how meditation stimulates activity in parts of the striatum. According to Kandel, the striatum plays an essential role in creating contentment and a sense of safety in the brain. Our brain-scan study showed increased striatal dopamine release during meditation, which helps explain the sense of relaxation, happiness, and peacefulness meditators experience. The striatum sends this information on to many parts of the brain, including the thalamus, which orchestrates our senses about the outside world. The brain perceives this as an internal state of reality, but another internal experience of reality is associated with the claustrum, which Crick considers to be the key to how our brain generates consciousness.

Here's where things become interesting: The claustrum is heavily interconnected with most of the cortex, *with the exception of the thalamus.* Kandel believes that the thalamus creates a holistic sense of reality, but obviously this sense of reality is disconnected from the sense of reality created by the striatum. In other words, there are two reality maps created by the brain, one conscious, the other subconscious, and they process incoming data about the world in very different ways. Now, they may somehow come together through other neural circuits, but the evidence collected from neurological disorders strengthens the argument that the brain has very different maps of reality. When you add to this model the discovery we've made that advanced meditators have unusual asymmetric activity in the thalamus, we are drawn to the conclusion that spiritual practices may create independent realms of separate realities, or they may help to unify separate realities that coexist in the brain.

We further hypothesize that thalamic asymmetry may make spiritual concepts feel objectively real, similar to other objects the brain perceives in the world. However, consciousness has so many elements associated with it that no single theory, or neural circuit, may lie at the core of this unique human experience. For example, recent research on the precuneus suggests that this part of the brain plays an essential role in increasing or decreasing our conscious awareness of the world, and as we will explain later in the book, yawning is one way to increase activity in the precuneus. See also:

Kandel E. *In Search of Memory: The Emergence of a New Science of Mind.* Norton, 2006.

Rogan MT, Leon KS, Perez DL, Kandel ER. Distinct neural signatures for safety and danger in the amygdala and striatum of the mouse. Neuron. 2005 Apr 21;46(2):309–20.

Crick FC, Koch C. What is the function of the claustrum? Philos Trans R Soc Lond B Biol Sci. 2005 Jun 29;360(1458):1271–9.

Stevens CF. Consciousness: Crick and the claustrum. Nature. 2005 Jun 23;435(7045):1040–1.

Edelstein LR, Denaro FJ. The claustrum: a historical review of its anatomy, physiology, cytochemistry and functional significance. Cell Mol Biol (Noisy-le-grand). 2004 Sep;50(6):675–702.

Cavanna AE. The precuneus and consciousness. CNS Spectr. 2007 Jul;12(7):545–52.

5. Altemeyer B. *The Authoritarians.* Published online by the University of Manitoba, 2006.

6. Pape R. *Dying to Win.* Gibson Square, 2007.

7. Over the past ten years the Southern Baptist membership has declined from 10 percent of the American population to six percent, while more liberal institutes have rapidly increased their memberships: Lyons L. Tracking U.S. Religious Preferences Over the Decades. Gallup News Service: Religion and Social Trends, May 24, 2005.

8. Carter J. *Our Endangered Values: America's Moral Crisis.* Simon and Schuster, 2005.

Archbishop Desmond Tutu on "God's Word and World Politics." United Nations Lecture Series, March 17, 2004.

9. Luke 6:26–28. New Testament, New International Version.

10. When people have attempted to leave authoritarian religious groups like Jehovah's Witnesses, some have been harassed to the point where they are cut off from family members. The practice, known as shunning, has numerous references in the New Testament. For example:

Thessalonians 3:6: "In the name of the Lord Jesus Christ, we command you, brothers, to keep away from every brother who is idle and does not live according to the teaching you received from us."

Thessalonians 3:14–15: "If anyone does not obey what we say in this letter, take note of that person and have nothing to do with him, that he may be ashamed. Do not regard him as an enemy, but warn him as a brother."

Romans 16:17: "I urge you, brothers, to watch out for those who cause divisions and put obstacles in your way that are contrary to the teaching you have learned. Keep away from them."

John 10–11, NASB: "If anyone comes to you and does not bring this teaching, do not receive him into your house, and do not give him a greeting; for the one who gives him a greeting participates in his evil deeds."

These passages have been used successfully in court to justify the act of shunning. As reported in *New York Times* on June 15, 1987, the Federal District Court ruled that "because the practice of shunning is a part of the faith of the

Jehovah's Witness, we find that the 'free exercise' provision of the United States Constitution . . . precludes [the ostracized individuals] from prevailing [in receiving punitive damages]. The defendants have a constitutionally protected privilege to engage in the practice of shunning."

11. Churches of Religious Science, Unitarian Universalists, Unity Churches, New Age congregations, many Eastern sects, and certain Sufi groups often combine a variety of spiritual philosophies in their teachings.

12. For a comprehensive evaluation and listing of religious extremist groups (as well as racist groups that masquerade as religious with titles like "Christian Identity"), see the Anti-Defamation League's website at http://www.ADL.org and click on the "extremism" link.

13. For an excellent overview of the history of American religion, see Gaustad, E.S. *The Religious History of America*. HarperOne, 2004.

14. Yoshii A, Constantine-Paton M. BDNF induces transport of PSD-95 to dendrites through PI3K-AKT signaling after NMDA receptor activation. Nat Neurosci. 2007 Jun;10(6):702–11.

15. Actually, the lowly sea slug did make it to the *New York Times* list. See: Kandel E. *In Search of Memory: The Emergence of a New Science of Mind*. Norton, 2006.

16. Gaiarsa JL, Caillard O, Ben-Ari Y. Long-term plasticity at GABAergic and glycinergic synapses: mechanisms and functional significance. Trends Neurosci. 2002;25(11): 564–570.

17. The Centre for Synaptic Plasticity provides an excellent online overview of neuroplasticity. The center is a joint venture between the Medical Research Council and the University of Bristol, advancing the understanding of synaptic plasticity in normal human functioning, especially during learning and memory and in certain pathological states such as Alzheimer's disease, memory loss, and epilepsy. For an online list of relevant research papers, see http://www.bris.ac.uk/synaptic/research/res2.html.

18. Polley DB, Kvasnak E, Frostig RD. Naturalisitic experience transforms sensory maps in the adult cortex of caged animals. Nature. 2004;429: 67–71.

Frostig RD. Functional organization and plasticity in the adult rat barrel cortex: moving out-of-the-box. Curr Opin Neurobiol. 2006; 16:1–6.

CHAPTER 2. DO YOU EVEN NEED GOD TO PRAY? (PAGES 22–40)

1. Charlton RA, McIntyre DJ, Howe FA, Morris RG, Markus HS. The relationship between white matter brain metabolites and cognition in normal aging: the GENIE study. Brain Res. 2007 Aug 20;1164:108–16.

2. Damoiseaux JS, Beckmann CF, Arigita EJ, Barkhof F, Scheltens P, Stam CJ, Smith SM, Rombouts SA. Reduced resting-state brain activity in the default network in normal aging. Cereb Cortex. 2007 Dec 5.

Allain P, Kauffmann M, Dubas F, Berrut G, Le Gall D. Executive functioning and normal aging: a study of arithmetic word-problem-solving. Psychol Neuropsychiatr Vieil. 2007 Dec;5(4):315–25.

Charlton RA, Barrick TR, McIntyre DJ, Shen Y, O'Sullivan M, Howe FA, Clark CA, Morris RG, Markus HS. White matter damage on diffusion tensor imaging correlates with age-related cognitive decline. Neurology. 2006 Jan 24;66(2):217–22.

Lamar M, Yousem DM, Resnick SM. Age differences in orbitofrontal activation: an fMRI investigation of delayed match and nonmatch to sample. Neuroimage. 2004 Apr;21(4):1368–76.

MacPherson SE, Phillips LH, Della Sala S. Age, executive function, and social decision making: a dorsolateral prefrontal theory of cognitive aging. Psychol Aging. 2002 Dec;17(4):598–609.

3. There are several versions of "sa-ta-na-ma" meditation, but its most popular form was introduced to Westerners by Yogi Bhajan, who came to the United States in 1969 to teach students a variety of kundalini and tantric yoga techniques drawn from various Eastern practices.

4. Sathyaprabha TN, Satishchandra P, Pradhan C, Sinha S, Kaveri B, Thennarasu K, Murthy BT, Raju TR. Modulation of cardiac autonomic balance with adjuvant yoga therapy in patients with refractory epilepsy. Epilepsy Behav. 2008 Feb;12(2):245–52.

Paul G, Elam B, Verhulst SJ. A longitudinal study of students' perceptions of using deep breathing meditation to reduce testing stresses. Teach Learn Med. 2007 Summer;19(3):287–92.

Brazier A, Mulkins A, Verhoef M. Evaluating a yogic breathing and meditation intervention for individuals living with HIV/AIDS. Am J Health Promot. 2006 Jan–Feb;20(3):192–5.

Mehling WE, Hamel KA, Acree M, Byl N, Hecht FM. Randomized, controlled trial of breath therapy for patients with chronic low-back pain. Altern Ther Health Med. 2005 Jul–Aug;11(4):44–52.

Cohen L, Warneke C, Fouladi RT, Rodriguez MA, Chaoul-Reich A. Psychological adjustment and sleep quality in a randomized trial of the effects of a Tibetan yoga intervention in patients with lymphoma. Cancer. 2004 May 15;100(10):2253–60.

5. Telles S, Raghuraj P, Maharana S, Nagendra HR. Immediate effect of three yoga breathing techniques on performance on a letter-cancellation task. Percept Mot Skills. 2007 Jun;104(3 Pt 2):1289–96.

Naveen KV, Nagarathna R, Nagendra HR, Telles S. Yoga breathing through a particular nostril increases spatial memory scores without lateralized effects. Psychol Rep. 1997 Oct;81(2):555–61.

Jella SA, Shannahoff-Khalsa DS. The effects of unilateral forced nostril breathing on cognitive performance. Int J Neurosci. 1993 Nov;73(1–2):61–8.

6. Sharma H, Datta P, Singh A, Sen S, Bhardwaj NK, Kochupillai V, Singh N. Gene expression profiling in practitioners of Sudarshan Kriya. J Psychosom Res. 2008 Feb;64(2):213–8.

Kochupillai V, Kumar P, Singh D, Aggarwal D, Bhardwaj N, Bhutani M, Das SN. Effect of rhythmic breathing (Sudarshan Kriya and Pranayam) on immune functions and tobacco addiction. Ann NY Acad Sci. 2005 Nov;1056:242–52.

Sharma H, Sen S, Singh A, Bhardwaj NK, Kochupillai V, Singh N. Sudarshan Kriya practitioners exhibit better antioxidant status and lower blood lactate levels. Biol Psychol. 2003 Jul;63(3):281–91.

7. Bernardi L, Sleight P, Bandinelli G, Cencetti S, Fattorini L, Wdowczyc-Szulc J, Lagi A. Effect of rosary prayer and yoga mantras on autonomic cardiovascular rhythms: comparative study. BMJ. 2001 Dec 22–29;323(7327):1446–9.

8. Different kundalini, kriya, and tantric yoga teachers may ascribe different meanings to the same mantra or sound. According to Dr. Dharma Singh Khalsa, *sa* means beginning, infinity, or absolute totality, while other teachers have ascribed the features of wisdom or knowledge. *Ta* symbolizes life, existence, and creativity to one teacher, but symbolizes patience to another. For Khalsa, *na* means death, change, and the transformation of consciousness. *Ma* means rebirth, regeneration, and resurrection to some teachers, while to others it stands for intuitive communication. According Yogi Bhajan, the *ah* part of the sound means "truth manifested" (*The Teachings of Yogi Bhajan,* Dutton, 1977). According to extensive studies by Herbert Benson and others, it appears to make no difference, in terms of the relaxation response, which sound or word you use. What matters is that is symbolizes something positive to the practitioner.

9. Novel and unusual sounds specifically heighten the neural pathways of consciousness. See, for example: Jaaskelainen IP, Ahveninen J, Bonmassar G, Dale AM, Ilmoniemi RJ, Levanen S, Lin FH, May P, Melcher J, Stufflebeam S, Tiitinen H, Belliveau JW. Human posterior auditory cortex gates novel sounds to consciousness. Proc Natl Acad Sci U S A. 2004 Apr 27;101(17):6809–14.

New research also shows that the cerebellum plays a key role in memory, attention, and coordination, and that repetitive activities, like finger tapping, play crucial roles in modulating cerebellar activity. See: Spencer RM, Verstynen T, Brett M, Ivry R. Cerebellar activation during discrete and not continuous timed movements: An fMRI study. Neuroimage. 2007 Jun;36(2):378–87; Akshoomoff NA, Courchesne E, Townsend J. Attention coordination and anticipatory control. Int Rev Neurobiol. 1997;41:575–98.

10. Toyoda H, Zhao MG, Xu H, Wu LJ, Ren M, Zhuo M. Requirement of extracellular signal-regulated kinase/mitogen-activated protein kinase for long-term potentiation in adult mouse anterior cingulate cortex. Mol Pain. 2007 Dec 1;3:36.

Malin EL, Ibrahim DY, Tu JW, McGaugh JL. Involvement of the rostral anterior cingulate cortex in consolidation of inhibitory avoidance memory: interaction with the basolateral amygdala. Neurobiol Learn Mem. 2007 Feb;87(2):295–302.

Fincham JM, Anderson JR. Distinct roles of the anterior cingulate and prefrontal cortex in the acquisition and performance of a cognitive skill. Proc Natl Acad Sci U S A. 2006 Aug 22;103(34):12941–6.

Teixeira CM, Pomedli SR, Maei HR, Kee N, Frankland PW. Involvement of the anterior cingulate cortex in the expression of remote spatial memory. J Neurosci. 2006 Jul 19;26(29):7555–64.

Lenartowicz A, McIntosh AR. The role of anterior cingulate cortex in working memory is shaped by functional connectivity. J Cogn Neurosci. 2005 Jul;17(7):1026–42.

11. Pardo JV, Lee JT, Sheikh SA, Surerus-Johnson C, Shah H, Munch KR, Carlis JV, Lewis SM, Kuskowski MA, Dysken MW. Where the brain grows old: decline in anterior cingulate and medial prefrontal function with normal aging. Neuroimage. 2007 Apr 15;35(3):1231–7.

Otsuka Y, Osaka N, Morishita M, Kondo H, Osaka M. Decreased activation of anterior cingulate cortex in the working memory of the elderly. Neuroreport. 2006 Oct 2;17(14):1479–82.

12. Holmes AJ, Pizzagalli DA. Spatiotemporal dynamics of error processing dysfunctions in major depressive disorder. Arch Gen Psychiatry. 2008 Feb;65(2):179–88.

Foster JA, MacQueen G. Neurobiological factors linking personality traits and major depression. Can J Psychiatry. 2008 Jan;53(1):6–13.

Cardoso EF, Fregni F, Martins Maia F, Boggio PS, Luis Myczkowski M, Coracini K, Lopes Vicira A, Melo LM, Sato JR, Antonio Marcolin M, Rigonatti SP, Cruz AC, Reis Barbosa E, Amaro E. rTMS treatment for depression in Parkinson's disease increases BOLD responses in the left prefrontal cortex. Int J Neuropsychopharmacol. 2007 Aug 21;:1–11

Langguth B, Wiegand R, Kharraz A, Landgrebe M, Marienhagen J, Frick U, Hajak G, Eichhammer P. Pre-treatment anterior cingulate activity as a predictor of antidepressant response to repetitive transcranial magnetic stimulation (rTMS). Neuro Endocrinol Lett. 2007 Oct;28(5):633–8.

Alexopoulos GS, Gunning-Dixon FM, Latoussakis V, Kanellopoulos D, Murphy CF. Anterior cingulate dysfunction in geriatric depression. Int J Geriatr Psychiatry. 2007 Nov 5.

13. Richards BA, Chertkow H, Singh V, Robillard A, Massoud F, Evans AC, Kabani NJ. Patterns of cortical thinning in Alzheimer's disease and frontotemporal dementia. Neurobiol Aging. 2008 Feb 6.

Marshall GA, Monserratt L, Harwood D, Mandelkern M, Cummings JL, Sultzer DL. Positron emission tomography metabolic correlates of apathy in Alzheimer disease. Arch Neurol. 2007 Jul;64(7):1015–20.

Matsui H, Nishinaka K, Oda M, Niikawa H, Komatsu K, Kubori T, Udaka F. Depression in Parkinson's disease. Diffusion tensor imaging study. J Neurol. 2007 Sep;254(9):1170–3.

Mito Y, Yoshida K, Yabe I, Makino K, Tashiro K, Kikuchi S, Sasaki H. Brain SPECT analysis by 3D-SSP and phenotype of Parkinson's disease. J Neurol Sci. 2006 Feb 15;241(1–2):67–72.

Ring HA, Bench CJ, Trimble MR, Brooks DJ, Frackowiak RS, Dolan RJ. Depression in Parkinson's disease. A positron emission study. Br J Psychiatry. 1994 Sep;165(3):333–9.

14. Kaufman Y, Anaki D, Binns M, Freedman M. Cognitive decline in Alzheimer disease: Impact of spirituality, religiosity, and QOL. Neurology. 2007 May 1;68(18):1509–14.

15. Pagnoni G, Cekic M. Age effects on gray matter volume and attentional performance in Zen meditation. Neurobiol Aging. 2007 Oct;28(10):1623–7.

16. Braam AW, Deeg DJ, Poppelaars JL, Beekman AT, van Tilburg W. Prayer and depressive symptoms in a period of secularization: patterns among older adults in the Netherlands. Am J Geriatr Psychiatry. 2007.

17. Obisesan T, Livingston I, Trulear HD, Gillum F. Frequency of attendance at religious services, cardiovascular disease, metabolic risk factors and dietary intake in Americans: an age-stratified exploratory analysis. Int J Psychiatry Med. 2006;36(4):435–48.

Hill TD, Angel JL, Ellison CG, Angel RJ. Religious attendance and mortality: an 8-year follow-up of older Mexican Americans. J Gerontol B Psychol Sci Soc Sci. 2005 Mar;60(2):S102–9.

Musick MA, House JS, Williams DR. Attendance at religious services and mortality in a national sample. J Health Soc Behav. 2004 Jun;45(2):198–213.

18. Ai AL, Peterson C, Tice TN, Huang B, Rodgers W, Bolling SF. The influence of prayer coping on mental health among cardiac surgery patients: the role of optimism and acute distress. J Health Psychol. 2007 Jul;12(4):580–96.

Jantos M, Kiat H. Prayer as medicine: how much have we learned? Med J Aust. 2007 May 21;186(10 Suppl):S51–3.

Rew L, Wong YJ, Sternglanz RW. The relationship between prayer, health behaviors, and protective resources in school-age children. Issues Compr Pediatr Nurs. 2004 Oct–Dec;27(4):245–55.

19. Pardo JV, Lee JT, Sheikh SA, Surerus-Johnson C, Shah H, Munch KR, Carlis JV, Lewis SM, Kuskowski MA, Dysken MW. Where the brain grows old: decline in anterior cingulate and medial prefrontal function with normal aging. Neuroimage. 2007 Apr 15;35(3):1231–7.

20. Riva G, Mantovani F, Gaggioli A. Presence and rehabilitation: toward second-generation virtual reality applications in neuropsychology. J Neuroeng Rehabil. 2004 Dec 8;1(1):9.

21. Csíkszentmihályi M. *Flow: The Psychology of Optimal Experience.* Harper and Row, 1990.

22. Chang C, Crottaz-Herbette S, Menon V. Temporal dynamics of basal ganglia response and connectivity during verbal working memory. Neuroimage. 2007 Feb 1;34(3):1253–69.

Tinaz S, Schendan HE, Schon K, Stern CE. Evidence for the importance of basal ganglia output nuclei in semantic event sequencing: an fMRI study. Brain Res. 2006 Jan 5;1067(1):239–49.

Nieoullon A. Dopamine and the regulation of cognition and attention. Prog Neurobiol. 2002 May;67(1):53–83.

Menon V, Anagnoson RT, Glover GH, Pfefferbaum A. Basal ganglia involvement in memory-guided movement sequencing. Neuroreport. 2000 Nov 9;11(16):3641–5.

23. Raz N, Rodrigue KM, Kennedy KM, Head D, Gunning-Dixon F, Acker JD. Differential aging of the human striatum: longitudinal evidence. AJNR Am J Neuroradiol. 2003 Oct;24(9):1849–56.

24. Shirai W, Ito S, Hattori T. Linear T2 Hyperintensity along the Medial Margin of the Globus Pallidus in Patients with Machado-Joseph Disease and Parkinson Disease, and in Healthy Subjects. AJNR Am J Neuroradiol. 2007 Oct 3.

25. Baym CL, Corbett BA, Wright SB, Bunge SA. Neural correlates of tic severity and cognitive control in children with Tourette syndrome. Brain. 2007 Dec 3.

Lewis SJ, Caldwell MA, Barker RA. Modern therapeutic approaches in Parkinson's disease. Expert Rev Mol Med. 2003 Mar 28;5(10):1–20.

Rosenblatt A, Leroi I. Neuropsychiatry of Huntington's disease and other basal ganglia disorders. Psychosomatics. 2000 Jan–Feb;41(1):24–30.

26. Pagnoni G, Cekic M. Age effects on gray matter volume and attentional per-formance in Zen meditation. Neurobiol Aging. 2007 Oct;28(10):1623–7.

Doraiswamy PM, Xiong GL. Does meditation enhance cognition and brain longevity? Ann NY Acad Sci. 2007 Sep 28.

27. The Trails test (Reitan and Wolfson 1985).

28. Bottiroli S, Cavallini E, Vecchi T. Long-term effects of memory training in the elderly: A longitudinal study. Arch Gerontol Geriatr. 2007 Oct 11.

29. Paul G, Elam B, Verhulst SJ. A longitudinal study of students' perceptions of using deep breathing meditation to reduce testing stresses. Teach Learn Med. 2007 Summer;19(3):287–92.

30. Barnes VA, Bauza LB, Treiber FA. Impact of stress reduction on negative school behavior in adolescents. Health Qual Life Outcomes. 2003 Apr 23;1(1):10.

See also: Rosaen C, Benn R. The experience of transcendental meditation in middle school students: a qualitative report. Explore (NY). 2006 Sep–Oct;2(5):422–5.

31. Wall RB. Tai Chi and mindfulness-based stress reduction in a Boston Public Middle School. J Pediatr Health Care. 2005 Jul–Aug;19(4):230–7.

32. Manjunath NK, Telles S. Spatial and verbal memory test scores following yoga and fine arts camps for school children. Indian J Physiol Pharmacol. 2004 Jul;48(3):353–6.

33. Sreenivasan KK, Jha AP. Selective attention supports working memory maintenance by modulating perceptual processing of distractors. J Cogn Neurosci. 2007 Jan;19(1):32–41.

34. Chang C, Crottaz-Herbette S, Menon V. Temporal dynamics of basal gan-glia response and connectivity during verbal working memory. Neuroimage. 2007 Feb 1;34(3):1253–69.

35. Nobel Laureate Eric Kandel wrote a simple autobiographical book, *In Search of Memory: The Emergence of a New Science of Mind* (Norton, 2006), that explains this neurological process.

36. Furukawa TA, Watanabe N, Omori IM, Churchill R. Can pill placebo aug-ment cognitive-behavior therapy for panic disorder? BMC Psychiatry. 2007 Dec 20;7:73.

See also: Harrington, A. (ed.). *The Placebo Effect.* Harvard University Press, 1999.

37. Bormann JE, Smith TL, Shively M, Dellefield ME, Gifford AL. Self-monitoring of a stress reduction technique using wrist-worn counters. J Healthcare Qual. 2007 Jan–Feb;29(1):45–52.

Bormann JE, Becker S, Gershwin M, Kelly A, Pada L, Smith TL, Gifford AL. Relationship of frequent mantram repetition to emotional and spiritual well-being in healthcare workers. J Contin Educ Nurs. 2006 Sep–Oct;37(5): 218–24.

Bormann JE, Smith TL, Becker S, Gershwin M, Pada L, Grudzinski AH, Nurmi EA. Efficacy of frequent mantram repetition on stress, quality of life, and spiritual well-being in veterans: a pilot study. J Holist Nurs. 2005 Dec;23(4):395–414.

38. Spencer RM, Verstynen T, Brett M, Ivry R. Cerebellar activation during discrete and not continuous timed movements: An fMRI study. Neuroimage. 2007 Jun;36(2):378–87.

Akshoomoff NA, Courchesne E, Townsend J. Attention coordination and anticipatory control. Int Rev Neurobiol. 1997;41:575–98.

39. Ranganathan VK, Siemionow V, Sahgal V, Liu JZ, Yue GH. Skilled finger movement exercise improves hand function. J Gerontol A Biol Sci Med Sci. 2001 Aug;56(8):M518–22.

40. Grant MD, Brody JA. Musical experience and dementia. Hypothesis. Aging Clin Exp Res. 2004 Oct;16(5):403–5.

41. Schlaug G, Norton A, Overy K, Winner E. Effects of music training on the child's brain and cognitive development. Ann N Y Acad Sci. 2005 Dec;1060: 219–30.

42. Baumgartner T, Esslen M, Jancke L. From emotion perception to emotion experience: emotions evoked by pictures and classical music. Int J Psychophysiol. 2006 Apr;60(1):34–43.

43. Blood AJ, Zatorre RJ. Intensely pleasurable responses to music correlate with activity in brain regions implicated in reward and emotion. Proc Natl Acad Sci U S A. 2001 Sep 25;98(20):11818–23.

Baumgartner T, Lutz K, Schmidt CF, Jancke L. The emotional power of music: how music enhances the feeling of affective pictures. Brain Res. 2006 Feb 23;1075(1):151–64.

44. Mitterschiffthaler MT, Fu CH, Dalton JA, Andrew CM, Williams SC. A functional MRI study of happy and sad affective states induced by classical music. Hum Brain Mapp. 2007 Feb 8;

45. Perry DW, Zatorre RJ, Petrides M, Alivisatos B, Meyer E, Evans AC. Localization of cerebral activity during simple singing. Neuroreport. 1999 Dec 16;10(18):3979–84.

46. Kalueff AV. Neurobiology of memory and anxiety: from genes to behavior. Neural Plast. 2007;:78171.

Wall PM, Messier C. Concurrent modulation of anxiety and memory. Behavioural Brain Research. 2000;109(2):229–241.

47. Peavy GM, Lange KL, Salmon DP, Patterson TL, Goldman S, Gamst AC, Mills PJ, Khandrika S, Galasko D. The Effects of Prolonged Stress and

APOE Genotype on Memory and Cortisol in Older Adults. Biol Psychiatry. 2007 Jun 1.

48. U.S. Government public domain.

49. Brown SM, Henning S, Wellman CL. Mild, short-term stress alters dendritic morphology in rat medial prefrontal cortex. Cereb Cortex. 2005 Nov;15(11):1714–22.

Cook SC, Wellman CL. Chronic stress alters dendritic morphology in rat medial prefrontal cortex. J Neurobiol. 2004 Aug;60(2):236–48.

Wellman CL. Dendritic reorganization in pyramidal neurons in medial prefrontal cortex after chronic corticosterone administration. J Neurobiol. 2001 Nov 15;49(3):245–53.

50. Brown SM, Henning S, Wellman CL. Mild, short-term stress alters dendritic morphology in rat medial prefrontal cortex. Cereb Cortex. 2005 Nov;15(11):1714–22.

51. Radley JJ, Rocher AB, Janssen WG, Hof PR, McEwen BS, Morrison JH. Reversibility of apical dendritic retraction in the rat medial prefrontal cortex following repeated stress. Exp Neurol. 2005 Nov;196(1):199–203.

52. Radley JJ, Rocher AB, Miller M, Janssen WG, Liston C, Hof PR, McEwen BS, Morrison JH. Repeated stress induces dendritic spine loss in the rat medial prefrontal cortex. Cereb Cortex. 2006 Mar;16(3):313–20.

53. Uylings HB, de Brabander JM. Neuronal changes in normal human aging and Alzheimer's disease. Brain Cogn. 2002;49:268–76.

de Brabander JM, Kramers RJ, Uylings HB. Layer-specific dendritic regression of pyramidal cells with ageing in the human prefrontal cortex. Eur J Neurosci. 1998;10:1261–9.

54. Dickstein DL, Kabaso D, Rocher AB, Luebke JI, Wearne SL, Hof PR. Changes in the structural complexity of the aged brain. Aging Cell. 2007 Jun;6(3):275–84.

55. Buell SJ, Coleman PD. Dendritic growth in the aged human brain and failure of growth in senile dementia. Science. 1979 Nov 16;206(4420):854–6.

56. The brain-scan technology we use to view neural activity during meditation measures cerebral blood flow, and this is associated with synaptic firing between neurons.

Jueptner M, Weiller C. Review: Does measurement of regional cerebral blood flow reflect synaptic activity? Implications for PET and fMRI. Neuroimage. 1995 Jun;2(2):148–56.

Wong TP, Marchese G, Casu MA, Ribeiro-da-Silva A, Cuello AC, De Koninck Y. Loss of presynaptic and postsynaptic structures is accompanied by compensatory increase in action potential-dependent synaptic input to layer

V neocortical pyramidal neurons in aged rats. J Neurosci. 2000 Nov 15;20(22):8596–606.

57. Carretti B, Borella E, De Beni R. Does strategic memory training improve the working memory performance of younger and older adults? Exp Psychol. 2007;54(4):311–20.

Bottiroli S, Cavallini E, Vecchi T. Long-term effects of memory training in the elderly: A longitudinal study. Arch Gerontol Geriatr. 2007 Oct 11.

O'Hara R, Brooks JO 3rd, Friedman L, Schroder CM, Morgan KS, Kraemer HC. Long-term effects of mnemonic training in community-dwelling older adults. J Psychiatr Res. 2007 Oct;41(7):585–90.

Willis SL, Tennstedt SL, Marsiske M, Ball K, Elias J, Koepke KM, Morris JN, Rebok GW, Unverzagt FW, Stoddard AM, Wright E; ACTIVE Study Group. Long-term effects of cognitive training on everyday functional outcomes in older adults. JAMA. 2006 Dec 20;296(23):2805–14.

Cheng ST, Chan AC, Yu EC. An exploratory study of the effect of mahjong on the cognitive functioning of persons with dementia. Int J Geriatr Psychiatry. 2006 Jul;21(7):611–7.

Ball K, Berch DB, Helmers KF, Jobe JB, Leveck MD, Marsiske M, Morris JN, Rebok GW, Smith DM, Tennstedt SL, Unverzagt FW, Willis SL. Advanced Cognitive Training for Independent and Vital Elderly Study Group. Effects of cognitive training interventions with older adults: a randomized controlled trial. JAMA. 2002 Nov 13;288(18):2271–81.

Brooks JO 3rd, Friedman L, Pearman AM, Gray C, Yesavage JA. Mnemonic training in older adults: effects of age, length of training, and type of cognitive pretraining. Int Psychogeriatr. 1999 Mar;11(1):75–84.

58. Derwinger A, Stigsdotter Neely A, Backman L. Design your own memory strategies! Self-generated strategy training versus mnemonic training in old age: an 8-month follow-up. Neuropsychol Rehabil. 2005 Mar;15(1):37–54.

Derwinger A, Stigsdotter Neely A, MacDonald S, Bäckman L. Forgetting numbers in old age: strategy and learning speed matter. Gerontology. 2005 Jul–Aug;51(4):277–84.

59. Small GW, Silverman DH, Siddarth P, Ercoli LM, Miller KJ, Lavretsky H, Wright BC, Bookheimer SY, Barrio JR, Phelps ME. Effects of a 14-day healthy longevity lifestyle program on cognition and brain function. Am J Geriatr Psychiatry. 2006 Jun;14(6):538–45.

60. Finucane A, Mercer SW. An exploratory mixed methods study of the acceptability and effectiveness of Mindfulness-Based Cognitive Therapy for patients with active depression and anxiety in primary care. BMC Psychiatry. 2006 Apr 7;6:14.

See also: Mark J, Williams G, Teasdale JD, Segal ZV, Kabat-Zinn J. *The Mindful Way Through Depression: Freeing Yourself from Chronic Unhappiness.* Guilford Press, 2007; and Segal ZV, Mark J, Williams G, Teasdale JD. *Mindfulness-Based Cognitive Therapy for Depression: A New Approach to Preventing Relapse.* Guilford Press, 2001.

61. Ritchie K, Carrière I, de Mendonca A, Portet F, Dartigues JF, Rouaud O, Barberger-Gateau P, Ancelin ML. The neuroprotective effects of caffeine: a prospective population study (the Three City Study). Neurology. 2007 Aug 7;69(6):536–45.

Van Gelder BM, Buijsse B, Tijhuis M, Kalmijn S, Giampaoli S, Nissinen A, Kromhout D. Coffee consumption is inversely associated with cognitive decline in elderly European men: the FINE Study. Eur J Clin Nutr. 2007 Feb;61(2):226–32.

Arendash GW, Schleif W, Rezai-Zadeh K, Jackson EK, Zacharia LC, Cracchiolo JR, Shippy D, Tan J. Caffeine protects Alzheimer's mice against cognitive impairment and reduces brain beta-amyloid production. Neuroscience. 2006 Nov 3;142(4):941–52.

Haskell CF, Kennedy DO, Wesnes KA, Scholey AB. Cognitive and mood improvements of caffeine in habitual consumers and habitual non-consumers of caffeine. Psychopharmacology (Berl). 2005 Jun;179(4):813–25.

Beaumont M, Batejat D, Pierard C, Coste O, Doireau P, Van Beers P, Chauffard F, Chassard D, Enslen M, Denis JB, Lagarde D. Slow release caffeine and prolonged (64-h) continuous wakefulness: effects on vigilance and cognitive performance. J Sleep Res. 2001 Dec;10(4):265–76.

62. Abel EL, Hendrix SO, McNeeley SG, Johnson KC, Rosenberg CA, Mossavar-Rahmani Y, Vitolins M, Kruger M. Daily coffee consumption and prevalence of nonmelanoma skin cancer in Caucasian women. Eur J Cancer Prev. 2007 Oct;16(5):446–452.

Hu G, Bidel S, Jousilahti P, Antikainen R, Tuomilehto J. Coffee and tea consumption and the risk of Parkinson's disease. Mov Disord. 2007 Nov 15;22(15):2242–8.

Choi HK, Willett W, Curhan G. Coffee consumption and risk of incident gout in men: a prospective study. Arthritis Rheum. 2007 Jun;56(6):2049–55.

Greenberg JA, Axen KV, Schnoll R, Boozer CN. Coffee, tea and diabetes: the role of weight loss and caffeine. Int J Obes (Lond). 2005 Sep;29(9):1121–9.

Michels KB, Willett WC, Fuchs CS, Giovannucci E. Coffee, tea, and caffeine consumption and incidence of colon and rectal cancer. J Natl Cancer Inst. 2005 Feb 16;97(4):282–92.

63. Lieberman HR, Tharion WJ, Shukitt-Hale B, Speckman KL, Tulley R. Effects of caffeine, sleep loss, and stress on cognitive performance and mood

during U.S. Navy SEAL training. Sea-Air-Land. Psychopharmacology (Berl). 2002 Nov;164(3):250–61.

See also: Tharion WJ, Shukitt-Hale B, Lieberman HR. Caffeine effects on marksmanship during high-stress military training with 72 hour sleep deprivation. Aviat Space Environ Med. 2003 Apr;74(4):309–14.

64. Ganmaa D, Willett WC, Li TY, Feskanich D, van Dam RM, Lopez-Garcia E, Hunter DJ, Holmes MD. Coffee, tea, caffeine and risk of breast cancer: a 22-year follow-up. Int J Cancer. 2008 May 1;122(9):2071–6.

Happonen P, Läärä E, Hiltunen L, Luukinen H. Coffee consumption and mortality in a 14-year follow-up of an elderly northern Finnish population. Br J Nutr. 2007 Dec 6;1–8.

Hino A, Adachi H, Enomoto M, Furuki K, Shigetoh Y, Ohtsuka M, Kumagae S, Hirai Y, Jalaldin A, Satoh A, Imaizumi T. Habitual coffee but not green tea consumption is inversely associated with metabolic syndrome: an epidemiological study in a general Japanese population. Diabetes Res Clin Pract. 2007 Jun;76(3):383–9.

Lopez-Garcia E, van Dam RM, Qi L, Hu FB. Coffee consumption and markers of inflammation and endothelial dysfunction in healthy and diabetic women. Am J Clin Nutr. 2006 Oct;84(4):888–93.

Iwai N, Ohshiro H, Kurozawa Y, Hosoda T, Morita H, Funakawa K, Okamoto M, Nose T. Relationship between coffee and green tea consumption and all-cause mortality in a cohort of a rural Japanese population. J Epidemiol. 2002 May;12(3):191–8.

65. Hering-Hanit R, Gadoth N. Caffeine-induced headache in children and adolescents. Cephalalgia. 2003 Jun;23(5):332–5.

Bic Z, Blix GG, Hopp HP, Leslie FM. In search of the ideal treatment for migraine headache. Med Hypotheses. 1998 Jan;50(1):1–7.

66. http://www.hsph.harvard.edu/nutritionsource/calcium.html.

67. Fujiyoshi N, Yoshioka T, Morimoto F, Suzuki Y, Sueyoshi K, Shibuya M, Shimazaki J. A case of caffeine poisoning, survived by percutaneous cardiopulmonary support. Chudoku Kenkyu. 2008 Jan;21(1):69–73.

Kerrigan S, Lindsey T. Fatal caffeine overdose: two case reports. Forensic Sci Int. 2005 Oct 4;153(1):67–9.

Holmgren P, Nordén-Pettersson L, Ahlner J. Caffeine fatalities—four case reports. Forensic Sci Int. 2004 Jan 6;139(1):71–3.

68. Haskell CF, Kennedy DO, Milne AL, Wesnes KA, Scholey AB. The effects of L-theanine, caffeine and their combination on cognition and mood. Biol Psychol. 2008 Feb;77(2):113–22.

Kuriyama S, Hozawa A, Ohmori K, Shimazu T, Matsui T, Ebihara S, Awata S, Nagatomi R, Arai H, Tsuji I. Green tea consumption and cognitive function: a cross-sectional study from the Tsurugaya Project 1. Am J Clin Nutr. 2006 Feb;83(2):355–61.

Hindmarch I, Rigney U, Stanley N, Quinlan P, Rycroft J, Lane J. A naturalistic investigation of the effects of day-long consumption of tea, coffee and water on alertness, sleep onset and sleep quality. Psychopharmacology (Berl). 2000 Apr;149(3):203–16.

69. Rogers PJ, Smith JE, Heatherley SV, Pleydell-Pearce CW. Time for tea: mood, blood pressure and cognitive performance effects of caffeine and theanine administered alone and together. Psychopharmacology (Berl). 2008 Jan;195(4):569–77.

70. Bryan J. Psychological effects of dietary components of tea: caffeine and L-theanine. Nutr Rev. 2008 Feb;66(2):82–90.

71. Petri NM, Dropulic N, Kardum G. Effects of voluntary fluid intake deprivation on mental and psychomotor performance. Croat Med J. 2006 Dec;47(6):855–61.

Wilson MM, Morley JE. Impaired cognitive function and mental performance in mild dehydration. Eur J Clin Nutr. 2003;57(Suppl 2):S24–9.

72. Adam GE, Carter R 3rd, Cheuvront SN, Merullo DJ, Castellani JW, Lieberman HR, Sawka MN. Hydration effects on cognitive performance during military tasks in temperate and cold environments. Physiol Behav. 2007 Nov 28.

Lieberman HR. Hydration and cognition: a critical review and recommendations for future research. J Am Coll Nutr. 2007 Oct;26(5 Suppl):555S–561S.

Patel AV, Mihalik JP, Notebaert AJ, Guskiewicz KM, Prentice WE. Neuropsychological performance, postural stability, and symptoms after dehydration. J Athl Train. 2007 Jan–Mar;42(1):66–75.

Szinnai G, Schachinger H, Arnaud MJ, Linder L, Keller U. Effect of water deprivation on cognitive-motor performance in healthy men and women. Am J Physiol Regul Integr Comp Physiol. 2005 Jul;289(1):R275–80.

73. Morgan J, Banerjee R. Post-event processing and autobiographical memory in social anxiety: the influence of negative feedback and rumination. J Anxiety Disord. 2008 Jan 9.

Kocovski NL, Endler NS, Rector NA, Flett GL. Ruminative coping and post-event processing in social anxiety. Behav Res Ther. 2005 Aug;43(8):971–84.

Lyubomirsky S, Caldwell ND, Nolen-Hoeksema S. Effects of ruminative and distracting responses to depressed mood on retrieval of autobiographical memories. J Pers Soc Psychol. 1998 Jul;75(1):166–77.

CHAPTER 3. WHAT DOES GOD DO TO YOUR BRAIN? (PAGES 41–63)

1. For a comprehensive list of studies relating the health benefits of church attendance and spirituality, see http://www.dukespiritualityandhealth.org/resources/pdfs/Research%20-%20latest%20outside%20Duke.pdf.

2. Luu P, Posner MI. Anterior cingulate cortex regulation of sympathetic activity. Brain. 2003 Oct;126(Pt 10):2119–20.

   Critchley HD, Mathias CJ, Josephs O, O'Doherty J, Zanini S, Dewar BK, Cipolotti L, Shallice T, Dolan RJ. Human cingulate cortex and autonomic control: converging neuroimaging and clinical evidence. Brain. 2003 Oct;126(Pt 10):2139–52.

   Paus T. Primate anterior cingulate cortex: where motor control, drive and cognition interface. Nat Rev Neurosci. 2001 Jun;2(6):417–24.

   The anterior cingulate cortex lends a hand in response selection. Nat Neurosci. 1999 Oct;2(10):853–4.

3. Deckro GR, Ballinger KM, Hoyt M, Wilcher M, Dusek J, Myers P, Greenberg B, Rosenthal DS, Benson H. The evaluation of a mind/body intervention to reduce psychological distress and perceived stress in college students. J Am Coll Health. 2002 May;50(6):281–7.

   Stefano GB, Fricchione GL, Slingsby BT, Benson H. The placebo effect and the relaxation response: neural processes and their coupling to constitutive nitric oxide. Brain Res Rev, 2001;35:1–19.

   Goodale IL, Domar AD, Benson H. Alleviation of premenstrual syndrome symptoms with the relaxation response. Obstet Gynecol. 1990 Apr;75(4):649–55.

   Leserman J, Stuart EM, Mamish ME, Benson H. The efficacy of the relaxation response in preparing for cardiac surgery. Behav Med. 1989 Fall;15(3):111–7.

   Kass JD, Friedman R, Leserman J, Zuttermeister PC, Benson H. Health outcome and a new index of spiritual experience. J Sci Stud Religion 1991;30:203–11.

   Benson H, Lehmann JW, Malhotra MS, Goldman RF, Hopkins J, Epstein MD. Body temperature changes during the practice of g tum-mo (heat) yoga. Nature 1982;295:234–6.

   Hoffman JW, Benson H, Arns PA, Stainbrook GL, Landsberg L, Young JB, Gill A. Reduced sympathetic nervous system responsivity associated with the relaxation response. Science 1982;215:190–2.

   Benson H, McCallie DP Jr. Angina pectoris and the placebo effect. N Engl J Med 1979;300:1424–9.

Beary JF, Benson H. A simple psychophysiologic technique which elicits the hypometabolic changes of the relaxation response. Psychosom Med 1974;36: 115–20.

Benson H, Beary JF, Carol MP. The relaxation response. Psychiatry 1974;37: 37–46.

Wallace RK, Benson H, Wilson AF. A wakeful hypometabolic physiologic state. Am J Physiol 1971;221:795–9.

4. Galvin JA, Benson H, Deckro GR, Fricchione GL, Dusek JA. The relaxation response: reducing stress and improving cognition in healthy aging adults. Complement Ther Clin Pract. 2006 Aug;12(3):186–91.

5. Roof W. *A Generation of Seekers.* HarperCollins, 1993.

6. The twenty references to meditation, from the King James version of the *Bible,* can be found in: Genesis 24:63, Joshua 1:8, Psalm 1:2, Psalm 5:1, Psalm 19:14, Psalm 49:3, Psalm 63:6, Psalm 77:12, Psalm 104:34, Psalm 119:15, Psalm 119:23, Psalm 119:48, Psalm 119:78, Psalm 119:97, Psalm 119:99, Psalm 119:148, Psalm 143:5, Isaiah 33:18, Luke 21:14, and 1 Timothy 4:15.

7. For a comprehensive overview of Christian meditative practices, see the online *Catholic Encyclopedia:* http://www.newadvent.org/cathen/index.html.

8. The author of this Christian mystical text is unknown, although it has been attributed to an English cloistered monk living in the fourteenth century. The excerpt cited here is from Evelyn Underwood's adaptation, *A Book of Contemplation Which Is Called the Cloud of Unknowing, In Which a Soul is One with God,* edited from a British Museum manuscript and published by John M. Watkins in 1922.

9. Keating T. *Intimacy With God.* New York: Crossroad Publishing Co, 1994.

10. For a complete history and description of the Centering Prayer, see http://www.centeringprayer.com.

11. Newberg A, Pourdehnad M, Alavi A, d'Aquili EG. Cerebral blood flow during meditative prayer: preliminary findings and methodological issues. Percept Mot Skills. 2003 Oct;97(2):625–30.

12. For a complete description of the similarities, see Newberg, A.; Waldman, M. *Born to Believe.* The Free Press, 2007.

13. Gödel K. "Ontological Proof," in *Collected Works: Unpublished Essays & Lectures* (vol. III), Oxford University Press, 1995; 403–4.

14. Creswell JD, Way BM, Eisenberger NI, Lieberman MD. Neural correlates of dispositional mindfulness during affect labeling. Psychosom Med. 2007 Jul–Aug;69(6):560–5.

15. Newberg A, Waldman M. *Born to Believe.* The Free Press, 2007.

16. V. S. Ramachandran and Michael Persinger are the two leading researchers who argue that religious and paranormal experiences might be related to temporal lobe dysfunction, but only a few rare examples have been found.

The majority of people who have religious experiences show no signs of neural dysfunction. See: Persinger MA, Valliant PM. Temporal lobe signs and reports of subjective paranormal experiences in a normal population: a replication. Percept Mot Skills 1985;60(3): 903–9; and Ramachandran VS, Blakeslee S. *Phantoms in the Brain.* New York: William Morrow, 1998.

17. Shalom DB, Poeppel D. Functional anatomic models of language: assembling the pieces. Neuroscientist. 2008 Feb;14(1):119–27.

18. Hölzel BK, Ott U, Hempel H, Hackl A, Wolf K, Stark R, Vaitl D. Differential engagement of anterior cingulate and adjacent medial frontal cortex in adept meditators and non-meditators. Neurosci Lett. 2007 Jun 21;421(1):16–21.

   Critchley HD, Melmed RN, Featherstone E, Mathias CJ, Dolan RJ. Brain activity during biofeedback relaxation: a functional neuroimaging investigation. Brain. 2001 May;124(Pt 5):1003–12.

   Lazar SW, Bush G, Gollub RL, Fricchione GL, Khalsa G, Benson H. Functional brain mapping of the relaxation response and meditation. Neuroreport. 2000 May 15;11(7):1581–5.

19. Pujol J, López A, Deus J, et al. Anatomical variability of the anterior cingulate gyrus and basic dimensions of human personality. Neuroimage 2002; 15: 847–855.

20. Gündel H, López-Sala A, Ceballos-Baumann AO, Deus J, Cardoner N, Marten-Mittag B, Soriano-Mas C, Pujol J. Alexithymia correlates with the size of the right anterior cingulate. Psychosom Med. 2004 Jan–Feb;66(1):132–40.

21. Berthoz S, Artiges E, Van De Moortele PF, Poline JB, Rouquette S, Consoli SM, Martinot JL. Effect of impaired recognition and expression of emotions on frontocingulate cortices: an fMRI study of men with alexithymia. Am J Psychiatry. 2002 Jun;159(6):961–7.

22. Lamm C, Batson CD, Decety J. The neural substrate of human empathy: effects of perspective-taking and cognitive appraisal. J Cogn Neurosci. 2007 Jan;19(1):42–58.

   Singer T. The neuronal basis of empathy and fairness. Novartis Found Symp. 2007;278:20–30.

   Seitz RJ, Nickel J, Azari NP. Functional modularity of the medial prefrontal cortex: involvement in human empathy. Neuropsychology. 2006 Nov;20(6): 743–51.

23. Milad MR, Quirk GJ, Pitman RK, Orr SP, Fischl B, Rauch SL. A role for the human dorsal anterior cingulate cortex in fear expression. Biol Psychiatry. 2007 Aug 16.

   Rudebeck PH, Walton ME, Millette BH, Shirley E, Rushworth MF, Bannerman DM. Distinct contributions of frontal areas to emotion and social behaviour in the rat. Eur J Neurosci. 2007 Oct;26(8):2315–26.

24. Etkin A, Wager TD. Functional neuroimaging of anxiety: a meta-analysis of emotional processing in PTSD, social anxiety disorder, and specific phobia. Am J Psychiatry. 2007 Oct;164(10):1476–88.

25. Knippenberg JM, Maes JH, Kuniecki MJ, Buyse BA, Coenen AM, van Luijtelaar G. N150 in amygdalar ERPs in the rat: Is there modulation by anticipatory fear? Physiol Behav. 2007 Aug 29.

Kumari V, ffytche DH, Das M, Wilson GD, Goswami S, Sharma T. Neuroticism and brain responses to anticipatory fear. Behav Neurosci. 2007 Aug;121(4):643–52.

26. Shim YS, Kim JS, Shon YM, Chung YA, Ahn KJ, Yang DW. A serial study of regional cerebral blood flow deficits in patients with left anterior thalamic infarction: Anatomical and neuropsychological correlates. J Neurol Sci. 2008 Mar 15;266(1–2):84–91.

Schroeter ML, Raczka K, Neumann J, von Cramon DY. Neural networks in frontotemporal dementia—a meta-analysis. Neurobiol Aging. 2008 Mar;29(3):418–26.

Sziklas V, Petrides M. Contribution of the anterior thalamic nuclei to conditional learning in rats. Hippocampus. 2007;17(6):456–61.

Edelstyn NM, Hunter B, Ellis SJ. Bilateral dorsolateral thalamic lesions disrupts conscious recollection. Neuropsychologia. 2006;44(6):931–8.

Cheung CC, Lee TM, Yip JT, King KE, Li LS. The differential effects of thalamus and basal ganglia on facial emotion recognition. Brain Cogn. 2006 Aug;61(3):262–8.

Graham DI, Adams JH, Murray LS, Jennett B. Neuropathology of the vegetative state after head injury. Neuropsychol Rehabil. 2005 Jul–Sep;15(3–4):198–213.

Dagenbach D, Kubat-Silman AK, Absher JR. Human verbal working memory impairments associated with thalamic damage. Int J Neurosci. 2001;111(1–2):67–87.

27. Kjaer TW, Bertelsen C, Piccini P, Brooks D, Alving J, Lou HC. Increased dopamine tone during meditation-induced change of consciousness. Brain Res Cogn Brain Res. 2002 Apr;13(2):255–9.

28. Gianotti LR, Mohr C, Pizzagalli D, Lehmann D, Brugger P. Associative processing and paranormal belief. Psychiatry Clin Neurosci. 2001 Dec;55(6):595–603.

29. Kurup RK, Kurup PA. Hypothalamic digoxin, hemispheric chemical dominance, and spirituality. Int J Neurosci. 2003 Mar;113(3):383–93.

30. Orme-Johnson D. Evidence that the Transcendental Meditation program prevents or decreases diseases of the nervous system and is specifically beneficial for epilepsy. Med Hypotheses. 2006;67(2):240–6.

Jaseja H. Meditation potentially capable of increasing susceptibility to epilepsy—a follow-up hypothesis. Med Hypotheses. 2006;66(5):925–8.

Solberg EE, Holen A, Ekeberg Ø, Østerud B, Halvorsen R, Sandvik L. The effects of long meditation on plasma melatonin and blood serotonin. Med Sci Monit. 2004 Mar;10(3):CR96–101.

Bujatti M, Riederer P. Serotonin, noradrenaline, dopamine metabolites in Transcendental Meditation-technique. J Neural Transm. 1976;39(3):257–67.

31. Toneatto T, Nguyen L. Does mindfulness meditation improve anxiety and mood symptoms? A review of the controlled research. Can J Psychiatry. 2007 Apr;52(4):260–6.

Finucane A, Mercer SW. An exploratory mixed methods study of the acceptability and effectiveness of Mindfulness-Based Cognitive Therapy for patients with active depression and anxiety in primary care. BMC Psychiatry. 2006 Apr 7;6:14. PMID.

Grossman P, Niemann L, Schmidt S, Walach H. Mindfulness-based stress reduction and health benefits. A meta-analysis.J Psychosom Res. 2004 Jul;57(1):35–43.

32. Streeter CC, Jensen JE, Perlmutter RM, Cabral HJ, Tian H, Terhune DB, Ciraulo DA, Renshaw PF. Yoga Asana sessions increase brain GABA levels: a pilot study. J Altern Complement Med. 2007 May;13(4):419–26.

33. Infante JR, Torres-Avisbal M, Pinel P, Vallejo JA, Peran F, Gonzalez F, Contreras P, Pacheco C, Roldan A, Latre JM. Catecholamine levels in practitioners of the transcendental meditation technique. Physiol Behav. 2001 Jan;72(1–2):141–6.

34. Between 1969 and 1996 extensive research was conducted on the use of psychedelic drugs and reported in the *Journal of Transpersonal Psychology*. The overall consensus concluded that fewer and fewer people reported spiritual or psychological insights after 1973, the year that LSD gained popularity as a recreational drug.

35. O'Leary DS, Block RI, Turner BM, Koeppel J, Magnotta VA, Ponto LB, Watkins GL, Hichwa RD, Andreasen NC. Marijuana alters the human cerebellar clock. Neuroreport. 2003 Jun 11;14(8):1145–51.

36. Block RI, O'Leary DS, Hichwa RD, Augustinack JC, Ponto LL, Ghoneim MM, Arndt S, Ehrhardt JC, Hurtig RR, Watkins GL, Hall JA, Nathan PE, Andreasen NC. Cerebellar hypoactivity in frequent marijuana users. Neuroreport. 2000 Mar 20;11(4):749–53.

37. Ghaffar O, Feinstein A. Multiple sclerosis and cannabis. A cognitive and psychiatric study. Neurology. 2008 Feb 13.

D'Souza DC, Braley G, Blaise R, Vendetti M, Oliver S, Pittman B, Ranganathan M, Bhakta S, Zimolo Z, Cooper T, Perry E. Effects of haloperidol on the behavioral, subjective, cognitive, motor, and neuroendocrine effects of Delta-9-tetrahydrocannabinol in humans. Psychopharmacology (Berl). 2008 Jan 29.

Fisk JE, Montgomery C. Real-world memory and executive processes in cannabis users and non-users. J Psychopharmacol. 2008 Jan 21.

Senn R, Keren O, Hefetz A, Sarne Y. Long-term cognitive deficits induced by a single, extremely low dose of tetrahydrocannabinol (THC): Behavioral, pharmacological and biochemical studies in mice. Pharmacol Biochem Behav. 2008 Jan;88(3):230–7.

Solowij N. *Cannabis and Cognitive Functioning.* Cambridge University Press, 1998.

38. de Sola Llopis S, Miguelez-Pan M, Peña-Casanova J, Poudevida S, Farre M, Pacifici R, Böhm P, Abanades S, García AV, Zuccaro P, de la Torre R. Cognitive performance in recreational ecstasy polydrug users: a two-year follow-up study. J Psychopharmacol. 2008 Jan 21.

Bedi G, Redman J. Ecstasy use and higher-level cognitive functions: weak effects of ecstasy after control for potential confounds. Psychol Med. 2008 Jan 29:1–12.

Schilt T, Win MM, Jager G, Koeter MW, Ramsey NF, Schmand B, van den Brink W. Specific effects of ecstasy and other illicit drugs on cognition in poly-substance users. Psychol Med. 2007 Nov 8;:1–9.

Montgomery C, Fisk JE. Everyday memory deficits in ecstasy-polydrug users. J Psychopharmacol. 2007 Sep;21(7):709–17.

Rodgers J, Buchanan T, Scholey AB, Heffernan TM, Ling J, Parrott AC. Patterns of drug use and the influence of gender on self-reports of memory ability in ecstasy users: a Web-based study. J Psychopharmacol. 2003 Dec;17(4):389–96.

Rodgers J. Cognitive performance amongst recreational users of "ecstasy." Psychopharmacology (Berl). 2000 Jul;151(1):19–24.

39. Lerner M, Lyvers M. Values and beliefs of psychedelic drug users: a cross-cultural study. J Psychoactive Drugs. 2006 Jun;38(2):143–7.

40. Hartung J, Skorka D. The HIT clinical profile of psychedelic drug users. J Pers Assess. 1980 Jun;44(3):237–45.

41. Vollenweider FX, Leenders KL, Scharfetter C, Maguire P, Stadelmann O, Angst J. Positron emission tomography and fluorodeoxyglucose studies of metabolic hyperfrontality and psychopathology in the psilocybin model of psychosis. Neuropsychopharmacology. 1997 May;16(5):357–72.

42. Griffiths RR, Richards WA, McCann U, Jesse R. Psilocybin can occasion mystical-type experiences having substantial and sustained personal mean-

ing and spiritual significance. Psychopharmacology (Berl). 2006 Aug;187(3): 268–83.

43. Bonn-Miller MO, Bernstein A, Sachs-Ericsson N, Schmidt NB, Zvolensky MJ. Associations between psychedelic use, abuse, and dependence and lifetime panic attack history in a representative sample. J Anxiety Disord. 2007;21(5):730–41.

44. Newberg A., and Waldman, M. *Born to Believe.* The Free Press, 2007.

45. Helmut Hanisch: The graphic development of the God picture with children and young people: An empirical comparative investigation with religious and non-religiously educating at the age of 7–16. Stuttgart and Leipzig 1996. http://www.uni-leipzig.de/~rp/vortraege/hanisch01.html.

46. For a comprehensive list of studies relating the health benefits of prayer, meditation, church attendance, and spirituality, see http://www.dukespirituality andhealth.org/resources/pdfs/Research%20-%20latest%20outside%20Duke .pdf.

47. Gillum RF, Ingram DD. Frequency of attendance at religious services, hypertension, and blood pressure: the Third National Health and Nutrition Examination Survey. Psychosom Med. 2006 May–Jun;68(3):382–5.

48. Shermer M. Hope Springs Eternal: Science, the Afterlife & the Meaning of Life. http://www.skeptic.com/reading_room/debates/afterlife.html.

49. Sloan, R. *Blind Faith: The Unholy Alliance of Religion and Medicine.* St. Martin's Press, 2006.

50. Musick MA, House JS, Williams DR. Attendance at religious services and mortality in a national sample. J Health Soc. 2004;45 (2):198–213.

51. Hill TD, Angel JL, Ellison CG, Angel RJ. Religious attendance and mortality: an 8-year follow-up of older Mexican Americans. J Gerontol B Psychol Sci Soc Sci. 2005 Mar;60(2):S102–9.

52. Obisesan T, Livingston I, Trulear HD, Gillum F. Frequency of attendance at religious services, cardiovascular disease, metabolic risk factors and dietary intake in Americans: an age-stratified exploratory analysis. Int J Psychiatry Med. 2006;36(4):435–48.

53. Oman D, Kurata JH, Strawbridge WJ, Cohen RD. Religious attendance and cause of death over 31 years. Int J Psychatr Med. 2002;32(1):69–89.

54. Gillum RF. Frequency of attendance at religious services and cigarette smoking in American women and men: the Third National Health and Nutrition Examination Survey. Prev Med. 2005 Aug;41(2):607–13.

55. Whooley MA, Boyd AL, Gardin JM, Williams DR. Religious involvement and cigarette smoking in young adults: the CARDIA study (Coronary Artery Risk Development in Young Adults) study. Arch Intern Med. 2002 Jul 22;162(14):1604–10.

56. Pargament KI, Koenig HG, Tarakeshwar N, Hahn J. Religious struggle as a predictor of mortality among medically ill elderly patients: a 2-year longitudinal study. Archives of Internal Medicine. 2001 Aug 13–27;161(15):1881–5.

57. Koenig HG, Pargament KI, Nielsen J. Religious coping and health status in medically ill hospitalized older adults. J Nerv Ment Dis. 1998 Sep;186(9):513–21.

58. Pargament, K.I. *The Psychology of Religion and Coping: Theory, Research, Practice.* Guilford Press, 1997.

Koenig HG, Pargament KI, Nielsen J. Religious coping and health status in medically ill hospitalized older adults. J Nerv Ment Dis. 1998;186:513–521.

Fitchett G, Rybarczyk BD, DeMarco GA, Nicholas JJ. The role of religion in medical rehabilitation outcomes: a longitudinal study. Rehab Psychol. 1999;44:1–22.

59. Pargament KI, Koenig HG, Tarakeshwar N, Hahn J. Religious coping methods as predictors of psychological, physical and spiritual outcomes among medically ill elderly patients: a two-year longitudinal study. J Health Psychol. 2004 Nov;9(6):713–30.

60. Creswell JD, Way BM, Eisenberger NI, Lieberman MD. Neural correlates of dispositional mindfulness during affect labeling. Psychosom Med. 2007 Jul–Aug;69(6):560–5.

Pagnoni G, Cekic M. Age effects on gray matter volume and attentional performance in Zen meditation. Neurobiol Aging. 2007 Oct;28(10):1623–7.

Brefczynski-Lewis JA, Lutz A, Schaefer HS, Levinson DB, Davidson RJ. Neural correlates of attentional expertise in long-term meditation practitioners. Proc Natl Acad Sci U S A. 2007 Jul 3;104(27):11483–8.

Hölzel BK, Ott U, Hempel H, Hackl A, Wolf K, Stark R, Vaitl D. Differential engagement of anterior cingulate and adjacent medial frontal cortex in adept meditators and non-meditators. Neurosci Lett. 2007 Jun 21;421(1): 16–21.

61. Brefczynski-Lewis JA, Lutz A, Schaefer HS, Levinson DB, Davidson RJ. Neural correlates of attentional expertise in long-term meditation practitioners. Proc Natl Acad Sci U S A. 2007 Jul 3;104(27):11483–8.

62. Goleman, D. *Destructive Emotions.* Bantam Books, 2003.

63. Slagter HA, Lutz A, Greischar LL, Francis AD, Nieuwenhuis S, Davis JM, Davidson RJ. Mental training affects distribution of limited brain resources. PLoS Biol. 2007 Jun;5(6):e138.

Lutz A, Greischar LL, Rawlings NB, Ricard M, Davidson RJ. Long-term meditators self-induce high-amplitude gamma synchrony during mental practice. Proc Natl Acad Sci U S A. 2004 Nov 16;101(46):16369–73.

64. Lazar SW, Kerr CE, Wasserman RH, Gray JR, Greve DN, Treadway MT, McGarvey M, Quinn BT, Dusek JA, Benson H, Rauch SL, Moore CI, Fischl B. Meditation experience is associated with increased cortical thickness. Neuroreport. 2005 Nov 28;16(17):1893–7.

CHAPTER 4. WHAT DOES GOD FEEL LIKE? (PAGES 67–82)

1. Ganzel B, Casey BJ, Glover G, Voss HU, Temple E. The aftermath of 9/11: effect of intensity and recency of trauma on outcome. Emotion. 2007 May;7(2):227–38.

   Wessa M, Flor H. Posttraumatic stress disorder and trauma memory—a psychobiological perspective. Psychosom Med Psychother. 2002;48(1):28–37. German.

2. Yokoyama S, Miyamoto T, Riera J, Kim J, Akitsuki Y, Iwata K, Yoshimoto K, Horie K, Sato S, Kawashima R. Cortical mechanisms involved in the processing of verbs: an fMRI study. J Cogn Neurosci. 2006 Aug;18(8):1304–13.

3. Newport F, Who Believes in God and Who Doesn't? Gallup News Service, June 23, 2006.

4. Larson EJ, Witham L. Scientists Are Still Keeping the Faith. Nature. 1997 April;386:435–36.

5. Gunn H. Web-based Surveys: Changing the Survey Process. First Monday. 2002 Dec;7(12), http://www.firstmonday.org/Issues/issue7_12/gunn/index .html.

6. Nobel prize winner Francis Crick argues that the claustrum is the "orchestra conductor" that brings together unity of consciousness, whereas Nobel prizewinner Eric Kandel argues that the thalamus is key to the processing of a holistic sense of reality. However, the claustrum is heavily interconnected with most of the cortex, with the exception of the thalamus.

   Crick FC, Koch C. What is the function of the claustrum? Philos Trans R Soc Lond B Biol Sci. 2005 Jun 29;360(1458):1271–9.

   Kandel, E. *In Search of Memory: The Emergence of a New Science of Mind.* Norton, 2006.

7. Aldous Huxley, Ken Wilbur, and Huston Smith are three well-known authors who have written extensively on the topic of perennial philosophy. See: Cousineau P. (ed.) *The Way Things Are: Conversations with Huston Smith on the Spiritual Life.* University of California Press, 2005.

8. Ens C, Bond JB Jr. Death anxiety in adolescents: the contributions of bereavement and religiosity. Omega (Westport). 2007;55(3):169–84.

   Al-Sabwah MN, Abdel-Khalek AM. Religiosity and death distress in Arabic college students. Death Stud. 2006 May;30(4):365–75.

Wink P, Scott J. Does religiousness buffer against the fear of death and dying in late adulthood? Findings from a longitudinal study. J Gerontol B Psychol Sci Soc Sci. 2005 Jul;60(4):P207–14.

Roff LL, Butkeviciene R, Klemmack DL. Death anxiety and religiosity among Lithuanian health and social service professionals. Death Stud. 2002 Nov;26(9):731–42.

Suhail K, Akram S. Correlates of death anxiety in Pakistan. Death Stud. 2002 Jan;26(1):39–50.

Fortner BV, Neimeyer RA. Death anxiety in older adults: a quantitative review. Death Stud. 1999 Jul–Aug;23(5):387–411.

9. Waldman M. The Case of Julia: Kundalini or Psychosis? J Transpers Psychol. 1992;24(2).

10. American Psychiatric Association. *1994 Diagnostic and Statistical Manual* (4th ed.). APA, Washington, DC.

11. James W. *The Varieties of Religious Experience: A Study in Human Nature.* Longman, 1902.

12. Keup J. Understanding the Role of Religion and Spirituality in the UCLA Undergraduate Experience. http://www.sairo.ucla.edu/2005Reports/Religion%20%Spirituality%20in%20the%20UCLA%20Undergraduate%20Experience%20Oct%202005.pdf. See also: http://www.spirituality.ucla.edu.

13. Although 80 to 90 percent of Americans believe in God, and faith is the second most important value in most American's lives (Barna, March 14, 2006), only 30 to 40 percent attend church regularly (Gallup, January 3 and 10, 2006); 43 percent don't attend any religious institution at all (Gallup, October 11, 2005).

14. Barna's Annual Tracking Study Shows Americans Stay Spiritually Active, But Biblical Views Wane. Barna Research Group. May 21, 2007.

15. Islamic Extremism: Common Concern for Muslim and Western Publics. Pew Global Attitudes Project. 2005. http://pewglobal.org/reports/display.php?PageID=809.

A Rising Tide Lifts Mood in the Developing World: Sharp Decline in Support for Suicide Bombing in Muslim Countries. Pew Global Attitudes Project. 2007. http://pewglobal.org/reports/display.php?ReportID=257.

CHAPTER 5. WHAT DOES GOD LOOK LIKE? (PAGES 83–105)

1. Wilson DS. *Darwin's Cathedral.* University of Chicago Press, 2002.

2. Kensinger EA, Schacter DL. Processing emotional pictures and words: effects of valence and arousal. Cogn Affect Behav Neurosci. 2006 Jun;6(2):110–26.

3. Alia-Klein N, Goldstein RZ, Tomasi D, Zhang L, Fagin-Jones S, Telang F, Wang GJ, Fowler JS, Volkow ND. What is in a word? No versus yes dif-

ferentially engage the lateral orbitofrontal cortex. Emotion. 2007 Aug;7(3): 649–59.

4. Solso R. Brain activities in a skilled versus a novice artist: An fMRI study. Leonardo 34.1 (2001) 31–34.

5. Heller D. *The Children's God.* University of Chicago Press, 1988.

6. Ladd K, McIntosh DN, Spilka B. Children's god concepts: Influences of denomination, age, and gender. International J for the Psychology of Religion. 1998; 8(1): 49–56.

7. Harms E.: The development of religious experience in children. American Journal of Sociology. 1944;(50).

Siegenthaler H.: Die Entwicklung des Gottesbildes bei Kindern und Jugendlichen, in: entwurf, hg. von der Fachgemeinschaft evangelischer Religionslehrer in Württemberg und vom Fachverband evangelischer Religionslehrer in Baden e. V. 3/1980.

Hanisch H. 1996. [German translation: The graphic development of the God picture with children and young people: An empirical comparative investigation with religious and non-religiously educating at the ages of 7–16]. Stuttgart and Leipzig. See also: Hanisch H. 2002. Children's and Young People's Drawings of God (lecture given at the University of Gloucestershire): http://www.uni-leipzig.de/~rp/vortraege/hanisch01.html.

Ladd K, McIntosh DN, Spilka B. Children's god concepts: Influences of denomination, age, and gender. Int J Psychol Rel. 1998; 8(1):49–56.

8. Szpunar KK, Watson JM, McDermott KB. Neural substrates of envisioning the future. Proc Natl Acad Sci U S A. 2007 Jan 9;104(2):642–7.

Addis DR, Wong AT, Schacter DL. Remembering the past and imagining the future: common and distinct neural substrates during event construction and elaboration. Neuropsychologia. 2007 Apr 8;45(7):1363–77.

9. Hofer A, Siedentopf CM, Ischebeck A, Rettenbacher MA, Verius M, Felber S, Wolfgang Fleischhacker W. Sex differences in brain activation patterns during processing of positively and negatively valenced emotional words. Psychol Med. 2007 Jan;37(1):109–19.

10. The first fifty words tend to be names of important persons, foods, nouns relating to activities like taking a bath, action words and verbs, and simple directions, like up, down, open, or go. See: Bremner JG, Slater A, Butterworth G. *Infant Development: Recent Advances.* Erlbaum, 1997.

11. Ravid D. Semantic development in textual contexts during the school years: noun scale analyses. J Child Lang. 2006 Nov;33(4):791–821.

Ogura T, Dale PS, Yamashita Y, Murase T, Mahieu A. The use of nouns and verbs by Japanese children and their caregivers in book-reading and toy-playing contexts. J Child Lang. 2006 Feb;33(1):1–29.

12. As neuroimaging technology improves, some of the assumptions concerning a child's language acquisition have been called into question. Furthermore, languages from various cultures may be learned and neurologically processed in different ways. See:

    Li P, Jin Z, Tan LH. Neural representations of nouns and verbs in Chinese: an fMRI study. Neuroimage. 2004 Apr;21(4):1533–41.

    Bassano D. Early development of nouns and verbs in French: exploring the interface between lexicon and grammar. J Child Lang. 2000 Oct;27(3):521–59.

13. Federmeier KD, Segal JB, Lombrozo T, Kutas M. Brain responses to nouns, verbs and class-ambiguous words in context. Brain. 2000 Dec;123 Pt 12:2552–66.

14. Pobric G, Mashal N, Faust M, Lavidor M. The role of the right cerebral hemisphere in processing novel metaphoric expressions: a transcranial magnetic stimulation study. J Cogn Neurosci. 2008 Jan;20(1):170–81.

15. Vinckier F, Naccache L, Papeix C, Forget J, Hahn-Barma V, Dehaene S, Cohen L. "What" and "where" in word reading: ventral coding of written words revealed by parietal atrophy. J Cogn Neurosci. 2006 Dec;18(12):1998–2012.

    Sestieri C, Di Matteo R, Ferretti A, Del Gratta C, Caulo M, Tartaro A, Olivetti Belardinelli M, Romani GL. "What" versus "where" in the audiovisual domain: an fMRI study. Neuroimage. 2006 Nov 1;33(2):672–80.

16. Shafritz KM, Gore JC, Marois R. The role of the parietal cortex in visual feature binding. Proc Natl Acad Sci U S A. 2002 August 6; 99(16): 10917–10922.

17. http://www.religiousscience.org.

18. http://www.rsint.org.

19. Fowler, J. Stages of Faith: The Psychology of Human Development. HarperSanFrancisco, 1981.

20. In 1961, the Unitarian and Universalist denominations consolidated to form Unitarian Universalism. However, Unitarian Universalism does not adhere to traditional Unitarian or Universalist beliefs and now embraces humanistic, interfaith, secular, and nondiscriminatory policies.

21. Benson PL, Donahue MJ, Erickson JA. Adolescence and religion: A review of the literature from 1970 to 1986. Res Soc Sci Study Rel. 1989;1: 153–181.

    King V, Elder GH, Whitbeck LB. Religious involvement among rural youth: an ecological and life-course perspective. J Res Adolesc. 1997;7: 431–456.

22. Banschick M. God representations in adolescence. In Finn M, Gartner J, (eds). Object Relations Theory and Religion. New York: Praeger, 1992.

23. Levenson MR, Aldwin CM, D'Mello M, Religious Development from Adolescence to Middle Adulthood. In Handbook of the Psychology of Religion and Spirituality, Guilford Press, 2005.

24. Smith C, Denton ML, Faris R,Regnerus M. Mapping American adolescent religious participation. J Sci Study Rel. 2002;13: 175–195.

   Markstrom CA. Religious involvement and adolescent psychosocial development. J Adolesc 1999;22(2):205–21.

25. Levenson MR, op cit.

26. The Barna Group. Most Twentysomethings Put Christianity on the Shelf Following Spiritually Active Teen Years. September 11, 2006. http://www.barna.org/FlexPage.aspx?Page=BarnaUpdate&BarnaUpdateID=245.

27. The Barna Group. Barna finds four mega-themes in recent research. December 3, 2007, http://www.barna.org/FlexPage.aspx?Page=BarnaUpdate&BarnaUpdateID=285.

28. Kinnaman D. *unChristian: What a New Generation Really Thinks about Christianity . . . and Why It Matters.* Baker Books, 2007.

29. Borg M. *The Heart of Christianity.* HarperOne, 2003.

30. Harrington GS, Farias D, Davis CH, Buonocore MH. Comparison of the neural basis for imagined writing and drawing. Hum Brain Mapp. 2007 May;28(5):450–9.

31. Taylor KI, Regard M. Language in the right cerebral hemisphere: contributions from reading studies. News Physiol Sci. 2003 Dec;18:257–61.

32. Sabsevitz DS, Medler DA, Seidenberg M, Binder JR. Modulation of the semantic system by word imageability. Neuroimage. 2005 Aug 1;27(1):188–200.

   Taylor KI, Regard M. Language in the right cerebral hemisphere: contributions from reading studies. News Physiol Sci. 2003 Dec;18:257–61.

33. Einstein, A. A Symposium, by the Conference on Science, Philosophy and Religion in Their Relation to the Democratic Way of Life. In *Science, Philosophy and Religion,* 1940. The website http://www.sahajayoga.asso.fr/news_sahaja-yoga_france/documents/Albert%20Einstein%20-%20Contemplating%20the%20cosmos.pdf also contains several other informative essays by Einstein on religion.

34. Kandinsky W. *Concerning the Spiritual in Art.* Project Gutenberg E Book, 2004.

35. Quiroga RQ, Reddy L, Kreiman G, Koch C, Fried I. Invariant visual representation by single neurons in the human brain. Nature. 2005 Jun 23;435(7045):1102–7.

36. Buber M. *The Way of Response* (Glatzer, ed.). Schocken, 1971.

37. Wilson D. Beyond Demonic Memes: Why Richard Dawkins Is Wrong About Religion. *eSkeptic,* July 14, 2007.

38. The Centre for Synaptic Plasticity provides an excellent online overview of neuroplasticity. The center is a joint venture between the Medical Research Council and the University of Bristol, advancing the understanding of

synaptic plasticity in normal human functioning, especially during learning and memory and in certain pathological states such as Alzheimer's disease, memory loss, and epilepsy. For an online list of relevant research papers, see www.bris.ac.uk/synaptic/research/res2.html.

39. Chklovskii DB, Mel BW, Svoboda K. Cortical rewiring and information storage. Nature. 2004 Oct 14;431(7010):782–8.

40. Yoshii A, Constantine-Paton M. BDNF induces transport of PSD-95 to dendrites through PI3K-AKT signaling after NMDA receptor activation. Nature Neuroscience. 2007;10, 702. Quotation cited in Medical Science News. 2007 May 20.

41. Frostig RD. Functional organization and plasticity in the adult rat barrel cortex: moving out-of-the-box. Curr Opin Neurobiol. 2006;16:1–6.

42. Polley DB, Kvasnak E, Frostig RD. Naturalisitic experience transforms sensory maps in the adult cortex of caged animals. Nature. 2004;429: 67–71.

43. Jacobs B, Scheibel AB. A quantitative dendritic analysis of Wernicke's area in humans. I. Lifespan changes. J Comp Neurol. 1993 Jan 1;327(1):83–96.

    Allman, J. *Evolving Brains*. Scientific American Library, 2000.

44. Muotri AR, Marchetto MC, Coufal NG, Gage FH. The necessary junk: new functions for transposable elements. Hum Mol Genet. 2007 Oct 15;16 Spec No. 2:R159–67.

    Garcia-Perez JL, et. al. LINE-1 retrotransposition in human embryonic stem cells. Hum Mol Genet. 2007 Jul 1;16(13):1569–77.

    Muotri AR, et al. Somatic mosaicism in neuronal precursor cells mediated by L1 retrotransposition. Nature. 2005 Jun 16;435(7044):903–10.

45. Deacon, C. *The Symbolic Species: The Co-Evolution of Language and the Brain*. Norton, 1998.

CHAPTER 6. DOES GOD HAVE A HEART? (PAGES 106–130)

1. American Piety in the 21st Century: New Insights to the Depth and Complexity of Religion in the U.S. Selected findings from the Baylor Religion Survey. September 2006. Research group: Christopher Bader, Kevin Dougherty, Paul Froese, Byron Johnson, F. Carson Mencken, Jerry Z. Park, Rodney Stark. http://www.baylor.edu/content/services/document.php/33304.pdf.

2. Zogby International. University Of Rochester And Zogby International Release Global Poll On Religious Beliefs, Practices And Priorities. October 16, 2003, http://www.zogby.com/NEWS/ReadNews.dbm?ID=746.

3. Buber M. *I and Thou*. Scribner, 1958.

4. Wuthnow R. *Sharing the Journey*. The Free Press, 1994.

5. Beliefs: General Religious. Barna Group. 2007, 2008, http://www.barna.org/FlexPage.aspx?Page=Topic&TopicID=2. See also: Barna, G. *Index of Leading Spiritual Indicators*. Thomas Nelson, 1996.

6. This quote appeared in the *New York Times Magazine* on November 9, 1930. It also appears in Einstein's book, *The World as I See It,* Philosophical Library, 1949.

7. For an excellent overview of the history of American religion, see Gaustad, E.S. *The Religious History of America.* HarperOne, 2004.

8. Atkinson W. *Thought Vibration or the Law of Attraction in the Thought World.* New Thought Publishing Company, 1906. Essay first published in 1901.

9. Torrey RA (ed.). *The Fundamentals: A Testimony to the Truth, 1910–15.* Baker Book House, 1994.

10. Department of Justice, Federal Bureau of Investigation, Crime in the United States, 2004. See also: FBI, 2006 Hate Crimes Statistics.

11. U.S. Government, 2004. Chart in public domain.

12. BNET Research Center poll: Americans shun conversion goals. *Christian Century,* May 8, 2002.

13. Borg MJ. *The Heart of Christianity.* HarperSanFrancisco, 2002.

14. http://www.dioceseofnewark.org/jsspong/reform.html. See also: Spong J. *Why Christianity Must Change or Die.* HarperOne, 1998.

15. A New Generation Expresses Its Skepticism and Frustration with Christianity. Barna Research Group. September 24, 2007, http://www.barna.org/FlexPage.aspx?Page=BarnaUpdate&BarnaUpdateID=280.

16. Tracking U.S. Religious Preferences Over the Decades: A Gallup Survey. May 24, 2005, http://www.gallup.com/poll/16459/Tracking-US-Religious-Preferences-Over-Decades.aspx.

17. Byrne, R. *The Secret.* Atria Books/Beyond Words, 2006 (DVD directed by Drew Heriot).

18. Spirituality and the Professoriate: A National Study of Faculty Beliefs, Attitudes, and Behaviors. Higher Education Research Institute, Graduate School of Education and Information Studies, University of California, Los Angeles. Alexander W. Astin, co-principal investigator.

19. Minkkinen M. Early care and education: Our social experiment. J Coll Teaching Learning, 2005;2(7): 1–6.

20. The neurobiology of romantic love involves different parts of the brain than other emotional conditions: areas in the frontal cortex, the anterior cingulate, and many areas within the limbic system. But love is also controlled by our thoughts and the evaluation of rewards or rejection, and by a constantly changing balance of neurochemicals and hormones, including oxytocin, vasopressin, dopamine, and opioids. See, for instance:

Zeki S. The neurobiology of love. FEBS Lett. 2007 Jun 12;581(14):2575–9.

Fisher HE, Aron A, Brown LL. Romantic love: a mammalian brain system for mate choice. Philos Trans R Soc Lond B Biol Sci. 2006 Dec 29;361(1476): 2173–86.

Romantic love: a mammalian brain system for mate choice. Philos Trans R Soc Lond B Biol Sci. 2006 Dec 29;361(1476):2173–86.

Kendrick KM. The neurobiology of social bonds. J Neuroendocrinol. 2004 Dec;16(12):1007–8.

Bartels A, Zeki S. The neural correlates of maternal and romantic love. Neuroimage. 2004 Mar;21(3):1155–66.

Marazziti D, Cassano GB. The neurobiology of attraction. J Endocrinol Invest. 2003;26(3 Suppl):58–60.

Bartels A, Zeki S. The neural basis of romantic love. Neuroreport. 2000 Nov 27;11(17):3829–34.

21. Bernier P, Be'dard A, Vinet J, Le'vesque M, Parent P. Newly generated neurons in the amygdala and adjoining cortex of adult primates. Proceedings of the National Academy of Sciences. PNAS 2002;99;11464–11469.

22. Allman JM, Hakeem A, Erwin JM, Nimchinsky E, Hof P. The anterior cingulate cortex. The evolution of an interface between emotion and cognition. Ann N Y Acad Sci. 2001 May;935:107–17.

Kasai K, Yamasue H, Gilbertson MW, Shenton ME, Rauch SL, Pitman RK. Evidence for acquired pregenual anterior cingulate gray matter loss from a twin study of combat-related posttraumatic stress disorder. Biol Psychiatry. 2008 Mar 15;63(6):550–6.

Javadapour A, Malhi GS, Ivanovski B, Chen X, Wen W, Sachdev P. Increased anterior cingulate cortex volume in bipolar I disorder. Aust N Z J Psychiatry. 2007 Nov;41(11):910–6.

Onoda K, Okamoto Y, Toki S, Ueda K, Shishida K, Kinoshita A, Yoshimura S, Yamashita H, Yamawaki S. Anterior cingulate cortex modulates preparatory activation during certain anticipation of negative picture. Neuropsychologia. 2007 Aug 15.

23. Bartolomeo P, Zieren N, Vohn R, Dubois B, Sturm W. Neural correlates of primary and reflective consciousness of spatial orienting. Neuropsychologia. 2007 Jul 19.

24. Saarela MV, Hlushchuk Y, Williams AC, Schürmann M, Kalso E, Hari R. The compassionate brain: humans detect intensity of pain from another's face. Cereb Cortex. 2007 Jan;17(1):230–7.

25. Alexopoulos GS, Gunning-Dixon FM, Latoussakis V, Kanellopoulos D, Murphy CF. Anterior cingulate dysfunction in geriatric depression. Int J Geriatr Psychiatry. 2007 Nov 5.

26. Seeley WW, Allman JM, Carlin DA, Crawford RK, Macedo MN, Greicius MD, Dearmond SJ, Miller BL. Divergent social functioning in behavioral variant frontotemporal dementia and Alzheimer disease: reciprocal net-

works and neuronal evolution. Alzheimer Dis Assoc Disord. 2007 Oct–Dec;21(4):S50–7.

Hof PR, Van Der Gucht E. Structure of the cerebral cortex of the humpback whale, *Megaptera novaeangliae* (Cetacea, Mysticeti, Balaenopteridae). Anat Rec A Discov Mol Cell Evol Biol. 2006 Nov 27.

27. Gross JJ. *Handbook of Emotion Regulation*. Guilford Press, 2006.

28. Siegrist J, Menrath I, Stöcker T, Klein M, Kellermann T, Shah NJ, Zilles K, Schneider F. Differential brain activation according to chronic social reward frustration. Neuroreport. 2005 Nov 28;16(17):1899–903.

29. Seeley WW, Allman JM, Carlin DA, Crawford RK, Macedo MN, Greicius MD, Dearmond SJ, Miller BL. Divergent social functioning in behavioral variant frontotemporal dementia and Alzheimer disease: reciprocal networks and neuronal evolution. Alzheimer Dis Assoc Disord. 2007 Oct–Dec;21(4):S50–7.

Seeley WW, Carlin DA, Allman JM, Macedo MN, Bush C, Miller BL, Dearmond SJ. Early frontotemporal dementia targets neurons unique to apes and humans. Ann Neurol. 2006 Dec;60(6):660–7.

Allman, J. *Evolving Brains*. Scientific American Library, 2000.

30. Eisenberger NI, Gable SL, Lieberman MD. Functional magnetic resonance imaging responses relate to differences in real-world social experience. Emotion. 2007 Nov;7(4):745–54.

Rudebeck PH, Walton ME, Millette BH, Shirley E, Rushworth MF, Bannerman DM. Distinct contributions of frontal areas to emotion and social behaviour in the rat. Eur J Neurosci. 2007 Oct;26(8):2315–26.

Eisenberger NI, Taylor SE, Gable SL, Hilmert CJ, Lieberman MD. Neural pathways link social support to attenuated neuroendocrine stress responses. Neuroimage. 2007 May 1;35(4):1601–12.

31. This quote, like the previous one cited, first appeared in the *New York Times Magazine* on November 9, 1930, and also appears in Einstein's book, *The World As I See It* (Citadel, 2001).

32. Slagter H, Lutz A, Greischar L, Francis A, Nieuwenhuis S, Davis J, Davidson R. Mental Training Affects Distribution of Limited Brain Resources. PLoS Biol 2007, Vol. 5, No. 6. http://biology.plosjournals.org/perlserv/?request=get-document&doi=10.1371/journal.pbio.0050138.

33. Stein J. Just Say Om. Time. Sunday, Jul. 27, 2003.

34. Stukin S. The best you now: Well-being and health—along with a growing appreciation for the age you are now—have come together in an era of unprecedented longevity. Los Angeles Times. July 29, 2007.

35. Halman L, Draulans V. How secular is Europe? Br J Sociol. 2006 Jun;57(2):263–88.

CHAPTER 7. WHAT HAPPENS WHEN GOD GETS MAD? (PAGES 131–146)

1. Davidson RJ, Lewis DA, Alloy LB, Amaral DG, Bush G, Cohen JD, Drevets WC, Farah MJ, Kagan J, McClelland JL, Nolen-Hoeksema S, Peterson BS. Neural and behavioral substrates of mood and mood regulation, Biol Psychiatry, 2002 Sep 15;52(6):478–502.

2. For the most comprehensive overview of anger published to date, see Lerner JS, Tiedens LZ. Portrait of the angry decision maker: How appraisal tendencies shape anger's influence on cognition. J Behavioral Decision Making. 2006:19: 115–137.

   Tiedens LZ, Linton S. Judgment under emotional certainty and uncertainty: the effects of specific emotions on information processing. J Pers Soc Psychol. 2001 Dec;81(6):973–88.

   Lerner JS, Goldberg JH, Tetlock PE. Sober second thought: the effects of accountability, anger and authoritarianism on attributions of responsibility. Personality and Social Psychology Bulletin. 1998;24(6), 563–74.

3. Maner JK, Kenrick DT, Becker DV, Robertson TE, Hofer B, Neuberg SL, Delton AW, Butner J, Schaller M. Functional projection: how fundamental social motives can bias interpersonal perception. J Pers Soc Psychol. 2005 Jan;88(1):63–78.

4. Hugenberg K, Bodenhausen GV. Facing prejudice: implicit prejudice and the perception of facial threat. Psychol Sci. 2003 Nov;14(6):640–3.

5. Lerner JS, Keltner D. Fear, anger, and risk. J Pers Soc Psychol. 2001 Jul;81(1):146–59.

6. Thomas KS, Nelesen RA, Dimsdale JE. Relationships between hostility, anger expression, and blood pressure dipping in an ethnically diverse sample. Psychosom Med. 2004 May–Jun;66(3):298–304.

   Chang PP, Ford DE, Meoni LA, Wang NY, Klag MJ. Anger in young men and subsequent premature cardiovascular disease. Arch Intern Med 2002;162:901–6.

   Gallacher JE, Yarnell JW, Sweetnam PM, Elwood PC, Stansfeld SA. Anger and incident heart disease in the caerphilly study. Psychosom Med. 1999 Jul–Aug;61(4):446–53.

   Bongard S, al'Absi M, Lovallo WR. Interactive effects of trait hostility and anger expression on cardiovascular reactivity in young men. Int J Psychophysiol. 1998 Mar;28(2):181–91.

   Shapiro D, Goldstein IB, Jamner LD. Effects of cynical hostility, anger out, anxiety, and defensiveness on ambulatory blood pressure in black and white college students. Psychosom Med. 1996 Jul–Aug;58(4):354–64.

Shapiro D, Goldstein IB, Jamner LD. Effects of anger/hostility, defensiveness, gender, and family history of hypertension on cardiovascular reactivity. Psychophysiology. 1995 Sep;32(5):425–35.

7. Lerner JS, Tiedens LZ. Portrait of the angry decision maker: How appraisal tendencies shape anger's influence on cognition. J Behavioral Decision Making,. 2006:19: 115–137.

8. Anderson CA, Carnagey NL, Eubanks J. Exposure to violent media: the effects of songs with violent lyrics on aggressive thoughts and feelings. J Pers Soc Psychol. 2003 May;84(5):960–71.

Warm TR. The role of teasing in development and vice versa. J Dev Behav Pediatr. 1997 Apr;18(2):97–101.

Ueno Y. [The relation between the attitude toward humor, aggression and altruism] Shinrigaku Kenkyu. 1993 Oct;64(4):247–54.

Prerost FJ. Locus of control and the aggression inhibiting effects of aggressive humor appreciation. J Pers Assess. 1983 Jun;47(3):294–9.

Sinnott JD, Ross BM. Comparison of aggression and incongruity as factors in children's judgments of humor. J Genet Psychol. 1976 Jun;128(2d Half): 241–9.

9. Beaver JD, Lawrence AD, Passamonti L, Calder AJ. Appetitive motivation predicts the neural response to facial signals of aggression. J Neurosci. 2008 Mar 12;28(11):2719–25.

10. Dougal S, Phelps EA, Davachi L. The role of medial temporal lobe in item recognition and source recollection of emotional stimuli. Cogn Affect Behav Neurosci. 2007 Sep;7(3):233–42.

Landis T. Emotional words: what's so different from just words? Cortex. 2006 Aug;42(6):823–30.

Nakic M, Smith BW, Busis S, Vythilingam M, Blair RJ. The impact of affect and frequency on lexical decision: the role of the amygdala and inferior frontal cortex. Neuroimage. 2006 Jul 15;31(4):1752–61.

11. Hamann S, Mao H. Positive and negative emotional verbal stimuli elicit activity in the left amygdala. Neuroreport. 2002 Jan 21;13(1):15–9.

12. Reynolds SJ, Ceranic TL. The effects of moral judgment and moral identity on moral behavior: an empirical examination of the moral individual. J Appl Psychol. 2007 Nov;92(6):1610–24.

13. Eldakar OT, Farrell DL, Wilson DS. Selfish punishment: altruism can be maintained by competition among cheaters. J Theor Biol. 2007 Nov 21;249(2):198–205.

Nakamaru M, Iwasa Y. The coevolution of altruism and punishment: role of the selfish punisher. J Theor Biol. 2006 Jun 7;240(3):475–88.

Fowler JH. Altruistic punishment and the origin of cooperation. Proc Natl Acad Sci U S A. 2005 May 10;102(19):7047–9.

Fehr E, Rockenbach B. Human altruism: economic, neural, and evolutionary perspectives. Curr Opin Neurobiol. 2004 Dec;14(6):784–90.

Jaffe K. Altruism, altruistic punishment and social investment. Acta Biotheor. 2004;52(3):155–72.

Fehr E, Gächter S. Altruistic punishment in humans. Nature. 2002 Jan 10;415(6868):137–40.

14. Abe N, Suzuki M, Mori E, Itoh M, Fujii T. Deceiving others: distinct neural responses of the prefrontal cortex and amygdala in simple fabrication and deception with social interactions. J Cogn Neurosci. 2007 Feb;19(2):287–95.

Grèzes J, Berthoz S, Passingham RE. Amygdala activation when one is the target of deceit: did he lie to you or to someone else? Neuroimage. 2006 Apr 1;30(2):601–8.

Langleben DD, Loughead JW, Bilker WB, Ruparel K, Childress AR, Busch SI, Gur RC. Telling truth from lie in individual subjects with fast event-related fMRI. Hum Brain Mapp. 2005 Dec;26(4):262–72.

Grèzes J, Frith C, Passingham RE. Brain mechanisms for inferring deceit in the actions of others. J Neurosci. 2004 Jun 16;24(24):5500–5.

15. Lotze M, Veit R, Anders S, Birbaumer N. Evidence for a different role of the ventral and dorsal medial prefrontal cortex for social reactive aggression: An interactive fMRI study. Neuroimage. 2007 Jan 1;34(1):470–8.

16. de Quervain DJ, Fischbacher U, Treyer V, Schellhammer M, Schnyder U, Buck A, Fehr E. The neural basis of altruistic punishment. Science. 2004 Aug 27;305(5688):1254–8.

17. The earliest printed version of the "two wolves" tale that I could find dates to 1965 (see Bisagno reference below). However, in one Internet link (http://answers.google.com/answers/threadview?id=321024), a sixty-year-old man recalled hearing a version of the story when he attended a Sunday school class in 1958 at a Cherokee Baptist Church in Oklahoma. Missionary traditions often transformed indigenous folktales into Christian parables and teaching stories, so it's quite possible that the "two dogs" metaphor used by Bisagno was rooted in the Plains Indian tradion.

18. Bisagno J. *The Power of Positive Praying.* Zondervan, 1965.

19. Graham B. *The Holy Spirit: Activating God's Power in Your Life.* Word Publishing Group, 1978.

20. Sapolsky, R. *Why Zebras Don't Get Ulcers,* Third Edition. New York: Owl Books, 2004.

Goleman D. *Destructive Emotions.* New York: Bantam, 2003.

21. Buston PM, Balshine S. Cooperating in the face of uncertainty: a consistent framework for understanding the evolution of cooperation. Behav Processes. 2007 Oct;76(2):152–9.

Lehmann L, Keller L. The evolution of cooperation and altruism—a general framework and a classification of models. J Evol Biol. 2006 Sep;19(5): 1365–76.

Sachs JL, Mueller UG, Wilcox TP, Bull JJ. The evolution of cooperation. Q Rev Biol. 2004 Jun;79(2):135–60.

Marshall JA, Rowe JE. Kin selection may inhibit the evolution of reciprocation. J Theor Biol. 2003 Jun 7;222(3):331–5.

22. Batson CD, Thompson ER, Seuferling G, Whitney H, Strongman JA. Moral hypocrisy: appearing moral to oneself without being so. J Personal Soc Psychol. 1999; 77(3):525–37.

23. Shariff AF, Norenzayan A. God is watching you: priming God concepts increases prosocial behavior in an anonymous economic game. Psychol Sci. 2007 Sep;18(9):803–9.

24. Muris P, Merckelbach H, Ollendick TH, King NJ, Bogie N. Children's nighttime fears: parent-child ratings of frequency, content, origins, coping behaviors and severity. Behav Res Ther. 2001 Jan;39(1):13–28.

25. Mohammed NA, Eapen V, Bener A. Prevalence and correlates of childhood fears in Al-Ain, United Arab Emirates. East Mediterr Health J. 2001 May;7(3):422–7.

26. Huelsman MA, Piroch J, Wasieleski D. Relation of religiosity with academic dishonesty in a sample of college students. Psychol Rep. 2006 Dec;99(3): 739–42.

27. Storch EA, Storch JB. Organizational, nonorganizational, and intrinsic religiosity and academic dishonesty. Psychol Rep. 2001 Apr;88(2):548–52.

28. Sider D. *The Scandal of the Evangelical Conscience.* Baker Books, 2005.

29. Takahashi T, Ikeda K, Hasegawa T. Social evaluation-induced amylase elevation and economic decision-making in the dictator game in humans. Neuro Endocrinol Lett. 2007 Oct;28(5):662–5.

30. de Waal FB. Putting the altruism back into altruism: the evolution of empathy. Annu Rev Psychol. 2008;59:279–300.

Rilling J, Gutman D, Zeh T, Pagnoni G, Berns G, Kilts C. A neural basis for social cooperation. Neuron. 2002 Jul 18;35(2):395–405.

31. Kaplan JT, Freedman J, Iacoboni M. Us versus them: Political attitudes and party affiliation influence neural response to faces of presidential candidates. Neuropsychologia. 2007 Jan 7;45(1):55–64.

32. Eek D, Gärling T. Prosocials prefer equal outcomes to maximizing joint outcomes. Br J Soc Psychol. 2006 Jun;45(Pt 2):321–37.

Joireman J, Duell B. Mother Teresa versus Ebenezer Scrooge: mortality salience leads proselfs to endorse self-transcendent values (unless proselfs are reassured). Pers Soc Psychol Bull. 2005 Mar;31(3):307–20.

33. Turner RN, Hewstone M, Voci A. Reducing explicit and implicit outgroup prejudice via direct and extended contact: The mediating role of self-disclosure and intergroup anxiety. J Pers Soc Psychol. 2007 Sep;93(3):369–88.

Henry PJ, Hardin CD. The contact hypothesis revisited: status bias in the reduction of implicit prejudice in the United States and Lebanon. Psychol Sci. 2006 Oct;17(10):862–8.

Harris LT, Fiske ST. Dehumanizing the lowest of the low: neuroimaging responses to extreme out-groups. Psychol Sci. 2006 Oct;17(10):847–53.

Wheeler ME, Fiske ST. Controlling racial prejudice: social-cognitive goals affect amygdala and stereotype activation. Psychol Sci. 2005 Jan;16(1):56–63.

Paolini S, Hewstone M, Cairns E, Voci A. Effects of direct and indirect cross-group friendships on judgments of Catholics and Protestants in Northern Ireland: the mediating role of an anxiety-reduction mechanism. Pers Soc Psychol Bull. 2004 Jun;30(6):770–86.

Ensari N, Miller N. The out-group must not be so bad after all: the effects of disclosure, typicality, and salience on intergroup bias. J Pers Soc Psychol. 2002 Aug;83(2):313–29.

34. Oyamot CM Jr, Borgida E, Fisher EL. Can values moderate the attitudes of right-wing authoritarians? Pers Soc Psychol Bull. 2006 Apr;32(4):486–500.

35. Fowler JH, Johnson T, Smirnov O. Human behaviour: Egalitarian motive and altruistic punishment. Nature. 2005 Jan 6;433(7021):1.

36. Dawes CT, Fowler JH, Johnson T, McElreath R, Smirnov O. Egalitarian motives in humans. Nature. 2007 Apr 12;446(7137):794–6.

37. Feather NT. Acceptance and rejection of arguments in relation to attitude strength, critical ability, and intolerance of inconsistency. J Abnor and Soc Psychol. 1964: 69: 127–136.

38. Miller A. (ed.). *The Social Psychology of Good and Evil*. Guilford Press, 2004.

39. Cohen TR, Montoya RM, Insko CA. Group morality and intergroup relations: cross-cultural and experimental evidence. Pers Soc Psychol Bull. 2006 Nov;32(11):1559–72.

40. Tajfel H, Flament MC, Billig M, Bundy RP. Social categorization and intergroup behavior. Euro J Soc Psychol 1971;1:149–178.

41. Fiske ST. Bias against outgroups. In Miller, *The Social Psychology of Good and Evil*. Guilford Press, 2004.

42. Wheeler ME, Fiske ST. Controlling racial prejudice: social-cognitive goals affect amygdala and stereotype activation. Psychol Sci. 2005; 16(1):56–63.

Hart AJ, Whalen PJ, Shin LM, McInerney SC, Fischer H, Rauch SL. Differential response in the human amygdala to racial outgroup vs ingroup face stimuli. Neuroreport. 2000; 11(11):2351–5.

43. For a comprehensive analysis of the neural varieties of morality and prejudice, see Chapter 6 in Newberg and Waldman, *Born to Believe* (The Free Press, 2007).

44. Aronson E. Reducing hostility and building compassion: Lessons from the jigsaw classroom. In Miller, *The Social Psychology of Good and Evil.* Guilford Press, 2004.

45. Davis JA, et al., General Social Survey, 2000. National Opinion Research Center. See also the Barna Update, "A New Generation of Pastors Places Its Stamp on Ministry," February 17, 2004.

46. The Fundamentalism Project incorporated hundreds of experts on religion and culture, was conducted under the auspices of the American Academy of Arts and Sciences, and funded by the John D. and Catherine T. MacArthur Foundation. Five encyclopedic volumes were edited by Marty Appleby and published by the University of Chicago Press, volumes 1 through 5, 1991–95. You can read several seminal papers at http://www.illuminos.com/mem/ selectPapers/contentsSelectList.html.

47. Hood RW, Hill PC, Williamson WP. *The Psychology of Religious Fundamentalism.* Guilford Press, 2005.

48. Flannelly KJ, Koenig HG, Ellison CG, Galek K, Krause N. Belief in life after death and mental health: findings from a national survey. J Nerv Ment Dis. 2006 Jul;(7):524–9.

    Murphy PE, Ciarrocchi JW, Piedmont RL, Cheston S, Peyrot M, Fitchett G. The relation of religious belief and practices, depression, and hopelessness in persons with clinical depression. J Consult Clin Psychol. 2000 Dec;68(6): 1102–6.

    Alvarado KA, Templer DI, Bresler C, Thomas-Dobson S. The relationship of religious variables to death depression and death anxiety. J Clin Psychol. 1995 Mar;51(2):202–4.

49. Vasegh S, Mohammadi MR. Religiosity, anxiety, and depression among a sample of Iranian medical students. Int J Psychiatry Med. 2007;37(2): 213–27.

50. Hovey JD, Seligman LD. Religious coping, family support, and negative affect in college students. Psychol Rep. 2007 Jun;100(3 Pt 1):787–8.

51. Kalkhoran MA, Karimollahi M. Religiousness and preoperative anxiety: a correlational study. Ann Gen Psychiatry. 2007 Jun 29;6:17.

    Grzesiak-Feldman M. Conspiracy thinking and state-trait anxiety in young Polish adults. Psychol Rep. 2007 Feb;100(1):199–202.

ENDNOTES

Altemeyer, B. *The Authoritarians*. Online publication: University of Manitoba, 2006.

52. Kreindler SA. A dual group processes model of individual differences in prejudice. Pers Soc Psychol Rev. 2005;9(2):90–107.

53. Phelps EA. Human emotion and memory: interactions of the amygdala and hippocampal complex. Curr Opin Neurobiol. 2004 Apr;14(2):198–202.

54. Sander D, Grandjean D, Pourtois G, Schwartz S, Seghier ML, Scherer KR, Vuilleumier P. Emotion and attention interactions in social cognition: brain regions involved in processing anger prosody. Neuroimage. 2005 Dec;28(4):848–58.

55. Stein MB, Goldin PR, Sareen J, Zorrilla LT, Brown GG. Increased amygdala activation to angry and contemptuous faces in generalized social phobia. Arch Gen Psychiatry. 2002 Nov;59(11):1027–34.

56. Hariri AR, Tessitore A, Mattay VS, Fera F, Weinberger DR. The amygdala response to emotional stimuli: a comparison of faces and scenes. Neuroimage. 2002 Sep;17(1):317–23.

57. Wild B, Erb M, Bartels M. Are emotions contagious? Evoked emotions while viewing emotionally expressive faces: quality, quantity, time course and gender differences. Psychiatry Res. 2001 Jun 1;102(2):109–24.

58. Kirsh SJ, Mounts JR, Olczak PV. Violent media consumption and the recognition of dynamic facial expressions. J Interpers Violence. 2006 May;21(5): 571–84.

Yukawa S, Yoshida F. The effect of media violence on aggression: Is aggressive behavior mediated by aggressive cognitions and emotions? Shinrigaku Kenkyu. 1999 Jun;70(2):94–103.

59. Fischer P, Greitemeyer T. Music and aggression: the impact of sexual-aggressive song lyrics on aggression-related thoughts, emotions, and behavior toward the same and the opposite sex. Pers Soc Psychol Bull. 2006 Sep;32(9):1165–76.

60. Anderson CA, Carnagey NL, Eubanks J. Exposure to violent media: the effects of songs with violent lyrics on aggressive thoughts and feelings. J Pers Soc Psychol. 2003 May;84(5):960–71.

61. Carnagey NL, Anderson CA. The effects of reward and punishment in violent video games on aggressive affect, cognition, and behavior. Psychol Sci. 2005 Nov;16(11):882–9.

Anderson CA, Bushman BJ. Effects of violent video games on aggressive behavior, aggressive cognition, aggressive affect, physiological arousal, and prosocial behavior: a meta-analytic review of the scientific literature. Psychol Sci. 2001 Sep;12(5):353–9.

62. Anderson CA. An update on the effects of playing violent video games. J Adolesc. 2004 Feb;27(1):113–22.

63. Kisley MA, Wood S, Burrows CL. Looking at the sunny side of life: age-related change in an event-related potential measure of the negativity bias. Psychol Sci. 2007 Sep;18(9):838–43.

64. Duhachek A, Zhang S, Krishnan S. Anticipated group interaction: coping with valence asymmetries in attitude shift. Journal Of Consumer Research. 2007 Oct;(34).

65. Magnée MJ, Stekelenburg JJ, Kemner C, de Gelder B. Similar facial electromyographic responses to faces, voices, and body expressions. Neuroreport. 2007 Mar 5;18(4):369–72.

66. Tamura R, Kameda T. Are facial expressions contagious in the Japanese? Shinrigaku Kenkyu. 2006 Oct;77(4):377–82.

Ilies R, Wagner DT, Morgeson FP. Explaining affective linkages in teams: individual differences in susceptibility to contagion and individualism-collectivism. J Appl Psychol. 2007 Jul;92(4):1140–8.

Lundqvist LO. Facial EMG reactions to facial expressions: a case of facial emotional contagion? Scand J Psychol. 1995 Jun;36(2):130–41.

67. Moody EJ, McIntosh DN, Mann LJ, Weisser KR. More than mere mimicry? The influence of emotion on rapid facial reactions to faces. Emotion. 2007 May;7(2):447–57.

68. Sonnby-Borgström M. [The facial expression says more than words. Is emotional "contagion" via facial expression the first step toward empathy?] Lakartidningen. 2002 Mar 27;99(13):1438–42.

69. Bond AJ, Verheyden SL, Wingrove J, Curran HV. Angry cognitive bias, trait aggression and impulsivity in substance users. Psychopharmacology (Berl). 2004 Jan;171(3):331–9.

70. Wachs K, Cordova JV. Mindful relating: exploring mindfulness and emotion repertoires in intimate relationships. J Marital Fam Ther. 2007 Oct;33(4):464–81.

Carson JW, Carson KM, Gil KM, Baucom DH. Self-expansion as a mediator of relationship improvements in a mindfulness intervention. J Marital Fam Ther. 2007 Oct;33(4):517–28.

Barnes S, Brown KW, Krusemark E, Campbell WK, Rogge RD. The role of mindfulness in romantic relationship satisfaction and responses to relationship stress. J Marital Fam Ther. 2007 Oct;33(4):482–500.

71. Block-Lerner J, Adair C, Plumb JC, Rhatigan DL, Orsillo SM. The case for mindfulness-based approaches in the cultivation of empathy: does nonjudgmental, present-moment awareness increase capacity for perspective-taking and empathic concern? J Marital Fam Ther. 2007 Oct;33(4):501–16.

72. Lester E. Roberts PS. Learning about World Religions in Public Schools: The Impact on Student Attitudes and Community Acceptance in Modesto, Cali-

fornia. First Amendment Center, 2006. You can read and download the entire report by going to http://www.firstamendmentcenter.org/about.aspx?id= 16863.

73. For a comprehensive overview, go to http://www.prisonexp.org, where you can see video footage of the actual experiment.

74. Krakovsky M. (interviewer). Zimbardo Unbound. Stanford Magazine. May/June 2007.

75. Mancuso S. Tolerance in Terror: Terror Management Theory. Oberlin College, unpublished paper.

76. Greenberg J, Jonas E. Psychological motives and political orientation—the left, the right, and the rigid: comment on Jost et al. Psychol Bull. 2003 May;129(3):376–82.

Jost JT, Glaser J, Kruglanski, AW, Sulloway FJ. Political conservatism as motivated social cognition. Psychol Bull. 2003;129:339–75.

77. Crowson HM, Thoma SJ, Hestevold N. Is political conservatism synonymous with authoritarianism? J Soc Psychol. 2005 Oct;145(5):571–92.

78. Evans J, Heron J, Lewis G, Araya R, Wolke D. Negative self-schemas and the onset of depression in women: longitudinal study. Br J Psychiatry. 2005 Apr;186:302–7.

79. Exline JJ, Yali AM, Sanderson WC. Guilt, discord, and alienation: the role of religious strain in depression and suicidality. J Clin Psychol. 2000 Dec;56(12):1481–96.

CHAPTER 8. EXERCISING YOUR BRAIN (PAGES 149–169)

1. Ohayon MM, Vecchierini MF. Normative sleep data, cognitive function and daily living activities in older adults in the community. Sleep. 2005 Aug 1;28(8):981–9.

2. Frauscher B, Gschliesser V, Brandauer E, Ulmer H, Poewe W, Högl B. The relation between abnormal behaviors and REM sleep microstructure in patients with REM sleep behavior disorder. Sleep Med. 2008 Mar 21.

3. Baulk SD, Biggs SN, Reid KJ, van den Heuvel CJ, Dawson D. Chasing the silver bullet: measuring driver fatigue using simple and complex tasks. Accid Anal Prev. 2008 Jan;40(1):396–402.

Jones CB, Dorrian J, Jay SM, Lamond N, Ferguson S, Dawson D. Self-awareness of impairment and the decision to drive after an extended period of wakefulness. Chronobiol Int. 2006;23(6):1253–63.

4. Song S, Howard JH Jr, Howard DV. Sleep does not benefit probabilistic motor sequence learning. J Neurosci. 2007 Nov 14;27(46):12475–83.

Lockley SW, Barger LK, Ayas NT, Rothschild JM, Czeisler CA, Landrigan CP; Harvard Work Hours, Health and Safety Group. Effects of health care provider work hours and sleep deprivation on safety and performance. Jt Comm J Qual Patient Saf. 2007 Nov;33(11 Suppl):7–18.

Zeitzer JM, Duffy JF, Lockley SW, Dijk DJ, Czeisler CA. Plasma melatonin rhythms in young and older humans during sleep, sleep deprivation, and wake. Sleep. 2007 Nov 1;30(11):1437–43.

Turner TH, Drummond SP, Salamat JS, Brown GG. Effects of 42 hr of total sleep deprivation on component processes of verbal working memory. Neuropsychology. 2007 Nov;21(6):787–95.

5. Calhoun PS, Wiley M, Dennis MF, Means MK, Edinger JD, Beckham JC. Objective evidence of sleep disturbance in women with posttraumatic stress disorder. J Trauma Stress. 2007 Dec;20(6):1009–18.

Perez-Chada D, Perez-Lloret S, Videla AJ, Cardinali D, Bergna MA, Fernández-Acquier M, Larrateguy L, Zabert GE, Drake C. Sleep disordered breathing and daytime sleepiness are associated with poor academic performance in teenagers. A study using the Pediatric Daytime Sleepiness Scale (PDSS). Sleep. 2007 Dec 1;30(12):1698–703.

Palermo TM, Toliver-Sokol M, Fonareva I, Koh JL. Objective and subjective assessment of sleep in adolescents with chronic pain compared to healthy adolescents. Clin J Pain. 2007 Nov–Dec;23(9):812–20.

Comella CL. Sleep disorders in Parkinson's disease: an overview. Mov Disord. 2007 Sep;22 Suppl 17:S367–73.

Blackwell T, Yaffe K, Ancoli-Israel S, Schneider JL, Cauley JA, Hillier TA, Fink HA, Stone KL; Study of Osteoporotic Fractures Group. Poor sleep is associated with impaired cognitive function in older women: the study of osteoporotic fractures. J Gerontol A Biol Sci Med Sci. 2006 Apr;61(4):405–10.

6. Brain Basics: Understanding Sleep. National Institute of Neurological Disorders and Stroke. http://www.ninds.nih.gov/disorders/brain_basics/understanding_sleep.htm.

7. Okun MS, Bowers D, Springer U, Shapira NA, Malone D, Rezai AR, Nuttin B, Heilman KM, Morecraft RJ, Rasmussen SA, Greenberg BD, Foote KD, Goodman WK. What's in a "smile?" Intra-operative observations of contralateral smiles induced by deep brain stimulation. Neurocase. 2004 Aug;10(4):271–9.

8. Hanh T. *Being Peace*. Parallax Press, 1987.

9. Tamura R, Kameda T. Are facial expressions contagious in the Japanese? Shinrigaku Kenkyu. 2006 Oct;77(4):377–82. Japanese.

Wild B, Erb M, Eyb M, Bartels M, Grodd W. Why are smiles contagious? An fMRI study of the interaction between perception of facial affect and facial movements. Psychiatry Res. 2003 May 1;123(1):17–36.

Wild B, Erb M, Bartels M. Are emotions contagious? Evoked emotions while viewing emotionally expressive faces: quality, quantity, time course and gender differences. Psychiatry Res. 2001 Jun 1;102(2):109–24.

10. Oliver C, Horsler K, Berg K, Bellamy G, Dick K, Griffiths E. Genomic imprinting and the expression of affect in Angelman syndrome: what's in the smile? J Child Psychol Psychiatry. 2007 Jun;48(6):571–9.

11. Hennenlotter A, Schroeder U, Erhard P, Castrop F, Haslinger B, Stoecker D, Lange KW, Ceballos-Baumann AO. A common neural basis for receptive and expressive communication of pleasant facial affect. Neuroimage. 2005 Jun;26(2):581–91.

12. Okun MS, Bowers D, Springer U, Shapira NA, Malone D, Rezai AR, Nuttin B, Heilman KM, Morecraft RJ, Rasmussen SA, Greenberg BD, Foote KD, Goodman WK. What's in a "smile?" Intra-operative observations of contralateral smiles induced by deep brain stimulation. Neurocase. 2004 Aug;10(4):271–9.

13. Moody EJ, McIntosh DN, Mann LJ, Weisser KR. More than mere mimicry? The influence of emotion on rapid facial reactions to faces. Emotion. 2007 May;7(2):447–57.

Falkenberg I, Bartels M, Wild B. Keep smiling! Facial reactions to emotional stimuli and their relationship to emotional contagion in patients with schizophrenia. Eur Arch Psychiatry Clin Neurosci. 2008 Feb 23.

O'Doherty J, Winston J, Critchley H, Perrett D, Burt DM, Dolan RJ. Beauty in a smile: the role of medial orbitofrontal cortex in facial attractiveness. Neuropsychologia. 2003;41(2):147–55.

14. Finzi E, Wasserman E. Treatment of depression with botulinum toxin A: a case series. Dermatol Surg. 2006 May;32(5):645–9. This study was highly criticized by Alastair Carruthers, president of the American Society for Dermatologic Surgery, because of the brief follow-up period, small number of participants, lack of a comparison group, and the use of the patient's subjective reports. In other words, it may be a placebo effect brought about by the patient's belief that a prettier face will improve social interactions, thus promising a more optimistic future. On the other hand, any interruption of a behavior associated with negative mood may alter neural circuits that generate that mood.

15. Wild B, Rodden FA, Rapp A, Erb M, Grodd W, Ruch W. Humor and smiling: cortical regions selective for cognitive, affective, and volitional components. Neurology. 2006 Mar 28;66(6):887–93.

16. Bartolo A, Benuzzi F, Nocetti L, Baraldi P, Nichelli P. Humor comprehension and appreciation: an FMRI study. J Cogn Neurosci. 2006 Nov;18(11):1789–98.

17. Moran JM, Wig GS, Adams RB Jr, Janata P, Kelley WM. Neural correlates of humor detection and appreciation. Neuroimage. 2004 Mar;21(3):1055–60.

Watson KK, Matthews BJ, Allman JM. Brain activation during sight gags and language-dependent humor. Cereb Cortex. 2007 Feb;17(2):314–24.

18. Hayashi T, Tsujii S, Iburi T, Tamanaha T, Yamagami K, Ishibashi R, Hori M, Sakamoto S, Ishii H, Murakami K. Laughter up-regulates the genes related to NK cell activity in diabetes. Biomed Res. 2008 Dec;28(6):281–5.

Hayashi T, Urayama O, Hori M, Sakamoto S, Nasir UM, Iwanaga S, Hayashi K, Suzuki F, Kawai K, Murakami K. Laughter modulates prorenin receptor gene expression in patients with type 2 diabetes. J Psychosom Res. 2007 Jun;62(6):703–6.

Hayashi T, Urayama O, Kawai K, Hayashi K, Iwanaga S, Ohta M, Saito T, Murakami K. Laughter regulates gene expression in patients with type 2 diabetes. Psychother Psychosom. 2006;75(1):62–5. Erratum in: Psychother Psychosom. 2006;75(2):106.

Bennett MP, Zeller JM, Rosenberg L, McCann J. The effect of mirthful laughter on stress and natural killer cell activity. Altern Ther Health Med. 2003 Mar–Apr;9(2):38–45.

Takahashi K, Iwase M, Yamashita K, Tatsumoto Y, Ue H, Kuratsune H, Shimizu A, Takeda M. The elevation of natural killer cell activity induced by laughter in a crossover designed study. Int J Mol Med. 2001 Dec;8(6):645–50.

19. Mitterschiffthaler MT, Fu CH, Dalton JA, Andrew CM, Williams SC. A functional MRI study of happy and sad affective states induced by classical music. Hum Brain Mapp. 2007 Nov;28(11):1150–62.

Blood AJ, Zatorre RJ. Intensely pleasurable responses to music correlate with activity in brain regions implicated in reward and emotion. Proc Natl Acad Sci U S A. 2001 Sep 25;98(20):11818–23.

20. Gallagher LM, Lagman R, Walsh D, Davis MP, Legrand SB. The clinical effects of music therapy in palliative medicine. Support Care Cancer. 2006 Aug;14(8):859–66.

21. Jacobs R, Harvey AS, Anderson V. Executive function following focal frontal lobe lesions: impact of timing of lesion on outcome. Cortex. 2007 Aug;43(6):792–805.

Counts SE, Nadeem M, Lad SP, Wuu J, Mufson EJ. Differential expression of synaptic proteins in the frontal and temporal cortex of elderly subjects with mild cognitive impairment. J Neuropathol Exp Neurol. 2006 Jun;65(6):592–601.

22. Elston GN. Pyramidal cells of the frontal lobe: all the more spinous to think with. J Neurosci. 2000 Sep 15;20(18):RC95.

23. Hall PA, Fong GT, Epp LJ, Elias LJ. Executive function moderates the intention-behavior link for physical activity and dietary behavior. Psychol Health. 2008;23(3):309–26.

24. Carretti B, Borella E, De Beni R. Does strategic memory training improve the working memory performance of younger and older adults? Exp Psychol. 2007;54(4):311–20.

Bottiroli S, Cavallini E, Vecchi T. Long-term effects of memory training in the elderly: A longitudinal study. Arch Gerontol Geriatr. 2007 Oct 11.

O'Hara R, Brooks JO 3rd, Friedman L, Schroder CM, Morgan KS, Kraemer HC. Long-term effects of mnemonic training in community-dwelling older adults. J Psychiatr Res. 2007 Oct;41(7):585–90.

Willis SL, Tennstedt SL, Marsiske M, Ball K, Elias J, Koepke KM, Morris JN, Rebok GW, Unverzagt FW, Stoddard AM, Wright E; ACTIVE Study Group. Long-term effects of cognitive training on everyday functional outcomes in older adults. JAMA. 2006 Dec 20;296(23):2805–14.

Cheng ST, Chan AC, Yu EC. An exploratory study of the effect of mahjong on the cognitive functioning of persons with dementia. Int J Geriatr Psychiatry. 2006 Jul;21(7):611–7.

Derwinger A, Stigsdotter Neely A, MacDonald S, Bäckman L. Forgetting numbers in old age: strategy and learning speed matter. Gerontology. 2005 Jul–Aug;51(4):277–84.

Derwinger A, Stigsdotter Neely A, Backman L. Design your own memory strategies! Self-generated strategy training versus mnemonic training in old age: an 8-month follow-up. Neuropsychol Rehabil. 2005 Mar;15(1):37–54.

Ball K, Berch DB, Helmers KF, Jobe JB, Leveck MD, Marsiske M, Morris JN, Rebok GW, Smith DM, Tennstedt SL, Unverzagt FW, Willis SL; Advanced Cognitive Training for Independent and Vital Elderly Study Group. Effects of cognitive training interventions with older adults: a randomized controlled trial. JAMA. 2002 Nov 13;288(18):2271–81.

Brooks JO 3rd, Friedman L, Pearman AM, Gray C, Yesavage JA. Mnemonic training in older adults: effects of age, length of training, and type of cognitive pretraining. Int Psychogeriatr. 1999 Mar;11(1):75–84.

25. Willis SL, Tennstedt SL, Marsiske M, Ball K, Elias J, Koepke KM, Morris JN, Rebok GW, Unverzagt FW, Stoddard AM, Wright E; ACTIVE Study Group. Long-term effects of cognitive training on everyday functional outcomes in older adults. JAMA. 2006 Dec 20;296(23):2805–14.

Wadley VG, Benz RL, Ball KK, Roenker DL, Edwards JD, Vance DE. Development and evaluation of home-based speed-of-processing training for older adults. Arch Phys Med Rehabil. 2006 Jun;87(6):757–63.

26. Hambrick DZ, Salthouse TA, Meinz EJ. Predictors of crossword puzzle proficiency and moderators of age-cognition relations. J Exp Psychol Gen. 1999 Jun;128(2):131–64.

MacKay DG, Abrams L. Age-linked declines in retrieving orthographic knowledge: empirical, practical, and theoretical implications. Psychol Aging. 1998 Dec;13(4):647–62.

27. Gimmig D, Huguet P, Caverni JP, Cury F. Choking under pressure and working memory capacity: when performance pressure reduces fluid intelligence. Psychon Bull Rev. 2006 Dec;13(6):1005–10.

28. Azari NP, Nickel J, Wunderlich G, Niedeggen M, Hefter H, Tellmann L, Herzog H, Stoerig P, Birnbacher D, Seitz RJ. Neural correlates of religious experience. Eur J Neurosci. 2001 Apr;13(8):1649–52.

29. Grüsser SM, Thalemann R, Albrecht U, Thalemann CN. [Excessive computer usage in adolescents—results of a psychometric evaluation] Wien Klin Wochenschr. 2005 Mar;117(5–6):188–95.

30. Bioulac S, Arfi L, Bouvard MP. Attention deficit/hyperactivity disorder and video games: a comparative study of hyperactive and control children. Eur Psychiatry. 2008 Mar;23(2):134–41.

Chan PA, Rabinowitz T. A cross-sectional analysis of video games and attention deficit hyperactivity disorder symptoms in adolescents. Ann Gen Psychiatry. 2006 Oct 24;5:16.

31. Tejeiro Salguero RA, Morán RM. Measuring problem video game playing in adolescents. Addiction. 2002 Dec;97(12):1601–6.

32. Grüsser SM, Thalemann R, Griffiths MD. Excessive computer game playing: evidence for addiction and aggression? Cyberpsychol Behav. 2007 Apr;10(2):290–2.

33. Carnagey NL, Anderson CA. The effects of reward and punishment in violent video games on aggressive affect, cognition, and behavior. Psychol Sci. 2005 Nov;16(11):882–9.

Anderson CA. An update on the effects of playing violent video games. J Adolesc. 2004 Feb;27(1):113–22.

Anderson CA, Bushman BJ. Effects of violent video games on aggressive behavior, aggressive cognition, aggressive affect, physiological arousal, and prosocial behavior: a meta-analytic review of the scientific literature. Psychol Sci. 2001 Sep;12(5):353–9.

34. Phillips H. Video game brain damage claim criticized. *New Scientist*. July 11, 2002. NewScientist.com news service.

35. Jimison H, Pavel M. Embedded assessment algorithms within home-based cognitive computer game exercises for elders. Conf Proc IEEE Eng Med Biol Soc. 2006;1:6101–4.

36. Gillam RB, Loeb DF, Hoffman LM, Bohman T, Champlin CA, Thibodeau L, Widen J, Brandel J, Friel-Patti S. The efficacy of Fast ForWord Language intervention in school-age children with language impairment: a

randomized controlled trial. J Speech Lang Hear Res. 2008 Feb;51(1): 97–119.

Valentine D, Hedrick MS, Swanson LA. Effect of an auditory training program on reading, phoneme awareness, and language. Percept Mot Skills. 2006 Aug;103(1):183–96.

Cohen W, Hodson A, O'Hare A, Boyle J, Durrani T, McCartney E, Mattey M, Naftalin L, Watson J. Effects of computer-based intervention through acoustically modified speech (Fast ForWord) in severe mixed receptive-expressive language impairment: outcomes from a randomized controlled trial. J Speech Lang Hear Res. 2005 Jun;48(3):715–29.

37. Ball K, Edwards JD, Ross LA. The impact of speed of processing training on cognitive and everyday functions. J Gerontol B Psychol Sci Soc Sci. 2007 Jun;62 Spec No 1:19–31.

Mahncke HW, Connor BB, Appelman J, Ahsanuddin ON, Hardy JL, Wood RA, Joyce NM, Boniske T, Atkins SM, Merzenich MM. Memory enhancement in healthy older adults using a brain plasticity-based training program: a randomized, controlled study. Proc Natl Acad Sci U S A. 2006 Aug 15;103(33):12523–8.

Mahncke HW, Bronstone A, Merzenich MM. Brain plasticity and functional losses in the aged: scientific bases for a novel intervention. Prog Brain Res. 2006;157:81–109.

Ball K, Berch DB, Helmers KF, Jobe JB, Leveck MD, Marsiske M, Morris JN, Rebok GW, Smith DM, Tennstedt SL, Unverzagt FW, Willis SL; Advanced Cognitive Training for Independent and Vital Elderly Study Group. Effects of cognitive training interventions with older adults: a randomized controlled trial. JAMA. 2002 Nov 13;288(18):2271–81.

Edwards JD, Wadley VG, Myers RS, Roenker DL, Cissell GM, Ball KK. Transfer of a speed of processing intervention to near and far cognitive functions. Gerontology. 2002 Sep–Oct;48(5):329–40.

See also an article on Dr. Michael Merzenich's research in *The Journal of Life Sciences,* March 6, 2008, http://www.tjols.com/printer_article-534-4.html.

38. Krout RE. The effects of single-session music therapy interventions on the observed and self-reported levels of pain control, physical comfort, and relaxation of hospice patients. Am J Hosp Palliat Care. 2001 Nov–Dec;18(6): 383–90.

39. Schellenberg EG, Hallam S. Music listening and cognitive abilities in 10- and 11-year-olds: the blur effect. Ann N Y Acad Sci. 2005 Dec;1060:202–9.

Aoun P, Jones T, Shaw GL, Bodner M. Long-term enhancement of maze learning in mice via a generalized Mozart effect. Neurol Res. 2005 Dec;27(8):791–6.

Bangerter A, Heath C. The Mozart effect: tracking the evolution of a scientific legend. Br J Soc Psychol. 2004 Dec;43(Pt 4):605–23.

40. Wlodarczyk N. The effect of music therapy on the spirituality of persons in an in-patient hospice unit as measured by self-report. J Music Ther. 2007 Summer;44(2):113–22.

41. Boone DR, McFarlane SC. A critical view of the yawn-sigh as a voice therapy technique. J Voice. 1993 Mar;7(1):75–80.

42. Platek SM, Mohamed FB, Gallup GG Jr. Contagious yawning and the brain. Brain Res Cogn Brain Res. 2005 May;23(2–3):448–52.

Schürmann M, Hesse MD, Stephan KE, Saarela M, Zilles K, Hari R, Fink GR. Yearning to yawn: the neural basis of contagious yawning. Neuroimage. 2005 Feb 15;24(4):1260–4.

43. Cavanna AE. The precuneus and consciousness. CNS Spectr. 2007 Jul;12(7):545–52.

Cavanna AE, Trimble MR. The precuneus: a review of its functional anatomy and behavioural correlates. Brain. 2006 Mar;129(Pt 3):564–83.

44. Lou HC, Nowak M, Kjaer TW. The mental self. Prog Brain Res. 2005;150:197–204.

45. Karas G, Scheltens P, Rombouts S, van Schijndel R, Klein M, Jones B, van der Flier W, Vrenken H, Barkhof F. Precuneus atrophy in early-onset Alzheimer's disease: a morphometric structural MRI study. Neuroradiology. 2007 Dec;49(12):967–76.

46. Schulte-Rüther M, Markowitsch HJ, Fink GR, Piefke M. Mirror neuron and theory of mind mechanisms involved in face-to-face interactions: a functional magnetic resonance imaging approach to empathy. J Cogn Neurosci. 2007 Aug;19(8):1354–72.

Castellanos FX, Margulies DS, Kelly C, Uddin LQ, Ghaffari M, Kirsch A, Shaw D, Shehzad Z, Di Martino A, Biswal B, Sonuga-Barke EJ, Rotrosen J, Adler LA, Milham MP. Cingulate-precuneus interactions: a new locus of dysfunction in adult attention-deficit/hyperactivity disorder. Biol Psychiatry. 2008 Feb 1;63(3):332–7.

Völlm BA, Taylor AN, Richardson P, Corcoran R, Stirling J, McKie S, Deakin JF, Elliott R. Neuronal correlates of theory of mind and empathy: a functional magnetic resonance imaging study in a nonverbal task. Neuroimage. 2006 Jan 1;29(1):90–8.

Uddin LQ, Kaplan JT, Molnar-Szakacs I, Zaidel E, Iacoboni M. Self-face recognition activates a frontoparietal "mirror" network in the right hemisphere: an event-related fMRI study. Neuroimage. 2005 Apr 15;25(3):926–35.

47. Zilli I, Giganti F, Salzarulo P. Yawning in morning and evening types. Physiol Behav. 2007 Jun 8;91(2–3):218–22.

Guggisberg AG, Mathis J, Herrmann US, Hess CW. The functional relationship between yawning and vigilance. Behav Brain Res. 2007 Apr 16;179(1):159–66.

48. Giganti F, Hayes MJ, Cioni G, Salzarulo P. Yawning frequency and distribution in preterm and near term infants assessed throughout 24-h recordings. Infant Behav Dev. 2007 Dec;30(4):641–7.

Seki Y, Nakatani Y, Kita I, Sato-Suzuki I, Oguri M, Arita H. Light induces cortical activation and yawning in rats. Behav Brain Res. 2003 Mar 18;140(1–2):65–73.

49. Matikainen J, Elo H. Does yawning increase arousal through mechanical stimulation of the carotid body? Med Hypotheses. 2008;70(3):488–92.

Kita I, Kubota N, Yanagita S, Motoki C. Intracerebroventricular administration of corticotropin-releasing factor antagonist attenuates arousal response accompanied by yawning behavior in rats. Neurosci Lett. 2008 Mar 15;433(3):205–8.

Kita I, Seki Y, Nakatani Y, Fumoto M, Oguri M, Sato-Suzuki I, Arita H. Corticotropin-releasing factor neurons in the hypothalamic paraventricular nucleus are involved in arousal/yawning response of rats. Behav Brain Res. 2006 Apr 25;169(1):48–56.

Walusinski O. [Yawning: from birth to senescence] Psychol Neuropsychiatr Vieil. 2006 Mar;4(1):39–46.

Kasuya Y, Murakami T, Oshima T, Dohi S. Does yawning represent a transient arousal-shift during intravenous induction of general anesthesia? Anesth Analg. 2005 Aug;101(2):382–4.

Sato-Suzuki I, Kita I, Seki Y, Oguri M, Arita H. Cortical arousal induced by microinjection of orexins into the paraventricular nucleus of the rat. Behav Brain Res. 2002 Jan 22;128(2):169–77.

Alóe F. Yawning. Arq Neuropsiquiatr. 1994 Jun;52(2):273–6.

Askenasy JJ. Is yawning an arousal defense reflex? J Psychol. 1989 Nov;123(6):609–21.

50. Walusinski O. Yawning: unsuspected avenue for a better understanding of arousal and interoception. Med Hypotheses. 2006;67(1):6–14.

Platek SM, Mohamed FB, Gallup GG Jr. Contagious yawning and the brain. Brain Res Cogn Brain Res. 2005 May;23(2–3):448–52.

51. Schürmann M, Hesse MD, Stephan KE, Saarela M, Zilles K, Hari R, Fink GR. Yearning to yawn: the neural basis of contagious yawning. Neuroimage. 2005 Feb 15;24(4):1260–4.

52. Wong A. Why do we yawn when we are tired? And why does it seem to be contagious? Scientific American. August 12, 2002.

53. Sherer DM, Smith SA, Abramowicz JS. Fetal yawning in utero at 20 weeks gestation. J Ultrasound Med. 1991;10:68.

54. Giganti F, Hayes MJ, Cioni G, Salzarulo P. Yawning frequency and distribution in preterm and near term infants assessed throughout 24-h recordings. Infant Behav Dev. 2007 Dec;30(4):641–7.

55. Giganti F, Hayes MJ, Akilesh MR, Salzarulo P. Yawning and behavioral states in premature infants. Dev Psychobiol. 2002 Nov;41(3):289–96.

56. Gallup A, Gallup G. Yawning as a Brain Cooling Mechanism: Nasal Breathing and Forehead Cooling Diminish the Incidence of Contagious Yawning. Evolutionary Psychology. http://www.epjournal.net—2007. 5(1): 92–101.

57. Senju A, Maeda M, Kikuchi Y, Hasegawa T, Tojo Y, Osanai H. Absence of contagious yawning in children with autism spectrum disorder. Biol Lett. 2007 Dec 22;3(6):706–8.

Wong A. Why do we yawn when we are tired? And why does it seem to be contagious? Scientific American. August 12, 2002.

58. Paukner A, Anderson JR. Video-induced yawning in stumptail macaques (*Macaca arctoides*). Biol Lett. 2006 Mar 22;2(1):36–8.

59. Anderson JR, Myowa-Yamakoshi M, Matsuzawa T. Contagious yawning in chimpanzees. Proceedings of the Royal Society: Biological Sciences. 2004;271, Biology Letters Supplement 6: S468–S470.

Platek SM, Critton SR, Myers TE, and Gallup GG. Jr. Contagious yawning: the role of self-awareness and mental state attribution. Cogn Brain Res. 2003;17:223–7.

60. Platek SM, Mohamed FB, Gallup GG Jr. Contagious yawning and the brain. Brain Res Cogn Brain Res. 2005 May;23(2–3):448–52.

61. Opar A. (Quoting psychologist Robert Provine of the University of Maryland). Scientists aren't exactly sure why we yawn, but they know yawns are contagious. Seed. May 5, 2006.

62. Provine RR. Yawning. American Scientist, 2005 Nov–Dec;93(6):532–49.

63. Kita I, Kubota N, Yanagita S, Motoki C. Intracerebroventricular administration of corticotropin-releasing factor antagonist attenuates arousal response accompanied by yawning behavior in rats. Neurosci Lett. 2008 Mar 15;433(3):205–8.

Giménez-Llort L, Cañete T, Guitart-Masip M, Fernández-Teruel A, Tobeña A. Two distinctive apomorphine-induced phenotypes in the Roman high- and low-avoidance rats. Physiol Behav. 2005 Nov 15;86(4):458–66.

Díaz-Romero M, Arias-Montaño JA, Eguibar JR, Flores G. Enhanced binding of dopamine D1 receptors in caudate-putamen subregions in High-Yawning Sprague-Dawley rats. Synapse. 2005 May;56(2):69–73.

Nasello AG, Tieppo CA, Felicio LF. Apomorphine-induced yawning in the rat: influence of fasting and time of day. Physiol Behav. 1995 May;57(5): 967–71.

64. Singer OC, Humpich MC, Lanfermann H, Neumann-Haefelin T. Yawning in acute anterior circulation stroke. J Neurol Neurosurg Psychiatry. 2007 Nov;78(11):1253–4.

Wicks P. Excessive yawning is common in the bulbar-onset form of ALS. Acta Psychiatr Scand. 2007 Jul;116(1):76.

D'Andrea G, Nordera GP, Perini F, Allais G, Granella F. Biochemistry of neuromodulation in primary headaches: focus on anomalies of tyrosine metabolism. Neurol Sci. 2007 May;28 Suppl 2:S94–6.

Gutiérrez-Alvarez AM. Do your patients suffer from excessive yawning? Acta Psychiatr Scand. 2007 Jan;115(1):80–1.

65. Perriol MP, Monaca C. One person yawning sets off everyone else. J Neurol Neurosurg Psychiatry. 2006 Jan;77(1):3.

66. Daquin G, Micallef J, Blin O. Yawning. Sleep Med Rev. 2001 Aug;5(4):299–312.

67. Walusinski O. Yawning: unsuspected avenue for a better understanding of arousal and interoception. Med Hypotheses. 2006;67(1):6–14.

Goessler UR, Hein G, Sadick H, Maurer JT, Hormann K, Verse T. Physiology, role and neuropharmacology of yawning (German). Laryngorhinootologie. 2005 May;84(5):345–51.

Argiolas A, Melis MR. The neuropharmacology of yawning. Eur J Pharmacol. 1998 Feb 5;343(1):1–16.

68. Swenson AJ, Leira EC. Paroxysmal sneezing at the onset of lateral medullary syndrome: cause or consequence? Eur J Neurol. 2007 Apr;14(4):461–3.

69. Leigh J, Bowen S, Marlatt GA. Spirituality, mindfulness and substance abuse. Addict Behav. 2005 Aug;30(7):1335–41.

70. Society for Neuroscience Press Release. November 13, 2005.

71. Yates LB, Djoussé L, Kurth T, Buring JE, Gaziano JM. Exceptional longevity in men: modifiable factors associated with survival and function to age 90 years. Arch Intern Med. 2008 Feb 11;168(3):284–90.

72. Barclay L. Exercise May Have Neuroprotective Effect. Medscape Medical News (medscape.com).

73. Lolak S, Connors GL, Sheridan MJ, Wise TN. Effects of progressive muscle relaxation training on anxiety and depression in patients enrolled in an outpatient pulmonary rehabilitation program. Psychother Psychosom. 2008;77(2):119–25.

74. Knobf MT, Musanti R, Dorward J. Exercise and quality of life outcomes in patients with cancer. Semin Oncol Nurs. 2007 Nov;23(4):285–96.

75. Ospina MB, Bond K, Karkhanch M, Tjosvold L, Vandermeer B, Liang Y, Bialy L, Hooton N, Buscemi N, Dryden DM, Klassen TP. Meditation practices for health: state of the research. Evid Rep Technol Assess (Full Rep). 2007 Jun;(155):1–263.

76. Sivasankaran S, Pollard-Quintner S, Sachdeva R, Pugeda J, Hoq SM, Zarich SW. The effect of a six-week program of yoga and meditation on brachial artery reactivity: do psychosocial interventions affect vascular tone? Clin Cardiol. 2006 Sep;29(9):393–8.

77. Sahay BK. Role of yoga in diabetes. J Assoc Physicians India. 2007 Feb;55: 121–6.

Malhotra V, Singh S, Tandon OP, Sharma SB. The beneficial effect of yoga in diabetes. Nepal Med Coll J. 2005 Dec;7(2):145–7.

Manjunatha S, Vempati RP, Ghosh D, Bijlani RL. An investigation into the acute and long-term effects of selected yogic postures on fasting and post-prandial glycemia and insulinemia in healthy young subjects. Indian J Physiol Pharmacol. 2005 Jul–Sep;49(3):319–24.

Singh S, Malhotra V, Singh KP, Madhu SV, Tandon OP. Role of yoga in modifying certain cardiovascular functions in type 2 diabetic patients. J Assoc Physicians India. 2004 Mar;52:203–6.

78. Booth-LaForce C, Thurston RC, Taylor MR. A pilot study of a Hatha yoga treatment for menopausal symptoms. Maturitas. 2007 Jul 20;57(3):286–95.

79. Standaert CJ. Is yoga an effective therapy for chronic low back pain? Clin J Sport Med. 2007 Jan;17(1):83–4.

Sherman KJ, Cherkin DC, Erro J, Miglioretti DL, Deyo RA. Comparing yoga, exercise, and a self-care book for chronic low back pain: a randomized, controlled trial. Ann Intern Med. 2005 Dec 20;143(12):849–56.

Williams KA, Petronis J, Smith D, Goodrich D, Wu J, Ravi N, Doyle EJ Jr, Gregory Juckett R, Munoz Kolar M, Gross R, Steinberg L. Effect of Iyengar yoga therapy for chronic low back pain. Pain. 2005 May;115(1–2):107–17.

Galantino ML, Bzdewka TM, Eissler-Russo JL, Holbrook ML, Mogck EP, Geigle P, Farrar JT. The impact of modified Hatha yoga on chronic low back pain: a pilot study. Altern Ther Health Med. 2004 Mar–Apr;10(2):56–9.

80. John PJ, Sharma N, Sharma CM, Kankane A. Effectiveness of yoga therapy in the treatment of migraine without aura: a randomized controlled trial. Headache. 2007 May;47(5):654–61.

81. Streeter CC, Jensen JE, Perlmutter RM, Cabral HJ, Tian H, Terhune DB, Ciraulo DA, Renshaw PF. Yoga Asana Sessions Increase Brain GABA Levels: A Pilot Study. J Altern Complement Med. 2007 May;13(4):419–26. See also: Harinath K, Malhotra AS, Pal K, Prasad R, Kumar R, Kain TC, Rai L, Sawhney RC. Effects of Hatha yoga and Omkar meditation on cardiorespi-

ratory performance, psychologic profile, and melatonin secretion. J Altern Complement Med. 2004 Apr;10(2):261–8.

82. Duraiswamy G, Thirthalli J, Nagendra HR, Gangadhar BN. Yoga therapy as an add-on treatment in the management of patients with schizophrenia— a randomized controlled trial. Acta Psychiatr Scand. 2007 Sep;116(3):226–32.

83. Telles S, Praghuraj P, Ghosh A, Nagendra HR. Effect of a one-month yoga training program on performance in a mirror-tracing task. Indian J Physiol Pharmacol. 2006 Apr–Jun;50(2):187–90.

Manjunath NK, Telles S. Improved performance in the Tower of London test following yoga. Indian J Physiol Pharmacol. 2001 Jul;45(3):351–4.

Telles S, Hanumanthaiah BH, Nagarathna R, Nagendra HR. Plasticity of motor control systems demonstrated by yoga training. Indian J Physiol Pharmacol. 1994 Apr;38(2):143–4.

Telles S, Hanumanthaiah B, Nagarathna R, Nagendra HR. Improvement in static motor performance following yogic training of school children. Percept Mot Skills. 1993 Jun;76(3 Pt 2):1264–6.

84. White LJ, Castellano V. Exercise and brain health—implications for multiple sclerosis : part 1—neuronal growth factors. Sports Med. 2008;38(2):91–100.

85. Vaynman S. and F. Gomez-Pinilla (2005). License to run: Exercise impacts functional plasticity in the intact and injured central nervous system by using neurotrophins. Neurorehabilitation and Neural Repair 19(4): 283–295.

86. McMorris T, Collard K, Corbett J, Dicks M, Swain JP. A test of the catecholamines hypothesis for an acute exercise-cognition interaction. Pharmacol Biochem Behav. 2008 Mar;89(1):106–15.

Hillman CH, Erickson KI, Kramer AF. Be smart, exercise your heart: exercise effects on brain and cognition. Nat Rev Neurosci. 2008 Jan;9(1):58–65.

Tomporowski PD. Effects of acute bouts of exercise on cognition. Acta Psychol. 2003 Mar;112(3): 297–324.

87. Radak Z, Kumagai S, Taylor AW, Naito H, Goto S. Effects of exercise on brain function: role of free radicals. Appl Physiol Nutr Metab. 2007 Oct;32(5):942–6.

88. Cotman CW, Berchtold NC, Christie LA. Exercise builds brain health: key roles of growth factor cascades and inflammation. Trends Neurosci. 2007 Sep;30(9):464–72.

Dishman RK, Berthoud HR, Booth FW, Cotman CW, Edgerton VR, Fleshner MR, Gandevia SC, Gomez-Pinilla F, Greenwood BN, Hillman CH, Kramer AF, Levin BE, Moran TH, Russo-Neustadt AA, Salamone JD, Van Hoomissen JD, Wade CE, York DA, Zigmond MJ. Neurobiology of exercise. Obesity (Silver Spring). 2006 Mar;14(3):345–56.

89. Campisi J, Leem TH, Greenwood BN, Hansen MK, Moraska A, Higgins K, Smith TP, Fleshner M. Habitual physical activity facilitates stress-induced HSP72 induction in brain, peripheral, and immune tissues. Am J Physiol Regul Integr Comp Physiol. 2003 Feb;284(2):R520–30.

90. Trejo JL, Llorens-Martín MV, Torres-Alemán I. The effects of exercise on spatial learning and anxiety-like behavior are mediated by an IGF-I-dependent mechanism related to hippocampal neurogenesis. Mol Cell Neurosci. 2008 Feb;37(2):402–11.

Guszkowska M. Effects of exercise on anxiety, depression and mood. Psychiatr Pol. 2004 Jul–Aug;38(4):611–20.

Scully D, Kremer J, Meade MM, Graham R, Dudgeon K. Physical exercise and psychological well being: a critical review. Br J Sports Med. 1998 Jun;32(2):111–20.

Byrne A, Byrne DG. The effect of exercise on depression, anxiety and other mood states: a review. J Psychosom Res. 1993 Sep;37(6):565–74.

Petruzzello SJ, Landers DM, Hatfield BD, Kubitz KA, Salazar W. A meta-analysis on the anxiety-reducing effects of acute and chronic exercise. Outcomes and mechanisms. Sports Med. 1991 Mar;11(3):143–82.

91. Broocks A, Ahrendt U, Sommer M. Physical training in the treatment of depressive disorders. Psychiatr Prax. 2007 Sep;34 Suppl 3:S300–4.

Meeusen R. Exercise and the brain: insight in new therapeutic modalities. Ann Transplant. 2005;10(4):49–51.

92. Blumenthal JA, Babyak MA, Doraiswamy PM, Watkins L, Hoffman BM, Barbour KA, Herman S, Craighead WE, Brosse AL, Waugh R, Hinderliter A, Sherwood A. Exercise and pharmacotherapy in the treatment of major depressive disorder. Psychosom Med. 2007 Sep–Oct;69(7):587–96.

93. Interestingly, cognitive behavior therapy was more effective than psychodynamic therapy or exercise, as the following study demonstrated: Pinquart M, Duberstein PR, Lyness JM. Effects of psychotherapy and other behavioral interventions on clinically depressed older adults: A meta-analysis. Aging Ment Health. 2007 Nov;11(6):645–57.

94. Colcombe SJ, Erickson KI, Raz N, Webb AG, Cohen NJ, McAuley E, Kramer AF. Aerobic fitness reduces brain tissue loss in aging humans. J Gerontol A Biol Sci Med Sci. 2003 Feb;58(2):176–80.

95. Adlard PA, Perreau VM, Pop V, Cotman CW. Voluntary exercise decreases amyloid load in a transgenic model of Alzheimer's disease. J Neurosci. 2005 Apr 27;25(17):4217–21.

96. Booth FW, Laye MJ, Lees SJ, Rector RS, Thyfault JP. Reduced physical activity and risk of chronic disease: the biology behind the consequences. Eur J Appl Physiol. 2007 Nov 7.

97. Ornish D, Brown SE, Scherwitz LW, Billings JH, Armstrong WT, Ports TA, McLanahan SM, Kirkeeide RL, Brand RJ, Gould KL. Can lifestyle changes reverse coronary heart disease? The Lifestyle Heart Trial. Lancet. 1990 Jul 21;336(8708):129–33.

98. Yanek LR, Becker DM, Moy TF, Gittelsohn J, Koffman DM. Project Joy: faith based cardiovascular health promotion for African American women. Public Health Rep. 2001;116 Suppl 1:68–81.

99. Deacon, T. *The Symbolic Species: The Co-evolution of Language and the Brain.* Norton, 1997.

100. Green AF, Rebok G, Lyketsos CG. Influence of social network characteristics on cognition and functional status with aging. Int J Geriatr Psychiatry. 2008 May 1.

Holtzman RE, Rebok GW, Saczynski JS, Kouzis AC, Wilcox Doyle K, Eaton WW. Social network characteristics and cognition in middle-aged and older adults. J Gerontol B Psychol Sci Soc Sci. 2004 Nov;59(6):P278–84.

Seeman TE, Lusignolo TM, Albert M, Berkman L. Social relationships, social support, and patterns of cognitive aging in healthy, high-functioning older adults: MacArthur studies of successful aging. Health Psychol. 2001 Jul;20(4):243–55.

Unger JB, McAvay G, Bruce ML, Berkman L, Seeman T. Variation in the impact of social network characteristics on physical functioning in elderly persons: MacArthur Studies of Successful Aging. J Gerontol B Psychol Sci Soc Sci. 1999; 54(5):S245–S251.

Bassuk SS, Glass TA, Berkman LF. Social disengagement and incident cognitive decline in community-dwelling elderly persons. Ann Intern Med. 1999;131(3):165–173.

101. Note: Since it is often inappropriate to conduct isolation experiments on humans, nonhuman experiments from many fields of inquiry are used to demonstrate that similar damage is caused to people who are placed in situations of social isolation.

Ibi D, Takuma K, Koike H, Mizoguchi H, Tsuritani K, Kuwahara Y, Kamei H, Nagai T, Yoneda Y, Nabeshima T, Yamada K. Social isolation rearing-induced impairment of the hippocampal neurogenesis is associated with deficits in spatial memory and emotion-related behaviors in juvenile mice. J Neurochem. 2008 May;105(3):921–32.

Bock J, Murmu RP, Ferdman N, Leshem M, Braun K. Refinement of dendritic and synaptic networks in the rodent anterior cingulate and orbitofrontal cortex: critical impact of early and late social experience. Dev Neurobiol. 2008 Apr;68(5):685–95.

Fone KC, Porkess MV. Behavioural and neurochemical effects of post-weaning social isolation in rodents-Relevance to developmental neuropsychiatric disorders. Neurosci Biobehav Rev. 2008 Mar 18.

Pibiri F, Nelson M, Guidotti A, Costa E, Pinna G. Decreased corticolimbic allopregnanolone expression during social isolation enhances contextual fear: A model relevant for posttraumatic stress disorder. Proc Natl Acad Sci U S A. 2008 Apr 8;105(14):5567–72.

102. Frankl, V. *Man's Search for Meaning.* Washington Square Press, 1959.

103. See our last book, *Born to Believe,* for an in-depth look at the placebo effect and the power that beliefs have on our physiological health.

104. Sharot T, Riccardi AM, Raio CM, Phelps EA. Neural mechanisms mediating optimism bias. Nature. 2007 Nov 1;450(7166):102–5.

105. http://www.mayoclinic.com/health/positive-thinking/SR00009.

Kung S, Rummans TA, Colligan RC, Clark MM, Sloan JA, Novotny PJ, Huntington JL. Association of optimism-pessimism with quality of life in patients with head and neck and thyroid cancers. Mayo Clin Proc. 2006 Dec;81(12):1545–52.

106. Evans P, Forte D, Jacobs C, Fredhoi C, Aitchison E, Hucklebridge F, Clow A. Cortisol secretory activity in older people in relation to positive and negative well-being. Psychoneuroendocrinology. 2007 Sep–Nov;32(8–10):922–30.

Schlotz W, Schulz P, Hellhammer J, Stone AA, Hellhammer DH. Trait anxiety moderates the impact of performance pressure on salivary cortisol in everyday life. Psychoneuroendocrinology. 2006 May;31(4):459–72.

Lai JC, Evans PD, Ng SH, Chong AM, Siu OT, Chan CL, Ho SM, Ho RT, Chan P, Chan CC. Optimism, positive affectivity, and salivary cortisol. Br J Health Psychol. 2005 Nov;10(Pt 4):467–84.

107. Treharne GJ, Lyons AC, Booth DA, Kitas GD. Psychological well-being across 1 year with rheumatoid arthritis: coping resources as buffers of perceived stress. Br J Health Psychol. 2007 Sep;12(Pt 3):323–45.

Steptoe A, Marmo M, Wardle J. Positive affect and psychosocial processes related to health. Br J Psychol. 2007 Jun 27.

Martínez-Correa A, Reyes del Paso GA, García-León A, González-Jareño MI. [Relationship between dispositional optimism/pessimism and stress coping strategies] Psicothema. 2006 Feb;18(1):66–72.

Nes LS, Segerstrom SC. Dispositional optimism and coping: a meta-analytic review. Pers Soc Psychol Rev. 2006;10(3):235–51.

Schou I, Ekeberg Ø, Ruland CM. The mediating role of appraisal and coping in the relationship between optimism-pessimism and quality of life. Psychooncology. 2005 Sep;14(9):718–27.

108. Brummett BH, Helms MJ, Dahlstrom WG, Siegler IC. Prediction of all-cause mortality by the Minnesota Multiphasic Personality Inventory Optimism-Pessimism Scale scores: study of a college sample during a 40-year follow-up period. Mayo Clin Proc. 2006 Dec;81(12):1541–4.

109. http://www.ppc.sas.upenn.edu/aboutus.htm.

110. Gillath O, Bunge SA, Shaver PR, Wendelken C, Mikulincer M. Attachment-style differences in the ability to suppress negative thoughts: exploring the neural correlates. Neuroimage. 2005 Dec;28(4):835–47.

111. Ray RD, Ochsner KN, Cooper JC, Robertson ER, Gabrieli JD, Gross JJ. Individual differences in trait rumination and the neural systems supporting cognitive reappraisal. Cogn Affect Behav Neurosci. 2005 Jun;5(2):156–68.

112. Orndorff, RL, et al. Quantum Dot Ex Vivo Labeling of Neuromuscular Synapses. Nano Lett. 2008 Feb 1.

113. Lei Y, Tang H, Yao L, Yu R, Feng M, Zou B. Applications of mesenchymal stem cells labeled with tat Peptide conjugated quantum dots to cell tracking in mouse body. Bioconjug Chem. 2008 Mar–Apr;19(2):421–7.

114. There are, however, a small group of scientists who hope to link quantum properties with consciousness, but at the moment, the research is theoretical. Even if evidence is found, there would be no way of telling if, or how, such properties influence our thoughts, let alone something that exists outside of our bodies and brains. At most, the theories suggest that quantum dynamics might explain the extraordinary shifts in consciousness that happen every second of our waking lives. However, I believe that simpler neuroscientific models can explain the same phenomena we observe when it comes to tracing the pathways of human awareness. For more on this, go to pubmed.gov and read the abstracts of the following:

Basar E, Güntekin B. A breakthrough in neuroscience needs a "Nebulous Cartesian System": Oscillations, quantum dynamics and chaos in the brain and vegetative system. Int J Psychophysiol. 2007 Apr;64(1):108–22.

Persinger MA, Koren SA. A theory of neurophysics and quantum neuroscience: implications for brain function and the limits of consciousness. Int J Neurosci. 2007 Feb;117(2):157–75.

Bob P. Chaos, brain and divided consciousness. Acta Univ Carol Med Monogr. 2007;153:9–80.

Schwartz JM, Stapp HP, Beauregard M. Quantum physics in neuroscience and psychology: a neurophysical model of mind-brain interaction. Philos Trans R Soc Lond B Biol Sci. 2005 Jun 29;360(1458):1309–27.

Sieb RA. The emergence of consciousness. Med Hypotheses. 2004;63(5):900–4.

Korn H, Faure P. Is there chaos in the brain? II. Experimental evidence and related models. C R Biol. 2003 Sep;326(9):787–840.

Pastor-Gómez J. Quantum mechanics and brain: a critical review. Rev Neurol. 2002 Jul 1–15;35(1):87–94.

John ER. The neurophysics of consciousness. Brain Res Brain Res Rev. 2002 Jun;39(1):1–28.

115. Attwood J, Attwood C. *The Passion Test.* Hudson Street Press, 2007.

116. Taylor SE, Lerner JS, Sherman DK, Sage RM, McDowell NK. Are self-enhancing cognitions associated with healthy or unhealthy biological profiles? J Pers Soc Psychol. 2003 Oct;85(4):605–15.

117. Taylor SE, Kemeny ME, Reed GM, Bower JE, Gruenewald TL. Psychological resources, positive illusions, and health. Am Psychol. 2000 Jan;55(1):99–109.

118. Fournier M, De Ridder D, Bensing J. Optimism and adaptation to chronic disease: The role of optimism in relation to self-care options of type 1 diabetes mellitus, rheumatoid arthritis and multiple sclerosis. Br J Health Psychol. 2002 Nov;7(Part 4):409–432.

119. Weinstein ND. Unrealistic optimism about susceptibility to health problems. J Behav Med. 1982 Dec;5(4):441–60.

120. Cohen S, Alper CM, Doyle WJ, Treanor JJ, Turner RB. Positive emotional style predicts resistance to illness after experimental exposure to rhinovirus or influenza a virus. Psychosom Med. 2006 Nov–Dec;68(6):809–15.

121. Dillard AJ, McCaul KD, Klein WM. Unrealistic optimism in smokers: implications for smoking myth endorsement and self-protective motivation. J Health Commun. 2006;11 Suppl 1:93–102.

122. Groot W, van den Brink HM. Optimism, pessimism and the compensating income variation of cardiovascular disease: a two-tiered quality of life stochastic frontier model. Soc Sci Med. 2007 Oct;65(7):1479–89.

123. Weber H, Vollmann M, Renner B. The spirited, the observant, and the disheartened: social concepts of optimism, realism, and pessimism. J Pers. 2007 Feb;75(1):169–97.

124. Sharot T, Riccardi AM, Raio CM, Phelps EA. Neural mechanisms mediating optimism bias. Nature. 2007 Nov 1;450(7166):102–5.

125. van der Velden PG, Kleber RJ, Fournier M, Grievink L, Drogendijk A, Gersons BP. The association between dispositional optimism and mental health problems among disaster victims and a comparison group: A prospective study. J Affect Disord. 2007 Sep;102(1–3):35–45.

Pinquart M, Fröhlich C, Silbereisen RK. Optimism, pessimism, and change of psychological well-being in cancer patients. Psychol Health Med. 2007 Aug;12(4):421–32.

126. Maruta T, Colligan RC, Malinchoc M, Offord KP. Optimists vs pessimists: survival rate among medical patients over a 30-year period. Mayo Clin Proc. 2000 Feb;75(2):140–3. Erratum in: Mayo Clin Proc 2000 Mar;75(3):318.

Maruta T, Colligan RC, Malinchoc M, Offord KP. Optimism-pessimism assessed in the 1960s and self-reported health status 30 years later. Mayo Clin Proc. 2002 Aug;77(8):748–53.

CHAPTER 9. FINDING SERENITY (PAGES 170–214)

1. Lou HC, Nowak M, Kjaer TW. The mental self. Prog Brain Res. 2005;150: 197–204.

2. Brefczynski-Lewis JA, Lutz A, Schaefer HS, Levinson DB, Davidson RJ. Neural correlates of attentional expertise in long-term meditation practitioners. Proc Natl Acad Sci U S A. 2007 Jul 3;104(27):11483–8.

3. Musick MA, House JS, Williams DR. Attendance at religious services and mortality in a national sample. Journal of Health and Social Behavior. 2004;45 (2):198–213.

4. Hill TD, Angel JL, Ellison CG, Angel RJ. Religious attendance and mortality: an 8-year follow-up of older Mexican Americans. J Gerontol B Psychol Sci Soc Sci. 2005 Mar;60(2):S102–9.

5. Obisesan T, Livingston I, Trulear HD, Gillum F. Frequency of attendance at religious services, cardiovascular disease, metabolic risk factors and dietary intake in Americans: an age-stratified exploratory analysis. Int J Psychiatry Med. 2006;36(4):435–48.

6. Rostosky SS, Danner F, Riggle. (ed.). Is religiosity a protective factor against substance use in young adulthood? Only if you're straight! J Adolesc Health. 2007 May;40(5):440–7. The above longitudinal study contradicted earlier research showing that religion had a moderate buffering effect on the use of alcohol and marijuana. See: Stewart C. The influence of spirituality on substance use of college students. J Drug Educ. 2001;31(4):343–51.

7. Koenig HG, Pargament KI, Nielsen J. Religious coping and health status in medically ill hospitalized older adults. J Nerv Ment Dis. 1998 Sep;186(9): 513–21.

8. Pargament KI, Koenig HG, Tarakeshwar N, Hahn J. Religious struggle as a predictor of mortality among medically ill elderly patients: a 2-year longitudinal study. Arch Intern Med. 2001 Aug 13–27;161(15):1881–5.

9. Ray RD, Wilhelm FH, Gross JJ. All in the mind's eye? Anger rumination and reappraisal. J Pers Soc Psychol. 2008 Jan;94(1):133–45.

McLaughlin KA, Borkovec TD, Sibrava NJ. The effects of worry and rumination on affect states and cognitive activity. Behav Ther. 2007 Mar;38(1): 23–38.

Peled M, Moretti MM. Rumination on anger and sadness in adolescence: fueling of fury and deepening of despair. J Clin Child Adolesc Psychol. 2007 Mar;36(1):66–75.

McCullough ME, Orsulak P, Brandon A, Akers L. Rumination, fear, and cortisol: an in vivo study of interpersonal transgressions. Health Psychol. 2007 Jan;26(1):126–32.

Lavender A, Watkins E. Rumination and future thinking in depression. Br J Clin Psychol. 2004 Jun;43(Pt 2):129–42.

10. Ray RD, Ochsner KN, Cooper JC, Robertson ER, Gabrieli JD, Gross JJ. Individual differences in trait rumination and the neural systems supporting cognitive reappraisal. Cogn Affect Behav Neurosci. 2005 Jun;5(2):156–68.

11. Jerath R, Edry JW, Barnes VA, Jerath V. Physiology of long pranayamic breathing: neural respiratory elements may provide a mechanism that explains how slow deep breathing shifts the autonomic nervous system. Med Hypotheses. 2006;67(3):566–71.

12. Kjaer TW, Bertelsen C, Piccini P, Brooks D, Alving J, Lou HC. Increased dopamine tone during meditation-induced change of consciousness. Brain Res Cogn Brain Res. 2002 Apr;13(2):255–9.

13. Settergren G, Angdin M, Astudillo R, Gelinder S, Liska J, Lundberg JO, Weitzberg E. Decreased pulmonary vascular resistance during nasal breathing: modulation by endogenous nitric oxide from the paranasal sinuses. Acta Physiol Scand. 1998 Jul;163(3):235–9.

Lundberg JO, Settergren G, Gelinder S, Lundberg JM, Alving K, Weitzberg E. Inhalation of nasally derived nitric oxide modulates pulmonary function in humans. Acta Physiol Scand. 1996 Dec;158(4):343–7.

14. Pinto VL, Brunini TM, Ferraz MR, Okinga A, Mendes-Ribeiro AC. Depression and cardiovascular disease: role of nitric oxide. Cardiovasc Hematol Agents Med Chem. 2008 Apr;6(2):142–9.

Workman JL, Trainor BC, Finy MS, Nelson RJ. Inhibition of neuronal nitric oxide reduces anxiety-like responses to pair housing. Behav Brain Res. 2008 Feb 11;187(1):109–15.

Spiacci A Jr, Kanamaru F, Guimarães FS, Oliveira RM. Nitric oxide-mediated anxiolytic-like and antidepressant-like effects in animal models of anxiety and depression. Pharmacol Biochem Behav. 2008 Jan;88(3):247–55.

15. Gallup A, Gallup G. Yawning as a brain cooling mechanism: nasal breathing and forehead cooling diminish the incidence of contagious yawning. Evolutionary Psychology. 2007. 5(1): 92–101. http://www.epjournal.net/filestore/ep0592101.pdf.

16. Benson H. *Timeless Healing.* Scribner, 1996.

17. Bormann JE, Giffor AL, Shively M Smith TL, Rdwien L, Kelly A, et al. Effects of spiritual mantram repetition on HIV outcomes: A randomized clinical trial. Journal of Behavioral Medicine. 2006;29:359–376.

18. Bormann JE, Becker S, Gershwin M, Kelly A, Pada L, Smith TL, Gifford AL. Relationship of frequent mantram repetition to emotional and spiritual well-being in healthcare workers. J Contin Educ Nurs. 2006 Sep–Oct;37(5):218–24.

   Bormann JE, Oman D, Kemppainen JK, Becker S, Gershwin M, Kelly A. Mantram repetition for stress management in veterans and employees: a critical incident study. J Adv Nurs. 2006 Mar;53(5):502–12.

   Bormann JE, Smith TL, Becker S, Gershwin M, Pada L, Grudzinski AH, Nurmi EA. Efficacy of frequent mantram repetition on stress, quality of life, and spiritual well-being in veterans: a pilot study. J Holist Nurs. 2005 Dec;23(4):395–414.

19. Stevens SE, Hynan MT, Allen M, Braun MM, McCart MR. Are complex psychotherapies more effective than biofeedback, progressive muscle relaxation, or both? A meta-analysis. Psychol Rep. 2007 Feb;100(1):303–24.

   Kwekkeboom KL, Gretarsdottir E. Systematic review of relaxation interventions for pain. J Nurs Scholarsh. 2006;38(3):269–77.

   Nickel C, Kettler C, Muehlbacher M, Lahmann C, Tritt K, Fartacek R, Bachler E, Rother N, Egger C, Rother WK, Loew TH, Nickel MK. Effect of progressive muscle relaxation in adolescent female bronchial asthma patients: a randomized, double-blind, controlled study. J Psychosom Res. 2005 Dec;59(6):393–8.

   de Paula AA, de Carvalho EC, dos Santos CB. The use of the "progressive muscle relaxation" technique for pain relief in gynecology and obstetrics. Rev Lat Am Enfermagem. 2002 Sep–Oct;10(5):654–9.

   Matsumoto M, Smith JC. Progressive muscle relaxation, breathing exercises, and ABC relaxation theory. J Clin Psychol. 2001 Dec;57(12):1551–7.

20. Lolak S, Connors GL, Sheridan MJ, Wise TN. Effects of progressive muscle relaxation training on anxiety and depression in patients enrolled in an outpatient pulmonary rehabilitation program. Psychother Psychosom. 2008;77(2):119–25.

   Yoo HJ, Ahn SH, Kim SB, Kim WK, Han OS. Efficacy of progressive muscle relaxation training and guided imagery in reducing chemotherapy side effects in patients with breast cancer and in improving their quality of life. Support Care Cancer. 2005 Oct;13(10):826–33.

21. Krystal AD. Treating the health, quality of life, and functional impairments in insomnia. J Clin Sleep Med. 2007 Feb 15;3(1):63–72.

   Simeit R, Deck R, Conta-Marx B. Sleep management training for cancer patients with insomnia. Support Care Cancer. 2004 Mar;12(3):176–83.

Waters WF, Hurry MJ, Binks PG, Carney CE, Lajos LE, Fuller KH, Betz B, Johnson J, Anderson T, Tucci JM. Behavioral and hypnotic treatments for insomnia subtypes. Behav Sleep Med. 2003;1(2):81–101.

Means MK, Lichstein KL, Epperson MT, Johnson CT. Relaxation therapy for insomnia: nighttime and day time effects. Behav Res Ther. 2000 Jul;38(7):665–78.

22. Hernández-Ruiz E. Effect of music therapy on the anxiety levels and sleep patterns of abused women in shelters. J Music Ther. 2005 Summer;42(2):140–58.

23. Carrico DJ, Peters KM, Diokno AC. Guided Imagery for Women with Interstitial Cystitis: Results of a Prospective, Randomized Controlled Pilot Study. J Altern Complement Med. 2008 Jan 16.

Menzies V, Taylor AG, Bourguignon C. Effects of guided imagery on outcomes of pain, functional status, and self-efficacy in persons diagnosed with fibromyalgia. J Altern Complement Med. 2006 Jan–Feb;12(1):23–30.

Fors EA, Sexton H, Götestam KG. The effect of guided imagery and amitriptyline on daily fibromyalgia pain: a prospective, randomized, controlled trial. J Psychiatr Res. 2002 May–Jun;36(3):179–87.

24. León-Pizarro C, Gich I, Barthe E, Rovirosa A, Farrús B, Casas F, Verger E, Biete A, Craven-Bartle J, Sierra J, Arcusa A. A randomized trial of the effect of training in relaxation and guided imagery techniques in improving psychological and quality-of-life indices for gynecologic and breast brachytherapy patients. Psychooncology. 2007 Nov;16(11):971–9.

Sloman R. Relaxation and imagery for anxiety and depression control in community patients with advanced cancer. Cancer Nurs. 2002 Dec;25(6):432–5.

Thompson MB, Coppens NM. The effects of guided imagery on anxiety levels and movement of clients undergoing magnetic resonance imaging. Holist Nurs Pract. 1994 Jan;8(2):59–69.

25. Mackenzie A, Frawley GP. Preoperative hypnotherapy in the management of a child with anticipatory nausea and vomiting. Anaesth Intensive Care. 2007 Oct;35(5):784–7.

Omlor G, Kiewitz S, Pietschmann S, Roesler S. Effect of preoperative visualization therapy on postoperative outcome after inguinal hernia surgery and thyroid resection. Zentralbl Chir. 2000;125(4):380–5.

26. Lengacher CA, Bennett MP, Gonzalez L, Gilvary D, Cox CE, Cantor A, Jacobsen PB, Yang C, Djeu J. Immune responses to guided imagery during breast cancer treatment. Biol Res Nurs. 2008 Jan;9(3):205–14.

Gruzelier JH. A review of the impact of hypnosis, relaxation, guided imagery and individual differences on aspects of immunity and health. Stress. 2002 Jun;5(2):147–63.

27. Peres JF, Newberg AB, Mercante JP, Simão M, Albuquerque VE, Peres MJ, Nasello AG. Cerebral blood flow changes during retrieval of traumatic memories before and after psychotherapy: a SPECT study. Psychol Med. 2007 Oct;37(10):1481–91.

28. Sinha R, Lacadie C, Skudlarski P, Wexler BE. Neural circuits underlying emotional distress in humans. Ann N Y Acad Sci. 2004 Dec;1032:254–7.

29. Weydert JA, Shapiro DE, Acra SA, Monheim CJ, Chambers AS, Ball TM. Evaluation of guided imagery as treatment for recurrent abdominal pain in children: a randomized controlled trial. BMC Pediatr. 2006 Nov 8;6:29.

30. Meyers AW, Whelan JP, Murphy SM. Cognitive behavioral strategies in athletic performance enhancement. Prog Behav Modif. 1996;30:137–64.

Blumenstein B, Bar-Eli M, Tenenbaum G. The augmenting role of biofeedback: effects of autogenic, imagery and music training on physiological indices and athletic performance. J Sports Sci. 1995 Aug;13(4):343–54.

31. Hudetz JA, Hudetz AG, Reddy DM. Effect of relaxation on working memory and the Bispectral Index of the EEG. Psychol Rep. 2004 Aug;95(1):53–70.

Hudetz JA, Hudetz AG, Klayman J. Relationship between relaxation by guided imagery and performance of working memory. Psychol Rep. 2000 Feb;86(1):15–20.

32. Williams M, Teasdale J, Segal Z, Kabat-Zinn-J. *The Mindful Way through Depression.* Guilford Press, 2007.

Hayes SC, et al. (eds.). *Mindfulness and Acceptance.* Guilford Press, 2004.

33. The author of this Christian mystical text is unknown, although it has been attributed to an English cloistered monk living in the fourteenth century. See Evelyn Underwood's adaptation, *A Book of Contemplation the Which Is Called The Cloud of Unknowing, in Which a Soul is One with God,* edited from a British Museum manuscript and published by John M. Watkins in 1922.

34. Keating T. *Intimacy With God.* Crossroad Publishing Co, 1994.

35. van Uffelen JG, Chinapaw MJ, van Mechelen W, Hopman-Rock M. Walking or vitamin B for cognition in older adults with mild cognitive impairment? A randomized controlled trial. Br J Sports Med. 2008 May;42(5): 344–51.

van Uffelen JG, Chin A Paw MJ, Hopman-Rock M, van Mechelen W. The effect of walking and vitamin B supplementation on quality of life in community-dwelling adults with mild cognitive impairment: a randomized, controlled trial. Qual Life Res. 2007 Sep;16(7):1137–46.

36. Andel R, Crowe M, Pedersen NL, Fratiglioni L, Johansson B, Gatz M. Physical exercise at midlife and risk of dementia three decades later: a population-based study of Swedish twins. J Gerontol A Biol Sci Med Sci. 2008 Jan;63(1): 62–6.

Rovio S, Kåreholt I, Helkala EL, Viitanen M, Winblad B, Tuomilehto J, Soininen H, Nissinen A, Kivipelto M. Leisure-time physical activity at midlife and the risk of dementia and Alzheimer's disease. Lancet Neurol. 2005 Nov;4(11):705–11.

37. Ernst E, Canter PH. The Alexander technique: a systematic review of controlled clinical trials." Forsch Komplementarmed Klass Naturheilkd. 2003 Dec; 10(6):325–29.

Netz Y, Lidor R. Mood alterations in mindful versus aerobic exercise modes. J Psychol. 2003 Sep; 137(5):405–419.

Stallibrass C, Sissons P, Chalmers C. Randomized controlled trial of the Alexander technique for idiopathic Parkinson's disease. Clin Rehabil. 2002 Nov; 16(7):695–708.

Malmgren-Olsson EB, Bränholm IB. A comparison between three physiotherapy approaches with regard to health-related factors in patients with non-specific musculoskeletal disorders. Disabil Rehabil. 2002 Apr 15; 24(6): 308–17.

Johnson SK, Frederick J, Kaufman M, Mountjoy B. A controlled investigation of bodywork in multiple sclerosis. J Altern Complement Med. 1999 Jun; 5(3):237–43.

Laumer U, Bauer M, Fichter M, Milz H. Therapeutic effects of the Feldenkrais method "awareness through movement" in patients with eating disorders. Psychother Psychosom Med Psychol. 1997 May;47(5):170–80.

Stallibrass C. An evaluation of the Alexander technique for the management of disability in Parkinson's disease—a preliminary study. Clin Rehabil. 1997 Feb; 11(1):8–12.

38. Cacciatore TW, Horak FB, Henry SM. Improvement in automatic postural coordination following Alexander technique lessons in a person with low back pain. Phys Ther. 2005 Jun;85(6):565–78.

Dunn PA, Rogers DK. Feldenkrais sensory imagery and forward reach. Percept Mot Skills. 2000 Dec;91(3 Pt 1):755–7.

39. Seurinck R, Vingerhoets G, Vandemaele P, Deblaere K, Achten E. Trial pacing in mental rotation tasks. Neuroimage. 2005 May 1;25(4):1187–96.

Seidler RD, Noll DC. Neuroanatomical correlates of motor acquisition and motor transfer. J Neurophysiol. 2008 Feb 13.

Kiefer M, Sim EJ, Liebich S, Hauk O, Tanaka J. Experience-dependent plasticity of conceptual representations in human sensory-motor areas. J Cogn Neurosci. 2007 Mar;19(3):525–42.

40. Anh-Huong N, Hanh T. *Walking Meditation*. Sounds True, 2006.

41. Spencer RM, Verstynen T, Brett M, Ivry R. Cerebellar activation during discrete and not continuous timed movements: An fMRI study. Neuroimage. 2007 Mar 23.

Bormann JE, Smith TL, Shively M, Dellefield ME, Gifford AL. Self-monitoring of a stress reduction technique using wrist-worn counters. J Healthc Qual. 2007 Jan–Feb;29(1):45–52.

Bernardi L, Sleight P, Bandinelli G, Cencetti S, Fattorini L, Wdowczyc-Szulc J, Lagi A. Effect of rosary prayer and yoga mantras on autonomic cardiovascular rhythms: comparative study. BMJ. 2001 Dec 22–29;323(7327): 1446–9.

Akshoomoff NA, Courchesne E, Townsend J. Attention coordination and anticipatory control. Int Rev Neurobiol. 1997;41:575–98.

42. Perry DW, Zatorre RJ, Petrides M, Alivisatos B, Meyer E, Evans AC. Localization of cerebral activity during simple singing. Neuroreport. 1999 Dec 16;10(18):3979–84.

43. Levine S. *Healing into Life and Death.* Doubleday, 1987.

44. Dua JK, Swinden ML. Effectiveness of negative-thought-reduction, meditation and placebo training treatment in reducing anger. Scand J Psychol. 1992;33(2):135–46.

45. Dua J, Price I. Effectiveness of training in negative thought reduction and positive thought increment in reducing thought-produced distress. J Genet Psychol. 1993 Mar;154(1):97–109.

46. Goleman D. *Destructive Emotions.* Bantam, 2003.

47. Guszkowska M. Effects of exercise on anxiety, depression and mood. Psychiatr Pol. 2004 Jul–Aug;38(4):611–20.

Scully D, Kremer J, Meade MM, Graham R, Dudgeon K. Physical exercise and psychological well being: a critical review. Br J Sports Med. 1998 Jun;32(2):111–20.

Byrne A, Byrne DG. The effect of exercise on depression, anxiety and other mood states: a review. J Psychosom Res. 1993 Sep;37(6):565–74.

Petruzzello SJ, Landers DM, Hatfield BD, Kubitz KA, Salazar W. A meta-analysis on the anxiety-reducing effects of acute and chronic exercise. Outcomes and mechanisms. Sports Med. 1991 Mar;11(3):143–82.

48. Grodnitzky GR, Tafrate RC. Imaginal exposure for anger reduction in adult outpatients: a pilot study. J Behav Ther Exp Psychiatry. 2000 Sep–Dec;31(3–4):259–79.

49. Maio GR, Thomas G, Fincham FD, Carnelley KB. Unraveling the role of forgiveness in family relationships. J Pers Soc Psychol. 2008 Feb;94(2): 307–19.

50. Levenson MR, Aldwin CM, Yancura L. Positive emotional change: mediating effects of forgiveness and spirituality. Explore (NY). 2006 Nov–Dec;2(6):498–508.

51. Rye MS, Pargament KI. Forgiveness and romantic relationships in college: can it heal the wounded heart? J Clin Psychol. 2002 Apr;58(4):419–41.

52. Worthington EL Jr, Witvliet CV, Pietrini P, Miller AJ. Forgiveness, health, and well-being: a review of evidence for emotional versus decisional forgiveness, dispositional forgivingness, and reduced unforgiveness. J Behav Med. 2007 Aug;30(4):291–302.

    Friedberg JP, Suchday S, Shelov DV. The impact of forgiveness on cardiovascular reactivity and recovery. Int J Psychophysiol. 2007 Aug;65(2):87–94.

    Lawler KA, Younger JW, Piferi RL, Jobe RL, Edmondson KA, Jones WH. The unique effects of forgiveness on health: an exploration of pathways. J Behav Med. 2005 Apr;28(2):157–67.

    Lawler KA, Younger JW, Piferi RL, Billington E, Jobe R, Edmondson K, Jones WH. A change of heart: cardiovascular correlates of forgiveness in response to interpersonal conflict. J Behav Med. 2003 Oct;26(5):373–93.

53. Mullet E, Barros J, Frongia L, Usaï V, Neto F, Shafighi SR. Religious involvement and the forgiving personality. J Pers. 2003 Feb;71(1):1–19.

54. Spiers A. Forgiveness as a secondary prevention strategy for victims of interpersonal crime. Australas Psychiatry. 2004 Sep;12(3):261–3.

55. Harris AH, Luskin F, Norman SB, Standard S, Bruning J, Evans S, Thoresen CE. Effects of a group forgiveness intervention on forgiveness, perceived stress, and trait-anger. J Clin Psychol. 2006 Jun;62(6):715–33. See also research links at http://www.forgiving.org.

56. Luskin F. Data on Effective Forgiveness Methodologies, Stanford Forgiveness Projects—Research Applications. Press release of ongoing research: http://www.forgiving.org/campaign/press/doefm_fredluskin.asp.

57. Ritskes R, Ritskes-Hoitinga M, Stødkilde-Jørgensen H, Bærentsen K, Hartman T. MRI scanning during Zen meditation: The picture of enlightenment? Proceedings of the International conference of the Transnational Network for the study of Physical, Psychological and Spiritual Wellbeing, Sydney, Australia, July 2002.

CHAPTER 10. COMPASSIONATE COMMUNICATION (PAGES 215–240)

1. Sheffield M, Carey J, Patenaude W, Lambert MJ. An exploration of the relationship between interpersonal problems and psychological health. Psychol Rep. 1995 Jun;76(3 Pt 1):947–56.

2. Lamm C, Nusbaum HC, Meltzoff AN, Decety J. What Are You Feeling? Using Functional Magnetic Resonance Imaging to Assess the Modulation of

Sensory and Affective Responses during Empathy for Pain. PLoS ONE. 2007 Dec 12;2(12):e1292.

Saarela MV, Hlushchuk Y, Williams AC, Schürmann M, Kalso E, Hari R. The compassionate brain: humans detect intensity of pain from another's face. Cereb Cortex. 2007 Jan;17(1):230–7.

3. Güroğlu B, Haselager GJ, van Lieshout CF, Takashima A, Rijpkema M, Fernández G. Why are friends special? Implementing a social interaction simulation task to probe the neural correlates of friendship. Neuroimage. 2008 Jan 15;39(2):903–10.

Völlm BA, Taylor AN, Richardson P, Corcoran R, Stirling J, McKie S, Deakin JF, Elliott R. Neuronal correlates of theory of mind and empathy: a functional magnetic resonance imaging study in a nonverbal task. Neuroimage. 2006 Jan 1;29(1):90–8.

Farrow TF, Zheng Y, Wilkinson ID, Spence SA, Deakin JF, Tarrier N, Griffiths PD, Woodruff PW. Investigating the functional anatomy of empathy and forgiveness. Neuroreport. 2001 Aug 8;12(11):2433–8.

4. Steffen PR, Masters KS. Does compassion mediate the intrinsic religion-health relationship? Ann Behav Med. 2005 Dec;30(3):217–24.

5. Morrison I, Downing PE. Organization of felt and seen pain responses in anterior cingulate cortex. Neuroimage. 2007 Aug 15;37(2):642–51. May 24.

Lamm C, Batson CD, Decety J. The neural substrate of human empathy: effects of perspective-taking and cognitive appraisal. J Cogn Neurosci. 2007 Jan;19(1):42–58.

Shafritz KM, Collins SH, Blumberg HP. The interaction of emotional and cognitive neural systems in emotionally guided response inhibition. Neuroimage. 2006 May 15;31(1):468–75.

Lawrence EJ, Shaw P, Giampietro VP, Surguladze S, Brammer MJ, David AS. The role of "shared representations" in social perception and empathy: an fMRI study. Neuroimage. 2006 Feb 15;29(4):1173–84.

Morrison I, Lloyd D, di Pellegrino G, Roberts N. Vicarious responses to pain in anterior cingulate cortex: is empathy a multisensory issue? Cogn Affect Behav Neurosci. 2004 Jun;4(2):270–8.

6. Bartels A, Zeki S. The neural basis of romantic love. Neuroreport. 2000 Nov 27;11(17):3829–34.

7. Moriguchi Y, Decety J, Ohnishi T, Maeda M, Mori T, Nemoto K, Matsuda H, Komaki G. Empathy and judging other's pain: an fMRI study of alexithymia. Cereb Cortex. 2007 Sep;17(9):2223–34.

Berthoz S, Artiges E, Van De Moortele PF, Poline JB, Rouquette S, Consoli SM, Martinot JL. Effect of impaired recognition and expression of emotions on frontocingulate cortices: an fMRI study of men with alexithymia. Am J Psychiatry. 2002 Jun;159(6):961–7.

8. Waldman MR (ed.). *The Art of Staying Together.* Tarcher/Putnam, 1998.

Waldman MR. *Love Games.* Tarcher/Putnam, 2000.

9. Grepmair L, Mitterlehner F, Loew T, Nickel M. Promotion of mindfulness in psychotherapists in training: preliminary study. Eur Psychiatry. 2007 Nov;22(8):485–9.

Grepmair L, Mitterlehner F, Loew T, Bachler E, Rother W, Nickel M. Promoting mindfulness in psychotherapists in training influences the treatment results of their patients: a randomized, double-blind, controlled study. Psychother Psychosom. 2007;76(6):332–8.

10. Brock RL, Lawrence E. A longitudinal investigation of stress spillover in marriage: does spousal support adequacy buffer the effects? J Fam Psychol. 2008 Feb;22(1):11–20.

Heffner KL, Kiccolt-Glaser JK, Loving TJ, Glaser R, Malarkey WB. Spousal support satisfaction as a modifier of physiological responses to marital conflict in younger and older couples. J Behav Med. 2004 Jun;27(3):233–54.

Cohan CL, Bradbury TN. Negative life events, marital interaction, and the longitudinal course of newlywed marriage. J Pers Soc Psychol. 1997 Jul;73(1):114–28.

Huston TL, Vangelisti AL. Socioemotional behavior and satisfaction in marital relationships: a longitudinal study. J Pers Soc Psychol. 1991 Nov;61(5): 721–33.

11. Downs AC, Hillje ES. Reassessment of the Miller Social Intimacy Scale: use with mixed- and same-sex dyads produces multidimensional structures. Psychol Rep. 1991 Dec;69(3 Pt 1):991–7.

Miller RS, Lefcourt HM. The assessment of social intimacy. J Pers Assess. 1982 Oct;46(5):514–8.

12. Toussaint L, Webb JR. Gender differences in the relationship between empathy and forgiveness. J Soc Psychol. 2005 Dec;145(6):673–85.

13. Singer T, Seymour B, O'Doherty JP, Stephan KE, Dolan RJ, Frith CD. Empathic neural responses are modulated by the perceived fairness of others. Nature. 2006 Jan 26;439(7075):466–9.

14. Block-Lerner J, Adair C, Plumb JC, Rhatigan DL, Orsillo SM. The case for mindfulness-based approaches in the cultivation of empathy: Does nonjudgmental, present-moment awareness increase capacity for perspective-taking and empathic concern? J Marital Fam Ther. 2007 Oct;33(4):501–16.

15. Carson JW, Carson KM, Gil KM, Baucom DH. Self-expansion as a mediator of relationship improvements in a mindfulness intervention. J Marital Fam Ther. 2007 Oct;33(4):517–28.

16. Block-Lerner J, Adair C, Plumb JC, Rhatigan DL, Orsillo SM. The case for mindfulness-based approaches in the cultivation of empathy: does nonjudgmental, present-moment awareness increase capacity for perspective-taking and empathic concern? J Marital Fam Ther. 2007 Oct;33(4):501–16.

Barnes S, Brown KW, Krusemark E, Campbell WK, Rogge RD. The role of mindfulness in romantic relationship satisfaction and responses to relationship stress. J Marital Fam Ther. 2007 Oct;33(4):482–500.

Wachs K, Cordova JV. Mindful relating: exploring mindfulness and emotion repertoires in intimate relationships. J Marital Fam Ther. 2007 Oct;33(4): 464–81.

Allen NB, Chambers R, Knight W; Melbourne Academic Mindfulness Interest Group. Mindfulness-based psychotherapies: a review of conceptual foundations, empirical evidence and practical considerations. Aust N Z J Psychiatry. 2006 Apr;40(4):285–94.

17. Dumas JE. Mindfulness-based parent training: strategies to lessen the grip of automaticity in families with disruptive children. J Clin Child Adolesc Psychol. 2005 Dec;34(4):779–91.

Singh NN, Lancioni GE, Winton AS, Singh J, Curtis WJ, Wahler RG, McAleavey KM. Mindful parenting decreases aggression and increases social behavior in children with developmental disabilities. Behav Modif. 2007 Nov;31(6):749–71.

18. Byrne, R. *The Secret*. Atria Books/Beyond Words, 2006 (DVD directed by Drew Heriot).

19. We did find one interesting incongruency in our studies. When Compassionate Communication was introduced to a group of community college students who were taking a course in the anthropology of religion, most maintained their interest in outer goals and pursuits. Getting better grades, completing school, and finding a career were the most commonly cited desires, whereas qualities like happiness, contentment, or peace were rarely mentioned. When they were, the person was usually female. Overall, the measurement of intimacy only slightly improved, and the desire of some students to openly dialogue with strangers declined. Several things might account for the difference from the religious groups we've studied. First, age: younger people have less experience with communication and intimacy, and thus may not be able to improve much with strangers. Second, college students are less focused on issues of intimacy usually associated with long-term relationships and marriage. They're in class because they want to graduate. In contrast, the adults at our workshops are there because they are explicitly interested in the experiments we conduct. Third, the day we "tested" the students, the air-conditioning wasn't working. The

room was 97 degrees, certainly not the ideal environment in which to practice meditation.

20. Gobet F, Clarkson G. Chunks in expert memory: evidence for the magical number four . . . or is it two? Memory. 2004 Nov;12(6):732–47.

    Cowan N. The magical number 4 in short-term memory: a reconsideration of mental storage capacity. Behav Brain Sci. 2001 Feb;24(1):87–114.

21. Grewen KM, Anderson BJ, Girdler SS, Light KC. Warm partner contact is related to lower cardiovascular reactivity. Behav Med. 2003 Fall;29(3): 123–30.

    Grewen KM, Girdler SS, Amico J, Light KC. Effects of partner support on resting oxytocin, cortisol, norepinephrine, and blood pressure before and after warm partner contact. Psychosom Med. 2005 Jul–Aug;67(4):531–8.

    Light KC, Grewen KM, Amico JA. More frequent partner hugs and higher oxytocin levels are linked to lower blood pressure and heart rate in premenopausal women. Biol Psychol. 2005 Apr;69(1):5–21.

22. Hayes SC, et al. (eds.). *Mindfulness and Acceptance*. Guilford Press, 2004.

23. Ost LG. Efficacy of the third wave of behavioral therapies: A systematic review and meta-analysis. Behav Res Ther. 2007 Dec 23.

    Dalrymple KL, Herbert JD. Acceptance and commitment therapy for generalized social anxiety disorder: a pilot study. Behav Modif. 2007 Sep;31(5): 543–68.

    Roemer L, Orsillo SM. An open trial of an acceptance-based behavior therapy for generalized anxiety disorder. Behav Ther. 2007 Mar;38(1):72–85.

24. Carlson LE, Speca M, Patel KD, Faris P. One year pre-post intervention follow-up of psychological, immune, endocrine and blood pressure outcomes of mindfulness-based stress reduction (MBSR) in breast and prostate cancer outpatients. Brain Behav Immun. 2007 Nov;21(8):1038–49.

    Toneatto T, Nguyen L. Does mindfulness meditation improve anxiety and mood symptoms? A review of the controlled research. Can J Psychiatry. 2007 Apr;52(4):260–6.

    Jain S, Shapiro SL, Swanick S, Roesch SC, Mills PJ, Bell I, Schwartz GE. A randomized controlled trial of mindfulness meditation versus relaxation training: effects on distress, positive states of mind, rumination, and distraction. Ann Behav Med. 2007 Feb;33(1):11–21.

    Hoppes K. The application of mindfulness-based cognitive interventions in the treatment of co-occurring addictive and mood disorders. CNS Spectr. 2006 Nov;11(11):829–51.

    Finucane A, Mercer SW. An exploratory mixed methods study of the acceptability and effectiveness of Mindfulness-Based Cognitive Therapy for patients with active depression and anxiety in primary care. BMC Psychiatry. 2006 Apr 7;6:14.

Smith JE, Richardson J, Hoffman C, Pilkington K. Mindfulness-based stress reduction as supportive therapy in cancer care: systematic review. J Adv Nurs. 2005 Nov;52(3):315–27. Review. Erratum in: J Adv Nurs. 2006 Mar;53(5):618.

Plews-Ogan M, Owens JE, Goodman M, Wolfe P, Schorling J. A pilot study evaluating mindfulness-based stress reduction and massage for the management of chronic pain. J Gen Intern Med. 2005 Dec;20(12):1136–8.

Kreitzer MJ, Gross CR, Ye X, Russas V, Treesak C. Longitudinal impact of mindfulness meditation on illness burden in solid-organ transplant recipients. Prog Transplant. 2005 Jun;15(2):166–72.

McComb JJ Robert, Tacon A, Randolph P, Caldera Y. A pilot study to examine the effects of a mindfulness-based stress-reduction and relaxation program on levels of stress hormones, physical functioning, and submaximal exercise responses. J Altern Complement Med. 2004 Oct;10(5):819–27.

Grossman P, Niemann L, Schmidt S, Walach H. Mindfulness-based stress reduction and health benefits. A meta-analysis. J Psychosom Res. 2004 Jul;57(1):35–43.

Gross CR, Kreitzer MJ, Russas V, Treesak C, Frazier PA, Hertz MI. Mindfulness meditation to reduce symptoms after organ transplant: a pilot study. Altern Ther Health Med. 2004 May–Jun;10(3):58–66.

Carlson LE, Speca M, Patel KD, Goodey E. Mindfulness-based stress reduction in relation to quality of life, mood, symptoms of stress and levels of cortisol, dehydroepiandrosterone sulfate (DHEAS) and melatonin in breast and prostate cancer outpatients. Psychoneuroendocrinology. 2004 May;29(4):448–74.

Roth B, Robbins D. Mindfulness-based stress reduction and health-related quality of life: findings from a bilingual inner-city patient population. Psychosom Med. 2004 Jan–Feb;66(1):113–23.

Singh NN, Wahler RG, Adkins AD, Myers RE. Soles of the feet: a mindfulness-based self-control intervention for aggression by an individual with mild mental retardation and mental illness. Res Dev Disabil. 2003 May–Jun;24(3):158–69.

Rosenzweig S, Reibel DK, Greeson JM, Brainard GC, Hojat M. Mindfulness-based stress reduction lowers psychological distress in medical students. Teach Learn Med. 2003 Spring;15(2):88–92.

Majumdar M, Grossman P, Dietz-Waschkowski B, Kersig S, Walach H. Does mindfulness meditation contribute to health? Outcome evaluation of a

German sample. J Altern Complement Med. 2002 Dec;8(6):719–30; discussion 731–5.

Bishop SR. What do we really know about mindfulness-based stress reduction? Psychosom Med. 2002 Jan–Feb;64(1):71–83.

Roth B, Stanley TW. Mindfulness-based stress reduction and healthcare utilization in the inner city: preliminary findings. Altern Ther Health Med. 2002 Jan–Feb;8(1):60–2, 64–6.

Speca M, Carlson LE, Goodey E, Angen M. A randomized, wait-list controlled clinical trial: the effect of a mindfulness meditation-based stress reduction program on mood and symptoms of stress in cancer outpatients. Psychosom Med. 2000 Sep–Oct;62(5):613–22.

Reibel DK, Greeson JM, Brainard GC, Rosenzweig S. Mindfulness-based stress reduction and health-related quality of life in a heterogeneous patient population. Gen Hosp Psychiatry. 2001 Jul–Aug;23(4):183–92.

25. Davis LW, Strasburger AM, Brown LF. Mindfulness: an intervention for anxiety in schizophrenia. J Psychosoc Nurs Ment Health Serv. 2007 Nov;45(11): 23–9.

26. Björgvinsson T, Hart J, Heffelfinger S. Obsessive-compulsive disorder: update on assessment and treatment. J Psychiatr Pract. 2007 Nov;13(6):362–72.

Masedo AI, Rosa Esteve M. Effects of suppression, acceptance and spontaneous coping on pain tolerance, pain intensity and distress. Behav Res Ther. 2007 Feb;45(2):199–209.

Gifford EV, Ritsher JB, McKellar JD, Moos RH. Acceptance and relationship context: a model of substance use disorder treatment outcome. Addiction. 2006 Aug;101(8):1167–77.

Lau MA, McMain SF. Integrating mindfulness meditation with cognitive and behavioural therapies: the challenge of combining acceptance- and change-based strategies. Can J Psychiatry. 2005 Nov;50(13):863–9.

McCracken LM, Vowles KE, Eccleston C. Acceptance-based treatment for persons with complex, long standing chronic pain: a preliminary analysis of treatment outcome in comparison to a waiting phase. Behav Res Ther. 2005 Oct;43(10):1335–46.

27. Heffner KL, Loving TJ, Kiecolt-Glaser JK, Himawan LK, Glaser R, Malarkey WB. Older spouses' cortisol responses to marital conflict: associations with demand/withdraw communication patterns. J Behav Med. 2006 Aug;29(4):317–25.

Kiecolt-Glaser JK, Loving TJ, Glaser R, Malarkey WB. Spousal support satisfaction as a modifier of physiological responses to marital conflict in younger and older couples. J Behav Med. 2004 Jun;27(3):233–54.

Marchand JF. Husbands' and wives' marital quality: the role of adult attachment orientations, depressive symptoms, and conflict resolution behaviors. Attach Hum Dev. 2004 Mar;6(1):99–112.

Kiecolt-Glaser JK, Bane C, Glaser R, Malarkey WB. Love, marriage, and divorce: newlyweds' stress hormones foreshadow relationship changes. J Consult Clin Psychol. 2003 Feb;71(1):176–88.

Kiecolt-Glaser JK, Glaser R, Cacioppo JT, Malarkey WB. Marital stress: immunologic, neuroendocrine, and autonomic correlates. Ann N Y Acad Sci. 1998 May 1;840:656–63.

Kiecolt-Glaser JK, Glaser R, Cacioppo JT, MacCallum RC, Snydersmith M, Kim C, Malarkey WB. Marital conflict in older adults: endocrinological and immunological correlates. Psychosom Med. 1997 Jul–Aug;59(4):339–49.

Kiecolt-Glaser JK, Newton T, Cacioppo JT, MacCallum RC, Glaser R, Malarkey WB. Marital conflict and endocrine function: are men really more physiologically affected than women? J Consult Clin Psychol. 1996 Apr;64(2):324–32.

Malarkey WB, Kiecolt-Glaser JK, Pearl D, Glaser R. Hostile behavior during marital conflict alters pituitary and adrenal hormones. Psychosom Med. 1994 Jan–Feb;56(1):41–51.

28. Grandjean D, Sander D, Pourtois G, Schwartz S, Seghier ML, Scherer KR, Vuilleumier P. The voices of wrath: brain responses to angry prosody in meaningless speech. Nat Neurosci. 2005 Feb;8(2):145–6.

Sander D, Grandjean D, Pourtois G, Schwartz S, Seghier ML, Scherer KR, Vuilleumier P. Emotion and attention interactions in social cognition: brain regions involved in processing anger prosody. Neuroimage. 2005 Dec;28(4):848–58.

29. Rota G, Veit R, Nardo D, Weiskopf N, Birbaumer N, Dogil G. Processing of inconsistent emotional information: an fMRI study. Exp Brain Res. 2007 Dec 20.

Mitchell RL. How does the brain mediate interpretation of incongruent auditory emotions? The neural response to prosody in the presence of conflicting lexico-semantic cues. Eur J Neurosci. 2006 Dec;24(12):3611–8.

30. Ghika-Schmid F, Ghika J, Vuilleumier P, Assal G, Vuadens P, Scherer K, Maeder P, Uske A, Bogousslavsky J. Bihippocampal damage with emotional dysfunction: impaired auditory recognition of fear. Eur Neurol. 1997;38(4):276–83.

Sachdev P, Smith JS, Matheson J, Last P, Blumbergs P. Amygdalo-hippocampectomy for pathological aggression. Aust N Z J Psychiatry. 1992 Dec;26(4):671–6.

31. Clark AJ. Forgiveness: a neurological model. Med Hypotheses. 2005;65(4): 649–54.

32. Carson JW. Carson KM. Gil KM. Baucom DH. Mindfulness-Based Relationship Enhancement. Behavior Ther. 2004;35: 471–494.

33. Hyde C. *Pay It Forward.* Simon and Schuster, 2000.

34. Bowen W. *A Complaint-Free World.* Doubleday, 2007.

INDEX

Page numbers in **bold** represent photos or illustrations.

plan, implementing, 238

problem, sitting with for a week, 238

progress report, getting, 238–39

critical God

and intolerance, 121

percentage of Americans who believe in, 108–9, **109**, 121

D

Dalai Lama, 13, 178

danger zone

recognizing, 235–36

Darwin, Charles, 5, 65

Davidson, Richard, 62

Dawkins, Richard, 5, 6, 13

Deacon, Terrance, 105

demons (sitting with)

as brain enhancement exercise, 201–5

dendrites, **37**

exercising, 36–37

Descent of Man, The (Darwin), 65

diabetes

caffeine and, 39

dialogue, constructive (three strategies for beginning), 233–36

kindness, opening dialogue with, 234

location, finding the best, 234

right time, picking the, 233–34

dialogue with others

as a best way to exercise your brain, 162–63

distant God

percentage of Americans who believe in, **109**, 109–10

dopamine levels

meditation and, 55–56, 159

drugs

and neural function, 150, 150n

E

Ecstasy (MDMA)

cognitive functions, impairing, 57–58

Einstein, Albert, 1, 100, 116–17

emotions, disruptive (six strategies for containing), 234–36

anger and danger zone, monitoring and recognizing, 235–36

don't blame, 235

nonverbal communication, be aware of, 235–36

provocative language, avoiding, 234

time-out, calling, 236

tone of voice, softening, 234–35

empathy and social awareness, 17–18

strokes and, 59

End of Faith, The (Harris), 6

epileptic seizures

meditation and, 170n

Escher, M. C., 100

Evangelicals, 82

See also fundamentalism

exercising your brain, 9, 149–69

affirmation, principles of, 165–68

neural function, drugs and supplements and, 150

sleep and, 150–51

video-game playing, 154

exercising your brain (eight best ways), 151–65

aerobic exercise, 160–62

consciously relaxing, 155

dialogue with others, 162–63

faith, 163–65

meditation, 159–60

smiling, 151–52

ABOUT THE AUTHORS

Andrew Newberg, M.D., is an associate professor in the Departments of Radiology and Psychiatry at the Hospital of the University of Pennsylvania and an adjunct professor in the Department of Religious Studies. He is the founder and director of the Center for Spirituality and the Mind, and the director of the Center for the Integrated Study of Spirituality and the Neurosciences at the University of Pennsylvania. He is board-certified in internal medicine, nuclear medicine, and nuclear cardiology.

Dr. Newberg has published over one hundred articles, essays, and book chapters, and is the co-author of *Born to Believe, Why We Believe What We Believe, Why God Won't Go Away,* and *The Mystical Mind.* An overview of his work can be viewed at www.andrewnewberg.com.

Mark Robert Waldman is an associate fellow at the Center for the Spirituality and the Mind, at the University of Pennsylvania. He is the co-author of *Born to Believe, Why We Believe What We Believe,* and nine other books and anthologies covering the fields of psychology and creativity. He was the founding editor of the academic literature review journal, *Transpersonal Review,* and his professional papers have been published in journals throughout the world. He has a counseling practice in southern California, specializing in relationship dynamics and awareness-based therapies. An overview of his current research and workshop/lecture schedule can be viewed at www.markrobertwaldman.com.

ABOUT THE TYPE

This book was set in Granjon, a modern recutting of a typeface produced under the direction of George W. Jones, who based Granjon's design upon the letter forms of Claude Garamond (1480–1561). The name was given to the typeface as a tribute to the typographic designer Robert Granjon.